M000279883

International Relations in the Cyber Age

International Relations in the Cyber Age

The Co-Evolution Dilemma

Nazli Choucri and David D. Clark

The MIT Press
Cambridge, Massachusetts
London, England

© 2018 Massachusetts Institute of Technology

All rights reserved. No part of this book may be reproduced in any form by any electronic or mechanical means (including photocopying, recording, or information storage and retrieval) without permission in writing from the publisher.

This book was set in Stone Serif by Westchester Publishing Services. Printed and bound in the United States of America.

Library of Congress Cataloging-in-Publication Data

Names: Choucri, Nazli, author. | Clark, David D. (David Dana), 1944– author.
Title: International relations in the cyber age : the co-evolution dilemma / Nazli Choucri and David D. Clark.
Description: Cambridge, MA : The MIT Press, [2018] | Includes bibliographical references and index.
Identifiers: LCCN 2018010197 | ISBN 9780262038911 (hardcover : alk. paper)
Subjects: LCSH: Internet and international relations. | Internet—Political aspects. | Internet—Security measures. | Computer networks—Security measures.
Classification: LCC JZ1254 .C49 2018 | DDC 327—dc23 LC record available at https://lccn.loc.gov/2018010197

10 9 8 7 6 5 4 3 2 1

Contents

Preface

The research for this book, as well as the reframing and revisions of the manuscript, were undertaken as a core initiative of the project on Explorations in Cyber International Relations (ECIR), a joint MIT–Harvard collaboration of the Minerva Program, US Department of Defense, funded by the Office of Naval Research under award number N00014-09-1-0597. Any opinions, findings, conclusions, or recommendations expressed in this book are ours alone and do not necessarily reflect the views of the Office of Naval Research.

Our book addresses and attempts to answer two broad questions centered respectively in the theory and practice of international relations and in the technology and utilization of cyberspace, and on this basis we then develop the framework for an *integrated joint cyber-IR system*.

With respect to international relations, the question is twofold: first, does cyberspace influence structure and process in international relations? If so, how? If not, why not? And second, what are the impacts, if any, of international relations on the cyber domain as broadly defined? With respect to cyberspace itself, with its current core, the Internet, we ask how its specific character shapes the nature of contention, which actors are empowered or not by its structure, and how to reason about its characteristic features as a built artifact. In this book we propose ways of thinking about the issues— modes of reasoning, methods of analysis, qualitative and quantitative inquiry, case studies, and the like that can improve our understanding and guide thinking about cyberspace and international relations—and we do so in a global geopolitical and strategic context.

Our book presents several models that can be used to understand the cyber domain, anchored in the Internet but supported and enabled by a wide range of institutional mechanisms. By the same token, we engage in empirical analysis of the international system, the whole and the parts, and the dynamics of transformation and change. We use the models to highlight different future scenarios for what we shall call the co-evolution of cyberspace and international relations—given the growing importance of global contention in the shared space.

In the course of our investigations, it became clear that these two domains, while seemingly independent or autonomous, were becoming increasingly interconnected in many different and unexpected ways. This realization created a new challenge: how to capture these interconnections and how to represent their characteristic features. The new "reality" is that we are now dealing with one highly complex system. By combining cyberspace and process, we constructed a model of this new "reality."

Acknowledgments

We would like to thank the joint ECIR project team for insights into the conduct of multidisciplinary research as well as critical reviews of disciplinary assumptions in a cross-disciplinary context. We are grateful to our MIT colleagues Stuart Madnick, John Mallery, Silvio Micali, Michael Siegel, Patrick Winston, and the late Roger Hurwitz and our collaborators at Harvard, Jack Goldsmith, Joseph S. Nye, Venkatesh Narayanamurti, and Melissa Hathaway who joined halfway through the project period as well as Richard Clarke and Eric Rosenbach who left the project early on for public service.

Special appreciation is due to the members of the regular ECIR Seminar on Cyber International Relations—held at MIT with companion sessions at Harvard Kennedy School of Government—for their views of emergent new "realities" in the traditional as well as virtual contexts. In particular, we would like to thank Scott Bradner for insights into the institutional complexities that sustain the Internet. We would also like to thank ECIR research associates whose work contributed to the framing of this book, most notably, Daniel Goldsmith, Shirley Hung, Robert Reardon, Aadya Shukla, Sinead Cheung, Chintan Vaishnav, and Cindy Williams. Special thanks are due to ECIR graduate research assistants Jeremy Ferwerda, Robert Ramirez, Jesse Sowell, and Josephine Wolff.

We are grateful to Gaurav Agarwal for research support, for analysis and reanalysis of empirical data—notably data fraught with ambiguities in definition and provenance—and for the joint effort with Kathleen Searle to resolve all matters related to copyright, from the most simple to the most thorny. Finally, for insightful reactions and suggestions, special thanks are due to Sandra Braman for an excellent review and overall critique.

I Cyberspace and International Relations

1 Context and Co-Evolution

1.1 Introduction

Almost everyone recognizes that cyberspace is a fact of daily life. Given its ubiquity, scale, and scope, cyberspace—including the Internet, the billions of computers it connects, its management, and the experiences it enables—has become a central feature of the world we live in and has created a fundamentally new reality for almost everyone in the developed world and rapidly growing numbers of people in the developing world.

At the same time, information and communication—foundations of all human societies and social interactions—have been accorded rather limited attention in all major theories of international relations. Despite the centrality of all forms of information exchange—in all contexts and cultures, conditions or situations—content of communication, conduits, and forms of connectivity remain more marginal than might be appropriate in world politics or in international relations more broadly defined.

In this book we view cyberspace as a global domain of human interaction that (1) is created through the interconnections of billions of computers by a global network, today the Internet; (2) is built as a layered construct where physical elements enable a logical framework of interconnection; (3) permits the processing, manipulation, exploitation, augmentation of information, and the interaction of people and information; (4) is enabled by institutional intermediation and organization; and (5) is characterized by decentralization and interplay among actors, constituencies, and interests.

If knowledge is power, as is commonly argued, then harnessing the power of knowledge becomes an intensely political activity. The flow of data now defines the international landscape as much as the flow of material and people. But the implications of data flows have not become an important issue in world politics, nor central to theory, policy, and practice. More often than not, communications in world politics harbor some form of contention over how bits—knowledge, commercial content, criminal content, or speech—flow in cyberspace. There are, of course, many ways that nations contend to excel at the creation and exploitation of knowledge. Sometimes the roles change. Sometimes the tools of contention change, based on the details of the circumstance. But all of these activities center on, and to a considerable extent are directly acted out in, cyberspace.

Until recently cyberspace was considered largely a matter of "low politics," the term used to denote background conditions and routine decisions and processes. By contrast, "high politics" is about national security, core institutions, and decision systems that are critical to the state, its interests, and its underlying values. Nationalism, political participation, political contentions, conflict, violence, and war are among the most often cited aspects of high politics. But low politics do not always remain below the surface. If the cumulative effects of normal activities shift the established dynamics of interaction, then the seemingly routine becomes increasingly politicized.

Cyberspace is now a matter of high politics. This new domain of interaction is a source of vulnerability, a potential threat to national security, and a disturber of the familiar international order. So critical has cyberspace become that the United States has created a Cyber Command in the U.S. Department of Defense in recognition of potential cyber threats that can undermine the security and welfare of the nation. The new practice of turning off the Internet during times of unrest in various countries, the effective leakage of confidential government documents on WikiLeaks, the cyber-attacks that accompanied past conflict in Georgia and Estonia, the use of cyber-based attacks to degrade Iran's nuclear capabilities, and the Russian interference with the U.S. presidential elections in 2016 all illustrate that state actors cannot ignore the salience of cyberspace and its capabilities. We see many incidents of power and politics, conflict and competition, violence and war—all central features of world politics—increasingly manifested via cyber venues.

Today, the influence of cyberspace is evident in all aspects of contemporary society, in almost all parts of the world. The result is a powerful disconnect between twentieth-century international relations and the realities of the twenty-first century. Starkly stated, this book is about the emergent

Cyberspace   International
                                    relations

Figure 1.1
Cyberspace and international relations.

interconnections and joint evolution of two domains fundamental to the
defining realities of the twenty-first century, the international system with
its actors and entities, structures and processes, and cyberspace, with its core,
the Internet, and its rapidly growing users and participants, and the formal
and informal institutions that seek to provide forms of order in the cyber
arena.

This book is framed by the question mark in figure 1.1. The challenge
is to reduce the disconnect between cyberspace and the conventional venues of international relations, and help create the fundamentals for aligning
contemporary international relations theory, policy, and practice with the
emergent complexities of the twenty-first century. We recognize that each
of these two domains—the cyber and the international—is defined by different core principles and characterized by distinct features of structure and
process that enable, and are enabled by, a wide range of actors and activities.

We examine the pervasiveness of power and politics in the cyber domain
as well as the resort to various modes of leverage and control. Invariably
when such issues arise, propensities for conflict and contention are not
far behind. In addition, we realize that traditional theory in international
relations, notably the surrounding concepts of deterrence and defense, for
example, are not readily portable to cyberspace. It goes without saying that
all of this forces us to reassess conventional perspectives on security.

If the reality of cyberspace is changing the character of international
relations, so are concerns of various states changing the character of cyberspace. It is already apparent that political pressures impinge upon the current Internet in various parts of the world to render its architecture more in
line with power and politics. Recognizing this reality, this book also seeks to
sensitize computer scientists to the inherent but sometimes hidden influence of power and politics that bear on new architecture, new construction
of the Internet, and new frontiers of cyberspace. We seek also to improve

the awareness of computer scientists of the potential for influence and leverage enabled, or even created, by the architecture of the Internet and all the attendant and operational features that sustain the core of cyberspace.

At a higher level of abstraction, our purpose is to build a conceptual and empirical framework to guide policy and practice for international relations in the cyber age. We have used the term "co-evolution" in the title of the book to describe the mutual influence that cyberspace and international relations have on each other. Clearly any reference to co-evolution involves matters of growth, development, security, stability, profit, control, governance, crime, and a wide range of related issues surrounding connectivity, conduit, and content as well as emergent views of alternative futures—all elements we consider later on as we introduce the overall framework of the book and the individual chapters.

Framed in this broad context, this book is the second of three books devoted to the interconnections of cyberspace and world politics. The first book, *Cyberpolitics in International Relations* (Choucri 2012), focused largely on the ubiquity of cyberspace at the different levels of analysis in international relations and pointed to some ways in which traditional theory and practice require reassessments and reframing. The second, this book, takes the position that this ubiquity calls for a meta-analysis, an overarching investigation of *contours and interconnections of cyberspace and international relations* (and international cyber relations) in order to identify the linkages between the international system (and international relations), on the one hand, and technological change (and cyberspace), on the other—in analytical, empirical, and observable terms. The third book consists of the basic studies foundational to our understanding of twenty-first-century international relations where cyberspace is so critical to all aspects of our interactions.

Our purpose in this first chapter is to provide terms of reference within which to situate the remainder of this book. We begin with tradition in international relations and turn to some observations about theory and policy in this domain. Then we introduce cyberspace and signal some of the discontinuities with tradition and implications for the state system and international relations. A seemingly minor, but relevant, digression takes us to some relevant features of evolution in the scientific tradition. All of this leads us to define the critical imperatives—core challenges—addressed in this book.

1.2 Tradition and Order

The state system, established by the Peace of Westphalia in 1648, was designed as much by necessity—a response to the challenges of the time—as by the power of human ingenuity. Traditional perspectives on international relations—theory, policy, and practice—assume the state to be the central, if not the only, actor of any significance in the international domain. The organizing principle of sovereignty is the anchor upon which the entire system rests. Thus, by definition, all other actors and entities are derivative, legitimized at their origin by the state. Contemporary international relations theory and practice evolved from the Westphalian state system, which established the modern world order. The gradual recognition of other actors on the world scene is usually accompanied by stressing their subservience to the state system, despite the growing influence of multinational corporations, varieties of nongovernmental entities, the emergence of robust international organizations, the growth of informal if not illegitimate actors, and the increasing evidence of a worldwide civil society.

Over time, some "rules" of expected state behavior emerged, loosely framed, with relatively limited empirical verification. The experience of World War I, the interwar period, World War II, and its immediate aftermath all reflect the leading theoretical perspectives at the time. In 1945, there were 45 independent states; by the end of the twentieth century there were 196 states. This expansion of the Westphalian system is far from trivial, especially if we consider the attendant generativity in structure and process. Most features of the traditional international system remain in place today. The "old" is especially important because it is the framework within which the "new" has evolved, and, in so doing, is challenging the most foundational features of the twentieth century.

Tradition in world politics recognizes the state the only actor with monopoly over the use of force. The individual is accounted for by the institution of citizenship. So, too, theory, policy, practice, and empirical analysis all bypass the individual as well as groups or other actors, recognizing them only as part of the state.

Given that international politics is generally considered the pursuit of power and wealth, the traditional system hosts a wide range of nonstate actors—anchored or "licensed" by the state—that engage in economic, social, and other pursuits, for profit or not for profit. Multinational corporations, as familiar to us as is the state, operate within and across state boundaries and, by necessity, encounter the rules and regulations thereof. Entities that evolve into multinational corporations always come into being within some state jurisdiction. The key point is that the identity of the state, as well as the identity of other actors, is known. Aside from the "illegitimates," ambiguity of identity is not a defining feature of traditional world politics.

The international system has generally been viewed as anarchical in nature, with no overarching source of authority to control all of its constituent parts. Dominant patterns of interaction in this system devoid of central authority revolve around propensities for and patterns of conflict, on the one hand, and modes of coordination and cooperation, on the other. These are seldom mutually exclusive, because conflict often involves a degree of cooperation, and almost all forms of cooperation harbor latent or even overt conflict.

The number of states, the relative power distributions, and the strategic and security relations that link them together shape the broader contour of world politics. States, as well as private entities, develop and grow; some decay and decline. Although the state system is "permanent" so far, the number of states changes over time. Generally, formal recognition by the United Nations is the mechanism for state creation. States are usually compared by wealth (levels of economic development—high, medium, low) and/or by type of political system (democratic, despotic, etc., depending on the labels used). These are two of the most common ways of characterizing states. In this book, we shall introduce other ways of representing states and the state system.

1.2.1 Poles, Power, and Private Actors

Depending on the prevailing distribution of power and capability, the international system takes on diverse structural forms generally described in terms of "poles." During the immediate post–World War II period, the international system was characterized as a tight bipolar system—with the United States leading the free world pole and the Soviet Union leading the communist pole. This arrangement was followed by the defection of France from the U.S. pole and of China from the U.S.S.R. group.

Gradually, the international system evolved into a multipolar system, when the newly independent countries defined themselves as nonaligned. The demise of the Soviet Union and the creation of a number of independent states rendered the multipolar system obsolete. Over time, the traditional system of twentieth-century international relations—generally characterized by hierarchical power relations—was replaced by new structural configurations characterized by different types of asymmetries and relatively weak hierarchy, if any.

Among the important legacies of the twentieth century are the end of the Cold War, the consolidation of the United States as the only hegemon, and the growth in the number of sovereign states (some due to the decolonization process, others to the breakup of the Soviet Union, and still others by common consensus), all with new claims on the international community. Until very recently the rest of the world was viewed as a residual and was expected to conform to major power rules and principles.

Various types of nonstate actors—such as those focusing on development assistance and humanitarian needs, religious groups, those with various ideological or political agendas, and the like—seem to be growing faster than our ability to track and assess their roles and responsibilities, constraints, and contributions, as well as threat potential. Each actor or entity shapes and is shaped by its own system of interaction, with its rules and expectations created by their dominant organizing principle (i.e., profit vs. not for profit, legal vs. nonlegal, etc.). Interestingly, the private sector in the cyber domain—for profit and not for profit—appears to prefer, even converge, around the notion of stakeholders in contrast to the more common notion of stockholders.

An important feature of the second part of the twentieth century is the repositioning of private and public interests, economic and political. We have seen the expansion of private and public interests coupled with the creation of new markets, and innovative practices that shape new interests and ever-fluid "playing fields" of alliances and counter alliances—each governed by distinctive rules and regulations. All of this is making it ever more difficult to understand and track the various systems of interaction. In some cases, we observe something akin to different entities behaving as if they were competing "sovereignties" seeking to expand their control and establish their legitimacy within and across the same territorial domains.

We have seen new regional centers of power with new political aspirations and new competitions on a global scale. As a result, there are new demands on national and international entities. These are invariably accompanied by the development and deployment of prevailing capabilities.

We now recognize the diversity of state and nonstate actors in the international system, as well as attendant demands and capabilities. New asymmetries and their complexities are already taking shape, potentially undermining in many ways the well-known "vertically organized" structures of power and influence. In addition, the evolution of new norms and the proliferation of international organizations—with diverse functions and responsibilities to facilitate development and sustainability—provide a legitimate basis for intrusion and influence deep into the structure of the state system.

1.2.2 Expanding Influence—Intersecting Interests

The shifting character of international relations has also created interests and with these come new vulnerabilities for the state—all without reducing any of the traditional ones. With the expansion of the private sector in almost all parts of the world and on almost all issues, the interests and activities of such entities invariably intersect, and, if unresolved, a wide variety of contentions generally ensue.

These vulnerabilities differ in scale and scope, and so do their implications. For example, we are familiar with the potential disruptions in the world oil market—almost entirely managed by the private sector—and the role of the state in response to interruptions in the flow of petroleum upon which modern economies depend. Each of the private and the public entities operates within their mandated systems of interaction, and in this example, their spheres of interests and activities are converging, if not overlapping, due to the exigencies of the situation.

Many of these features are manifestations of lateral pressure, that is, the propensity of organized entities to expand behavior beyond established boundaries. When this propensity is realized, then we generally observe the intersection of political interests and activities. Such intersection often leads to competition, hostilities, conflict—and the proverbial spiral of action and reaction. Although generally framed in the context of the state system, we observe analogous processes in the competitive commercial contexts (Choucri 1995). The propensity to expand is an empirical phenomenon; it is not contingent on any particular theory of international relations.

All of this contributes to an increasingly complicated policy challenge, exacerbated by an additional issue in the late twentieth century, namely, the introduction of the environmental domain into the political and social discourse at all levels of decision. We also observe a gradual appreciation of the unintended consequences of economic growth as the prime target for all future developments, and a shift toward a quest for sustainable development—an improvement or "progress" in the human condition devoid of the most damaging byproducts of growth. The transition toward sustainability is now a central feature of the international agenda.

We witness changes in the nature of conflict and war in all parts of the world. Large-scale war among major powers no longer seems likely, but we see the state seeking to retain control in its efforts to contain or prevent the evolution of new types of conflict and violence with varying degrees of formal organization. For example, wars for national liberation from colonial rule have gradually been superseded by conflicts waged by nonstate actors, expansion of civil conflicts, and a wide range of terrorist initiatives. Conflicts between major powers over spheres of influence are replaced by contentions over control of these spheres by various local entities. (Afghanistan is a good case in point.)

None of the foregoing is due to the construction of cyberspace or to the expansion of cyber access. Each one of these changes in traditional international relations is embedded in its own situational context and is important in its own right. Jointly they are fundamental features of our world today. And each, in different ways, creates pressures on the established forms of international interactions and on the traditional mechanisms of assessing threats and framing responses. Jointly they constitute the context within which the construction of cyberspace contributes to new and unprecedented shifts in power and influence, and forges new types of threats and new forms of vulnerabilities.

With that background as preamble, we turn to the new arena of interaction that we call cyberspace and draw attention to specific features of structure and process that challenge tradition in international relations—the nature of which provides powerful anchors for all the chapters that follow. At the risk of stating the obvious, the construction of the Internet and the salience of cyber-based actions and interactions will go down in history as such a powerful legacy of the twentieth century, so powerful as to define the very essence of the twenty-first century.

Cyberspace is a global fabric, with few tools to define jurisdictional boundaries. Traditionally jurisdiction, inherent in sovereignty, is understood in physical and geographical terms (with the usual correlates of diplomatic and extraterritorial arrangements). In cyberspace, *who* is recognized to have the legitimate right to adjudicate or govern *what, when,* and *how?*

1.3 Cyberspace—New Complexities

The United States made the decision to explore, initiate, design, and finance the new space. The construction, operation, and management of the new domain were done by nonstate actors. If we take into account the salience of cyberspace—especially the dramatic expansion of cyber access in all parts of the world, the growth in cyber participation, as well as the new opportunities provided by uses of cyber venues—then we can appreciate the fundamental departures from tradition in international structures and processes, and that the world is now much more complex.

We already see that the rapid diffusion of cyber access and participation worldwide has created new patterns of power and leverage, new interests, and new opportunities, and this occurred far more rapidly than would have been anticipated by traditional theory. The new cyber domain has become a critical driver of the ongoing realignments in power and influence, as well as the mechanisms through which different actors at different levels of analysis pursue their objectives. Most important of all, cyber venues have assumed constitutive capabilities of their own.

Then too we observe the cyber-based mobilization of civil society (the aggregations of individuals in their private capacity as well as organized elements of the private sector) and its potential empowerment across jurisdictions, in all parts of the world. Later in this book we consider these developments more closely. The new patterns of power have now begun to challenge the prevailing U.S.-led cyber order and its governing principles—not only from ascending states as traditionally defined but also from civil society, nonstate actors, and a wide range of cross-border interests.

Such sketchy rendering notwithstanding, it is clear to see the potential disconnects between conventional principles and the character and ubiquity of cyberspace. There are inherent tensions that are yet to be addressed. If there is international law for cyberspace, it is still in the making. Especially important here is that characteristic features of cyberspace stand in sharp contrast to our traditional conceptions of social systems, generally, and of the state system in particular. Accordingly, in table 1.1 we draw attention to seven

Table 1.1
Characteristics of cyberspace.

Temporality	Introduces near instantaneity in human interactions
Virtuality	Transcends constraints of location and geography
Permeation	Penetrates boundaries and jurisdictions
Fluidity	Sustains shifts and reconfigurations
Participation	Reduces barriers to activism and political expression
Attribution	Obscures actor identity and links to action
Accountability	Bypasses established mechanisms of accountability

Source: Based on Choucri (2012, 4).

critical disconnects between important features of cyberspace and defining features of the state system. To be clear, these are properties of cyberspace from a user perspective in the most general terms (Choucri 2012).

To date, none of these features are usually considered particularly problematic from a computer science perspective or as seen by the original architects of the Internet. However, they can be seen as undermining the power and sovereignty of states and the traditional norms of social order that sustain it. A major concern to the state system and to traditional international relations theory, policy, and practice is the fact that cyberspace—with its ubiquity, pervasiveness, and global reach—has been constructed and continues to be managed at the global level almost entirely by the private sector. Closely related is the "myth of the Internet," derived from early views that the rules of digital technology are so elusive as to remain beyond the reach of formal state authority. Highlighting excerpts from a 2001 article in *Technology Review*, the editors remind us of what we now recognize as a persistent myth, namely that "information wants to be free" (C. C. Mann 2001, 44).

Early in the twenty-first century, it was already apparent that the cyber domain shapes new parameters of international relations and new dimensions of international politics. Among the most salient new features is the previously noted creation of new actors—some with formal identities and others without—and their cyber empowerment, which is altering the traditional international decision landscape in potentially significant ways. Concurrently, we see the growing use of cyber venues by nonstate groups whose objectives are to undermine the state or to alter its foundations. The recent WikiLeaks episodes showed in unambiguous ways the politicization and disruptiveness of cyberspace. Responses varied across the international landscape, but in general, most, if not all, countries viewed this episode as a threat to their sovereignty and to their security and are becoming more and more aware of their own vulnerabilities.

In addition, the growth in the number of cyber-centered actors increases the density of decision entities—each with new interests and new capabilities to pursue their interests—and thus increases the potential for intersections in spheres of influence, with possibilities for new and different types of contentions and possible conflicts.

With the benefit of hindsight, we now observe how seemingly transparent and relatively "simple" was the world of the nineteenth century through most of the twentieth century. Gradually it became more "complicated" as the victors' design for the postwar period required major innovations in the management of international activities. In retrospect, once more, what we had understood as "complicated" is more accurately described as "complex." With increasing cross-border interactions, entanglements that were initially viewed as "interdependence" during the twentieth century took on dynamics of their own, shaping what we refer to as "globalization."

All of this remained, until recently, in the low politics domain. As cyberspace shifted to the realm of high politics, it altered the international political ecology, topography, and demography in profound ways. Whereas globalization—reinforced by interactions in the cyber domain—is well recognized, less attention has been given to localization in international relations or in the cyber domain. (The term "globalization" crept into the political lexicon long before the consolidation of cyber venues.)

Interactions in cyberspace have shifted the balance of power among different actors, including the traditional state powers, and enabled weaker actors to influence or even threaten stronger actors. (Note press reports of anonymous penetration incidences of U.S. government computer systems.) This sort of shift has little precedent in world politics. We might view this situation—the players and their capabilities—as emergent new asymmetries. However framed, we are witnessing a potentially powerful shift in the nature of the game. The increased influence of nonstate entities may well undermine the sanctity of sovereignty as the defining principle for the international system. The forgoing calls into question the effectiveness of traditional policy tools and responses crafted to deal with state-to-state interactions in a geopolitical world—with known threat actors and an arsenal of expected diplomatic or military responses.

All of this creates an added and inescapable problem for the state, the state system, and international relations, that is, the emergence of unprecedented forms of threat to security. These threats carry a new label (cyber threats) to signal new vulnerabilities (cybersecurity) and—most vexing of all—emanating from unknown sources (attribution problem). Invariably these trends further reinforce the politicization of cyberspace and its salience in emergent policy discourses.

1.4   The Co-Evolution Dilemma

The subtitle of this book, *The Co-Evolution Dilemma*, reflects the growing politicization of cyberspace and its implications for international relations. We proceed from the premise that the two domains are evolving into a system of interlocking and mutual influence that continues to shape each of these arenas, while creating added, joint effects on society, economy, politics, and all aspects of the human experience. The dilemma is rooted in the fact that the two systems are changing at different rates, and elements of each are also changing at different rates, thereby creating realities and uncertainties that are particularly difficult to anticipate or manage—let alone regulate.

In this book, we consider the dilemma "writ large" but often shaped by relatively minor matters, questions, or disconnects. For example, why is it, and how, that the sovereign state that supported the construction of cyberspace with its vision of openness and freedom is also engaged in various "denial of service" practices? How do different countries attempt to control data and information flows, monitor content, or sever connections? How is it and why is it that the "illegitimate" or damaging uses of the Internet are growing much faster than our ability to identify, let alone to control or prevent, them? Why is it that the power of the state—with its monopoly over the use of force, in theory at least—seems inadequate for responding to threats from the cyber domain? All of this is intensely political—in all contexts and at all levels of analysis.

1.4.1   New "Realities" for the State System

We continue to witness inevitable changes worldwide, the specific nature of which cannot be readily discerned with any degree of certainty. Some are driven in part by concerns that are traditionally viewed as low politics, such as population dynamics, resource uses, technological developments, and environmental changes. Others are shaped by high politics, such as strategic competition, conflict and warfare, and contentions over right and wrong. Still others are shaped by the competitive pressures of the newly forming and rapidly expanding markets surrounding the layers of the Internet.

It may well be that changes in one domain—cyberspace or the international system—induce changes in the other. It is unlikely that any change can be attributed entirely to endogenous factors. It goes without saying that differences in speed are foundational in any consideration of co-evolution. This is taken for granted. Yet to be developed are methods for capturing the differences. We do not anticipate, nor hypothesize mirror-image dynamics across physical and cyber domains, nor can we even consider the possibility of identical adjustments over time. Temporal differences go a long way in shaping the nature of co-evolution—the leads and lags, the feedback, and other critical systemic features.

Of relevance here is not just co-evolution but also its dilemma—for the state and the state system. We see today the possibility that cyberspace can "out-evolve" the tools of the state, leaving the state poorly equipped to address its needs. The state has not yet developed theories or practices that will allow it to maintain control over its core values while preserving the vital character of cyberspace. Indeed, the state has not yet understood the full implications of cyberspace and its properties.

Many facets of this constructed space are not well understood. There is considerable ambiguity by "the user" as well as "the state" about technical, managerial, operational, and governance factors that might directly or indirectly bear on the future of security and sustainability. Yet states must develop strategies, policies, and instruments to manage emergent challenges to their positions. They must protect the operational mechanisms that have evolved over the centuries and are considered fundamental anchors for the international system as a whole.

As noted, the dilemma is exacerbated by differences in rates of change: cyberspace is evolving much faster than are the tools the state has to regulate it. They both change, but at different rates. Furthermore, different features of cyberspace—in technical, management, or operational terms—change at different rates, thus making it more difficult to derive a "general" rate of change for the entire domain. The state system, by contrast, is not known for its rapid change in overall structure, functions, orientations, performance—or any other feature thereof. These embedded disjunctions will become more, rather than less, salient over time. Also important is the nature of the evolutionary drivers, that is, whether they are endogenous and generated by the R&D system, or exogenous to the R&D system and even the domain at hand.

The co-evolution dilemma invariably touches upon, and may even become dominated by, the activities of nonstate actors and their management of the Internet so far. Overall states recognize the dominance of the private sector in shaping the Internet, but few states are ready to accept or accommodate this reality. All are confronted with the uncertainties over control of the cyber domain—how, when, and why? More starkly, we ask these questions: *what* are the controls, *who* controls, and *where* are the control points?

To some extent, there is a general tendency among analysts of international relations to make simplifying assumptions about the character of cyberspace. Generally, these push toward similarity with the known "real" domain that in itself may be problematic. To the extent that the state determines that it must shape the character of cyberspace—irrespective of the wisdom of so proceeding—there are today few guideposts or theories as to how to proceed in order to achieve this objective. If cyberspace and international relations evolve a joint system, then differences must be addressed. Already we appreciate that they are held together by very different concepts and practices of organization and order.

A major barrier to effective understanding of these seemingly disconnected features is the dearth of concepts or approaches leading to an integrated framework that connects the two domains in a systematic way, provides critical linkages, and incorporates major actors and forms of activity. Such a framework is fundamental for understanding the mutual influences—their sources and consequences. And challenges abound. On the one hand, it goes without saying that we will continue to see changes in world politics that cannot always be attributed to cyberspace. On the other hand, cyberspace is constructed by human ingenuity; it is difficult to argue its autonomous status. We shall begin by considering these two domains individually, each shaped by their respective operational principles. Then we shall trace their interconnections.

How is the overall cyber domain managed—in pieces and in parts? What is the nature and character of critical cyber-centered organizations and institutional practices? New international arrangements are being established for the management of cyberspace. They are distinctly new additions to the global landscape. We cannot as yet determine their utility or effectiveness, or even their relative rate of evolution. Will they be able to evolve at the rate that cyberspace itself evolves, or will they themselves be "out evolved"?

Earlier in this chapter we alluded to characteristic features of our world today that appear highly inconsistent with traditional principles as well as facts on the ground. At issue here is not the quest for consistency but the signal that certain types of inconsistencies may fester and morph into drivers of instability, threats to security, and even conflict and violence. In other words, rooted in low politics, some inconsistencies may evolve into high politics. Inevitably, this raises added questions: What are the forms of cyber conflicts and what are the connections to the traditional modes of conflict systems? How do hostilities spill over across domains to shape overarching conflict? What mechanisms exist to resolve cyber conflicts?

1.4.2   Complexity of Co-Evolution

So far in this chapter we have alluded to a wide range of conditions that are generally complex—complexity is understood in the conventional sense of the term. More formally, however, a complex system consists of many interacting entities, "agents," whose incentives, roles, and functions are context specific (i.e., market, politics, trade, etc.). They are connected by shared information and networked relationships. In definitional as well as operational terms, the whole of a complex system is greater than the sum of its individual parts.

We are reminded that complexity science is "the study of phenomena which emerge from a collection of interacting objects..." (N. F. Johnson 2009, 3) and capable of adjusting to changing conditions. Complexity theory is about agents (actors) and networks, operating over time and space. It is also about the relationships between the parts and the whole of a system, that is, how interactions among the parts generate behaviors of a system, as well as how the system interacts with its broader context.

At a high level of abstraction, the evolution of social systems is usually considered more with reference to the generic biological mechanisms known as selection and variation, rather than with decision systems and agency, or to institutional choices and outcomes. Both idiom and known features of biological evolution provide important insights even in terms of reference for the challenges at hand. For example, writing in the *International Encyclopedia of the Social Sciences*, Lewontin (1968, 203) highlights the "hierarchy of principles" in evolutionary perspective to signal direct relevance to the social sciences.

In Lewontin's terms of reference, the hierarchy of principles consists of "change, order, direction, progress and perfectibility" (Lewontin 1968, 203). At first glance, these principles appear entirely abstract, devoid of empirical content. When viewed with reference to actors and entities, actions and behaviors, structures and processes, as well as conflict and cooperation, they provide necessary—but not sufficient—conceptual foundations for the inquiry at hand. So, if we consider the increasing interconnections of the cyberspace and international relations—and the co-evolution dilemma in its various facets—we will necessarily focus on critical anchors (or "hooks") to help frame and track evolution and co-evolution.

In this context, change, direction, and order are the most portable to the factors at hand. Change is inevitable, as are variations in rates of change noted earlier. However, variations in themselves are not neutral with respect to power relations, or technological contexts, and direction is of primary importance. Change is the defining feature of social life. Direction usually results from the relative influence of the drivers of change. It is a cumulative process, and it is path dependent; but it is also subject to sharp breaks by decision, innovation, or system overload relative to system capabilities. Order usually refers to structures and functions for governance, as well as overall system supports for sustainability and survival. Again, at this writing, we are observing emerging conflict over the nature of order for cyberspace in the international context. It should come as no surprise that China and Russia pursue a vision of order different from that of the United States and its allies.

Interactions among the parts and the whole of a system are shaped by two related but distinct processes, namely, path dependency and feedback dynamics. Both processes create bounds for discretionary actions, the nature of which depends on actors, situations, stakes, and general conditions. There might be a presumption of equilibrium-seeking behavior, but none of equilibrium as a system property.

Among the most important features of complexity are the emergent phenomena or properties of the system. Central to all evolutionary systems is "self-organization" (Kauffman 1996, 8). In this book, we shall point to the "self-generating" and "self-organizing" without any central authority or center of power, in both the cyber domain and the international system.

1.4.3   Complexity and Authority

In social science parlance, what keeps a system together is authority. Authority involves a claim of trust in social relationships in order to induce conformity and support for governing principles. So, too, there is a special relationship between author or source and subject, a relationship that is located in a particular definable domain. This relationship is based on consensus and is created by prevailing norms, rules, and practices. In this context, authority is institutionalized power authenticated by legitimacy. The directionality—on matters of substance as well as context—forges a set of obligations. All of this is social order.

The international system is a system of states. The state can rely on obedience of its citizens by establishing legal codes and punishing those who transgress. This, in conjunction with the inability of individuals to protect themselves from others, forges the special relationship between state and individuals. Generally, public authority dominates and social recognition of authority is expressed publically.

The twenty-first century has inherited an international system with a large number of actors that are not states and are not state based. They pursue their own interests, and not necessarily those of the state or those of the market. According to R. B. Hall and Biersteker (2002), private authority arises when there are gaps in capacity or in functionality. On this basis, nonstate actors have been accorded some form of legitimacy. They serve some other (often larger) public across state borders. They are strong enough to establish the rule of interaction over an issue area, and even control the agenda for policy deliberation. Today, private authority is strong and salient in many parts of the world and for many issue areas. This may well be a challenge to the assumption of state primacy.

In the cyber domain, the entire arena was constructed by private sector actors (albeit with support and funding from the dominant state). In this context, private authority is self-generated by the construction of the new domain. The foundations were functional (making sure the Internet works) but took on normative features early on (making sure that the architecture supports an open Internet). In this particular case, the state provided the support required for realization of the cyber vision.

Authority over the operation of the Internet is based on performance and capability. More specifically, authority in the cyber domain is derived from innovation of the system we call the Internet and the operational capacity demonstrated by effective control of essential activities. Often this authority continues to rest on evolving and often delegated capabilities—all in order to support relatively nonsubstitutable functions—with relatively nonsubstitutable actors, at least in the short run. Operational authority also calls for self-regulation. In short, the role of private authority is functional (and only partly normative) and is self-generated (rather than assigned).

At this writing, the governance of cyberspace has taken on a new salience due to efforts of a group of legal experts to extend international law to cyberspace. In general, international law refers to the corpus, or body, of law that governs the legal relations among states. This body is based on custom, treaties, or other formal arrangements that affect the rights and responsibilities of states to each other. It is strictly state based, anchored in principles of sovereignty. Authority, in the context, is derived from the past and legitimized by the sovereign system. It is not too difficult to imagine the contentions that will continue to surround such efforts.

1.5   What Lies Ahead?

This book is in two parts.

Part I, on *cyberspace and international relations*, focuses on salient features of the two domains, with special attention to structures and processes. As noted earlier, so far, cyberspace and the international system have been viewed as separate domains of interaction—each based on its own principles, defined by its own parameters. The first and probably most important challenge before us is to develop rules for framing the interconnections of the traditional (physical) international domain and the new (virtual) Internet-enabled domain. This means that we must first highlight the characteristic features of each system and then, on this basis, develop an integrated model of the joint domain. Such is the focus of chapters 2–5.

In chapter 2, we put forth a framework that distinguishes between the physical infrastructure of the Internet and its role as a carrier of information. To provide some structure and decomposition to the phenomenon, we will exploit a model familiar to technologists—a layered model of the Internet, the core of cyberspace. Although use of a layered model to describe the Internet is well understood, different models have been proposed, so we chose to frame a four-layer model that captures the features of interest for alignment purposes. Defined in some detail, the model consists of the physical layer, the platform layer, the information later, and the people layer.

We use layering to describe both the technology itself and the actors that make and shape it, and the functions they perform. To the extent relevant so early in this book, we shall also indicate the static versus the more dynamic features of each layer. We note that sophisticated controls at the information layer are required to address emergent international contentions.

Chapter 3 introduces the traditional hierarchical view of international relations, namely, levels of analysis—the individual, the state, and the international system. Anchored in the principle of sovereignty, this view distinguishes between the state and other entities and provides the legal basis for the modern system of international relations. The limits of the level of analysis in international relations are well recognized. Chapter 3 expands the conventional view by (1) specifying the global system as an overarching level of analysis, (2) extending the levels framework beyond the social domain to include the natural environment (of life-supporting properties) and the constructed environment (of Internet-enabled cyberspace), and (3) introducing different ways of looking at the international system, drawing on lateral pressure theory for an empirical and quantitative perspective on various dynamics of transformation and change due to the construction of cyberspace.

It is useful to signal that (1) unlike the layers structure, permeability of influences across levels of analysis is the rule, not the exception; (2) the extent to which situations and behaviors at one level influence structure and process across others varies considerably; and (3) despite evidence of increasing cyber access worldwide, the operational norms and practices vary considerably within levels and across jurisdictions.

In chapter 4, we attempt to tie these two frameworks together, connecting the levels of analysis in international relations and the layers of the Internet. This approach provides a view of the whole and the parts and helps contextualize actors and entities, interests and activities, as well as sources of change and potential impacts. In so doing we address the empirical features located at the intersection of levels and layers. Then, using the cyber layers and the international relations levels, we illustrate the joint framework with selected examples of how issues that arise in cyberspace affect the state and its interests.

These illustrations help us understand the connections between cyberspace and international relations and, as noted previously, provide the foundations for an integrated model of the two domains. We also focus on the ways in which the "pieces hang together." The alignment strategy gives us a model within which actors and actions can be positioned and evaluated. In principle, all actors and all cyber functions can be viewed within this framework. Drawing on lateral pressure theory, introduced earlier, we can then derive some basic principles for identifying sources and consequences of transformation.

This process should yield the interconnections between foundational features of cyberspace, on the one hand, and structure and process in international relations, on the other. It should provide a full census of major actors in conjunction with the modes of interaction in their respective contexts. In this way, we seek to enhance the capabilities and methods of social scientists and scholars, as well as analysts of international relations and other areas of social interactions, to understand and incorporate the larger role and character of cyberspace in diverse social contexts. A considerable literature is already developing around these issues, as scholars, analysts, practitioners, and policy makers seek to grapple with the new realities.

Chapter 5 highlights the scale and scope of evolving complexities due to the impacts of cyberspace on the international system—a system that consists today not only of the traditional parameters, actors, and entities noted in chapter 3, but also of a wide range of new actors, new processes, and new sources of conflict and of cooperation. The conventional view of international relations has morphed into a complex landscape hosting new actors, activities, and outcomes—all pressing on the state system and its foundations. A whole range of new entities and actors, experiences and interactions, institutions and agencies—some introduced in chapter 2 and chapter 4—and, most importantly, a wide range of operational, effective, and even powerful nonstate entities have assumed center stage. By mapping out the various aspects of the extended levels of analysis, we seek to unbundle international relations and highlight the various points at which there are obvious intersections with the cyber domain.

Cyber access empowers the individual, the first level of analysis. It provides new and powerful ways to articulate and aggregate their interests and mobilize for action. The individual begins to matter in the state-based sovereign system. From a theoretical perspective, this means that the first level in international relations theory is as privileged as other levels of analysis, a change from traditional theory. Theories of perception and misperception as well as constructivism in international relations are likely to be relevant at this level.

For the state, the second level of analysis, cyberspace creates new imperatives for the traditional security calculus by calling attention to the importance of cybersecurity—security of online information and knowledge, and protection against cyber threats, espionage, sabotage, crime, and fraud. All of these elements are relevant to the overall security of the state but to different degrees and extents. The state must now protect the security of its own cyber systems and capabilities, as well as defend against uses of cyberspace to undermine its overall security, stability, and sustainability. Recognizing that cyberspace has become a war-fighting domain and the world's major power, the United States established the U.S. Cyber Command. Other countries may well follow suit. Realism and neorealism may well be of relevance here.

The third level of analysis consists of the international system and its constituent parts anchored in the state. Cyberspace has accelerated the formation of private interests that become influential entities in their own right, with goals and objectives, priorities, and problems. It has also empowered international institutions with new tools to support communication and performance. At the same time, it is creating a new arena of conflict and contention for states and nonstates alike. Insights from institutionalism (including regime theory and other variants) can be useful here.

At the fourth level, the global system transcends and incorporates other levels. This level consists of the Earth's population and its global society, supported by all the life-supporting properties of nature. It now spans cyberspace, the most pervasive system of interaction ever constructed by human science and engineering—and challenges social, regulatory, and policy practices.

With such expansion comes the potential for contention and opportunities for conflict. We will highlight the specific ways in which cyberspace has already influenced the fabric of international relations, then propose some extensions and modifications to the levels perspective in order to integrate the important aspects of cyberspace into the overall fabric of international relations. Almost all international institutions have extended their reach and performance by using cyber tools and capabilities. Little in this trend is surprising, except perhaps the speed at which the use of cyber access is taking shape. Although states are the *stockholders* in international governance, nonstate actors and other *stakeholders* resort to cyber venues for interest articulation and aggregation decision forums. In this connection, civil society, a cross-level social construct, is an aggregation of individuals with demands and capabilities distinct, even separate, from those of the state or organized nonstate actors.

Part II is on the *complexities of co-evolution*. Conceptually and operationally, our goal in these chapters is to address the near decomposability of complex systems. Some might argue that, in the overall scheme of things "everything is related to everything else," but for pragmatic as well as policy reasons, it is important to identify those system segments that reflect tightly coupled relationships, that is, a high degree of interdependence. All of this is shaped by the interactive effects of structures and processes for cyberspace and international relations, as well as the emergent properties created by their co-evolution. All of this enables us to examine the dynamics of co-evolution and attendant complexities in considerable detail.

Given the ecosystem of the Internet—and the dynamics of cyberspace—with multitudes of options for control, it might seem that an organized actor could find some way to exercise control if that were his or her intention. Given the logic of layers and levels, it might seem that the cyber ecosystem conditions potentials for control. And given the diversity of power and influence of various traditional and cyber actors in international relations, it may appear almost impossible to map out *who* can control *what*, *when*, and *how*. These issues all pertain to the broad space of contention delineated as much by the architecture and manipulability of the Internet layers as by the distribution of power and capabilities across the levels of analysis in international relations. At this point we take on an added challenge, namely, identifying and understanding the control mechanisms in the cyber–international relations integrated system—who controls what? How? When? And with what consequences?

In chapter 6, we develop a method for addressing control in the cyber domain that we call control point analysis, and then demonstrate its utility in different contexts for different uses. This method is complementary to the levels and layers approach in part I. Chapter 6 identifies critical features of technology (structure and process) and actors (roles and functions) inherent in the pursuit of a particular task or objective. As we introduce this method, we shall focus on actors, actions, and outcomes given the structure and process of the Internet, as well as cyberspace more broadly defined.

For contextual purposes, we highlight some of the key actors that make the Internet experience. For example, the actors that actually construct, build, and operate regions of the Internet are Internet Service Providers (ISPs). Within their regions, they control topology and completion of connections (e.g., who talks to whom, under what circumstances). ISPs exercise ultimate operational control; if they do not forward packets, the operation fails. Other aspects of the Internet experience are controlled by other actors: those who develop operating systems, build browsers, make Web content, and so on. Governments can pass laws, and actors around the periphery of cyberspace can compete for power, but in the end, if these actions are to have any consequence, they must change the character of cyberspace itself in some way—they must change the experience of using the Internet or they are not material.

To illustrate control point analysis, chapter 6 presents a simple user task: the steps taken in the normal sequence of events to first create and then retrieve a selected Web page. Each step is a potential point of control, and we show which actors have immediate authority, access, or technological responsibility for each control point. We show the steps that are taken to prepare the computer for use on the Internet, steps taken by the content provider to ready a page for viewing on the Internet, and steps taken for actual retrieval. The purpose of this section is to focus more closely on the diversity of actors and actions that are taken and that the user usually does not track.

In chapter 7, we apply control point analysis to major actors in international relations and the cyber domain, namely the United States, China, and Google. These applications provide not only a common method across cases but also make it easier to identify the critical differences in the capabilities of the various actors. We illustrate the space of contention, its configuration, and the control options of key actors. In many ways, we can consider control as an operational manifestation of power and leverage. In general, few governments exercise direct control over cyberspace. They can exert great influence by their ability to influence other actors using regulation, legislation, investment (procurement and research), and standards, as well as other more direct means of leverage. In the United States, the government and the ISPs are separate entities in law and in practice. It would seem that the tussle over control is ongoing, with no lasting victory for any side. One actor designs an application, other actors hunt for points of control, others design mitigations to the controls, and so on.

If there is one lesson to be learned from chapters 6 and 7, it is about the intricacy of cyber operations given the role of diverse actors, on the one hand, and the complexity of structure, process, and operations, on the other hand. We note the ability of select actors (China) to manage all intricacies without resort to what are conventionally considered "private" actors. A related lesson is about the overarching management strategy within which all operational features are embedded. China's streamlined strategy stands in sharp contrast to the distributed approach of the U.S. case.

Chapter 8 examines two different aspects of the joint cyber-IR domain, namely, (1) conflict and contention and (2) cooperation and collaboration. We begin with conflict dynamics. The challenge is to understand various modalities and the ways in which different actors seek to exert influence and shape their environment to support their goals. We begin with cyber-based system threats and consider modes of adversarial interactions. We present two somewhat countervailing perspectives on cyber conflict at this point in time. The first perspective puts forth select "state-of-the-art" views of threats to cybersecurity—as well as cyber conflict and war. The second perspective reports on an initiative to engage in systematic comparisons across cases of cyber conflict. The purpose is to highlight central tendencies (as well as outlier features and idiosyncrasies). Overall, at this point we signal: "reader, beware"—there the evidence is incomplete, the data are inconsistent, and we must do our best with what there is.

These investigations—something of an experiment in the context of our joint MIT-Harvard project on *Explorations in Cyber International Relations*—is driven by one question: What systematic inferences, if any, can be drawn from a set of cases reported in narrative form? The results suggest that the "new normal" in world politics in the cyber age is one that transcends state actors and actions. The conduct of conflict, violence, and warfare in the cyber domain is significantly different from tradition in international relations. A wide range of nonstate entities—known and unknown—operate in a highly dynamic and volatile international context. At a minimum, the salience of nonstate actors, the potential influence of the individual, and the role of group activity may continue to be part of the "new normal."

Turning to examples of cooperation and collaboration, we focus on how the international community has begun to respond to the rapid growth of cyber conflicts and the spillover effects on traditional international relations. We consider different forms of responses, each with distinctive features, and reflecting different interests, priorities, and perspectives. It should come as no surprise that institutional responses to damaging cyber behavior have evolved gradually—in different contexts and with different effects—and that threat behaviors have grown at much faster rates than have response capabilities. Nonetheless, these responses are important as they reflect emergent capabilities to deal with new unknowns, especially when viewed in the broader strategic context.

Chapter 9 focuses on governance of the Internet, the core of cyberspace. How is the new arena of interaction managed, in its parts and in the whole? What are the basic principles? To raise a familiar question, adapted somewhat to this situation, this is about "who does what, when, and how." By extension, of course, one can begin to derive "who gets what, when, and how."

We present a mapping of the entire governance system for the Internet, albeit at a high level of resolution. What we see is a loosely connected ecosystem of ecosystems. The individual pieces are distinctive in their own right. The conjunction of mutual dependencies, the salience of consensus, and absence of coercive mechanisms—all in the course of managing and "running" a large-scale, cross-jurisdiction, distributed system—is a new and major institutional design.

We also examine emergent modes of international collaboration given the growing salience of cyberspace. We review the major mechanisms, the institutional innovations, and the private sector arrangements since the construction of cyberspace. This includes actors and actions designed to enable the workings of cyberspace and routinize the regulation of the cyber system; and other actors that reflect the state system and provide the interface with the traditional international system.

This chapter then situates three seminal global conferences to date, each with its motivation and message, as well as products and outcomes, namely: (1) the World Summit on the Information Society, a new intergovernmental initiative to pursue a global agenda, (2) the World Conference on International Telecommunications, a formal conference convened to update an operational treaty, and (3) NETmundial, in 2014, a notable and unexpected initiative that came at a time marked by a convergence of surprising events, including the Snowden revelations and their aftermath and the U.S. announcement of its "separation" from the Internet Corporation for Assigned Names and Numbers, a driver for consensus building around plans for managing this transition.

Finally, chapter 9 turns to international law for cyber activities, presented in *Tallinn Manual 2.0 on the International Law Applicable to Cyber Operations* (Schmitt 2017). Despite the daunting disconnect between the state-centric model of order articulated in international law, on the one hand, and the fluid, diffuse, and decentralized character of cyberspace, on the other, they share a joint feature, namely the territorial character of the physical layer of the Internet.

Chapter 10 focuses on the dynamics of transformation and change in the joint system of cyberspace and international relations. We will point to the powerful mismatch of the rates of change, a mismatch that derives from fundamental factors. The private sector and the state run at different rates, a fact that, in turn, points to inevitable struggle and tension between the dominance of the private sector and its operational private order, on the one hand, and the rights of the state and the principle of sovereign order, on the other. In addition, the variable and differential rates of change that dominate at various layers of the Internet reinforce the private-public contentions. And all of this takes place in a world that is increasingly complicated by interactions across levels of analysis—with a growing influence of individuals, the first level, and the consolidation of the common features of the global system, the fourth level. These levels are also subject to different rates of change.

The various elements of the cyber ecosystem—technology, standards, private sector, state, civil society, and international institutions—are each challenged to "maintain their fitness." Different parts of this ecosystem have very different natural rates of change, a fact that leads to major structural problems within the system. To illustrate, we focus on the differentials in the rates of change inherent in the cyber and in the state system. The institution of the state is anchored in continuity and stability, shaped by the bureaucratic logic, the legal system, participatory mechanisms, accounting imperatives, authorization requirements, and so forth. As we explore the drivers of change and the interacting dynamics of this system, we also look at the behavior of various actors through alternative lenses, to indicate potential trajectories of the co-evolution dilemma, not to predict what will happen. The state is the most assertive actor in world politics, in that it can take decisions and proceed accordingly. However, its power to take decisions does not imply its ability to maintain fitness for purpose.

In chapter 11, we turn to the consequences of co-evolution. Based on what we have developed to this point, what can we infer about the future of cyberspace? In this chapter, we paint a number of pictures of possible futures for this co-evolving system. We focus on several of our lenses to map out possible futures: (1) the layer model, (2) our levels of analysis model, (3) our control point analysis model, and (4) our analysis of the governance of cyberspace. These lenses are closely related but very distinct in their perspective and implication. We draw on the earlier chapters and use the models and frameworks developed to offer some inferences—clearly speculations—about the future. We do not predict the future—the drivers of change are too diverse and their interactions too unpredictable. But we can identify critical drivers and make some claims about likely directions.

Our inferences about the future are shaped by some general presumptions. Individuals and small groups of people can be very nimble at inventing unexpected and unpredictable innovations that may come to shape the future, for example, Bitcoin. The private sector can as well move quickly in certain circumstances (e.g., where capital or politics are not the gating factors) and will continue to be a powerful driver of the future.

Chapter 12 highlights further complexity for the co-evolution dilemma, given that systems that were once parallel and then gradually became joined have generated a new whole with features, dynamics, and an overall character that is greater than the sum of what were once its individual parts. What we may have once considered as parallel "realities," the virtual and the physical, have become inextricably interconnected. Even the term used earlier, "entanglement," may not accurately reflect the pervasive joint influences with attendant system-changing effects. We have witnessed the increased density of actors/users in cyberspace as well as the density of decision entities, in conjunction with the remarkable expansion of governance structures for the management of information and communication technologies and the support of development goals.

We begin this last chapter of the book with some highlights of our investigations presented in brief form. Then we turn to powerful parameters of the co-evolution dilemma and ask, what are theoretical implications of the new realities? In response, we put forth some critical imperatives that we consider fundamental for twenty-first-century international relations theory.

The term "imperatives" refers to the essential, even necessary, anchors for twenty-first-century theory, policy, and practice. Their effects permeate all levels of analysis in international relations—the individual, the state, the international system, and the global system—including transnational and nonstate actors, for profit and not for profit. These are grounded in the evolution of knowledge and evidence and the experiences of the past decades, not on assumptions or premises of twentieth-century politics and power. As imperatives, these are foundational for our understanding and management of emergent realities.

2 Cyberspace: Layers and Interconnections

In the previous chapter, we noted the distinct and separate developmental trajectories—the histories—of cyberspace, on the one hand, and of international relations, on the other. The separate histories are important in having shaped their own path dependence to date. This chapter focuses on the structures that define cyberspace, more specifically the Internet. We develop two models: one is structural, based on *layers*, and one is topological, based on the patterns of *interconnection* that make up the Internet. The patterns of regional interconnection are a reflection of the physical distribution of the Internet and provide an entry to understanding potential relationships between cyberspace and political issues such as jurisdiction. This narrative is largely devoid of reference to politics, power, or international relations.

In general terms, most scholars and practitioners share a working concept of cyberspace. It is a domain of interaction created by the collection of computing devices connected by networks in which electronic information is stored and utilized and communication takes place.[1] Another way to understand the nature of cyberspace is to articulate its purpose, which we will describe as the processing, manipulation, and exploitation of information, the facilitation and augmentation of communication among people, and the interaction of people and information. Both information and people are central to the power and venues of cyberspace.

Because it is the *connected* nature of cyberspace that gives its distinct character—not just that computing is now widespread but that essentially all computing is connected together by a common network, we focus here on the Internet as the core of cyberspace, but we stress that computing, both at the edges (personal computing, the so-called Internet of Things, and the like) and in the core (including so-called "cloud computing"), as well as embedded processing, and the cellular world are all necessary enablers of cyberspace—as are the institutions that govern the standards, operational norms, and attendant requisites.

Whereas it is common practice today to associate cyberspace with the Internet, with its particular approach to interconnection, there could be many alternative cyberspaces, driven by different visions and principles at different layers and defined (created and constructed) by different approaches to interconnection. Indeed, in *The Victorian Internet*, Tom Standage (1998) argues that the mode of interconnection created by the telegraph was as transformative in its time as the Internet is today. However, the structure (and the structural implications) and the scale and scope of use (and users) of the telegraph and the Internet could not be more different, as we will show later.

From a social science perspective, cyberspace is a domain or arena of interaction, an ecosystem with an emphasis on human construction of this domain (in contrast to the natural environment, an arena of interaction that is not created by humans). We shall return to this issue later on in this book when we consider diverse facets of the cyber domain.

The subtitle of this book, *The Co-Evolution Dilemma*, captures our view of the actors and actions in cyberspace. It is a dynamic ecosystem in which actors compete for success, where fitness for purpose is the metric of survival, and where the roles and structure of the ecosystem also evolve. The later chapters provide models that attempt to characterize the dynamics of the cyberspace ecosystem, but as a place to start, it useful to have a simple, static, or structural framework that shows the system and organizes the different actors by their salient characteristics and location in the overall system. A framework with structure for the Internet—the core of cyberspace—is particularly useful as an introduction to cyberspace because it allows us to understand contingencies and dependencies.

2.1   A Four-Layer Model

In this chapter, we will attempt to characterize the core of cyberspace, starting with the character of the Internet and all of its constituent features and support mechanisms. A commonly used framework to describe the Internet is a *layered model*, and we will follow that convention with a simple, four-layer model, as shown in figure 2.1, which we will use in the subsequent chapters of the book. We focus on the Internet as we introduce this model,

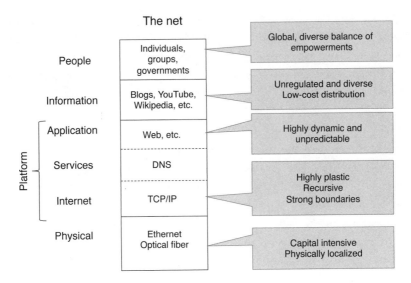

Figure 2.1
The layers of the Internet and their key attributes.

but it can be used as well to characterize other aspects of cyberspace, such as computing platforms and other sorts of networks. (Other analysts have used models with more layers, but for our purposes, the four-layer view provides all of the basics that are required.) From the top down, the important layers that are structurally and functionally differentiated are:

- *The people*—that is, the users and constituencies of cyber venues who participate in and shape the cyber experience—who communicate, work with information, make decisions and carry out plans, and who themselves transform the nature of cyberspace by working with its component services and capabilities, and by making direct and indirect demands for the construction of new functionalities.

- *The information*, in its various forms and manifestations, that is stored, transmitted, and transformed in cyberspace.

- *The platform layers* that provide the services that realize the structure of cyberspace.

- *The physical foundations* that support the logical elements, the fundamental physicality that enables the "virtual" manifestations of interactions.

Of course we recognize that the second, third, and fourth layers are enabled, if not operated by, people, but we differentiate here between those who are essentially users or "takers" who constitute the "demand" side and those who are central to the layer functions that jointly enable the "supply" side. When we consider the individual layers, the functionalities and dependencies become clear. Here we reverse the order, beginning with the foundational elements.

2.1.1   The Bottom Layer—The Physical Components

The foundation of the Internet, and hence of cyberspace, is the *physical* layer—the physical devices out of which it is built. Cyberspace is a space of interconnected computing devices, so its foundations are personal computers (PCs) and servers, supercomputers and grids, sensors and transducers, and various sorts of networks and communications channels. Communications may occur over wires or fibers, via radio transmission, or by the physical transport of the computing and storage devices from place to place. The physical layer is perhaps the easiest to grasp; because it is tangible, its physicality gives it a grounded sense of location. Physical devices such as routers or data centers exist in a place and thus sit within a jurisdiction. Some physical components, such as residential access networks, are capital intensive, and the industries that produce them are as much construction companies as telecommunications companies.

2.1.2   The Platform Layer

The next layer above the physical layer we call the *platform* layer. The structure of the platform layer is a series of *sublayers* that each provides services to the next sublayer above, hence our choice of the term *platform*. Low-level services include program execution environments, mechanisms for data transport, and standards for data formats. The basic transport service of the Internet, which moves packets of data from a source to a destination, is an essential element of this lowest sublayer of the platform layer. Out of these low-level components and services are built *applications*, such as a word processor, a database or the Web. In turn, by combining these, more complex services emerge. For example, by combining a database with the Web, we get dynamic content generation and active Web objects. On top of the Web, we now see services such as *Facebook* that are themselves platforms for further application development. Once the foundations are in place—the anchors set—then human creativity drives different forms of generativity, in functionalities, activities, and possibilities.

The physical foundations of cyberspace are fundamental. Cyberspace is a real artifact built out of real elements, not a domain without any physical grounding. But the nature of cyberspace, its strengths and its limitations, derive more from the decisions made at the platform layer than the physical layer. The Internet, for example, provides a set of capabilities that are to a great extent intentionally separated or divorced from the details of the technology that underpins it. The decisions that shape the Internet arise at this higher layer. If one wants to understand why some Internet vulnerabilities exist—why it allows phishing or denial of service attacks, for example—it is correct but not very useful to point out that computers and communications are subject to the laws of physics. It would have been possible to build a very different Internet within the constraints of the same physics. For the time being, however, we are captured by decisions at the platform level made earlier by the initial architects.

The layer model we have presented here does not automatically lead to the emergence of the Internet as we know it. One could build a very different system by taking a different approach to the logic of interconnection. Using the same sorts of physical elements, one could design a closed, essentially fixed function system such as an air traffic control system. Earlier examples of interconnected systems such as the telegraph and the early telephone system had this character. Both these systems predate the computer, and indeed predate essentially all of what we call electronics, not just the transistor but the vacuum tube and the relay. Prior to the invention of those elements, it was not possible to design a system with the generality, complexity, and modularity of the Internet. It is the interconnection that enables cyberspace, but it is the programmability and generality of the computer that makes possible the flexible logical structure we are associating with cyberspace.

The nature of cyberspace is the continuous and rapid evolution of new capabilities and services, based on the creation and combination of new logical constructs, all running on top of the physical foundations. Cyberspace is very *plastic*, and it can be described as *recursive*—platforms upon platforms upon platforms. The platforms may differ in detail, but they share the common feature that they are the foundation for the next platform above them. In a descriptive as well as operational sense, the structure is hierarchical— each platform layer depends on the layer below.

The drive for increased productivity and comparative competitive advantage shapes many aspects of cyberspace, but most particularly, it drives toward a characteristic that allows for rapid innovation, new patterns of exploitation, and so on. The platform layer—the "platform/plasticity" component of cyberspace—enhances this capability, and this fact in turn fuels the emphasis and attention given to this layer by the market and by developers of cyberspace. But we must not limit our focus to the platform layer, because another aspect of the drive for productivity is the expectations this rapid change implies for the "people" layer—rapid change will bring forward and advance people who can recognize new opportunities to exploit information and communications technology, who value rather than fear change, who demand new products and services, and who may contribute to new ways of doing things, and so on—as we shall note later on.

2.1.3   The Information Layer

Above the platform layer we find the *information* layer. The creation, capture, storage, and processing of information and "content" is central to the nature of cyberspace. Information in cyberspace takes many forms. It is the music and videos we share, the stored records of businesses, and all of the pages in the World Wide Web. It is online books and photographs. It is information about information (metadata). It is information created and retrieved as we search for other information (as is returned by Google). It is the implied meaning of information and content that is transmitted, shared, changed, augmented, and the like.

The character of information in cyberspace (or "on the net") has changed greatly since computers first started working with data sets. Data was processed by isolated computers well before we had capabilities for interconnection. Data lived in card decks, on tapes, and later on disks. Initially, data was normally thought of as static—stored and retrieved as needed. Books are static products of authors; images are static, and so on. Massive archives of static information still exist, such as corporate transaction records that are now stored in "data warehouses" and "mined" for further information. But more and more, information is created dynamically on demand, blurring the boundaries between storage and computation. Web pages are now often made on demand, tailored to each user, based on component information stored in databases. Information is now becoming more a personal experience, not a communal one. Issues of ownership, authenticity, and dependability are all critical as more and more information moves online. All of this points to the dynamic, emergent, creative formulations, and reformulations available to users.

2.1.4 The Top Layer—The Users

People are not just the passive users of cyberspace; they define and shape its character by the ways they choose to use it. They are active participants. The people and their character, which may vary from region to region, is an important part of the character of cyberspace. If people contribute to Wikipedia, then Wikipedia exists. If people tweet, then Twitter exists. This is a critically important, definitional feature of cyberspace.

Alfred Thayer Mahan (1894, 28) in *The Influence of Sea Power upon History*, wrote that the history of the "seaboard nations has been less determined by the shrewdness and foresight of governments than by conditions of position, extent, configuration, number and character of their people, by what are called, in a word, natural conditions." As we consider the characteristics of cyberspace, and the position of different countries with respect to their place and power in cyberspace, this same observation will certainly apply. We must recognize people as an important component of cyberspace, just as we must recognize wires and protocols. We see this reality as well with the increased understanding of environmental degradation due to human activities.

One of the reasons why the United States has led in the cyber revolution as a global phenomenon is our enthusiasm for innovation and experiment, our willingness to risk failure to find gain, and our respect for risk-takers. It is our enthusiasm for both individual ingenuity and the power of collaboration. This national trait should serve us well if advantage can be gained from "out innovating" friends and foes alike. The system of higher education has recognized the need for innovative thinking in response to the realities of the twenty-first century. The nation's entrepreneurs have continued to forge novelty with various forms and functions.

2.1.5 Layers in Context

All of these layers—characteristic features of the Internet—are critical for cyberspace. As a specific example, if one wants to understand the security of cyberspace, one cannot focus on just one of these layers. Attacks can come at all layers, from destruction of physical components to compromise of logical elements to corruption of information to deception of people. So defense must similarly be based on an understanding of all these layers.

Layering is a traditional approach used by technologists to design (or to understand) a system by breaking it up into parts, and by controlling the dependencies among those parts. In a system that is strictly defined by layers (in a technical sense), the upper layers build upon (or depend on) the lower layers, as a house sits on its foundation, but the lower layers do not depend upon the upper layers. The functional and technical dependency is from high to low, not the other way around.

In the broader frame of this chapter, the notion of "layer dependency" is much less precise. For example, people use information, but they create it. In the larger sociotechnical context, the system does not conform to this simple layered relationship at all: *all the "layers" depend on and influence each other*. The intervening factors may be roles, functions, or interests. Once we take into account all the modes of interaction—not just technical dependency but economic, regulatory, legislative, educational, and the like—all the "layers" should be seen as fully interdependent with *mutual influence*. A computer scientist might call this a "modularized" system rather than a layered one, but the layering image is consistent with the way networks are conceived, even as the modules are not fully autonomous. A social scientist would consider layering to reflect near-decomposability, an important feature of a complex system.

2.2   Identifying the Actors and Functions

The layered model just introduced was used to describe the components that make up cyberspace as we know it today. But from the perspective of international relations (and governance, more generally), as well as markets (and competition, more generally) the important questions center on the interests and activities of salient actors that make, shape, define, and govern the Internet. Whether in pursuit of power or the pursuit of wealth, these actors, in principle, are all sensitive to their constituencies. We now turn to this larger inquiry, continuing to use the layer architecture to the extent that it is relevant.

2.2.1   Those Who Create and Operate the Internet
Figure 2.2 provides an overview of the key actors.

At the *physical level*, we find companies that install fiber optics in the ground and undersea, put satellites in orbit, erect radio towers, install high-speed connections to the home, and so on. Some of these companies are also in the business of using these physical facilities to provide public Internet service, and have well-known names, like Verizon, AT&T, Comcast,

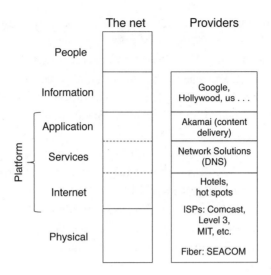

Figure 2.2
Illustrating a few examples of actors who create and operate the Internet and shape cyberspace.

British Telecom, and so on. However, the distinction between the physical assets (e.g., fiber-optic bundles) and the logical service (e.g., the Internet) is important. In one bundle of fibers, or using a common satellite, one can find a range of services, including the public Internet, private corporate networks, specialized services such as air traffic control, and military networks.

Some activities at the physical layer (such as satellite and undersea cables) may be structured as public-private partnerships, and physical construction may be more or less regulated and financed by government in different states, but to a large extent physical construction is a private sector activity. The business is capital intensive, and thus usually depends on private sector investment, which makes this business a creature of "Wall Street" or its equivalent in other countries.

At the lowest of the platform layers—that most proximate to the physical layer—we find *Internet service providers* (ISPs), who utilize physical assets to perform functions that make the Internet. The scope and boundaries of their business are defined by the protocols and standards of the Internet. The core data transport service of the Internet (specified by the so-called Internet protocol, or IP) defines a clear interface between the service it provides and the higher-layer services above it. That standard provides both a technical interface and an obvious point of cleavage in the industry structure.

Along a lateral dimension, ISPs interconnect among themselves to make the global Internet, and again it is standards and protocols (e.g., the Border Gateway Protocol, or BGP) that defines the technical means of interconnection. The business relationships among the ISPs are in turn shaped by the features and limitations of these protocols. ISPs (and the supporting actors that facilitate interconnection) are obviously a critical set of actors in the making of the Internet, and we discuss their structure in more detail in section 2.4.1.

Above this lowest logical layer, we find first some supporting services (such as the Domain Name System, or DNS) and then application providers. Applications come in many forms and structures, because the definition of IP has the effect of decoupling the design of applications from the structure of the IP sublayer. Specifically, given that ISPs are to some extent tied to the physical assets they use to build their part of the Internet, and thus seem physically localized, applications do not see the boundaries among these parts of the Internet and can be implemented with an internal structure that has nothing to do with the structure of the ISPs.

Email, a very old Internet application, is usually provided by ISPs as a part of their basic service offering. However, email is now also offered by Google, Microsoft, AOL, and the like, which are not primarily in the business of being ISPs. This simple fact illustrates the cross-layer opportunities pursued by actors as they expand the scale and scope of their businesses. The design of the Web allows it to be built up out of millions of independent providers of websites, supported by Web hosting companies, content delivery services such as Akamai, and the like. Some applications are highly centralized, such as Facebook, Twitter, and many multiplayer computer games. This pattern is often seen in applications developed by commercial developers, who use the centralization as a means to maintain control and sustain their commercial objectives—and thus protect their interests and profits.

At the information layers, we find a range of actors with diverse capabilities and providing different services. Google delivers a searchable index of the Web. Companies like Netflix, Google, and Apple iTunes provide music and video content over the Internet. Some applications are centralized from a control perspective, but highly distributed technically, for reasons of performance; these include high-volume content sources such as YouTube or

Netflix, which together (at the time of publication) generate over 50% of all consumer-destined traffic in the United States. The providers of Web pages are perhaps the most obvious example of "information layer actors"—they include commercial sales and marketing sites, "free" sites supported by advertising, government information and service portals, and so on. All of these businesses are based on the ingenuity and innovation, buttressed by market creation capability.

The two important points of this discussion are first, that the protocols and standards of the Internet define not just technical interfaces but interfaces between separate business entities, and second, that almost all of this vast universe of actors, large and small, are highly dynamic creatures of the private sector in many countries, but in others are empowered by the state. To date, the operators of the Internet, as defined earlier, are predominantly in the private sector, subject to principles of private order, not to the power of the state.

2.2.2 Suppliers of Hardware and Software

In support of the set of actors that make and operate the layers of the Internet, a set of equipment and software suppliers have grown to meet an expanding demand, with a rough structure that matches the layering of their customers. There is no fundamental reason why this set of actors would be structured along the same layering boundaries, but different core competencies, customary provider relationships, and the like have led to a fairly consistent mapping between providers and their customers. If there is an underlying logic, then it is one of market efficiency. Thus, companies such as Cisco, Juniper, and Huawei supply ISPs with routers, Corning supplies fiber optics, and Alcatel-Lucent sells wireless base stations.

Looking beyond the Internet to other aspects of cyberspace, operators of data centers tend to have their own preferred suppliers, again distinct from the makers of end-consumer PCs. The PC industry is itself layered, with Intel making chips, companies such as Dell making the computers, Microsoft and Apple making the lowest logical layer (the operating system), and other providers making application software. The theory of the firm is the relevant reference point here, given that the firms in question are all shaped by and shaping a highly dynamic, volatile, and virtual market environment, hooked together in many cases by standards and well-specified interfaces. Figure 2.3 shows the upward trend in the performance of select leading corporate entities

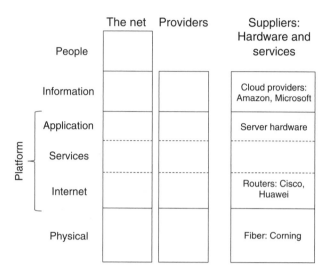

Figure 2.3
Illustrating a few examples of firms that supply technology for cyberspace.

in the cyber domain. The services that they provide have become an integral part of the daily experience for almost everyone and almost everywhere.

2.2.3   Governance Actors

In general, governance refers to the authoritative processes that provide order in social interactions, enable decision-making, and facilitate compliance. Governance will be a critical issue to which we will return several times in the course of this book. In this chapter, we focus on a subset of the governance actors—those that have emerged within the ecosystem of cyberspace to ensure stable operation and management. These include the organizations that set the standards that define the Internet, and the organizations that serve to facilitate its overall stable operation. Figure 2.4 illustrates a few of these actors.

2.2.3.1   Standards organizations   Standards bodies define the necessary technical agreements to which the providers and suppliers must comply for the Internet to interoperate. These groups (which embody a deep technical strength) tend to follow a layered model. The Institute of Electrical and Electronics Engineers (IEEE; through their 802 standards body) defines many standards at the physical level, including the well-known Ethernet and Wi-Fi standards. The Internet Engineering Task Force (IETF) establishes and

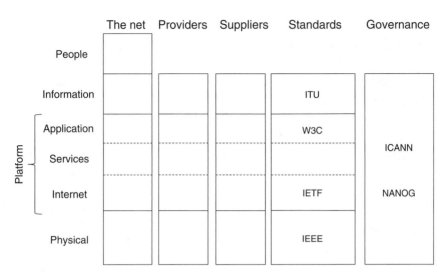

Figure 2.4
Illustrating a few of the organizations that set standards or provide aspects of Internet governance.

maintains most of the standards that define the Internet and its core services (DNS, email, and the like). The World Wide Web Consortium at MIT (the W3C) establishes the standards that define the Web. Other standards bodies define standards for media formats (audio and video), and so on.

The IETF is the earliest of the standards bodies that emerged in the definition of the Internet. It is an open technical community concerned with "the evolution of the Internet architecture and the smooth operation of the Internet" (Hovey and Bradner 1996, 2), whose first meeting was held in January 1986 (Arkko 2016; Gross 1986). The technical work of the IETF is done in its working groups, which are organized by topic into several areas such as routing, transport, and security. The IETF operates under the umbrella of the not-for-profit Internet Society.

2.2.3.2 Operations and management Different industry sectors tend to have their own associations to facilitate cooperation. For example, ISPs meet through the misnamed North American Network Operators Group (NANOG; misnamed because it is not restricted to operators from North America), which provides a venue for addressing pragmatic operational issues among ISPs. The Internet Corporation for Assigned Names and Numbers (ICANN) oversees the orderly allocation of domain names and Internet addresses.

ICANN is the focus of much attention at the time we are writing this book, and we will consider ICANN in detail in later chapters.

In these discussions, we have only begun to catalog the range of relevant actors that make up the Internet. If, for example, one looks at a particular subcomponent of the system, such as online video delivery, one can find hundreds of players involved in what business schools call the "value network"—operators, equipment suppliers, content providers, specialized distribution agents, ancillary commercial actors (e.g., the actors in the advertising industry), actors associated with enforcement of copyright, and so on. The space of actors is dense, interconnected, dynamic, and mostly unregulated by the state. This is the case in the United States and other many industrial countries. The situation may be different for the "latecomer" states to the cyber domain.

We are not the first to suggest that a layered model be used to organize and structure the process of governance and regulation of cyberspace. Much of the prior work in this area comes from the legal tradition. Much of it has been centered on one concern, the "open" Internet or network neutrality, and much of it is scoped to the domestic or state level. Lawrence Lessig (2001b) describes a three-layer model: physical, "code" (which is our Internet layer), and content. The different layers have different properties: the physical layer is private property (in most countries), much content is protected by copyright (in competitive Western societies and to some extent by international law), but his "code" layer is a "commons," which he believes should be protected.

Kevin Werbach (2002) describes a very similar model, with four layers: physical, logical, application, and content. His paper provides a good summary of the U.S. domestic (e.g., Federal Communications Commission) regulation of telecoms, and its potential relevance to the regulation of the Internet (which he describes as "square pegs in round holes" (Werbach 2002, 44). He stresses the importance of the open interfaces between the layers, and interfaces as potential points of control.

Solum and Chung (2003) propose a slightly more complex model, where they separate physical into link and physical, and they distinguish the two protocol layers, Transmission Control Protocol (TCP) and IP in the Internet. They provide an extensive tutorial on layering, suited for nontechnical audiences, and then propose their *layers principle*, which is "respect the integrity of the layers" (817). More specifically, they propose two corollaries: *layer separation* and *minimization of layer-crossing regulation* (Solum and

Chung 2003, 849). This corollary has much in common with the conclusion we will draw in a later chapter, which is that regulation imposed at the wrong layer will often be ineffective and perhaps even burdensome.

Richard Whitt (2004) also uses the four-layer model to look at a number of issues, both domestic and international. Scott Jordan (2007) argues that a layered approach to network neutrality regulation is appropriate to take into account the differences among the layers. With respect to network neutrality, he argues that because the application layer is more competitive, regulation should not focus there but on the lower Internet/physical layer.

2.2.4 Major Actors

In this chapter, we introduce many of the actors that are part of the Internet ecosystem, including operators and providers of applications and services, equipment providers, and operational governance organizations. These organizations, emerging organically as the Internet matures, tend to mirror the layered structure of the Internet itself—they support actors at specific layers (e.g., ISPs) and they develop expertise specific to these layers, so they tend to stay within their scope of competence. However, within their scope, they can become powerful entities that pursue their own interests.

Essentially all of these organizations, including the governance organizations we discussed, are creations of the private sector, not derived from sovereign state or international state-centric institutions. This fact is in sharp contrast to the earlier history of telecommunications in the telegraph and telephone era, when the International Telecommunication Union (ITU) set standards. The ITU, which today is a component of the United Nations, is by definition an international, state-centric organization with all attendant implications for state-directed motivations and interests. In contrast, the IETF is housed inside a private sector U.S. corporation set up for that purpose (the Internet Society), the IEEE is a professional society, and the World Wide Web Consortium (W3C) housed itself at an academic institution. ICANN is a notable "special case" in this situation, having been created as a private corporation by special action of the United States, and thus left in an ambiguous and contested form.

No other state has had any notable influence on the governance of the Internet. Although the Internet has its roots in the United States, most of these governance institutions have, by necessity and with the support of the United States, a strongly international (even global) character today. The authority, and even legitimacy, of these private sector actors is now being contested by some of the more state-centered institutions that either existed before (e.g., the ITU) or have come into existence to deal with specific issues around the Internet (such as the Internet Governance Forum). This contestation is supported by enough states to enable the ITU to proceed with its challenges. In chapter 8, we will return to a consideration of public versus private order. In that chapter, we will catalog a further set of actors, who are creations of the state system, not the organizations that emerged organically in the private sector to shape cyberspace.

2.2.5 Interactions among the Actors

The layered model is static in its form. It provides a framework to position many of the actors, but does not in itself provide a way to illustrate the interactions among the actors. As we will discuss in subsequent chapters, it is the dynamics of interaction, as well as the static structure of the actors, that define the essential character of cyberspace.

In figure 2.5, we augment our layer model by adding additional classes of actors—governments and different sorts of users—to provide a more

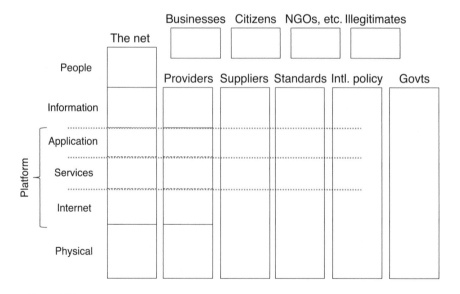

Figure 2.5

Illustrating the full set of actors relating to the layer model, including governments and different classes of users of the Internet.

Note: Dotted lines suggest the extent to which the layered structure can be found in the actors.

complete illustration. Using this figure, we can begin to illustrate how different actors use the tools and affordances at their disposal to influence other actors and improve their own situation.

An important and powerful class of actor is the providers, from the providers of physical assets and the platform providers who realize the Internet itself to the higher-level providers of information and services. We illustrate some of their actions in figure 2.6. These actors use their capabilities and position in the ecosystem to exercise influence over many other actors. Perhaps most directly, they spend money to deploy the technology that makes up the Internet. Whereas money is spent at all the layers, the capital that is spent to deploy the physical layer and the Internet itself are notable as major costs of the ecosystem. Providers at different layers can enter into partnerships and alliances, and can favor or discriminate against other actors in the ecosystem. They attempt to attract users through advertising, as well as (of course) by the quality of the service they offer. They purchase technology, thus influencing their suppliers, who in turn influence the standards bodies that define (in part) the behavior of the products they

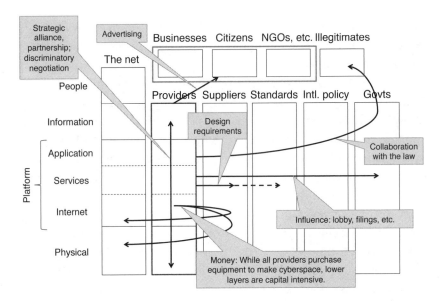

Figure 2.6
The providers of the Internet ecosystem exercise influence over many other actors through expenditure, alliance and competition, use of influence, and articulation of requirements.

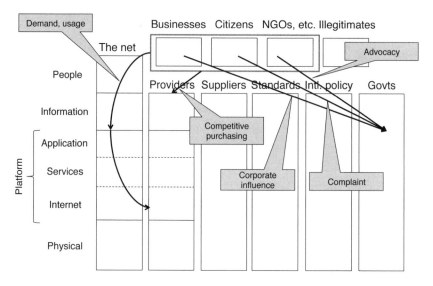

Figure 2.7
The users of the Internet exercise influence through their selective purchase and use of service, advocacy, and complaint.

purchase. They collaborate with governments to control the behavior of illegitimate actors, and they attempt to influence government by lobbying and similar approaches.

Another important class of actor is the legitimate user community, which includes businesses, individual citizens, and nonprofit organizations. Users directly influence the providers by their purchasing decisions. They generate the demand that justifies the investment that puts the technology of the Internet in place. Different sorts of users attempt to influence the government in different ways: consumers complain, businesses use their corporate influence, and advocacy groups advocate their causes (see figure 2.7).

A final set of actors that we illustrate is governments (see figure 2.8). Different governments exercise very different degrees of control over the character of the Internet, as we discuss in a later chapter. They can exercise direct control over providers by regulation, which in turn influences the providers and standards bodies, and thus the character of cyberspace itself. They can also exercise a similar set of influences by their purchasing decisions, which may be constrained by the standards that the government sets for the products they purchase (in the United States, called Federal

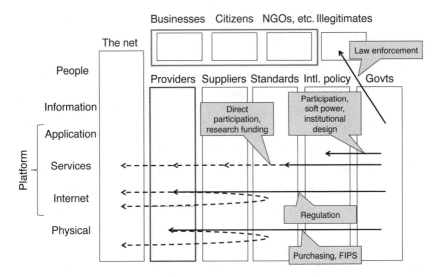

Figure 2.8
Governments exercise domestic influence through law and regulation, direct participation in standards setting and other processes, funding research, and their purchasing decisions. They exercise influence internationally by forms of soft power, direct
participation in international institutions, and the design of these institutions.

Information Processing Standards). They can fund research, directly participate in standards bodies, and participate in (and attempt to shape) international governance organizations. Finally, they use their law enforcement
powers to try to control the action of illegitimate users.

In subsequent chapters we develop more sophisticated models and tools
to better understand the dynamic character of cyberspace.

2.3   The Limits of the Layered Model

Although layering is a useful approach or description to make an initial division of the system into more comprehensible parts, as with all approaches
it has its limits. The layers are essentially a point of entry for analysis of the
Internet. Layering provides an internally consistent, clearly definable, and
easily tractable set of criteria for describing, observing, and analyzing actors
and action, functions and outcomes that shape the character of cyberspace,
but a layer model is not intended to be a map for all cyber-related activities or
issues that arise. We focus on layering for specific purposes, as noted earlier.

More specifically, the layers model is a useful device to (1) locate cyber actors and activities, (2) signal changes in strategies or orientations, (3) identify the conditions under which actors operate across layers or, alternatively, chose to concentrate their activities within a layer, and (4) thus help track and represent the processes of transformation and change within the cyber domain. At the same time, the solution to a recognized problem may be concentrated or, conversely, cut across layers. The structure of the layers model provides a degree of coherence and internal consistency in both conceptual and operational terms. In other words, the overall structure is layered, and their interconnections shape what we call cyberspace.

However, some critical aspects of complex systems are not easily represented in layered terms. For example, *security* of cyberspace is not best understood or achieved using a layered approach to the problem. Security is an overall emergent property of a system, shaped both by design (e.g., standards) and deployment (e.g., investment) decisions. It is also shaped by the actors, their intents, expectations, and capabilities. In theory, one can attempt a partial division of the security problem into layers, but in practice, for overall progress to occur all parties must agree to the terms of the division, and because any particular division has significant economic consequences, there is a strong motivation to throw problems "over the interface" into another entity's action and decision space. At the same time, we recognize that many security problems arise due to threat actors that are equally willing to "stay within their layer" or to cross layer boundaries and go "over" or "under" a layer-centric defense.

In many ways, these dynamics processes are central to competitive practices, among firms, between states, or even in individual behavior, as noted in chapter 1. In another context, in a later chapter we shall refer to this general propensity as a fundamental feature of transformation and change of complex systems. At issue here is the relative strength of two seemingly contradictory tendencies—those that are system supporting versus those that are system threatening.

Moreover, given the contested nature of the dense institutional structure that surrounds today's Internet and the broader cyber arena, the layer structure is a model for understanding the core of the cyber domain, not a mechanism for guiding solution strategies. In addition, the layers provide a useful way of framing and understanding the nature of cyber contentions, that is, those contentions among actors that have the goal of shaping the character of cyberspace itself. Usually such contentions are about the degree of openness, the areas in need of regulation, essential symbols, and the like. And, given the dominance of the private sector, such contentions are invariably about profit, or at a minimum remaining in business.

In sum, a critical feature of the layers is that they stand in a specific relation to each other; they cannot be reversed or randomly rearranged, and to some extent, the performance of each layer is contingent on the efficacy of the one that underpins it. At the same time, various actors noted herein operate within and across the different layers, albeit in uneven and unequal ways. These asymmetries reflect relative power and capability of different actors. In the context of system security, these asymmetries become especially relevant.

2.4   Topology and Interconnections

The previous sections addressed and explained the structure of the Internet in terms of layers. This is a useful model, and we will use it to connect to the levels of international relations in chapter 4. As well, there is another important structural model of the Internet, which is how it is made up of regions that are hooked together. This model captures the character of *interconnection* in the Internet, and is useful because in capturing the pattern of interconnection of the Internet, we capture the relationships (e.g., business relationships, authority connections, etc.) among the actors that make up the Internet. We focus on the role these actors play in enabling networks and facilitating flows. This alternative model is also anchored in structure, but its value lies in the flows that are facilitated and generated.

2.4.1   Internet Service Providers

Earlier, we discussed the role of the ISP. As a unique set of actors, ISPs share some common core functions but then vary in the extent to which they take on other activities. We seek to present something of a census of ISPs at this point in time, and highlight the variations in status, legal position, and responsibilities. From an international relations perspective, it is not clear how best to characterize them, whether as traffic cops, enablers and facilitators, border patrols, or business and revenue-raising entities—or other or all of the above.

Each ISP implements a region of the Internet. The specific term that is used to describe these parts of the Internet is autonomous system (AS). As of 2017, almost 58,000 ASs make up the Internet (Bates, Smith, and Huston 2017). Many of these are "edge" ASs: companies, schools, governments, and so on that connect to the Internet but do not provide services to others. It is hard to enumerate these exactly, because some institutions may provide a path to a small number of other institutions without actually being in the service business, but as an estimate, all but approximately 5000 ASs are "at the edge" of the Internet.

Within these 5000 remaining ASs, we find the familiar names that provide Internet service: AT&T, Comcast, Verizon, British Telecom, France Telecom, and so on. We also find providers of wide area connectivity, similar to what in the old telephone system were called long-distance providers: Level3, Cogent, Tata, and so on. In the specialized language of the Internet, these are called "Tier 1" providers, because they do not obtain service from other providers.

2.4.2 Interconnection—Peering and Transit

In the early days of the Internet, the structure of the Internet was somewhat hierarchical: smaller ISPs hooked to larger ISPs (sometimes called Tier 2 providers) that in turn hooked to Tier 1 providers to provide the overall connectivity. This is illustrated in figure 2.9.

In this picture, there are two sorts of interconnections illustrated, *transit* and *peering*. When a smaller ISP purchases an interconnection to the rest of the Internet from a larger ISP, this is called transit. A provider of transit, such

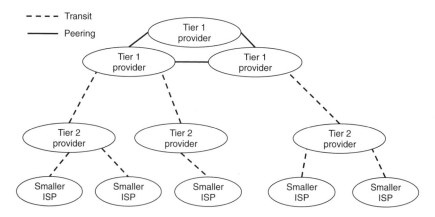

Figure 2.9
The hierarchical structure of the early Internet.

as the Tier 1 and Tier 2 providers in the figure, must themselves arrange to have access to the rest of the Internet in order to offer this service.

At the Tier 1 level, there are no higher-level providers, so the Tier 1 providers interconnect among themselves to exchange the traffic that each has for the other, a form of interconnection called peering. Peering connections differ from transit connections in two ways. First, they do not give access to all of the Internet, but just to the other provider and its customers. Second, peering has customarily been on a settlement-free or revenue-neutral basis—the parties do not pay each other. Peering is seen as mutually beneficial, not as a service of one ISP sold to another.

Figure 2.9 illustrates the early structure of the Internet; in the more recent past the structure has mutated. We have seen a move from a hierarchical structure to one that is more richly connected, with peering connections among the networks at lower levels. Peering can save both parties the cost of using a transit path to exchange traffic, so a rich mesh of peering connections has emerged in the Internet of today, as illustrated in figure 2.10.

In this more current pattern of interconnection, the Tier 1 providers are still important because they provide the "path of last resort" to distant parts of the Internet for which there is no path across a peering link. But they may be carrying a small part of the total traffic; modern ISPs may use

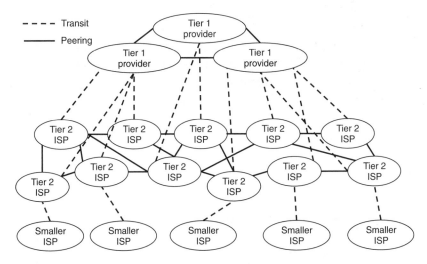

Figure 2.10

Illustrating a rich mesh of peering connections among lower-level autonomous systems.

peering connections to carry well over 90% of their off-net traffic, and may peer with tens if not hundreds of other ISPs. Further, large ISPs may have peering connections at multiple physical locations. So this picture in no way captures the actual density of the peering interconnections.

2.4.3   Facilitating Interconnection—New Actors and Their Roles

2.4.3.1   Co-location   To allow the implementation of this rich peering mesh at low cost, specialized physical facilities have come into existence: substantial buildings where different ISPs can co-locate equipment and interconnect. These buildings, which today can occupy a city block, are called co-location centers or carrier hotels. The providers of these facilities are yet another class of actor in the Internet ecosystem. Different carriers install routing equipment in these facilities and then negotiate to peer as appropriate. A large ISP today may install equipment in ten or more co-location facilities in different cities, both to get efficient paths and to provide resilience in case of a disaster that affects one of the buildings. Figure 2.11 illustrates a co-location facility. Four ISPs have each positioned a router inside the facility and then cross-connected them to implement a peering mesh.

2.4.3.2   Internet exchanges   There is an additional development that further reduces the cost of these rich peering interconnections, which is to install some sort of interconnection switch in a co-location facility, to which the various ASs there attach. The resulting facility is called an Internet exchange (IX). An IX allows multiple ASs to interconnect for the purpose of exchanging traffic. Exchanges are usually operated by a single, neutral party (i.e., not one of the ASs) and have a policy that encourages other ASs to join

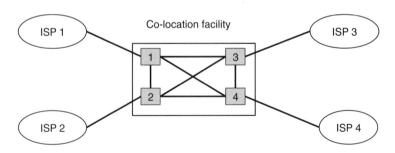

Figure 2.11
Four ISPs interconnect at a co-location facility.

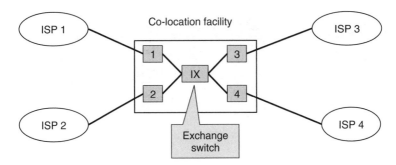

Figure 2.12
Use of an exchange switch to simplify interconnection.

for this purpose. Because the direct exchange of traffic on the Internet is known as peering, on occasion co-location facilities and IXs are referred to as *peering points*.

The advantages of an IX include reduced cost and potentially improved performance. The IX reduces cost by reducing the number of connections that each AS makes. In a simple co-location facility, a given AS must make a physical connection to each desired peer. With the equipment provided by an IX, each AS makes only one connection, to the switch, as illustrated in figure 2.12. The advantage of the IX with its exchange switch is that now there is only one connection on each router, rather than one for each peering partner, which saves the cost of connection ports.

The one connection from the router of each ISP to the switch now carries all the traffic to all the peering partners. This is beneficial if the total load is light and the traffic mix is variable. However, if two ISPs have a predictable, high-volume flow between them, it may not be optimal to route that traffic through the IX. In practice, a hybrid approach is often implemented in which the IX facility is used for low-volume flows; and a direct peering connection is used for a high-volume flow, as between ISPs 3 and 4 in figure 2.13.

IXs capture a relatively small fraction of all Internet traffic but can be significant because of their location and physicality. The location of an exchange point is by definition located within a formal jurisdiction. Even setting up the infrastructure usually involves interactions with the authorities at hand. This is a specific point where Internet services intersect with the state and its authority, as well as a control point that is formal, visible, and potentially subject to leverage.

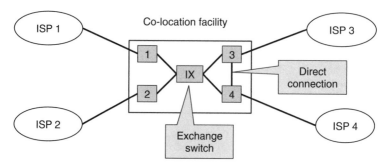

Figure 2.13
Using both an exchange switch and direct peering to interconnect.

The large number of IXs and their worldwide distribution support the decentralized nature of the Internet because they provide intervening locales through which multiple network providers can connect. Given that the physical infrastructure of the IX is shared by all of its connected ISPs, and their activity can affect one another, all IXs have requirements that an ISP must meet in order to connect to the IXs and exchange traffic. This is illustrative of the bottom-up organization of Internet management and the development of norms and rules for effective cooperative operations—in theory, efficient as well.

2.4.4   The Landscape of Exchanges

Exchanges differ in size from a rack in a closet to a building the size of a city block. Because there is no requirement that an Internet exchange point (IX) register in order to operate, there is no definitive census. The first IXs were established in the United States, in connection with the construction of the Internet. In 1989, the federal IXs were initiated on the East and West Coasts of the United States, followed by the first commercial IX on the West Coast, and the first metropolitan area exchange in the Washington, D.C. area. By the most recent estimate, there are one hundred and sixty-nine IXs in operation in North America, with a majority in the United States and some in Canada (CAIDA 2018b). In Europe, by contrast, there are currently three hundred and eighteen IXs (CAIDA, 2018b). The first European IXs were established in 1993 in the Nordic countries and Finland, and then in the other countries throughout the remainder of the decade. In Asia, the first IXs were established in Japan in 1998, followed by China two years later.

Although IXs are established in almost all countries of Latin America—one hundred and thirty-five IXs in total—Brazil and Argentina are especially noteworthy (CAIDA 2018b). Brazil's IXs were first made available to those other than research universities in 2004. IXs are located in all of the major Brazilian cities. Today they have thirty-six IXs in operation. In 1997, Argentina established locations for efficient peering. The country has made major strides in establishing IXs in a variety of locations including in rural locales. Although Africa remains behind, it has made notable advances in the past ten to fifteen years. Figure 2.14 shows the geographical location of the IXs according to CAIDA (2018c).

2.5 Cybersecurity

The goal of security, broadly defined, underpins the overall framing of this book—national security is a central theme of international relations. However, a narrower aspect of security relates to the actual security of cyberspace itself. Anyone who uses the Internet understands that there are manifest security risks in doing so, including malware, deceptive email (so-called "phishing"), identity theft, online fraud, and so on. And anyone who reads the news will have heard about larger consequences of poor Internet security, most commonly data breaches or theft of information (whether for economic benefit, traditional espionage, or public disclosure of private or confidential files). There are fears of attacks against a nation's critical infrastructure using cyberspace as the means. These events, and the fears of even more consequential harms, lead to questions as to why the Internet is insecure, or more definitive statements such as, "The Internet is broken." They lead as well to calls for a more secure, or trustworthy, or accountable Internet.

Abstractly, better security seems like a virtuous goal. Who would object to better security? However, a call for better security at this abstract level is aspirational, not actionable. To understand what it would actually mean for the Internet to be more secure, it is necessary to break the goal of security into smaller and better-defined subgoals. We can use both the layer model and the topology model as a way to sort out different aspects of security, and we will draw four conclusions from this exercise. First, and obviously, better security is not cost free. Second, some aspects of security are actually in conflict with each other. Third, different actors in the ecosystem must address different aspects of security; there is no one place (or one set of actors) to

Figure 2.14
Location of IXs across the globe, 2018.
Source: Based on CAIDA (2018c).

whom we can turn to make the Internet more secure. Finally, the security problems that plague us today are only partially technical. Issues of trust, and the betrayal of trust, are as central to cybersecurity as is better technology.

The layer model reminds us that different security problems are going to emerge at different layers, and (using the logic from earlier in this chapter), will have to be solved at the layer at which they emerge, or perhaps at a higher layer, but seldom at a lower layer. Consider the security (or lack thereof) in an interchange between a set of communicants. In the case of willing communicants, the traditional security goals are *confidentiality*, *integrity*, and *availability*; the communication should be private to the communicants, not corrupted in transit, and successful whenever communication is attempted. The Internet layer (the layer that forwards information from source to destination) is responsible for availability. However, in the layered design of the Internet, it is the application layer (or software running on its behalf in the end nodes of the communicants) that is responsible for confidentiality and integrity. There is no way to prevent an untrustworthy router from making a copy of a packet or changing it. The approach used in the Internet to improve confidentiality and integrity is to encrypt the information—encryption enhances confidentiality and provides a robust detection of violations of integrity. However, the decision to use encryption does not sit in the network itself but in the end nodes attached to the net, within the application layer, or in a service layer *above* the Internet layer. So there is a division of responsibility even within this subgoal of security.

The aspect of security we just discussed was the secure communication among willing communicants. But there is an equally relevant security problem—dealing with the case that one communicant uses the communication as an opportunity to attack another. What if the communicants are not mutually trustworthy? One might initially speculate that parties would not choose to communicate at all unless they deemed the other parties trustworthy, but in fact, much of what happens on the Internet is among parties that may be untrustworthy. Email continues to be used, even though users know that they may receive spam, malicious attachments (forgeries and malware), or mail with falsified sender identity. Users of the Web know (or should know) that going to a website may trigger the download of malware, or misdirection of the user to a malicious copy of the website, or the release of personal information. On balance, users continue to use email and the Web because the benefits seem to outweigh the risks, but the risks are real. Again, these risks arise at the application and information layer, not the Internet platform layer where packets are forwarded. It makes no more sense to expect the routers on the Internet to look inside a packet and detect malware than to expect a highway to look inside a car and detect robbers fleeing a bank robbery.

This limitation on what the Internet layer can do is greatly increased, of course, if the content being sent is encrypted. Encryption seems like an obvious thing to do between trusting communicants, but may well be the wrong idea if one party wants protection from another. A mail-forwarding agent cannot scan for spam or check attachments for malware if the email is encrypted. So optimal security in this space is a tradeoff; it will depend on the degree that the communicants choose to trust each other. However that variation is accomplished, it does not happen in the network but in the software running in computers attached to the network. When one hears a call for a more secure Internet, it is important to sort out if what is really being sought is more secure applications, or a more secure packet-forwarding layer, or a more secure operating system environment.

There are, of course, security problems at the network layer. The regional model, which describes the Internet as composed of interconnected autonomous systems, reminds us that of the 59,000 ASs interconnected on the Internet across the globe, not all of them are likely to be equally trustworthy. Perhaps the most common problem today that arises from this variation in trustworthy behavior is attacks on one part of the network by other parts, using falsified routing assertions to try to deflect traffic from its intended destination to an alternative point where it can be inspected, or a fake version of the end point has been installed.

One proposal to preventing this class of attack is to encrypt the routing assertions (or using cryptography to sign them in an authoritative manner). But encryption (or signing) only solves half the problem, just as in the case (once we look more closely) with the use of encryption to provide confidentiality between communicants. Encryption provides a secure channel, but by itself does not guarantee who the communicants are. The set of entities that are party to a particular communication is defined by the set of entities who share the encryption key. If a malicious entity has managed to obtain the key, they are part of the protected communication. If the wrong entity has obtained the key, a communicant may end up having an encrypted communication with the wrong end point. So the protection provided by encryption is no better than the associated scheme for key management, and key management is the weak point of almost all encryption schemes.

If two parties want to have a secure conversation, and share a key by writing it down on paper and sharing that paper, the key should be reasonably secure except in the case of physical theft (which is within scope of spycraft but not normal cybercrime). However, that sort of sharing does not scale to the size of the Internet. To provide secure (encrypted) communication to a website, the website operator must provide some form of key access to potentially millions of users. There is a powerful technical innovation that has made this possible, called asymmetric or public key systems, in which there is a *pair* of keys, one used for encryption and one for decryption, and knowing one does not help in guessing the other. So a website can give out its "public" key, keep its private key secret, and allow anyone to establish an encrypted connection to the site using the public key to encrypt what is sent.

This use of public keys is the basis for secure encryption at scale on the Internet today, but again, key management is the critical vulnerability. How can any of those potential users of the website know that they have actually received the correct public key, as opposed to a false key provided by a malicious clone of the site? To solve this problem, there is a service layer on the Internet called the Certificate Authority system, which is made of servers that will attempt to ensure that only valid public keys are handed out. But what has happened in practice, again given the global nature of the Internet, is that some of the Certificate Authority servers have turned out not to be trustworthy and have been handing out maliciously falsified information about public keys.

There are ways to use technology to improve this situation, but technology cannot solve this problem by itself. What is needed is a way to detect untrustworthy actors in the Internet ecosystem and arrange not to depend on them. This happens today within many parts of the Internet ecosystem— there are organizations that try to identify and fence off sources of malicious email, malicious websites, and so on. But of course, these efforts depend on those organizations themselves being trustworthy. It is not reasonable to expect ordinary users to make sophisticated decisions about the trust landscape of the Internet, but rather the overall system must somehow build up a high-level understanding of the landscape of trust so that users can know when they are doing something that is potentially risky. Technology can help here, but it cannot solve the problem by itself. A framework to manage the trust landscape of the global Internet is ultimately a social construction, not a technical construction.

Building the mechanisms that address these sorts of specific security concerns is costly. Actors will invest only if they see a reduction in risk that is a defensible return on investment. However, many of the security problems we face in the Internet today manifest what economists call "negative externalities"—that is, the cost of putting in some mechanism will be imposed on one set of actors, but the benefits will accrue to another set of actors. One of the reasons why some policy intervention may be justified in pursuit of better cybersecurity is to mitigate some of these externalities—to improve the relationship between cost and benefit for given classes of actor.

In summary, cybersecurity is a multidimensional space of goals, some in potential conflict with others. Different aspects of security require attention from different classes of actors, and the actors that build the Internet platform layer—the ISPs—do not in fact have the ability to address many of the most pressing problems of today. The problems of today more often arise at the application and information layer, or at service layers directly supporting those layers. It is to those layers, and the actors that provide them, that we must turn to see better overall Internet security. But if we expect them to improve security, we must ask if they face the right incentive structure to motivate them, and we must allow for the fact that in the global ecosystem of the Internet, there are and always will be actors that are untrustworthy or who have interests adverse to a given set of users. Management of trust and management of incentives are the keys to better cybersecurity.

2.6 Endnote: What Have We Learned?

In this chapter, we have begun to understand how complex even the most limited view of interactions in the cyber domain can be. We use the term "complex" intentionally, to signal more than just complicated. This means we can now identify with a considerable degree of specificity some basic features of both structure and process, and appreciate the points at which unimpeded operations of the cyber experience are contingent on decisions and actions made by actors that are usually not accounted for in traditional international relations but can now be identified in the combined cyber–international relations model.

Whereas layering is a useful approach or description to make an initial division of the system into more comprehensible parts, as with all approaches it has its limits. The layers are essentially a point of entry for analysis of the Internet. Layering provides an internally consistent, clearly definable, and easily tractable set of criteria for describing, observing, and analyzing actors and actions, functions and outcomes that shape the character of cyberspace. The structure of the layers model provides a degree of coherence and internal consistency in both conceptual and operational terms. In other words, the overall structure is layered, and their interconnections shape what we call cyberspace.

However, a layer model is not intended to be a map for all cyber-related activities or issues that arise. Some critical aspects of complex systems are not easily represented in layered terms. For example, security of cyberspace is not best understood or achieved using a layered approach to the problem. Security is an overall emergent property of a system, shaped both by design (e.g., standards) and deployment (e.g., investment) decisions. It is also shaped by the actors, their intents, expectations, and capabilities. In theory, one can attempt a partial division of the security problem into layers, but in practice for overall progress to occur all parties must agree to the terms of the division, and because any particular division has significant economic consequences, there is a strong motivation to throw problems "over the interface" into another entity's action and decision space.

At the same time, we recognize that many security problems arise due to threat actors that are equally willing to "stay within their layer" or to cross layer boundaries and go "over" or "under" a layer-centric defense. A topological perspective highlights actors and activities. A wide range of actors is involved in managing the layers of the Internet, with different interests, capabilities, and support systems. We shall address this and related issues in a later chapter.

With these foundations in place, the next chapter turns to international relations. In chapter 3, we shall present a highly stylized model of the international system, a simple but useful structure of world politics. In doing so, we seek to provide the terms of reference for understanding the ways in which this new cyber domain influences and is influenced by the realities in the international system, both old and new. We also provide a set of tools for analysts of cyberspace to help anticipate the ways in which world politics impinges on the Internet and on the overall cyber system, as we know it today.

3   International Relations: Levels of Analysis

It goes without saying that the international system is a complex arena and that the dynamics of international relations continue to change over time. The twentieth century has left us with a world that has been annotated, mapped, analyzed, metricized, and so forth. For the most part, we are familiar with the major actors and actions, and their positioning with respect to structures and processes. This chapter serves as an introduction to international relations in the most basic terms. Our purpose is to highlight the elements that are directly relevant to our strategy for integrating cyberspace and international relations. In many ways, chapter 3 can be seen as a counterpart to chapter 2.

In this chapter, we introduce the traditional levels of analysis view of international relations. Then we highlight the departures from traditional theory introduced by the lateral pressure theory. What follows are views of the international system without any "contaminating" effects due to the construction of cyberspace. In the following chapters, we shall focus specifically on the linkages between cyberspace and the international system and the ways in which today's "real" world politics is, and continues to be, transformed by the "virtual" domain and its physical underpinnings.

Without resorting to undue complexity, the fact remains that our world today is often depicted in different ways. Figure 3.1 shows the international system with sovereign states in 2017. This map provides a reference for other views of the international system discussed throughout this book.

3.1   Levels of Analysis—Reframed

In 1956, Kenneth Boulding published *The Image*, which contributed to the three levels of analysis framed by Kenneth N. Waltz (1959), namely as man (the individual), the state, and the international system (whose members are

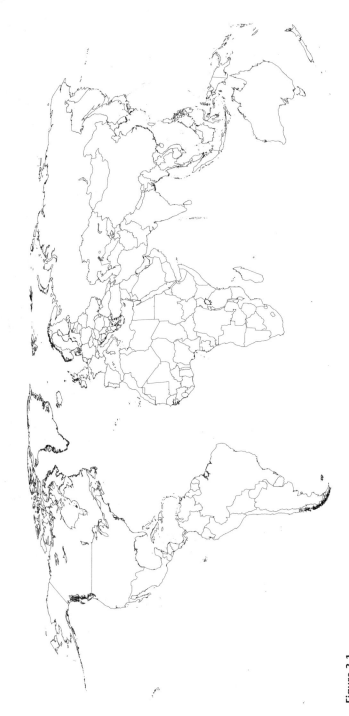

Figure 3.1
Political map of the world, 2017.
Source: Based on Natural Earth (2018).

states). At its roots, this notion is centered entirely on the social domain. This perspective is consistent with the evolution of the social sciences built by separating humans from their natural environment and then fragmenting the social into specialized areas, such as economics, political science, and so forth—each built on different assumptions. The result is a *view of the international system that consists of three levels of analysis and one domain of interaction*, the traditional way of framing international relations—with limited attention to dynamics and change.

Against this background, in this chapter we highlight three major extensions of tradition derived from lateral pressure theory and its causal logic. The first is to introduce the *global level* of analysis—to encompass the individual, the state, the international system, and the global system—and to specify critical aggregations and influences. We shall return to this issue later. The second is to appreciate that both *state* and *nonstate* actors shape all aspects of international relations. Although the state system is central, nonstate entities exert major, and sometimes dominant, influence in world politics. Third is to recognize that human activities—at all levels of analysis—are embedded in two distinct but closely coupled *systems of interaction*, that is, the *social* domain of human interactions and the *natural* environment of life-supporting properties. The logic of lateral pressure theory argues for their joint or co-dependence (even co-evolution), despite fundamental differences among them.

"Lateral pressure" refers to any *tendency* (or propensity) of individuals, states, firms, and societies to expand their activities and exert influence and control beyond their established boundaries, whether for economic, political, military, scientific, religious, or other purposes (Lofdahl 2002; North 1990; Choucri and North 1989; Choucri and North 1975). The theory posits that the overall dynamics of organized activities are rooted in internal drivers, the *master variables*—the most fundamental features of the social order; these *shape* the *demands* and the *capabilities* that, on the aggregate, define *state profiles*. In many ways, profiles shape the parameters of permissible behavior, that is, what states are able to do or not do.

These internal features create pressures pushing for *expansion*, but such tendencies can be blocked or prevented by internal or external conditions or moves by other actors. Alternatively, they can be realized and articulated through various modes of external behavior. The nature of the interactions shapes the dynamics of international relations—most notably, conflict, contention, collaboration, cooperation—and the associated generativity. All the familiar processes of military competition, arms races, and so on, follow at this point. The outcome may well alter the initial configuration of the internal drivers as well as the international position of the state.

Thus, the levels of analysis reframed and the assumptions upon which these rest yield *four levels of analysis and two domains of interaction.* The rest of this chapter focuses on interaction within and across each of the four stylized levels of analysis—the individual, the state, the international system, and the global system—and across two domains of interaction, the social context and the natural environment. All parts of this chapter refer to the traditional world of international relations. Cyberspace will be considered in chapter 5 as the third arena of interaction.

We now turn to a brief sketch of the causal logic and then turn to each of the levels of analysis, beginning with the individual level, the most basic unit in international relations.

3.2   The Causal Logic

The master variables are the core building blocks of theory. Lateral pressure stipulates that the causal logic runs from the *internal* drivers (that is, the master variables that shape the profiles of states) through the intervening variables (namely, aggregated and articulated demands given prevailing capabilities), to *external* behavior and international outcomes. Throughout this process, states may experience structural and other changes. Here, we can only briefly present the causal logic, not a detailed statement or the various forms of nonlinear interactions among the three master variables. The underlying causal logic is shown in figure 3.2.

This high-level view reminds us that the state profile contributes to propensities for external expansion—and eventually to international behavior. When expansion happens, states may intersect with others similarly engaged. This is the first stage in what usually becomes a complex dynamic process. At the same time, however, all states are experiencing differential rates of change in their master variables—foundations for unequal rates of growth and development—shaping differential rates and types of international activities.

Decisions take place from this point on: countries can pursue different strategies; they can engage in different forms of interactions; they can make friends and make enemies. All of this generates different outcomes. For

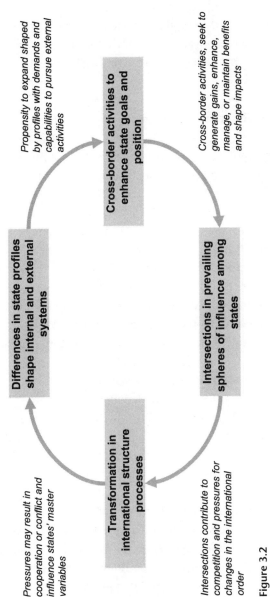

Figure 3.2

Simplified causal logic of lateral pressure theory.

Source: Choucri and Agarwal (2017). Reproduced by permission of Oxford University Press. Based on Choucri and Mistree (2010).

Note: This simplified view obscures feedback dynamics at each stage that may modify, alter, or reinforce the illustrated pathways.

example, if intersections are conflict oriented, when violence results, there are usually winners and losers. In each case, there could be a gain or loss in the master variable metrics, thereby potentially altering the profile of the state. On balance, then, the state profile is shaped by the state's own situation, as well as by the situations of all other states in the international system.

We now turn to each of the levels of analysis, beginning with the first level, the individual.

3.3 The Individual Level: Basis for Aggregation

Strictly construed, the individual, the first image, is the sole thinking, feeling, and acting entity in world politics, as we are reminded by Robert C. North in *War, Peace, Survival* (1990)—a reminder that echoes Herbert Simon's earlier arguments in *The Sciences of the Artificial* (Simon 1968). At the base of the social order are the core activities undertaken by individuals in their efforts to meet their needs and demands. Aggregated at the level of the state, the international system, and the global context, the most fundamental individual needs and wants are driven by the quest for security and survival.

Each individual is an *energy-using* and *information-processing* entity embedded in distinct domains, the social and the natural environments (North 1990)—and recently in the cyber domain. Further, human actions can affect the natural system in ways that feed back into the social system, and may have repercussions that are not susceptible to power-based instruments of control in the traditional international perspective. International relations theory recognizes the individual mainly in the context of states, formal decision-making position, or engaged in high-salience activity, or as being fundamental to critical functions such as military service. For the most part, it is in a particular role—as citizen, consumer, constituent, voter—that the individual is acknowledged.

The concepts of demands and capabilities provide the transition from the individual to the broader social entity, notably, the state. A *demand* is a determination that derives from a perceived (or felt) need, want, or desire for the purpose of narrowing or closing the gap between a perception of fact (what is) and a preference or value (what ought to be). Basic demands are usually for resource access, better living conditions, physical safety, and security, all of which are generally considered under the rubric of utility by economists. To meet demands—and to close the gap between the *is* and the *ought to be*, or possibly establish a preferred condition—individuals and societies must possess the required capabilities. The demands of individuals are shaped in large part by their respective capabilities.

Capabilities consist of the set of attributes that enable performance and allow individuals, groups, political systems, and entire societies to manage their demands. Given that states vary extensively in their capabilities, their environmental effects will also vary, as will the attendant pressures on the integrity of social systems, or the viability of the natural environment.

Demands combine with capabilities to produce *propensities* for actions. But actual *behavior* is contingent on intents, knowledge, skills, and access to resources, as well as capabilities. Social *outcomes* are often less the result of conscious value-maximizing choices than of inertia, habit, and a mixture of personal and organizational purposes and adaptations. In any case, social habit patterns are usually the outcome of some earlier discrete (conscious or unconscious) individual choices made by the members of the population at large or by an individual or individuals in a bureaucratic or government context.

At the aggregate level, the critical drivers of social activity—in all contexts and at all levels of development—can be traced to three basic, foundational interactive variables: population, resources, and technology. These are the fundamental *master variables*. They are the observed outcomes of a number of widely dispersed decisions made by individuals (e.g., investors and voters), all coordinated through *institutional* mechanisms, private and public, the fundamental channels through which the social order is managed. The efficacy of institutions is closely dependent on the characteristic features of, and interactions among, the master variables. These are the building blocks of the state. They are *interactive* foundational variables in the sense that if any one of these deteriorates or "goes to zero," the social system stagnates or loses its coherence. Each of these variables is obviously not a singular factor but a cluster of constructs (and attendant variables or subvariables).

Specifically, *population* includes changes in the size, distribution, and composition of populations. *Technology* refers to all applications of knowledge and skills in mechanical (equipment, machinery) as well as organizational (institutional) terms, and encompasses both soft and hard dimensions. Often the former is as important as the latter. Technology may require new resources, which often calls for the deployment of specialized capabilities. Herbert Simon has described technology as "stored knowledge" and has highlighted its key impacts on society (Simon 1968). *Resources* are conventionally defined as that which has value, and include all elements critical to human existence (such as water, air, etc.).

All of the above is contextual. None of the forgoing negates the role of the state as the basic organizing principle for authority in the international system. The state remains the major actor and the dominant level of analysis in international relations theory, policy, and practice, with security and survival as its overarching concern.

3.4   The State Level: Sovereignty and Authority

The state system we know today dates to the Peace of Westphalia in 1648. As noted earlier, it is anchored in the notion of sovereignty, the definition of territoriality, the role of authority, and jurisdictional reach—all with attendant challenges and opportunities.

The state encompasses a wide range of organizational entities through which individuals interact with each other and with their social, natural, and now cyber arenas. The only legal entity enfranchised to speak on behalf of its citizens in international forums, the state, is defined as sovereign in international law. Its primary goal is to ensure its own security and survival within its internationally recognized boundaries.

State borders are constructed—and often contested. In principle, they delineate jurisdictions of states and, by extension, the authority of government. Also in principle, borders are protected, and states are in full control of access, that is, entry and exit. In practice, this is seldom the case. Even the most cursory exposure to news coverage—in any media, anywhere, and on any day—reveals contentions over transgressions. Few states, if any, are able to fully control entry and exit of people, goods, or services. States cannot protect or regulate effluents or emissions that cross their borders. It goes without saying, also, that states cannot protect themselves against damage to their own environment caused by the activities of other states. As we shall see in chapter 5, the state system is seeking to find ways of controlling access to the cyber domain, for its citizens and for others as relevant.

Governance refers to legitimate structures and processes through which societies are managed. Government refers to the specific mechanisms for management. Initially framed in the context of the sovereign state, these definitions are generic in form, applicable to all countries, at all levels of development, and in all periods of time. Some similar mechanisms operate in other contexts and entities, such as corporations and nonprofit entities. Simple as this might seem, we shall note further along, in chapter 9, the complexity of governance in the cyber domain.

The generic governance challenge is how best to manage two counter-prevailing processes: (1) understanding pressures emanating from societal *demands* creating loads on the system, and (2) mobilizing *capacities* of government to respond to pressures, while avoiding large-scale disruption. It is not unusual for efforts to meet demand—or to expand capacity for purposes of meeting demands—to create unintended consequences that may undermine the government's own positions.[1] In this context, the management of demands and capabilities is the intervening process relating state profiles and their characteristics features to propensities for external behavior.

3.4.1 State Profiles

All states can be characterized by different combinations of population, resources, and technology—the master variables—and different combinations yield different state profiles as well as different impacts on the natural environment. The concept of the *state profile* provides an internally consistent "rule" for differentiating among states and a method for calculating the differences among them (Choucri and North 1989). Table 3.1 presents an operational definition of state profile. The table defines the six modal types of profiles, with the understanding that countries are distributed within and across these types and, as we show later on in this chapter, a state's profiles can change over time.

Table 3.1
State profiles defined.

Profile I	Resources > Population > *Technology*
Profile II	Population > Resources > *Technology*
Profile III	Population > *Technology* > Resources
Profile IV	Resources > *Technology* > Population
Profile V	*Technology* > Resources > Population
Profile IV	*Technology* > Population > Resources

Source: Based on Choucri (2012, 32).
Note: See Choucri and North (1993) and Lofdahl (2002) for the original specification; and Wickboldt and Choucri (2006) and Choucri and Agarwal (2017) for extension of the logic to differentiate empirically among countries within each profile group.

The logic of collective behavior and state action is mediated by institutions and instruments of governance. It goes without saying that the nature of collective action depends on its underlying logic. As new expectations are generated, larger amounts of resources are usually demanded. Access to resources often depends on the state's capabilities, power, and ability to muster and exert influence. Further, the increased knowledge intensity of economic activity points to the enhanced salience and politicization of knowledge. None of these are fixed, in the sense that the master variables are subject to change, some more readily than others. New resources can be discovered, new technologies can be imported, policies may be designed to constrain population growth, and so forth. For this reason, it is sometimes useful to look at the distribution of states over time. Further along in this chapter we shall present some empirical views of state profiles.

Each state accounts for a "share" of the global total for each of the individual master variables. The inequalities in table 3.1 apply to the individual shares for each state relative to the global aggregate. Different profiles generate different propensities for expansion. Here is the direct connection between *internal* attributes and *external* behavior. For simplification, we use population size (population), land area (resources) as suggested by Charles Kindleberger (1970), and gross domestic product (technology) as the master variables. We shall turn to the measurement of profiles later in this chapter.

Over time these "shares" of the global total change—as states grow and expand, or stagnate and "fail." The display in table 3.1 with technology in the diagonal is for convenience purposes only. The reorganization of each profile type in this table yields, by definition, to a population-driven display, or alternatively, a resource-driven display (each with the P or the R variable along the diagonals). Operationally, the master variables of each state constitute an individual "share" of the global total.

The state profile is a good predictor of both power indicators and attendant behavior patterns. The important point here is to note that *the driving variable is the one in which the state's power and influence is rooted*. Some countries are shaped by their population relative to the other master variables; others are shaped more by their other variables. The profile type is also a good indicator of environmental impacts, as we have shown elsewhere (Choucri and North 1993). Box 3.1 puts forth a stylistic but substantive description of the profile groups. Later we shall ask, is this approach relevant for understanding the implications of the cyber domain?

Box 3.1

State profiles: brief description

Profile I: Resources > Population > *Technology*

Defined largely as resource-rich and technologically constrained entities, these states are driven (and shaped) by traditional activities such as agriculture, grazing, lumbering, mining, and development of other natural resources.

Profile II: Population > Resources > *Technology*

In contrast to profile I, states in profile II are driven by the dominant strength of populations, followed by access to resources, with technology in third place. Technologically constrained, these states tend to be among the poorest and the least developed.

Profile III: Population > *Technology* > Resources

Similar to profile II, profile III states are shaped by population dynamics; however, their technologies surpass their resources. They exert strong pressures on their limited resources, at the risk of becoming seriously dependent on external sources for meeting needs and demands.

Profile IV: Resources > *Technology* > Population

Profile IV states are noteworthy for having large territories, reasonably advanced technologies, and relatively small populations. Their resource intensity calls for better methods of exploitation, access, and use.

Profile V: *Technology* > Resources > Population

Profile V countries are technology dominant, with resources greater than population. Both technology and resources are adequate relative to populations. To the extent that their populations increase, these countries will become candidates for profile VI. However, if technology declines substantially relative to their extensive resources and limited populations, they risk falling back into profile III.

Profile VI: *Technology* > Population > Resources

Profile VI states are driven by technology intensity, but their populations are large relative to their resources. Accordingly, they tend to exert maximum (yet ever-increasing) pressures on their (relatively) limited resource base.

Source: Based on Choucri (2012, 34–35).

Any change in the master variables—in levels or rates of change—generates changes *within* the state, which in turn create changes in the distribution of profiles *across* states. The nature of the changes depends on the particular master variable that drives the overall profile. For example, if growth in the technology variable (and its underlying knowledge assets) is greater than growth in the population or resources variable, then the state will be moving along a technology-led trajectory. It also depends on the roots of change, that is, the sources of influence that drive the changes in question. Moreover, changes at the state profile—because the state can travel across profile types—will have an impact on the overall structure of the international system. If we recognize that at each point in time a state is characterized by one set of master variables that define the empirical parameters of the polity and provide the basis for policy agenda as well (Choucri and North 1989), then normalizing each master variable to a share of the global total for that variable provides a simple and replicable approach to understanding, not only the position of an individual state, but shifts in the global total for any variable. This step ensures that the profiles of different states are comparable and meaningful. See appendix 3.1 for indicators and sources.

We illustrate later in this chapter how the location of states within profile type can change over time depending on changes in their own master variables and the master variables of other states (i.e., the global total). Figure 3.3 shows a map of the international system, differentiating states' profile groups. The inset in figure 3.3 presents changes in profiles over time.

These empirical views reflect *real* types of state profiles in the international system, traditionally defined. All of this leads us to a critical question: What is the profile distribution in the *cyber* domain? Are countries characterized by the same profile group in both the traditional system and the cyber arena? Does it matter? If so, how? If not, why not? We shall return to this question in chapter 5.

3.4.2 Propensity for Expansion

The propensity to expand behavior outside territorial boundaries is motivated by a desire to close the gap between the *actual* condition and the *preferred* situation. Because the strength of an entity's lateral pressure is generally taken to correlate positively with its power as conventionally understood, this logic reflects the assumption that sources of power and change are rooted *within* the state system. Pollins and Schweller (1999) as well as Wickboldt and Choucri (2006) remind us that when states extend their

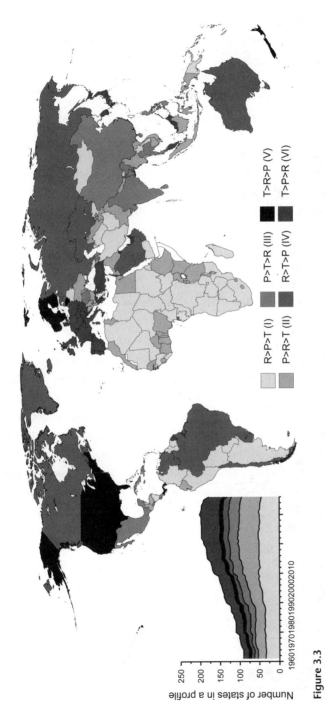

Figure 3.3

Distribution of states by real profile type, 2016. *Inset:* Number of states in each profile, 1960–2016.

Source: Based on data from World Bank (2017i).

behavior outside territorial boundaries, they will encounter other states similarly engaged. North (1990) reminds us that, in this process, modes of bargaining and leverage are shaped by each side's real or perceived capabilities. This assumption also holds for all other actors.

The theory of lateral pressure signals the *intersection of spheres of influence* as a significant point at which interactions are likely to evolve into competition, which in turn shapes hostilities that can rapidly evolve into spiraling conflicts—leading to military competition and eventually to violence and warfare and usually triggered by an overt act that is perceived as a provocation.

Clearly not all expansion leads to intersections of interests, nor do all intersections of interests harness a conflict spiral. This stylistic sketch is remarkably consistent with the historical record of the industrial west and the narratives developed over time to explain the outbreak of World War I and World War II. The quantitative investigations of lateral pressure theory, highlighted later in this chapter, signal the challenges as well as the opportunities and contentions inherent in, and surrounding, quantitative empirical analyses.

None of this is inevitable. At issue is how to navigate through the critical disconnects between their own demands and those of others, and their ability to meet their demands. The concepts of "soft" power and "smart" power—important additions to contemporary discourse—significantly broaden the theory and practice of leverage and influence (Nye, 2011). The core implication, however, is that the consequences of lateral pressure, actions, and the behavioral outcomes can influence the international system in various ways and, depending on the nature of the activities, shape the global system as well (Choucri and North 1989). Propensities for expansion may be blocked in various ways—by internal capabilities or by external conditions—leading to frustration, tension, conflict, and escalation of hostilities. (Much is contingent on the arena or domain within which expansion takes place.)

More recently, we developed the lateral pressure (LP) index to capture the propensity for expansion and, to the extent possible, to highlight the relative salience of the individual drivers. Given that the theory recognizes the high degree of *interaction* among the master variables[2] we framed the LP index, for state i at time j, as a function of the geometric mean of the master variables:[3]

$$LP\ Index_{i,j} = \sqrt[3]{P_{i,j} \times R_{i,j} \times T_{i,j}}$$

where $P_{i,j}$, $R_{i,j}$ and $T_{i,j}$ are population, resource, and technology master variables for state i at time j, respectively.

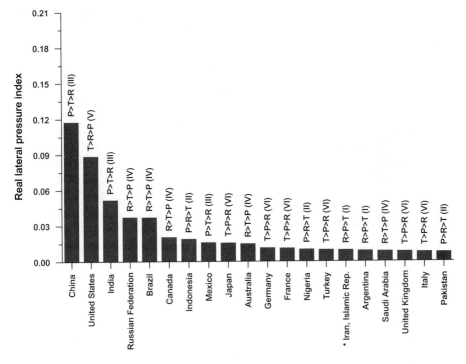

Figure 3.4
States ordered by real lateral pressure index and identified by real profile, 2016.
Source: Based on data from World Bank (2017i).
Note: * 2015 data.

When we consider the LP index of states and signal their profile type, as in figure 3.4, we can identify the state with the highest propensity for expansion and its profile type. This figure shows that *propensity to expand is not contingent on profile type*. It also identifies the most dominant of the three variables defining the profile, and hence the power base.

Figure 3.5 shows the propensity to extend behavior outside territorial boundaries for states in each of the six profile types. This figure highlights what is, at first glance, self-evident—namely, that technology drives U.S. expansion, and population drives China's expansion. But it also raises questions about the potential implications of China's technology development. Note, for example, that technology is not the most constraining variable for China. It is not surprising that population is the dominant variable. At the same time, population is the most

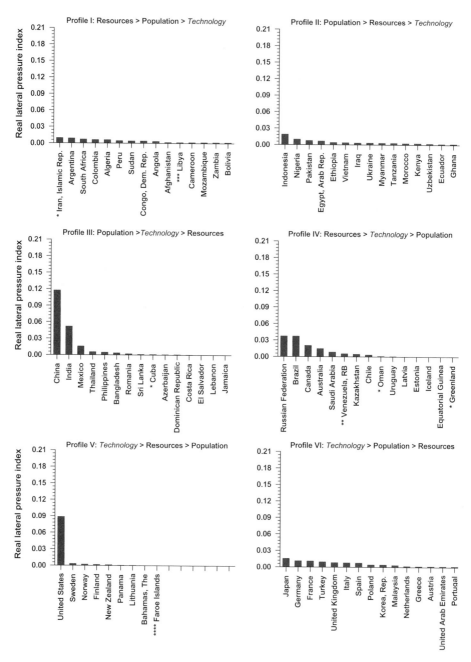

Figure 3.5

States ordered by real lateral pressure index and identified by real profile, 2016.

Source: Based on data from World Bank (2017i).

Note: * 2015 data; ** 2013 data; *** 2011 data; **** 2010 data. No 2014 and 2012 data are included.

constraining master variable for the United States. We shall return to these patterns again.

In general, the relationship between the sovereign state and private entities—for profit and not for profit—is framed by the characteristic features of the state's profile, on the one hand, and by the capabilities and propensity for expansion of private actors, on the other. We know that in early phases of development, a country generates neither outward nor inward organizational capability. Over time, as a state increases its capabilities and its private entities, it generates a range of cross-border activities and may even become a net outward investor. Eventually, the capabilities of private actors, such as firms, rather than the power and the profile of the home state can become more significant (Choucri 1995). In this process, a firm's strategies are increasingly decoupled from the home state and its profile type. At this point, all policies and practices are embedded in the firm's "organizational field" (Fligstein 1990, 5–11), a concept that carries much of the expansionist core of lateral pressure.

3.5   The International Level: Domain of Interaction

The third level, the international system, is formally defined as a system composed of sovereign states. Rooted in the Westphalian principle of sovereignty, the state remained for several centuries as the only constituent feature of the international system. Today international relations consist of interactions among sovereign states, intergovernmental organizations, nonstate entities (both for profit and not for profit), nongovernmental organizations, and many others. As a result, the sovereign state is embedded in a wide range of networks, formal and informal. Given that competition for power and influence is a generic feature of politics among nations, lateral pressure theory points to intersections among spheres of influences as a mechanism for setting off hostility, potentially initiating the dynamics of military competition leading to the well-known phenomenon of an arms race.

Clearly, the state is not the only actor, nor is it the only expansionist one. For a while, the generic imperatives in the international arena—pursuit of power and pursuit of wealth—were the prime goals of the sovereign state. Over time, state dominance eroded as other entities established relatively autonomous power. (These issues are addressed further along.) A wide range of nonstate actors are also extending their activities beyond their home borders. These transnational entities are private as well as public.[4] They operate horizontally, that is, connecting constituencies and interests across state boundaries, as well as vertically, connecting constituencies across all levels of interaction. These entities are not always controlled by the organs of the state or by those of the international system. Multinational corporations are among the most prominent (Choucri 1993c). Corporations conduct most of the world's economic activity, serving as producers, managers, and distributors of goods and services. Others include trade unions, scientific organizations, religious groups, and international cartels, to name only a few of the most obvious.

3.5.1 International Institutions

International institutions and their multilateral foundations are considered to be the formal mechanism of cooperation for the third level of analysis. They are the only venues for decision making among the member states—the ultimate actors, agents, voters, participants, and constituencies. The origins of intergovernmental institutions are usually traced back to the founding of the International Telecommunication Union toward the end of the nineteenth century. At the turn of the twentieth century, there were fewer than forty such institutions; by the onset of the twenty-first century, the number had increased to roughly four hundred (Zacher 2001).

This growth of international institutions represents a different modality of expansion. It is not a single state projecting influence beyond territorial boundaries (as discussed so far), rather it is the established state system expanding its power and influence across the international system and, generally, into the state and its boundaries. This modality is enabled and legitimized by the establishment of the United Nations. Figure 3.6 shows the growth trend in United Nations membership that mirrors almost perfectly the growth of independent states. The inset in figure 3.6 can be seen as companion developments. The trend in intergovernmental institutions requires no interpretation. In the absence of central authority, states have had little recourse other than to establish entities that can facilitate, if not ensure, coordinated action as needed.

Generally, changes in international institutional arrangements reflect changes in the distribution of influence throughout the international system. As Kratochwil and Ruggie (1986, 753) stated many years ago, international organizations as a subfield of international relations had "its ups and downs

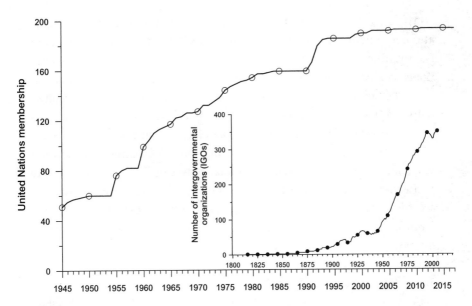

Figure 3.6
Trends in United Nations membership, 1945–2017. *Inset:* Leading intergovernmental organizations, 1800–2005.
Sources: Based on data from United Nations (1945a, 1945b); Pevehouse, Nordstrom, and Warnke (2004); Nordstrom, Pevehouse, and Shannon (2010).

throughout the post–World War II era and throughout this past century for that matter." Increasingly, however, we see evidence of institutional learning and development. Although the evidence may be subject to contention, a notable shift toward knowledge-based institutional policy appears to be emerging. Differences in institutional performance are to be expected, but a considerable degree of innovation is clearly taking place on matters of process, over and above matters of content.

What is now salient in international relations theory, policy, and practice, is growth in the provision of public goods, a trend that is not created by the construction of cyberspace. An immediate follow-up concern, then, pertains to the nature of the rules and institutional mechanisms for such provision. However, as we shall show in later chapters, when cyber venues are used to pursue global objectives via international institutions, a completely new set of challenges emerges. Yet to be seen is the extent to which this shapes *who gets what, when,* and *how*—as well as who decides on each of these issues.

The growth and expansion of nongovernmental institutions operating at the international level is a trend that consolidated in the second half of the twentieth century. It does not replace the formal state-based institutions. In some cases, it fills the gaps left by the state system; in others it "intrudes" to support state system initiatives; in others in serves as an alternative to established institutions; in still others it is a venue for consolidating, even empowering, civil society—at all levels of analysis.

The complexities of these arrangements and the expansion in scale and scope make it difficult to generate a total census of nonstate actors at any point in time. Late in the twentieth century, nonstate groups had been accorded observer status or otherwise allowed to participate in international forums, but the fact remains that only states are formal voters and decision makers.

3.5.2   Jurisdictions and Markets

Whereas the expansionist activities of corporations and those of the state represent two different trajectories of collective action—and their conceptual underpinnings and extensions developed separately—the behaviors of these entities are often interconnected. As a jurisdictional actor, the state undertakes investments and thus engages in state-firm interactions and often intervenes in economic sectors and other issue areas.

Now we return to an issue raised early on in this chapter, namely, the situation of the individual in international relations. Trends in population movements, shown in figure 3.7, are among the most common that shape and reshape the overall configuration of the master variables worldwide. At the same time, people are crossing state borders motivated by the search for a better life. Increasingly we appreciate the growth in the scale and scope of migration for employment. During 1990 and 2013, the total stock of migrant population has increased by 1.5 times to approximately 243 million, up from roughly 150 million in 1990, about 3% of the world population (United Nations: Department of Economic and Social Affairs 2015a, 2015b).

In figure 3.8, we show a different form of mobility, namely, trends in global trade of goods and services. By extension, the inset presents the manifold increase in the remittances from the migrant workers to their home country between 1990 and 2016.

Shifting issues and idiom somewhat, it is not surprising that we also see an international system characterized by a dense network of shipping

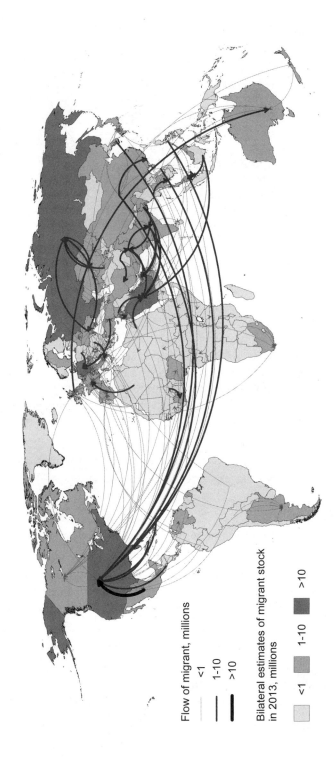

Flow of migrant, millions

<1

1-10

>10

Bilateral estimates of migrant stock
in 2013, millions

<1   1-10   >10

Figure 3.7

Total migrant stock and key flows of people across state boundaries, 2013.
Source: Based on data from World Bank (2016b).

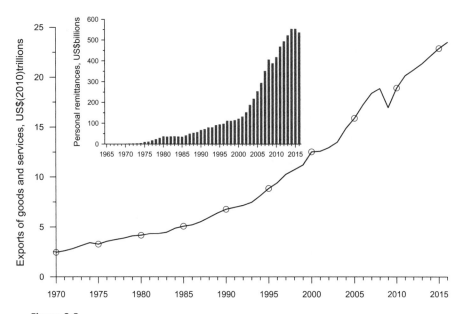

Figure 3.8
Trends in exports of goods and services, 1970–2016. *Inset:* Trends in personal remittances, 1970–2016.
Sources: Based on data from World Bank (2017b, 2017f).
Note: Personal remittances are the sum of personal transfers and compensation of employees, in current U.S. dollars.

routes in figure 3.9. In chapter 5, we draw attention to the networks of undersea cables, notably those carrying communication lines.

3.5.3 International Order

The views of the international system just discussed are all predicated on the existence of territorial boundaries. Central authority is exercised within, but does not cross, state borders (unless special provisions are made). Clearly, the international system is a highly fragmented and partitioned arena of interaction. At the same time, this international system functions, to some extent, by a set of rules and regulations all under the rubric of international law. As noted in chapter 1, international law is based on custom, practice, precedents, and general consensus evolving over centuries of interactions among sovereign entities. International law develops over time as scholars, decision makers, researchers, and others seek to formalize particular principles of order. In practice, sources of international law are

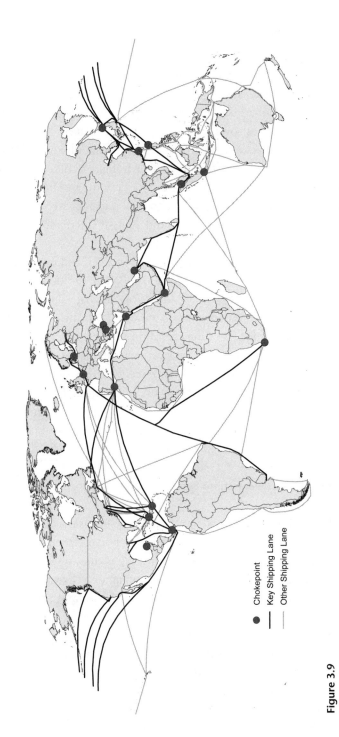

Figure 3.9

Maritime shipping routes.

Source: Based on CIA (2012) and its generalization by ESRI et al. (2013)

- ● Chokepoint
- —— Key Shipping Lane
- —— Other Shipping Lane

influenced by various legal and political theories that reflect the judgment of the community.

Public international law is concerned with the behavior of sovereign states and other analogous entities, such as the Holy See. With sovereignty and territorial jurisdiction comes state immunity. Public international law has grown in importance and use over the twentieth century, due to the increase in international trade, increases in international transportation, environmental conditions, responses to violations of human rights, and rapid increases in worldwide communication—to note only the most obvious. A growing number of issue-specific regimes (and legal imperatives) have developed to help manage international order and support international peace and security.

Although in principle all states are equal and sovereign and public international law is considered binding, international realities dictate a different logic—the authority of international law and its operational value is contingent on state willingness to observe and to enforce. With the proliferation of international organizations and the evolution of international law with specialized focus—international humanitarian law, international trade law, and gradual emergence of international environmental law, with treaties, protocols, agreements, and the like—the fabric of public international law has become more and more complex. Over time, select aspects of international law have extended to the behavior of corporations and of individuals. In a later chapter, we shall ask: Does international law extend to the cyber domain?

3.6   The Global Level: Overarching System

Transcending the international system, the global system is the overarching context for human life as we know it. A system of systems, it encompasses the social system and all its activities as well as the natural system with its life-supporting properties (and as discussed in chapter 5, cyberspace and all its functionalities as well as all generative properties and potentials). Almost all scholars and analysts of international relations now appreciate the interconnections between the natural and the human systems. Decisions and policies pertaining to the fourth image are made at the other levels of analysis, if and when the various constituencies recognize the need to make decisions. Embedded in the foregoing is a simple reality, that the fourth image is the "final aggregator" of human tensions and threats that have the potential for eroding life-supporting properties.

Once we recognize the global system as an overarching level of analysis, a set of new challenges emerge, at least four of which are especially compelling (Choucri 1993b). First, the basic biogeochemical characteristics of the global environment are broadly recognized, but uncertainties about *feedback effects* on both the geophysical and social processes remain daunting. Second, the social, environmental, and cyber-based processes operate at unequal and sometimes overlapping *time frames*, thus complicating the notion of temporality and the role of time. Third, are the *intergenerational impacts* of environmental change, whereby future generations incur the environmental burden created by the actions of past and present generations, with the challenges associated with long lead times. Fourth, are uncertainties due to *irreversibility*. Patterns of environmental alterations cannot readily be "undone." Underlying sources are not easily controlled or eliminated in short order—if at all. Needless to say, the construction of cyberspace creates its own pervasive challenges.

3.6.1 Basic Global Parameters
Turning briefly to select indicators of the master variables for the overarching global level, we point to overall trends at the most aggregate level.

We all know that the global population has been growing over time, as seen in figure 3.10. Although the rate of growth declined over time, the trends also show notable increase in population density (as seen the inset). In other words, given that the amount of land is limited, the rising population has placed pressures on the resources. Using gross domestic product (GDP) as a highly imperfect indicator of technology, we note that GDP per capita has increased over time, as shown in the inset in figure 3.10, despite fluctuations in rates of growth.

Generally, CO_2 emissions serve as a strong reference variable for human activity as well as for human impacts on the natural environment. The message in figure 3.11 is clear. Both per capita and absolute amount of greenhouse gases produced have increased, indicating a degradation of the environmental systems. Although generated by individuals and aggregated at the local level, once realized they are inherently global in their implications.

3.6.2 Globalization
Any reference to the global system as the fourth level invariably draws attention to globalization as a process. Globalization generally leads to new arenas of interaction with dynamics of its own.

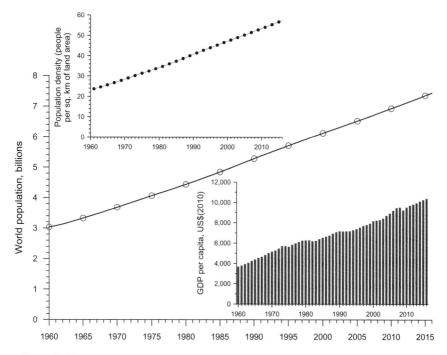

Figure 3.10

Trends in world population, 1960–2016. *Insets:* GDP per capita and population density, 1961–2016.

Sources: Based on data from World Bank (2017d, 2017h).

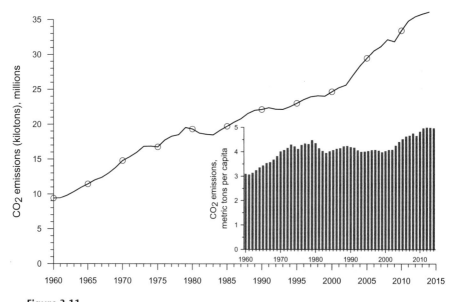

Figure 3.11

Trends in CO_2 emissions, 1960–2013.

Source: Based on data from World Bank (2017a).

Globalization unambiguously generates fundamental transformations in economic and social structures and processes worldwide, shaped by the large-scale movements of people, resources, and technologies across boundaries, and all of the attendant by-products. Earlier globalizations, which had created new spaces of interaction due to control or conquest (colonies, polar regions, outer space, for example), provided opportunities for the few and the powerful. Over time, the globalization processes became more complex and assumed new properties of unprecedented scale and scope. Such cross-border mobility influences the nature of national societies and economies and, under certain circumstances, may even alter them in fundamental ways. Inevitably, they also shape and reshape international exchanges and interactions.

The lateral pressure theory views globalization as an *empirical manifestation* of a process that is (1) generated by uneven growth and development within states, which (2) leads to the movement of goods, services, ideas, and effluents across national borders, such that (3) globalization contributes to transformations of socioeconomic and political structures, within and across states, (4) creates pressure on prevailing modes of governance, and (5) generates demands for changes in governance or expansion of behavior, and invariably these processes (6) create feedback dynamics driven by any one or a combination of the foregoing, that (7) shape changes in dominant processes and in the structures that govern them. If one or more of the above elements do not hold, then the interactions in question do not reflect globalization but are part of the international system.

To the extent that these processes are sufficiently pervasive and call for changes in dominant policy thrusts, it is reasonable to argue that the essence of globalization lies in the forging of common and overlapping territorial as well as policy spaces. In many ways, this view is consistent with that expressed in *The Oxford Companion to Politics of the World* by David Held and Anthony McGrew in their article "Globalization." They define globalization as the "process (or set of processes), which embodies a transformation in the spatial organization of social relations and transactions, expressed in transcontinental or interregional networks of activity, interaction, and power" (Held and McGrew 2001, 324).

3.6.3   What Does All This Amount To?

All of the foregoing is part of the world in which cyberspace was constructed. It is now "normal" to recognize the salience of environmental processes that were traditionally well beyond the purview of world politics.

Issues surrounding nature's life-supporting properties have clearly transitioned from the realm of low politics to that of high politics—where states compete and conflict over the nature of appropriate international strategies and policies. This process took well over thirty years.

There is a growing international consensus that present trends cannot continue unabated, that humans are destroying their life-supporting properties, that inequalities are dominating the international system, creating powerful contentions, and increasing conflict intensities. The prevailing focus on meeting short-term needs and demands is creating a "myopia effect" that, in itself, reinforces the damaging consequences of human activities.

This consensus has translated into a mounting international demand for some form of sustainability for people and societies everywhere. The conception of sustainable development commonly appears in the context of social systems, economies, enterprises, or states. Yet its fundamentals are relevant and applicable to other units and other levels of abstraction and with other forms of aggregation around various organizing principles.

These issues are all central to our consideration of individuals, states, and various entities in the international system. Are they also relevant in the constructed world of cyberspace? In a later chapter, we shall turn to the cyber domain and illustrate the ways the new realities have become part of our daily experience and, guided by lateral pressure theory, we explore the cyber arena and examine the actors and activities that shape the system and its interactions with the social and the natural systems.

3.7 Cyberspace—Literature Review 2000–2010

At this point, we turn to a review of the entire body of articles on cyberspace and international relations published in twenty-six major scholarly journals over the first ten years of the twenty-first century, 2000–2010 (Reardon and Choucri 2012). This review serves as something of a baseline. It was motivated by the Special Issue of the *International Political Science Review*, the first issue devoted entirely to the subject of cyberspace and international relations published by a major journal of international relations (Choucri 2000).

3.7.1 Approach and Method

Our review of twenty-six major journals is controlled, in the sense that it is bounded by time frame and content coverage. Of the twenty-six journals covered over a decade, eighteen are academic journals, and for comparative purposes, eight are policy-oriented journals. Of the academic journals, twelve focus on international relations, and the remaining six concentrate on political science more broadly.

With all due caveats and qualifications, the ten-year review provides something of a baseline against which we can consider the evolution of interest in, and knowledge about, the cyber arena in world politics. Only forty-nine articles published in these journals over this decade consider the matter of cyberspace—a rather limited number given the salience of the virtual in world politics at the time. Of these, thirty-three articles appeared in policy journals and sixteen in academic journals.

In general, we expected these journals to be dominated by realism and institutionalism, each focusing on a different aspect of this daunting domain. Further, we expected realist theorists to focus on cyber conflict, crisis management, and consider if cyberspace were stabilizing or destabilizing, or if cyber technologies will be a new source of conflict or of peace, or if states will engage in a cyber arms race, and so forth. Also, we expected realists to challenge those who argue that cyberspace empowers new international actors and undermines the authority of the state. By contrast, we expected institutionalism, in its various forms, to consider how access to cyberspace can promote the free flow of information, the spread of political ideas, the organization of civil society, and the development of transnational social networks, for example. We also expected institutional theorists to focus on matters of governance of cyberspace, behavioral cyber norms, acceptable conduct in the cyber arena, and the like. These expectations were not borne out.

Over the entire ten-year period, half of the articles on cyberspace were of a constructivist bent. Of these, half focused on security, an issue area that traditionally is associated with realism. This is rather paradoxical, given that realist theories of international relations are expected to contribute to our understanding of cybersecurity and related matters. Although many constructivists do not contest the idea that there is a material basis to security threats, they argue that the labeling of diverse activities as threats to national security is a product of intersubjective interpretation.

The constructivist literature raises questions of relevance here. First, what, exactly, is cybersecurity? And how many different "cybersecurities" (or facets thereof) are there? Are they separate or part of a larger whole? Second, to what degree should threats in cyberspace be considered important to our conception of national security? Is cyber security a military issue or a civilian one? The constructivists help to frame a set of important issues—perhaps the most important ones. Most of the articles draw upon the Cold War ethos, especially deterrence theory and the offense-defense balance. They place emphasis on the low cost of cyberattacks in contrast to the higher cost of defense and military activity.

Interestingly, the role of nonstate actors is largely ignored except by some authors who noted that the ease with which an attack can be launched allows even nonstate actors to threaten states. Constructivists are not concerned with cyber conflict as described in the policy literature, or with how nonstate actors can use novel cyber weapons crafted out of code to gain access to critical government or military networks and disrupt them, steal official secrets or intellectual property, or with the conduct acts of terrorism by disabling or hijacking critical systems—all part of the traditional domain of realist theories. Constructivists focus on competition for ideas, and how ideas shape alternatives and alter outcomes.

3.7.2   What Else Can Be Inferred?

Two issues cut across the entire set, 2001–2010. The first is *definitional*: There is *considerable ambiguity* about the nature of the new domain. That in itself signals an intellectual challenge, e.g., is it the Internet per se or social media? Is it "information" technology? Information and communications technology? Or is it just technology? Or networks? Is it the globalization process itself? The second pertains to *omission*: Very little attention, if any, is given to dynamics of *transformation and change*. At the core, these are driven by the constitutive power of decisions that were made early on about Internet architecture, from material structures to syntactic code to overall governance of implementation and deployment.

3.8   Endnote: What Have We Learned?

The issues addressed in chapter 3 are as fundamental to the international system as are the issues in chapter 2 to the cyber domain. Jointly, these two chapters constitute the essential building blocks for an integrated view of cyberspace and the international system.

This chapter begins with a formal map of the international system and a brief note on the traditional approach to the levels of analysis in international relations. We then reframe and expand the traditional view, briefly, by

(1) introducing a fourth level of analysis, (2) recognizing the importance of nonstate entities, and (3) differentiating between two domains of interaction, the social system and the natural system with its life-supporting properties. In later chapters we shall introduce other important theoretical extensions.

Then we focus on the characteristic elements of each level of analysis and present some informative empirical features. Our purpose is to provide a view of the world *before* the construction of the Internet—with prevailing assumptions and empirical manifestations. Later, in chapter 5, we revisit the international system and the levels of analysis *after* the forging of cyberspace.

Beginning with the first level, we assume that the *individual—Homo politicus* or *Homo economicus* or other—is an information-processing and energy-using entity. As primary actor and decision maker—constrained by situational, organizational, and institutional mechanisms—the individual is a *goal-seeking* entity; in this case, the goal is to close the gap between actual and desired situation. Further, all individuals and entities generate *demands* of various sorts and are characterized at any point in time by *capabilities*. Demands and capabilities are essential requisites for seeking to engage in *external activity*.

We introduce the concept of *state profile* to differentiate among states and create a consistent set of metrics to capture propensities for expansion. We find that China, the United States and India, in that order, are the states with the highest propensity for external expansion. For these, and all other states, we identify the dominant master variable that shapes the profile type and contributes to the propensity for expansion.

Clearly, the *state* remains the definitional entity for the international system but it is not the only significant actor in world politics. All states seek to enhance their *system-sustaining* properties and to reduce *system-threatening* conditions.

We then present several different views of the *international* system, the third level, in terms of structures (actors and entities) and processes (movements of people, goods, services, etc.). We observe the growth in number of international institutions, state and nonstate, which contributes to the dense fabric of international entities, for profit and not for profit. With the commensurate growth of international decision-making organizations and consolidation of the new policy priorities, we see more complex institutional ecosystems.

Finally, we turn to the *global* system, the all-encompassing fourth level that also spans two distinct domains, the human system and the natural environment. Consistent with the practice in this chapter, we show some empirically based views of this level. Some reflect expansion of scale, others carry generative properties with all the feedback dynamics that these imply.

The *causal logic* runs from master variables, the internal drivers that shape the profiles of states—through the intervening effects of socially aggregated and prevailing capabilities to shape propensity for expansion—in all contexts and at all levels of development. All features at all levels of analysis in this chapter are framed in a world long before the construction of the Internet and creation of cyberspace.

Later on, of course, we shall ask: Are these of relevance—directly or by analogy—to the world today, one near dominated by the ubiquity of cyberspace? And again, if so, how? If not, why not? At this writing the cyber domain is, nearly everywhere, part of the normal human experience. If twenty-first-century international relations theory is to take into account the constructed environment, then it must recognize its fundamental properties—pertaining to time, space, permeation, fluidity, participation, attribution, and accountability noted earlier—the very elements that undermine the traditional state. These elements define the essence of cyber politics, at all levels, distinguish between the real domains and the cyber arenas, and create new possibilities—as well as new constraints—in contentions over *who gets what, when*, and *how*. Throughout this chapter we recognize the importance of rates of change for critical parameters as well as feedback dynamics, and transformations of structures and processes.

In chapter 4 we build upon the layers of the Internet and the levels of analysis in international relations and develop an overarching model spanning both systems, with case-based "tests" to explore its utility and robustness. We put forth a model integrating cyberspace and international relations to create the joint *cyber-IR system*. And we ask: where are the intersection points of cyberspace and the international system?

Appendix 3.1
On *Real* Data

This appendix addresses data issues for *real* (or basic) master variables as well as *real* profile type and *real* lateral pressure index. See Choucri and Agarwal (2016, 2017) for details, and Choucri and North (1975) and Choucri, North, and Yamakage (1992) for earlier analyses.

Table 3.2
Indicators for real master variables.

Master Variable	Indicator	Measures
Population	Population	Size, distribution, composition, and rates of change.
Resource	Land area	Elements of value to society, including natural resources critical for human survival and those made available through applications of technology (such as drilling for petroleum, alternative energy sources, extracting raw materials and minerals, for example).
Technology	Gross domestic product	Productivity due to applications of knowledge and skills in mechanical (equipment, machinery, etc.) as well as organizational (institutional) terms.

Sources: See Choucri and North (1975), and Kindleberger (1970).

Indicators

Table 3.2 lists the indicators for real master variables and further used annually for state profile and lateral pressure index, 1960–2016.

Master Variables

Master variables of state i in year j, for *real* state profile and *real* lateral pressure index are defined as follows:

$$Real\ Population\ Index_{i,j} = \frac{Population_{i,j}}{Population_{world,j}}$$

where, $Population_{i,j}$ is the population for state i in year j, and $Population_{world,j}$ is the reported total world population in year j.

$$Real\ Resources\ Index_{i,j} = \frac{Land\ area_{i,j}}{Land\ area_{world,j}}$$

where $Land\ area_{i,j}$ is the total surface area for state i in year j, and $Land\ area_{world,j}$ is the reported total surface area of the world in year j.

$$Real\ Technology\ Index_{i,j} = \frac{GDP_{i,j}}{GDP_{world,j}}$$

where $GDP_{i,j}$ is the gross domestic product, in US\$(2010), for state i in year j, and $GDP_{world,j}$ is the reported world gross domestic product, in US\$(2010), in year j.

Prices are in constant 2010 U.S. dollars (see World Bank [2017j, 2017k]).

State Profiles
See table 3.1 for definition of state profiles.

Lateral Pressure Index
See section 3.4.2 for definition.

Data and Sources
Real population master variable:
Population, total: Mid-year estimates of total population, including all residents—except for refugees. See World Bank (2017i, SP.POP.TOTL).

Real resources master variable:
Surface area (sq. km): Total area of state, including areas under inland bodies of water and some coastal waterways. Variations due to revised data. See World Bank (2017i, AG.SRF.TOTL.K2).

Real technology master variable:
GDP (constant 2010 US$): The sum of gross value, purchaser's prices added by all resident producers plus any product taxes and minus any subsidies. GDP reported in 2010 U.S. dollars, converted from domestic currencies using 2010 official exchange rates if needed. If the official exchange rate does not reflect the rate applied to actual foreign exchange transactions, then an alternative conversion factor is used. See World Bank (2017i, NY.GDP.MKTP.KD).

4 The Cyber-IR System: Integrating Cyberspace and International Relations

So far we have introduced and reviewed briefly the *layers of the Internet*, the core of cyberspace (chapter 2) and the *levels of analysis*, a conventional view of the international system (chapter 3) as two different systems of interaction. Both levels and layers are human constructs. But their defining properties reinforce the propensity to consider them as two separate, possibly parallel systems. Given their increasing convergence, even interpenetration—in the sense that cyberspace has become an integral aspect of international relations, and world politics fuses into the cyber arena—the challenge at hand is to capture the interconnections between the two systems and, to the extent relevant, the mutual penetration across their respective components.

In some ways, the levels view shares with the layers model an important feature, namely mutual influences and dependencies. The difference is that the layers are hierarchical in architecture and functionality; the levels are hierarchical in construct with sovereignty as a defining feature. Whereas "reversing the levels" is a feature of the level view, reversing the layers is not an option in Internet architecture. Earlier in this book, we signaled that international relations and cyberspace are each governed by different principles of authority. The former is dominated by public authority (the state system) and the latter by private authority (the private sector, for profit and not for profit).

Chapter 4 puts forth the foundations for a view of twenty-first-century international relations (IR) that recognizes cyberspace as a new arena of interaction and integrates the cyber and the geopolitical arenas into one overarching framework. Our purpose here is to develop and illustrate the relationships and interdependence between the layer method of analysis and the levels approach. To the extent that an integrated view is instructive, it may even help frame a commensurate theory of international relations for the cyber age. Even more daunting is the companion challenge, namely, understanding the dynamics of their *joint* transformation and change—and implications for the international system and for the cyber domain.

We also consider key mechanisms that have evolved to enable Internet operations for seamless networking in a world defined by sovereignty and territoriality, on the one hand, and by market and competition, on the other. These mechanisms were rooted in technological imperatives, embedded in the realm of the apolitical—not even considered within the lowest of "low politics." However, given the co-evolution of cyberspace and international relations, this "privileged" position is not likely to persist. Finally, consistent with the question mark in figure 1.1, we consider "how the pieces hang together" in terms of the "parts" and the integrated "whole," and how elements that provide the "glue" are, in themselves, subject to pressures of transformation and change.

4.1   Integrated System

As a starting point, we build off the previous chapters and construct a matrix, a model that represents both the core of cyberspace and the traditional view of international relations—the layers and the levels. The matrix is constructed with the layers as its rows and the levels as its columns. We augment the traditional three levels of analysis with a fourth—the global level—and as well further augment it with two columns implied by the salience of the private sector in the construction of cyberspace. We have divided the private sector into two subcategories—profit-seeking and nonprofit—and demonstrate the importance of this distinction.

The matrix captures the intersection of the two domains and helps situate various actors and activities, current technology and innovations in information and communications, and varieties of policy issues and emergent dilemmas. Figure 4.1 shows the joint space in matrix form within which we situate examples of current issues. In doing so, we seek to respect the basic structural features of each domain. The extent to which these issues can or cannot be "pigeonholed" illustrates some of the power and nuances of the matrix. At a minimum, we can best consider this matrix as an entry point for issue concerns, with the understanding that initial positioning may not capture structural changes or evolution over time. Later in

	Individual	State	International	Global	Nonprofit	Profit-Seeking
People	Fake News	Digital divide			Advocacy	Off-shoring
Information	Privacy; peer production	Censorship	Protection of intellectual property	Spam; WikiLeaks and other leaks	Frameworks for peer production	Aggregation of personal data; search; advertising
Application	Peer production	Lawful intercept; blocking			Application design (example: TOR)	Control over character of application
Services		Blocking DNS		Authority over DNS	Operation of DNS; other services	Manipulation of service
Internet	Home network management	Network neutrality			Co-op network	Network neutrality
Physical	Home wiring	Facilities unbundling	Satellite orbit; spectrum			Facilities investment

Platform (Application, Services, Internet)

Figure 4.1

A selection of current issues and concerns, positioned in the matrix of levels and layers.

this book we consider matters of transformation and change and illustrate sources and consequences thereof. At this point our purpose is to highlight the basic reference model for the joint cyber-IR system.

The integrated framework—with the illustrative views presented in matrix form—provides an important first step, a useful baseline to help: (1) track changes in actors, functions, situations, standards, and other critical factors shaping current realities, altering these realities, or taking on new significance over time; (2) identify, explore, and anticipate potential futures— in conceptual, empirical, and perhaps even strategic terms; (3) signal emergent conflicts of interest or intersections in spheres of influence, and, especially important, (4) frame policy and practice on more transparent and robust, normative and empirical principles.

Despite its snapshot view, the model captures the key elements. For the levels, it is inspired by the complexity of the levels of analysis and linkages among the levels. For the layers, it highlights hierarchical dependencies, with the physical layer as a starting point, while recognizing the interconnections that arise among the other layers. Recall that in chapter 2, we introduced select key institutions that enable the operations of the cyber domain. Notable among those directly relevant are the Internet service providers (ISPs) that generate the first-order connectivity throughout the cyber arena. Later, in chapter 9, we shall examine the Internet institutional foundations and operations in greater depth.

4.2   Illustrating the Joint System—Cases in Context

In order to explore the integrative features in this matrix, we turn to several highly visible cases that have dominated the media, the government, the legal system, and the research community in various parts of the world. These cases reflect generic features of cyber-real international relations, not theoretical or contingency potentials or possibilities. One added interest in constructing this matrix is to determine if by positioning different problems or issues, and solution strategies, we can identify common attributes among issues that share a common location. Each of these cases, usually framed in cyber terms, can also carry potentially powerful implications for international relations.

4.2.1 WikiLeaks and the Disclosure of Classified Information

In the last few years, there have been a number of high-profile disclosures of classified information, perhaps most notably involving Chelsea Manning and Edward Snowden. These leaks raise serious challenges to the leadership of the United States, specifically with respect to its leadership of the future of cyberspace. However, from the perspective of tensions and conflict in cyberspace, an equally interesting phenomenon is the use of the Internet itself as a tool for the dissemination of leaked information. The institution most centrally associated with the posting of leaked information on the Internet is WikiLeaks. The WikiLeaks release of classified information is clearly an issue at the *information* layer of the cyberspace architecture initiated at the *individual* level of analysis. It might initially be seen as having consequences at the state level of analysis. However, it was in essence an international issue, in large part because the WikiLeaks operator was overseas. In general, it is very difficult to exercise influence or control over actors at the information layer, because they may be highly mobile (with respect to jurisdictions) and very small scale (a few people). States that have strong resistance to regulation of information (e.g., on "freedom of speech" or other grounds) make control at the information layer harder.

Some attempts were made to disable WikiLeaks by "attacking" it at lower layers. It has been speculated, but not confirmed, that the U.S. government brought influence to bear on the domestic provider of their Domain Name System (DNS) name (wikileaks.com) to disable it. In response, WikiLeaks registered a variant of their name in Switzerland. It also appeared that the U.S. government attempted an attack on WikiLeaks at the physical level, by bringing pressure on Amazon, the company hosting the website. In response, the data was moved overseas, and as well, a number of zealous advocates hosted copies of the information across the globe, more or less assuring that the information could never be suppressed.

The creator of WikiLeaks, Julian Assange, was called before the Swedish court for a sexual transgression—one can form different opinions as to whether this was in fact an "attack" at the *people* layer. In any event, at this time none of these actions have been effective in suppressing the leaked information; in fact they may have been counterproductive, as they drove the locus of the offense further from the offended jurisdiction and brought attention to it. There could have been other possible responses to the WikiLeaks incident; other tools could have been used. Our purpose here is to highlight the iterations at levels and layers.

Even with this skeletal review, we can already see the issue unfolding with movement across layers, diversity of actors, efforts at solutions, and contention between an individual and entities at the state and international levels. What began as a unilateral action evolved into a complicated, multilevel issue even engaging elements of civil society at the global level.

4.2.2 Network Neutrality

As noted earlier, in chapter 2, network neutrality is an issue at the overall *Internet* level—it has to do with whether ISPs can discriminate in the way they offer services to the services at the layer above. Currently, this issue seems to rest at the state level but can be expected to expand to international and global levels. Attempts to regulate ISPs depend on the details of domestic law. In the United States the Federal Communications Commission managed to impose neutrality regulations only after the courts twice rejected their approach as inconsistent with their authority, whereas in other countries the regulators seem to have more explicit powers.[1] Regulation also depends on the capacity of the state, its tools, and the extent of consensus among key actors—all elements of the second level of analysis, the state and its constituent elements.

Structurally, the consequence of a "nonneutral" ISP might be felt at the application layer (an ISP might discriminate against a specific application, such as a game) or at the information layer (an ISP might discriminate against one content provider, such as Netflix).

This type of issue will rise to the *international* level if there are calls for consistent imposition of norms and regulations across countries and as multinational firms start to enter or exit country-specific markets based on variation in local conditions. It will also arise if the state finds it necessary to close its border, so to speak.

Interestingly, to date the ISPs have yet to be acknowledged as potentially significant actors in world politics. Their function, generally described in operational terms, obscures the potential power of their "gatekeeping" or their capacity or willingness to conform to state instructions. From an international systems perspective, the ISPs create linkages—literally and figuratively—between the layers and the levels, yet to be fully explored.

4.2.3 Competition Policy and Monopolies

This issue is related to network neutrality, but with its roots at the *physical* layer and at the *international* level. Because some physical facilities are very costly, (for example, broadband access to the residence), there is a recurring fear that the market will not sustain adequate competition. One approach (in the United States) was to try to remove the need for regulation at the *Internet* layer by encouraging diversity at the physical layer (so-called *facilities-based competition* as between a cable and telephone company). Other countries have taken the tack of forcing providers to give their competitors access to their physical facilities, which in turn is seen as inhibiting investment, because the provider taking the investment risk gets no competitive advantage, given that their competitors will have full access to the resulting infrastructure.

The question of ownership and control of physical facilities is mostly at the *state* level, but takes on an international scope when facilities cross borders, as with the recent construction of an undersea fiber facility linking countries in Africa. Such initiatives are usually public/private partnerships, given the need for large amounts of capital, but also with strong need to assure the various states as to the terms under which they and their domestic providers could have access to this cable.

4.2.4 Pakistan and YouTube

This type of situation is typical of various *state-specific* (e.g., national level) attempts to block access by their citizens to content that they deem offensive, disruptive, or illegal for one or another reason. However, there was a *global* twist to this story. Pakistan, offended by a video degrading to Islam on YouTube, decided to block access to YouTube internally and instructed their domestic ISP to take this action. YouTube, of course, is a higher-level (information) service from the perspective of an ISP; ISPs have no control over YouTube (Google) and what they post. So, the Pakistan ISP took the approach of injecting a false routing assertion into the local region, which would redirect packets being sent to the address of YouTube to a local site that would inform the viewer that YouTube was blocked. However, due to a technical error, this false routing assertion leaked out of Pakistan and disrupted access to YouTube in various parts of the globe. In fact, a global effort was required to "fence off" Pakistan's disruption. This effort was carried out (in a matter of a few hours) by the collective and cooperative action of

ISPs across the globe. In other words, the response was not an *international* (multistate) action but a large-scale voluntary *global, nonstate* action carried out in a loose, nonhierarchical organization of ISPs. This case illustrates the complexities of the levels of analysis as well as the relevance and influence of ISPs, now an important addition to the expanding set of increasingly influential nonstate actors.

4.2.5 Spam

Spam is a problem that arises within email at the *application/information* layer. It seems to be of global scope, because spam arises from sources across the globe. Responses have been formulated at all scopes of analysis. At the *individual* level, control of spam has been somewhat effective by the use of local spam filters. Working at the state level, the United States has passed the CanSpam Act, which seems somewhat ineffective because of the mismatch of scope—the spammers can easily move themselves outside the jurisdiction. Although there may have been international conversations, they have mostly remained just that—conversations, not actions.

In contrast, a significant and somewhat effective response has arisen at the institutional *global, nonstate* scope: the private, not-for-profit organizations called Spamhaus and Messaging, Malware and Mobile Anti-Abuse Working Group (M³AAWG), which collect lists of sites known to be spammers and passes these lists on to email operators who then have the option of blocking email from those sites. Spamhaus is structurally lightweight (performing only this function, and having essentially no assets); it can easily position itself in jurisdictions that are unsympathetic to lawsuits from enraged spammers. Its small size and lack of physical assets is actually its major advantage. Spamhaus illustrates the emergence of private, voluntary entities concentrating on "self-policing" of the cyber arena. Allowing for differences in focus, scale, and scope, as well as domain of activity, this case prompts us to ask if we should consider Spamhaus to be in the same broad category of normatively driven nonstate actors such as Amnesty International. An alternative view is that they are vigilantes, acting without properly given authority and with potentially abusive power.

In figure 4.2, we use our matrix to illustrate some of the actors (in italics) and actions that are undertaken to control spam. We identify an actor we call a mail service provider that can filter email based on its characteristics. Individuals can also deploy such a spam filter. We illustrate (using

	Individual	State	International	Global	Nonprofit	Profit-Seeking
People						
Information	Filter	Pass laws; authorize private action	Discuss		Spamhaus; M³AAWG	*Mail service providers*: Filter; Goodmail
Application	Use alternate such as IM				Redesign email	*ISPs*: Block ports
Services		Block DNS				*ISPs*: Block DNS
Internet		Disconnect ISPs				*ISPs*: Block IP, Disconnect ISPs, Identify BOTs
Physical						

Platform (bracket spanning Application, Services, Internet)

Figure 4.2

Actors (in italics) and actions intended to block spam.

the arrows) the relationship between organizations that attempt to identify senders of spam, and the ISPs that can block those actors based on the information they receive.

4.2.6 Controlling Unauthorized Distribution
of Material Protected by Copyright

Holders of copyright on commercial content (most commonly music and videos) have been vigilant and forceful in attempting to block the unlicensed sharing of this content among users. They have taken a variety of steps, as we illustrate in figure 4.3.

There is an interesting contrast between the actors/actions in figure 4.2 (control of spam) and figure 4.3 (control of unauthorized sharing of copyright material). In the case of spam, there is a misalignment of interests between the sender of the spam and the receiver of the spam—the receiver does not wish to receive what the sender is sending. For this reason, the ISPs providing Internet access to the receiver have been willing to take unilateral (private) action to filter and block spam, consistent with the desires of their customers. However, in the case of unauthorized sharing of copyright material, the interests of the sender and receiver are aligned, and it is a third party, the rights holder, who wants to disrupt the sharing. ISPs showed a certain reluctance to act in the interests of the rights holders and thus act in ways that were not in the interests of their customers. For this reason, the rights holders had to seek the power of law (such as the Digital Millennium Copyright Act) to coerce other actors to act in their interest.

It is law and regulation that give the rights holders the power to force sites that host content to take down infringing content and force the blocking of access to sites that persist in hosting such content. The rights holders have also used their authority under copyright law to bring suit against users who share. But it is no doubt the lobbying efforts of the rights holders that brought these laws into existence.

4.2.7 Fueling Revolutionary Fervor

The "Arab Spring" of 2011 is the label given to the resistance movements in Tunisia and Egypt and to the eventual revolutions that seriously disrupted the normal course of politics in these countries for a notable period of time. The events in Egypt following the Tunisian initiative that called for regime change eventually led to the resignation of the president and his entire cabinet. The

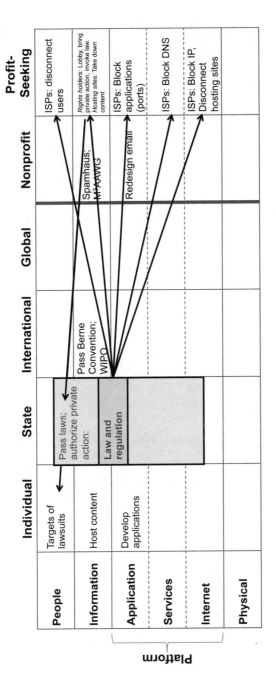

Figure 4.3

Actors and actions that relate to the prevention of the unauthorized sharing of material protected by copyright.

initial protest movement set in motion a political avalanche constrained only by the power of the military. This case combined a variety of actors, activities, interests, and outcomes, involving the mobilization of individuals, the concentration and expansion of activities in the people layer, with users who leveraged their Internet connection via various types of appliances to mobilize political protest and create a relatively nonviolent but dramatic demand for political change in the state. It also illustrates some contagion or demonstration effects, whereby activities in one state are said to influence the development of similar activities in other, contiguous, states.

It is fairly reasonable to assume that without access to the Internet the initial protests would not have had the momentum to hold their course and turn into revolution. At this writing, we are observing various efforts to use the Internet as a venue for organizing protest, most notably, with war in Syria, suppressed unrest in Bahrain, and to continued war in Yemen and militarization of Saudi Arabia.

These events fit into the layer model at the *people* layer, the users of the Internet. But, the people-user layer is overarching in scale and scope. It might (on first inspection) seem to fit into the levels of analysis model at the state level. But the key actors are individuals and aggregations thereof, not the instruments of the state. They demonstrate the consolidation of civil society. The cross-state effects have been well demonstrated, at least within the Arab region.

For a while, there was clearly a fear at the state level triggered by the ripple effect as this revolutionary fervor spilled from one country to another. Early on, Egypt tried (briefly and ineffectively) to quell the cyber-based aspect of the protest by turning off the Internet. China tends to act at the information layer by blocking search terms, and (at the people layer) the phenomenon is no longer a cyber event but a physical event in the streets and the seats of government. But as the problem spilled across states, there was no institution at the international level that could serve to address the fears of these worried states. The dynamics transcended the boundaries of one state, illustrating once more the lateral cross-level impacts. Clearly, the events had powerful spillover effects to other regions as well, namely China blocking such search terms as "Egypt" and "Arab Spring."

These cases are positioned in the integrated model that represents the structural joint view of cyberspace and international relations. Each case illustrates different types of dynamic interactions and situational evolution.

As presented, they are all shaped by current conditions. They are not about the potential effects of changes in information and communication technologies, economic pressures, the power of jurisdiction, operations of regulatory regimes, and the like. They are about interconnections of *actors* and *actions* at various *levels* of international analysis and *layers* of the Internet, the *mechanisms* and tools employed, relative scale and scope of *effects*, and potential *shift of power* and influence as cases unfold.

At the same time, however, all of these elements are embedded in their respective institutional contexts—some already in place, others still in the making—that shape parameters of permissible behaviors, enable and constrain the actors and their actions as well as instruments used, and leverage possibilities. Chapter 8 extends this discussion in the context of cyber conflict.

4.3   Institutional Frame of the Cyber-IR System

Institutions, formal and informal, are fundamental defining features of social systems, in all contexts. In the most general terms, they are designed to provide for order in social interaction, reduce transaction costs, and manage unnecessary uncertainties. In chapters 1 and 3, we referred to institutionalism, a theory (or perspective) of international relations. We now turn to the institutions central to the integrated system. Generally, their functions are to regularize and regulate behavior at the user-people layer, namely, all actors at all levels of international relations. In chapter 9, we shall consider in some depth the governance of the cyber domain and its distributed character.

In figure 4.1, we positioned a number of issues and problems in specific cells. The integrative figure—with levels and layers as its defining features—can also be used to highlight, locate, and position different institutions and salient actors. In figure 4.4 we illustrate, for purposes of example, actors and institutions that perform functions, to one degree or other, with some respect to standards organizations, regulators, facilitators, and enforcement. Accordingly, in figure 4.4 we illustrate how the actors and entities "map out" across the levels and layers, and indicate their relative scope of action within the integrated space. As such, it provides a view of the intersection between international relations and cyberspace.

Even the most cursory look at figure 4.4 captures the variety of entities that operate diverse features and functions of the cyber system, linkages

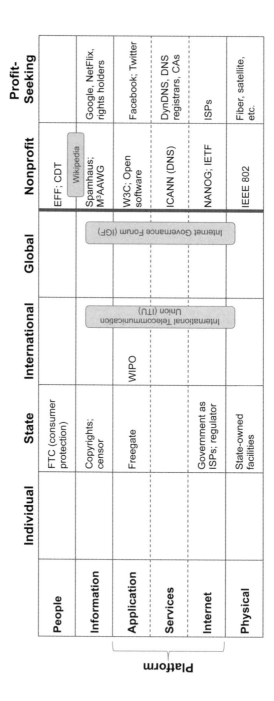

	Individual	State	International	Global	Nonprofit	Profit-Seeking
People		FTC (consumer protection)			EFF; CDT	
Information		Copyrights; censor		Internet Governance Forum (IGF)	Spamhaus; M³AAWG [Wikipedia]	Google, NetFlix, rights holders
Application		Freegate	WIPO	International Telecommunication Union (ITU)	W3C; Open software	Facebook; Twitter
Services					ICANN (DNS)	DynDNS, DNS registrars, CAs
Internet		Government as ISPs; regulator			NANOG; IETF	ISPs
Physical		State-owned facilities			IEEE 802	Fiber, satellite, etc.

Platform

Figure 4.4

A selection of institutions and activities in the integrated system of levels and layers.

with the traditional international system, scope and type of activity, as well as status in formal or informal terms. Many of the entities in this figure are "newcomers" in the sense of being of the cyber age. However, some of the most notable entities are of a long-standing nature in world politics.

The International Telecommunication Union is of particular distinction. Created toward the end of the nineteenth century in response to emergent technological changes, it spans all layers of the Internet, embodies the state system, and intersects with, if not manages to some extent, private sector entities central to the international communications and information systems. A very different entity is the Internet Governance Forum (IGF), established by the World Summit on the Information Society (WSIS) to provide a neutral space for multistakeholder deliberations on Internet governance and supported by the United Nations IGF Trust Fund.

Also listed in figure 4.4 are state-based entities where sovereignty, jurisdiction, and territoriality dominate. Note for example, state-owned physical facilities, or censors and enforcers of copyright, and so forth. Then, too, we note that a number of entities are not-for-profit private actors; others are profit-seeking private actors. We shall return to these and other entities in figure 4.4 in later chapters.

4.4 Complexity of Integration

At this point, we turn to particular contributions of the joint cyber-IR system that facilitate our understanding of such complex twenty-first-century realities—different problems have an empirical base or definitional positioning in this matrix of levels and layers, with some neatly fitting into one box and some less well constrained. Just as we used the matrix to track current issues, we can use location to position various institutions that propose to govern one or another aspect of cyberspace. It is instructive to compare the positioning of one or another problem in figure 4.1 with the positioning of various proposed solutions, both in terms of mechanism and operating organization.

Based on the few examples just discussed, we can draw some conclusions, perhaps tentative at this point, but at least they serve as hypotheses to inform further study.

- The lower layers of the Internet architecture are more amenable to state regulation, because they are territorial, and the actors at that level are fixed on the face of the earth by physical assets. The activities are also capital intensive and thus associated with large, established actors that are easy to find. The higher layers are often populated by private actors that are smaller or that can more easily escape from regulation and enforcement by moving. Even a large firm like Google can choose to leave China to avoid conforming to their regulation.

- An issue that naturally arises at one layer (e.g., the information layer) is most effectively dealt with at that layer. Attempts to deal with problems by imposing controls at another layer are less likely to be effective. In particular, moving to a lower layer as a potential point of control is problematic, because in the structure of the layering, lower layers are normally more general in order to provide a platform for a range of services above them. So, moving to a lower layer for a solution either fails because the adversary can use the generality of the layer to sidestep the control (e.g., trying to disable WikiLeaks by disabling its name in the DNS, which just triggered a move to a different provider of names), or have the "blunt instrument" outcome (e.g., turning off all of the Internet to block access to social networking sites such as Facebook and Twitter). Moving to a higher layer (e.g., finding the adversary and arresting him)—an action at the people layer—can be effective if the person can be identified.

- An issue that arises at one level (e.g., within a state or internationally) can often be mitigated at different levels. Going to a larger scope (e.g., trying to solve a domestic problem at the international level) will in general be ineffective, because the international system is less nimble and less aligned than a single domestic system. But, dealing with a problem of global scope can sometimes be effective at the domestic or individual level. A successful strategy involves finding an effective institution with a suitable scope of responsibility. Lack of an effective institution (which might imply having to create one to address the problem) is a signal that progress may be slow or ineffective.

- Problems and challenges will move across layers and levels over time. State problems may become global problems. Global problems may become state problems.

- In contrast to state-centered international organizations, the nonstate global organizations, sometimes with limited formal institutionalization, have shown the nimble and flexible character necessary to deal effectively with important issues. These nonstate organizations can position themselves, not necessarily intentionally but often very successfully, as competitors to traditional international institutions as the proper venue for oversight and governance of cyberspace.

- With respect to nonstate actors, international or global refers to scope of activity, not size of entity. Nonstate actors can be both global and small. Many of the important nonstate global actors seem to be positioned at the higher layers of the cyberspace architecture—they are more concerned with people and information than with fibers and simple packet transport. But this is by no means always true.

The foregoing points—directly and indirectly—to emergent properties of the integrated cyber-international system, one in which matters of power and politics are becoming more and more salient at all levels of analysis. We see the emergence of dilemmas inherent in the ubiquity of cyberspace in international relations that will shape local and global interactions throughout the remainder of the twenty-first century.

Implicit in these examples is the near-inevitable challenge to provide governance for all aspects of an integrated system—with its layers, levels, and linkages—given the existing policy spaces and the new ones as they begin to consolidate. The key point, however, is that the integrated system in itself calls for management and coordination—transcending the institutions targeted to manage the layers of the Internet and to cyberspace, or those managing the levels in international relations. This does not mean that we require one structure of governance, far from it, but that a functional distributed approach will provide more flexibility in aligning structure to function, and segregating or coordinating functions as deemed best.

Furthermore, the near decomposability of such a complex system is likely to provide important clues regarding *what* is to be governed, *why*, and *how*. (Invariably, such dilemmas will be amplified as the international community also considers its responses to worldwide increasing evidence of climate change due to human actions.)

Most of the cases in this chapter, as well as the initial conclusions noted previously, involve actors and entities that are usually not part of our traditional view of international relations. An entirely different ecosystem seems to have developed without authorization of, or control by, the conventional decision entities. To date, the construction and management of cyberspace remains largely in private hands. And international relations theories, as we noted earlier—have given little attention to the new reality of cyberspace.

Recognizing that the matrix model provides a largely static view of the intersection of two complex systems—the cyber and the international—nonetheless this view of the joint cyber-IR system provides added benefit. It generates a holistic rather than partial coverage of layers and levels, one that allows for more detailed focused investigations of segments thereof, without losing sight of the overall architecture of structures and processes.

4.5   How the Pieces "Hang Together"

We now turn to some of the glue through which various pieces—within and across levels and layers—provide overarching coherence for the complex whole. Clearly, the term "glue" does not evoke the most appropriate image, however, the point here is that the various elements are connected and interdependent in *nonreversible* ways. Drawing on the arguments, observations, and evidence in this book so far, we identify four factors that are especially significant in making international relations and cyberspace "hang together."

First, and most important, in the intersection of layers and levels are the *entanglements* of actors and processes created by decisions made at the layers and/or the levels or both. Some of these are the inevitable by-product of participating in the cyber domain in almost any capacity; some are connected to the built-in structural hierarchies in the layer system; and still others are anchored in the authority hierarchy of international relations. Of course, the nature of the entanglements varies a great deal. Some are contractual; others are embedded in supply chains; and others still in the logics of infrastructure or those of information transmission; as well as a wide range of situational factors. The key point here is that disentanglement is extremely difficult and often near impossible.

Second, is the authority of the state and its *jurisdiction* that, in principle, is implied at many points in the cyber domain. Jurisdictional authority can be evoked at any time. The physical layer is one of the most obvious manifestations of leveraged jurisdiction on the Internet. The physicality of ISP infrastructure and the location of Internet exchanges means that they cannot escape state jurisdiction. So far we have seen relatively little exercise of a definitional prerogative, but it would be surprising if we do not begin to see the hand of the state, given the emergent contentions surrounding the governance of cyberspace. Jurisdictional disputes are common in world politics. When combined with a powerful feature of law in international politics and in many national contexts, namely, precedent, then this second source of "glue" makes it very difficult to already entangled entities to "opt out."

Third, is a foundational feature of social interactions, in all contexts, namely the exercise of power manifested through the deployment of influence with the use of leverage at the most accessible *control points* to induce a desired outcome. All entities in all social interactions—including levels of international relations and layers of the Internet—invariably engage in such behavior, albeit with different intensity and variable effectiveness. However, power and control have not been a critical concern for computer scientists in general, nor were they for designers concerned with the architecture of the Internet more specifically.

Fourth, and central to twenty-first-century international relations, is the complexity of the joint system and the parameters of co-evolution shaped by *feedback dynamics*—positive and negative. Whatever the effects the forgoing might have on any actor or action at one point in time will be affected by previous experience and, in turn, influence conditions in the future. It is far easier to conceptualize the feedback relations than it is to anticipate, model, or predict them. As of yet, we have few empirical analyses of the feedback dynamics in other than anecdotal reports, and usually focused on specific issues.

These four factors are contextual, in the sense that they pertain to the conditions of the actors, their constraints and opportunities, and the arenas within which they operate. They are descriptors of critical features at the intersection of levels and layers, but as presented here they are in static mode. Individually or jointly, these factors all enable, situate, constrain, or delimit behavior. Based on different principles, instruments, or processes and with different degrees of manipulability, they can best be viewed as delineating parameters of readily permissible or allowable behavior. We shall return to these issues in a later chapter.

4.6 Endnote: What Have We Learned?

The construction of cyberspace is a powerful globalizing phenomenon in an already globalizing world—irrespective of how one views the globalization process itself. Its organization and management is under the control of a wide range of nonstate actors and its properties differ significantly from those of the social system and the environmental system.

This chapter draws attention to the elements that create the joint cyber-IR system. These were introduced earlier, directly or indirectly, but are noted explicitly as performing the function of ensuring coherence and continuity in a joint cyber-IR reality. Some features are relatively stable whereas others are highly dynamic. Jurisdiction, entanglements, controls, and feedback all contribute to the cohesion of this joint system. As indicated earlier, the first three factors are largely situational, and the fourth provides almost all of the intertemporal change.

The integration strategy presented here gives us a set of rules to connect the layers of the Internet and the levels of analysis in international relations. It should come as no surprise that the forgoing puts forth important extensions of the logics in chapters 1, 2, and 3—thus reflecting the co-evolution of cyberspace and international relations. The joint framework, with the illustrative tables, provides an important first step, a useful baseline and context to signal the evolution of cyberspace and its intersection with international relations. It has also provided a common platform within which all actors and all cyber functions can be located and their goals, objectives, and activities identified. We consider this framework as an initial baseline whose properties would change in response to actual (or simulated) external interventions to help articulate the dynamic processes.

Various features of the cyber-IR system are interconnected in largely nonreversible ways, in the sense that the "glue" consists of foundational features of our world as we understand it. Modes of entanglements, state jurisdiction, and differentials in power and leverage connect the cyber and the international domains, and, over time, feedback both reinforces and changes the nature of the connections.

Cyber-based interactions are already recognized as influencing human activities at all levels of analysis. The state finds itself embedded in an increasingly complex system of international relations, far different from the traditional structure of the nineteenth and twentieth centuries. However, the influence goes the other way as well. This chapter illustrates the various directionalities of influence. Evident in much of the issues raised so far—the cases, examples, results, all with caveats and qualifications—is the power of generativity, that is, the emergence of structures and processes in response to apparent barriers or bottlenecks, as well as discernable possibility and opportunity with respect to *who gets what, when,* and *how.* We shall return to actors and activities later in this book when we consider the matter of power and control.

Traditionally, in international relations we consider the contending entities in any situation in terms of the scale, scope, and range of their respective power, and usually connected to the potential resort to physical force. More recently, we have recognized more subtle forms of leverage accompanied by the companion feature now described as "soft power" (Nye 2004). In the chapters that follow, we shall introduce the control point method of analysis designed specifically to help us address the power relations—*who gets what, when,* and *how*—embedded in the architecture of the Internet and its operational manifestations.

It is with this set of "lenses" that we can begin to frame international relations in the cyber age. Any one of these factors is significant in its own right; jointly they create significant challenges for theory, policy, and analysis. Each of these features can also be considered as tools to explore particular linkages of cyberspace and international relations and may well create greater mutual sensitivity and interdependence among actors—the old and the new.

In this connection, we expect the integrated system and its attendant dynamics to help clarify situational context and boundary conditions for policy responses. These investigations will also allow us to locate potential errors in the baseline and suggest correctives for missed understandings or faulted framing. Clearly, all of this requires further elaboration, some of which is developed in subsequent chapters. These issues are all central in our effort to understand the nature of change and the transformative processes shaping the future of cyberspace and international relations.

5 Co-Evolution and Complexity in Twenty-First-Century International Relations

This chapter revisits the international system following the expansion of cyber access worldwide. We highlight the scale and scope of evolving complexities due to the impacts of cyberspace on the international system—a system that consists today not only of the traditional parameters, actors, and entities noted in chapter 1, but also of a wide range of new actors, new processes, and new sources of conflict and of cooperation.

5.1 Domains of Interaction

To note the self-evident once more, a powerful legacy of twentieth-century science and technology is the recognition that we are all embedded in three distinct but interconnected systems, each with its different properties, but all jointly shaping our twenty-first-century world—namely, the *social* system, the natural *environment* and now the *cyber* system. We cannot extract ourselves from any one of these systems, nor can we always rely on simplifying assumptions to minimize their interconnections or mutual impacts. By necessity, we also recognize implications for human security—at all levels of analysis. Figure 5.1 illustrates, albeit in a simplified manner, this new recognition.

The *social system*, the traditional order that we are all accustomed to, is the focus of the social sciences. Recall that the social sciences were built by carefully separating humans from their natural environment, and then segmenting areas of human activities into different, somewhat arbitrary modalities. This practice enabled the systematic development of knowledge under conditions that today would be considered somewhat constraining. The recent attention to the natural and the cyber systems signals an awareness of the potential limits of this common practice.

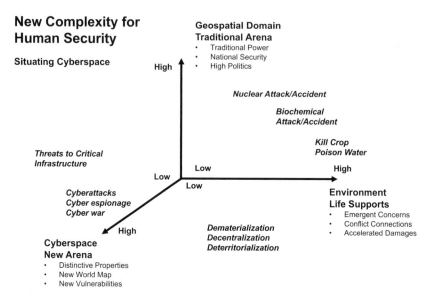

Figure 5.1
Systems of interaction—dimensions of security.

In recent years, as noted in chapter 3, the *natural environment* assumed an importance of its own as an all-encompassing context, after decades of conflict and contention in the scholarly, policy, and business communities over potential impacts of human activities on life-supporting properties. With improved measurement of carbon emissions, the impact of human agency in the growth of CO_2 is generally recognized. Deforestation, contamination of fresh water, depletion of marine life, and other such processes are among the most visible damages to nature's properties.

To say that there has been a major delay in our appreciation of the relevance of the natural environment for the social order is an understatement of major proportions. There is no such delay for cyberspace.

The challenge for the state now is to take account of the emergent cyber context and, to the extent possible, protect and pursue its interests in a new arena dominated by private, not sovereign, order. In sum, if there is one overarching proposition, it is this: *a state is secure only to the extent that it can guarantee security across all three domains—the human system, the natural environment, and the cyber domain* (see figure 5.1).

Framed in abstract and stylistic terms, this view of national security obscures the fact that the different components do not necessarily trend in the same direction and may interact with one another in unexpected ways. Such caveats aside, this three-dimensional view is likely to be more robust in the context of the twenty-first century than the traditional military-centered view of national security. On balance, the more robust the individual security components are, the stronger is the state's overall national security. We thus anticipate a greater complexity of policy processes for national security as we begin to explore the full ramifications of each of the constituent dimensions.

We now turn to some new features of international relations, those due almost entirely to the construction of the Internet and the growth and expansion of cyberspace.

5.2   The New Domain

Cyberspace introduced new conditions that are far from the normal traditional order. Paradoxically, it has become the new normal for almost everyone, almost everywhere. In other words, society broadly defined has accepted and incorporated the cyber area in its day-to-day interactions with its aggregation of interests, group formation, and the creation of new technologies to further enhance communication and accelerate information flows.

All of this has taken place much more rapidly than our ability to appreciate their full implications, and certainly faster than accommodated by the scholarly or the policy community. It is no secret that our understandings of the twenty-first century are filtered largely through the events, theories, policies, and practices of the twentieth century. The construction of cyberspace is forcing us to reconsider our general comfort zone of theory, methods, and policy.

Cyberspace remains a domain fraught with ambiguities whose features and dynamics remain to be fully charted. Terms like "virtual" versus "real," and nouns or verbs prefaced by "e-" became common currency. At this time one cannot understand and model the impacts of cyberspace by viewing it as a separate and parallel system to the traditional world but rather by seeing it as a deeply embedded aspect of that familiar world. The enabling power of cyberspace provides new and different parameters for potential behavior. If there is one powerful outcome of the forging of cyberspace, it is the expansion, enablement, and proliferation of actors and linkages, creating a remarkable density in networks of communication, and of interests.

As signaled earlier, *feedback dynamics* are fundamental to the joint system of cyberspace and international relations and its co-evolution. The features of the cyber domain allow for both constraints and opportunities rooted at the local level to extend within and across levels of analysis nearly unimpeded and to circulate through the global system. Overall, use of cyber venues facilitates both the demand for political participation and the supply of potential possibilities, at all levels of analysis. On the *demand* side, a growing number of Internet sites are being used as a conduit to express positions, make claims, and call for action. By the same token, there are growing trends in the *supply* of government services through cyber venues, for example.

We now turn to the effects of cyberspace within and across levels of analysis. Our purpose is to illustrate the cross-level effects and feedback dynamics within and across all levels of international relations—the individual, the state, the international system, and the global system—and all actors and entities, including cross-level nonstate actors, for profit and not for profit.

We begin with the individual level, and then move on to the state level where we highlight cyber-based implications for state and nonstate actors. Then we examine the international system and the ways in which its configuration has been influenced—shaped and reshaped—by the new arena. Finally, we focus on the overarching global system where territorial boundaries and sovereign principles of the international system are superseded by the power of the natural environment and its life-supporting properties and, paradoxically, by a growing civil society mobilized via cyber venues unrestricted by territoriality, jurisdiction, or sovereignty.

5.3   Individuals—New Power, New Influence

We consider the twenty-first century *Homo individualis*—the first level of analysis in international relations—as a human being embedded in the three systems of interaction in figure 5.1. Clearly, this perspective has little affinity with the traditional view of the individual situated exclusively in the social context, such as the standard *Homo economicus*, the isolated individual entering an impersonal market at a particular point in time. It is also at variance with *Homo politicus*, a not-too-distant cousin of economic man. In behavioral terms, the individual is both an economic and a political person as a function of a particular role at any point in time or in different contexts. Both the market and the polity are well understood with respect to properties and modes of behaviors. In essence, however, the *Homo* is far from simply *politicus* or *economicus*. Both are social beings traditionally seen in a physical context and yet an integral part of the all-encompassing natural environment.

The twenty-first-century *Homo individualis* is most surely also *Homo cybericus*, able to express both voice and views through cyber venues, despite various state efforts to control cyber access. Use of cyber venues increases the ability of individuals to express concern about their insecurity and to voice demands for safety. In international relations, security is generally considered in the context of the state (the second image).

5.3.1   Expansion of Cyber Access

Enabled by infrastructure developments, buttressed by institutional supports, and steered by policy directives, the individual today is endowed with access to cyber venues and enabled in ways that were not possible earlier. Figure 5.2 shows recent trends in individual users per 100 inhabitants recorded by the International Telecommunications Union (2017c).

Access to cyberspace and participation in cyber politics facilitates the formation and articulation of demands and enhances the development and deployment of capabilities. Often overlooked in conventional inquiry, these factors become especially important as we consider population growth and the different forms of aggregation and articulation of interests. But all of this is especially relevant to the international system today because the Internet provides a ready mechanism for expressing demands and demonstrating capabilities.

By participating in cyber venues, individuals transcend the bounds of sovereign territoriality and even formal identity. Individuals and groups have found many ways to use cyberspace to bypass the power of the state and pursue their own goals, thus drawing attention to units of decision other than the state itself, and to the gradual emergence of new organizational principles in world politics. All of this points to the reality of *Homo cybericus*, whose creation is due to cyberspace and whose persona may be either *economicus* or *politicus*, or other as the case may be.

In some parts of the world, notably democratic countries and aspiring democracies, political blogs have become mechanisms for the articulation of interests and for the aggregation of individuals or groups into a critical mass.

This kind of activity is possible when political rights of individuals are articulated, understood, and protected by the social contract and the principles of the political system. It is often difficult to differentiate the personal from the social, the political statement from an expression of threat, and so forth. Whereas we recognize that this global connectivity is used everywhere and anywhere to influence consumers, it is only recently that we appreciate the potentials for its use for politics.

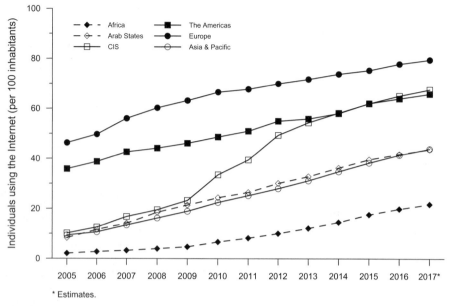

Figure 5.2
Individuals using the Internet (per 100 inhabitants), 2005–2016.
Source: Based on data from International Telecommunication Union (2017c).
Note: Aggregates are based on ITU regions, and UN M49 developed/developing coun-
try classification; see International Telecommunication Union (2017b).

Clearly, cyberspace does not eliminate the use of traditional modes of
interest articulation and aggregation within an established political process.
It does, however, serve as an effective venue of expression outside the established channels, even in ways that challenge the established order. In this
context, traditional theory in international relations seriously underestimates
the role of the individual and, in so doing, overlooks one of the most important features of twenty-first-century international relations. From a theoretical
perspective, this means that the first image in international relations theory
is as privileged as other levels of analysis. Under these conditions, *Homo
politicus* is fundamentally enabled by the capabilities of *Homo cybericus*. So,
too, cross-level effects are more rapidly mobilized than in the traditional
order.

We are increasingly aware of the cyber intrusions and impacts created by
individuals alone or in concert. Recall, for example, the "Snowden affair,"
when the actions of one individual reverberated across all levels of analysis. We have also seen the many ways in which the actions of an individual

(or collective) create costs for others. Even more daunting is the increasing recognition that we cannot always determine whether the individuals act alone or on behalf of a state.

Turning briefly to matters of theory, when compared to both realism and institutionalism (including all forms of regime theory), constructivism considers all structures and practices of international politics as socially constructed entities, buttressed by worldviews and ideas, rather than physical and geostrategic forces. Put simply, the cognitive dominates. Thus, communicative action can have an important effect on international relations that is independent of underlying material conditions.[1] Accordingly, the Internet experience is a subjective window onto a world seen by others as dominated by the objective.[2] With increased diversity in cyber access and uses, the subjective and its cultural and related underpinnings surface to high politics.

5.3.2   Emergent Diversity—Individuals and Aggregates

Early on in the history of the Internet, most people participating in the cyber experience were English speakers. This is no longer the case. English now shares the cyber domain with a large number of other languages, many of which are non-Western. Figure 5.3 shows the distribution of Internet

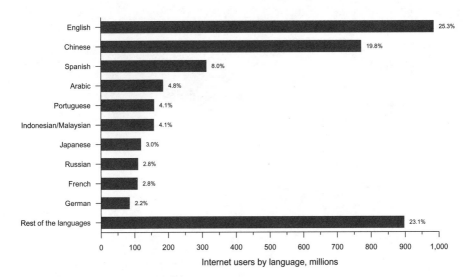

Figure 5.3
Internet users by language, 2017.
Source: Based on data from Internet World Stats (2017).
Note: Shown as percent of total online population worldwide.

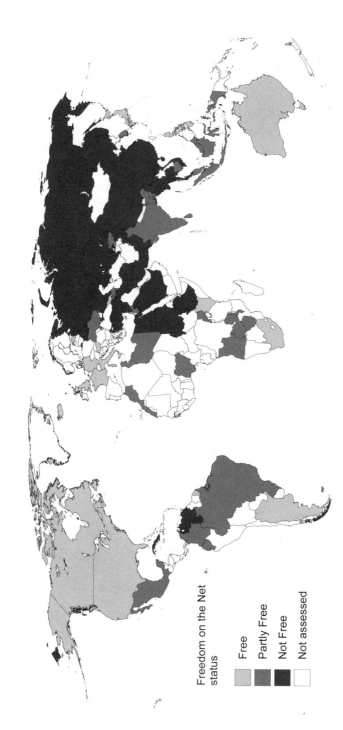

Figure 5.4

Freedom on the Internet, 2017.

Source: Based on data from Kelly et al. (2017).

users by language. The dominance of English is not surprising. Chinese, as the second language, is a noteworthy presence.

Figure 5.4 presents an assessment of Internet freedom based on Internet and digital media freedom for sixty-five states in 2016. State score is based on (1) obstacle to access, (2) limits on content, and (3) violation of user rights and is profiled into three groups—free, partly free, and not free—based on the level of censorship and monitoring practices used by the states in targeting of individual users.

Finally, we turn to figure 5.5, which shows the relationship of *empirical* freedom on the Internet indicators and *perceptions* of freedom in voice and accountability that capture "perceptions of the extent to which a country's citizens are able to participate in selecting their government, as well as freedom of expression, freedom of association, and a free media" (Kraay, Kaufmann,

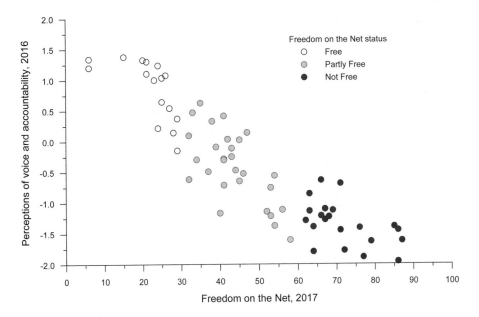

Figure 5.5
Freedom on the Internet, and voice and accountability.
Sources: Data from Kelly et al. (2017); Kraay, Kaufmann, and Mastruzzi (2010); World Bank (2016c).
Note: States scored as Free (0–30), Partly Free (31–60), or Not Free (61–100). Voice and Accountability (VA) index is based on a "standard normal units of the governance indicator, ranging from around –2.5 to 2.5" (Kraay, Kaufmann, and Mastruzzi 2010, 12).

and Mastruzzi 2010, 4). Only partial, to be sure, nonetheless the display along the two axes reflects some important differences across "freedom factors."

All these figures are about aggregates—of individual attributes within state boundaries. Jointly they reflect the emergence of *Homo cybericus* in the new domain of interaction.

5.4 States and Cyberspace—New Possibilities, New Challenges

The state is now confronted with new challenges and opportunities. Cyberspace has created a new context of interaction, one that allows action and reaction within and across levels of analysis and enables the transmission of content through mechanisms that were not available earlier. The constitutive pressures of cyber access are potentially powerful enough to alter the nature of interactions, if not the stakes themselves. All of this is reinforced by a varied population of stakeholders voicing new interests and aggregating and mobilizing for political action.

5.4.1 e-Government and e-Commerce

Increasingly we see the use of e-government to facilitate social services, the use of cyber facilities by candidates during electoral competitions, and the resort to cyberspace to pursue a wide range of political objectives—again at all levels of analysis. Many states have begun to routinize service delivery via cyber venues, with different levels of success. The degree of effectiveness depends on the reliability of cyber access, clarity of purpose, and specificity of instructions. Although we would expect industrial states to excel in the use of cyber venues, "leapfrogging" initiatives—states moving from lower to higher levels of development via rapid incorporation of ideas from industrial states—are already observable.

Because the international community is committed to enhancing e-readiness and e-participation in all countries, we would expect the capabilities of political systems to strengthen and the delivery of services to improve. We would also expect political participation and interest articulation to increase. Although the entire state system is engaged more and more in cyber venues, there is little uniformity in their operational cyber policies or even in their formal postures.

As framed by the United Nations, the *e-Governance Development Index* is a composite indicator based on (1) availability and quality of online services,

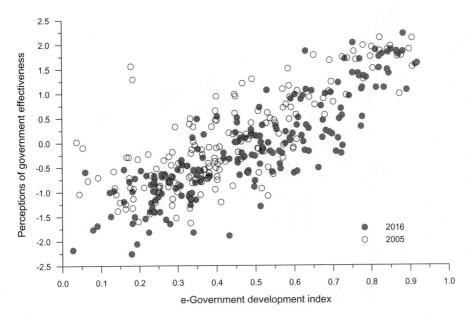

Figure 5.6
Perceptions of government effectiveness and e-government development index, 2005 and 2016.
Sources: Based on data from Kraay, Kaufmann, and Mastruzzi (2010), downloaded from World Bank (2016a); United Nations: Department of Economic and Social Affairs (2005, 2016).
Note: Government Effectiveness (GE) index is based on a "standard normal units of the governance indicator, ranging from around –2.5 to 2.5" (Kraay, Kaufmann, and Mastruzzi 2010, 12).

(2) telecommunication infrastructure, and (3) quality of human capital. Figure 5.6 indicates something that might be obvious but carries an important message: states that are leaders in the development of e-governance create perceptions of greater government effectiveness. *Government effectiveness* captures "perceptions of the quality of public services, the quality of the civil service and the degree of its independence from political pressures, the quality of policy formulation and implementation, and the credibility of the government's commitment to such policies" (Kraay, Kaufmann, and Mastruzzi 2010, 4).

Turning to trade in information and communication technologies, figure 5.7 shows the value of exports of information and communication goods and services. This figure also signals the diversity in the international system evidenced by these variables.

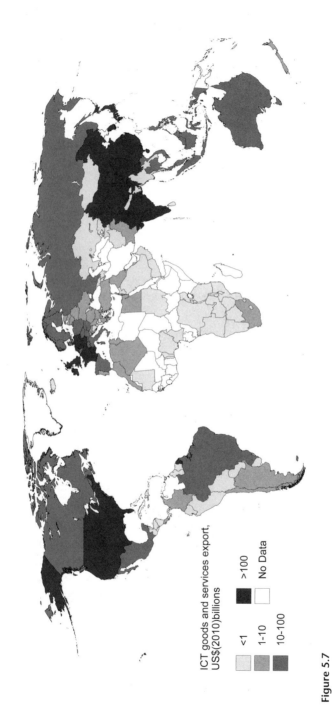

Figure 5.7

Exports of information and communication technology (ICT)—goods and services, 2015 (see appendix 5.1).

Source: Based on data from World Bank (2017c).

ICT goods and services export,
US$(2010)billions

<1   >100

1-10   No Data

10-100

5.4.2   Lateral Pressure—Real and Cyber

This leads us once more to the question: is the state's propensity to expand in the traditional domain similar to, or congruent with, the expansion propensity in the cyber arena?

Earlier in chapter 3, we ranked states by their expansionist tendencies in the traditional international relations arena and identified their real profile type. Figure 5.8 shows state rankings of propensity for expansion in the cyber arena and their cyber profiles. Among the results: China shows the greatest propensity for expansion in *both* real and cyber domains, the United States ranks second, and third is India. Interestingly, relative to its basic lateral pressure index, Saudi Arabia demonstrates little, if any, propensity for expansion in the cyber arena. There are other anomalies.

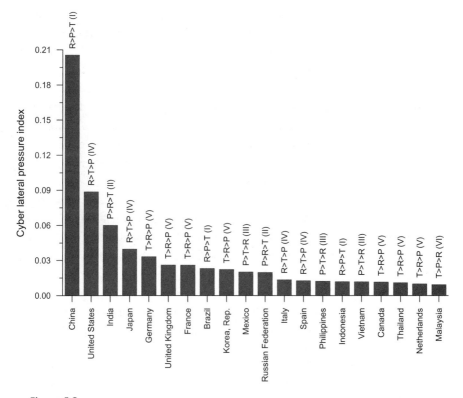

Figure 5.8
States ordered by cyber lateral pressure index and identified by cyber profile, 2015.
Sources: Based on data from World Bank (2017c, 2017g); International Telecommunication Union (2017a).

Figure 5.9 presents the top-ranking states for each profile group 2015, ordered by cyber LP Index, 2015. Note that, for China, Brazil, and Indonesia in cyber Profile I, cyber resources are dominant relative to population and technology. In Profile II, India, Russia, and Turkey, for example, are driven by their respective online populations and, secondarily, by access to cyber resources, and lastly by cyber technology. Online populations also dominate for Profile III states (such as Mexico, Philippines, and Vietnam), with cyber technology surpassing access to cyber resources. Further, figure 5.9 shows that for the United States, Japan, and other countries in cyber Profile IV, resources dominate compared to their share in global cyber technology or of online population. States in Profile V, such as Germany, the United Kingdom, and France, are dominant in cyber technology relative to cyber resources or online population. Finally, Profile VI states, such as Malaysia, Poland, Czech Republic and Norway, are characterized by strong cyber technology and by online populations larger than cyber resources.

This still leaves us with the question: are the lateral pressure patterns similar or different when they are manifested in conventional versus cyber contexts? The previous figures suggest that the answer is, it depends on the state, and in general there are variations among states, but some inferences can be derived by comparing expansion in these two domains. However, differences in indicators and metrics make it difficult to compare the measures and force us to focus on the within-domain inferences as well as the differences in states' posture, both within and across domains.

Figure 5.10 provides a *system wide view* in terms of a logarithmic distribution of the real lateral pressure (LP) index of the traditional international order and the cyber LP index. The inset shows the same in the original metrics. Clearly, the top rankings in lateral pressure, real and cyber, go to China, the United States, and India—in that order. The equality line in figure 5.10 signals the trajectory for similar propensities for expansion in both cyber and real domains. States situated above the line are those with greater lateral pressure in cyberspace than in the traditional international arena. States below the equality line demonstrate more lateral pressure in the real mode than they do in cyberspace. Tables 5.2 to 5.4 in appendix 5.2 to this chapter list states with *similar* and *different* cyber and real profiles, in each of *cyber* and *real* terms.

A closer look shows that states with dominant technology in their *real* profile—Profile V (T $>$ R $>$ P) and Profile VI (T $>$ P $>$ R)—such as the United

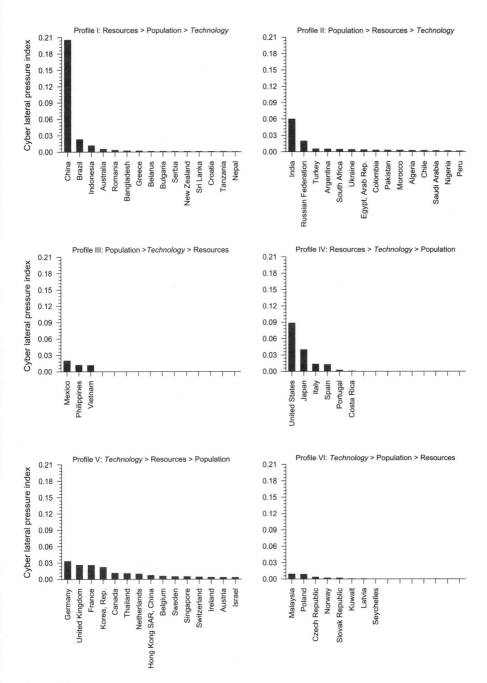

Figure 5.9
States ordered by cyber lateral pressure index for each cyber profile, 2015.
Sources: Based on data from World Bank (2017c, 2017g); International Telecommunication Union (2017a).

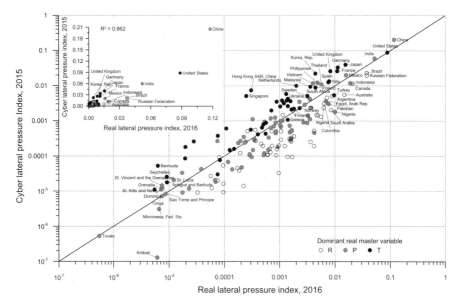

Figure 5.10

Comparison of lateral pressure index in real domain, 2016 and cyber domain, 2015. *Sources*: Based on data from World Bank (2017c, 2017g, 2017i); International Telecommunication Union (2017a).

States, Japan, Germany, the United Kingdom, and France, are leaders in the cyber domain. By contrast, states with real resource dominance—such as South Africa and Colombia in Profile I (R >P >T) and Russia, Brazil, Canada, Australia, and Saudi Arabia in Profile IV (R >T >P)—show less propensity for cyber than for real expansion. The same holds for countries with real Profile II (P >R >T) states whose population dominates, but resources are greater than technology, such as Indonesia, Nigeria, Pakistan, and Egypt. Profile III (P >T >R) countries, also with population dominance, but with technology greater than resources in real terms—such as China, India, Mexico, Thailand, and the Philippines—exhibit greater lateral pressure in cyberspace than in the traditional world.

On balance, several patterns are noteworthy: First, many states demonstrate different cyber versus real-type profiles. Second, states also differ in the dominant master variable that shape lateral pressure—real or cyber. Third, with notable exceptions, individual states also differ in the propensity to expand in the real versus the cyber world. Fourth, it is perhaps to be expected that real technology is the salient factor shaping lateral pressure in cyberspace. Finally, although these observations are state based, it is useful to signal some added inferences for the international system as a whole. For example, the cluster at bottom left of the inset in figure 5.10 situates states with limited, if any, lateral pressure—real or cyber. Concurrently, the correlation coefficient, also in the inset, points to more system-wide (or overall) convergence than divergence in lateral pressure, real versus cyber.

We have remained as close to the empirical data as possible, without resorting to added assumptions as the basis of statistical inferences or dynamic modeling in order to obtain new data. Parenthetically, we encountered the same challenge much earlier when we considered the impacts of states on the natural environment. At that time, scholars of international relations had not yet begun to address the environmental aspects of world politics—how the state system affects the natural environment, and how the natural environment can influence power and politics among states. Thus, the development of environmental metrics many years ago enabled our understanding of the state-environment interactions. Such holds for our understanding of the cyber domain.

5.4.3 New Complexity for National Security

The salience of cyberspace creates an overarching and inescapable challenge for the state, the state system, and international relations. Clearly, the state must now manage the entire security complex given the emergence of unprecedented forms of threat to security (cyber threats) that signal new vulnerabilities (undermining cybersecurity) and—most vexing of all—emanating from unknown sources (we refer to this as the attribution problem). These developments inevitably reinforce the politicization of cyberspace and its salience in emergent policy discourses. Recognizing that cyberspace has become a war-fighting domain, the world's major power, the United States, has strengthened its military system by creating the U.S. Cyber Command. Several other countries have followed suit.

Recall that in chapter 2 we introduced cybersecurity, focusing largely on the Internet. There is no general consensus about the precise definition of cybersecurity. At a minimum, cybersecurity refers to a state's ability to protect itself and its institutions against threats, sabotage, crime and fraud, identify theft, and various destructive e-interactions and e-transactions. It is fair to say that there is growing attention to cybersecurity in the research and scholarly community as well as a diversity of views and perspectives. Bayuk et al. (2012) have taken on the challenging task of providing a policy guidebook for cybersecurity largely in descriptive terms. Several edited books cover a wide range of issues pertaining to cybersecurity, generally without reference to a central theses or argument yet instructive and informative. Among these are Shane and Hunker (2013) and Yannakogeorgos and Lowther (2014).

Turning to matters of cyber war, especially informative is Singer and Friedman (2014) with their focus on *What Everyone Needs to Know*, the subtitle of their book *Cybersecurity and Cyberwarfare*. What we also need to know are some basics about ethics and conduct appropriate in international relations. Of relevance here is Lucas (2016), who is careful to differentiate between ethics and law as he addresses the highly normative aspects of this complex issue. Especially notable on international law of cyber operations is Schmitt (2013, 2017). We return to Schmit (2017) in chapter 9 this book.

From an operational perspective, a certain degree of precision is necessary. This means that cyber metrics must be developed and, to the extent possible, carry the same "meaning" as in the traditional domain. Once resolved, we can raise the same questions with respect to indices of lateral pressure. Given the recent construction of the cyber domain and the absence of compelling precedents, the matter of metrics will remain with us for some time to come.

Bryant (2016) aptly notes there is little scholarly work on the issue of cyberspace superiority in warfare. Cyberspace superiority is "… about achieving enough control of the cyberspace domain to enable the successful completion of your objectives, while blocking the enemy from achieving his objectives" (Bryant 2016, 183). "If a nation achieves cyberspace superiority during a conflict, then it gains a significant advantage for military operations ….at the tactical, organizational, and strategic levels" (Bryant 2016, 200). This concept is important as it helps focus on operational implications under different conditions in real time and space. Although it may be neither necessary nor sufficient for military performance, it provides major advantages in a combat situation.

5.5   The International System—New Actors, New Decisions

The expansion of cyber access continues to influence the Westphalian world in powerful ways. Today's international system hosts a complex of infrastructures, institutions, and operational features. Despite its importance, this ecology is not integrated in our overall understanding of international relations. Earlier, in chapter 2, we introduced some of the most salient features. At this point, we take a closer look at notable new elements from a state-based perspective.

5.5.1   Built Ecology of Connectivity

At this point, we illustrate the (1) the growth of allocated autonomous systems, and (2) the distribution of Internet protocol (IP) addresses. Earlier, in chapter 2, we introduced the autonomous system (AS), a collection of connected IP routing prefixes, located under the control of one or more network operators, on behalf of a single administrative entity, and with a common and clearly defined routing policy and practice. Figure 5.11 shows the growth of autonomous systems over time, and the inset lists the top ten countries ranked by number of autonomous systems (with their respective profile type). Of relevance are the differences in the number of ASs among states, on the one hand, and the dramatic rise of the global total, on the other.

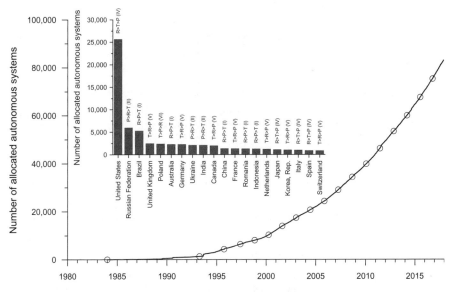

Figure 5.11

Growth of allocated autonomous systems, 1980–2017. *Inset:* States with cyber profiles in 2015, hosting the largest number of autonomous systems in 2017.

Sources: Based on data from American Registry for Internet Numbers (2017a); Réseaux IP Européens (2017a); LACNIC (2017); AFRINIC (2017a); APNIC (2017).

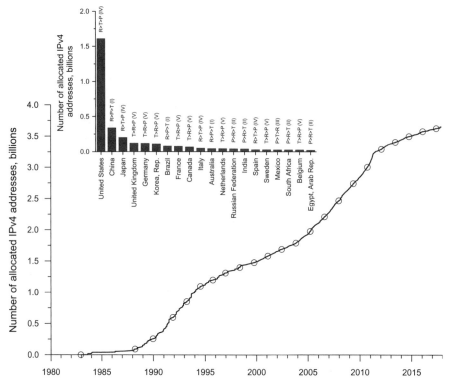

Figure 5.12

Growth of allocated IPv4 addresses, 1980–2017. *Inset:* States with cyber profiles in 2015, hosting the largest number of allocated IPv4 addresses in 2017.

Sources: Based on data from American Registry for Internet Numbers (2017a); Réseaux IP Européens (RIPE) (2017a); LACNIC (2017); AFRINIC (2017a); APNIC (2017).

We now turn to the IP address (abbreviated form of Internet Protocol address)—an identifier given to each device connected to a network (based on the IPs) in order to locate and identify the node in communications with other nodes. For contextual purposes, we signal briefly the well-known limits of the IPv4 address space (figure 5.12 shows trends and the inset shows distribution by state) and the conversion to nearly unlimited IPv6 space (figure 5.13 and inset). These figures clearly illustrate the growth of cyber access and the rapid accommodation to this growth.

Although construction of cyberspace opened up a new set of global opportunities for everyone almost everywhere, we do observe some continued inequalities in cyber access, coupled with technological constraints.

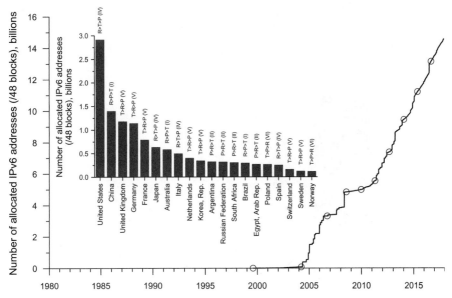

Figure 5.13
Growth of allocated IPv6 addresses, 1980–2017. *Inset:* States with cyber profiles in 2015, hosting the largest number of allocated IPv6 addresses in 2017.
Sources: Based on data from American Registry for Internet Numbers (2017a); Réseaux IP Européens (2017a); LACNIC (2017); AFRINIC (2017a); APNIC (2017).

Figure 5.14 shows the world map with states differentiated by average Internet connection speed, and the inset the total mobile Internet traffic (for 2017, first quarter). Given the message in the inset, at a minimum we can expect a push for the expansion of bandwidth by the less-advantaged states.

5.5.2 Internet-Based Services

As noted, among the new and increasingly powerful actors are the cyber-centered commercial entities, creators of new markets, proxies for state actors, cyber criminals (generally too varied to list and too anonymous to identify), as well as not-for-profit actors (faith groups, environmental interest groups, agenda setters, etc.) and anonymous actors—"good" and "bad" as the case may be—whose anonymity itself conflicts with traditional principles of international interactions.

It is near impossible to underestimate the role, structure, operations, and functions of the private entities—for profit and not for profit—that

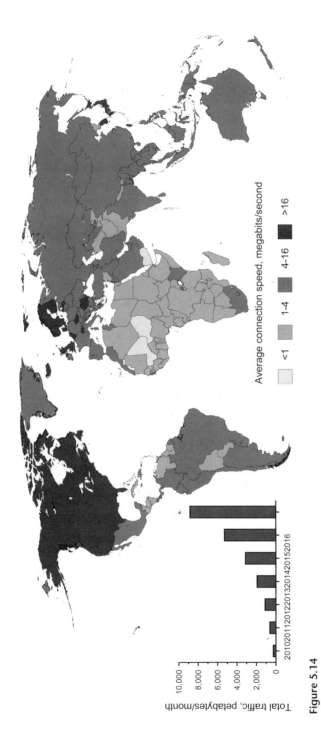

Figure 5.14

Average Internet connection speed, Q1, 2017. *Inset:* Total mobile Internet traffic, 2010–2016.

Sources: Based on data from Akamai (2017) and Ericsson AB (2017).

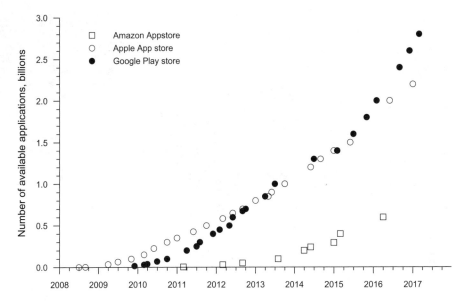

Figure 5.15
Rise in Internet-based services, 2008–2017.
Sources: Based on data from AppBrain (2017); Apple and AppleInsider (2017); Amazon and various sources (International Games Week Berlin 2017).

constructed the Internet and sustain the underpinnings of cyberspace or the scale and scope of stakeholders. There is no precedence for such salience in the modern era, and this situation further reinforces departures from the traditional structural polarities of the international system. We have also seen the growth of Internet firms creating and shaping markets in and for the cyber domain. Figure 5.15 shows the growth of three leading Internet-based service providers.

5.5.3 Anonymity Networks

Turning next to the anonymity supporting services: The technology of proxy networks is designed to obscure the identity of a user by masking his or her IP address. Data packets sent through the Internet must contain the IP address of the source as well as the destination. Therefore, the Internet service provider (or equivalent) can catalog both source and destination. Proxy networks are intended to prevent this sort of observation. The example we note here is the Tor system. The term "Tor" is an acronym for "The Onion Router," originally developed by the U.S. Naval Research Laboratory. Launched in 2006, the Tor

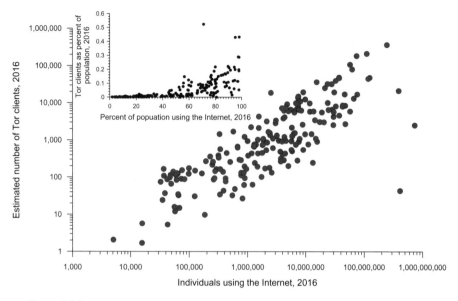

Figure 5.16
Average-daily Tor clients and Internet users per state, 2016.
Sources: Based on data from World Bank (2017g); Tor Metrics (2018a).

Project is funded by a wide variety of sources, notably Human Rights Watch, the University of Cambridge, Google, and others.

Tor is based on proxy principles extended by networks of computers that allow packets to travel across a path of proxy computers before reaching their final destination. It is this detour strategy that ensures a high degree of anonymity. The Tor system rests on relays (computers with Tor software), director authorities (servers designed to track the live relays), and bridges (Tor proxies not listed in the directory authorities). Anchored in the principle of extended intermediation, the entire system is based on and reinforces the distributed character of the Internet and its supporting architecture. The result obscures the identity of sender and receiver. Figure 5.16 shows a relatively close coupling of the estimated Tor clients and the number of Internet users. According to *Tor Metrics*, the largest numbers of Tor users in 2015 were from the United States and Russia, in that order.

Finally, in figure 5.17 we show states with the most Tor users and how they connect to it. So far we know more about the routing operations and the complexities for responding to increasingly large networks but considerably

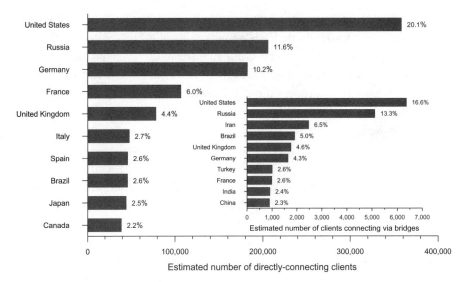

Figure 5.17
States with most estimated number and percent of total of directly-connecting Tor clients, daily average, 2016. *Inset:* States with most average daily Tor clients connecting via bridge, 2016, estimation.
Sources: Based on data from Tor Metrics (2018b, 2018c).
Note: Bridge is a nonpublic Tor relay and provides access for blocked clients, often in combination with pluggable transports, and is registered with bridge authority.

less about various efforts by government and private sector initiatives to "track and crack," so to speak.

5.5.4 Undersea Cable Networks

One of the least appreciated facts is that roughly 95 percent of global Internet communication—including classified and sensitive diplomatic and military orders, financial data for global markets, and so forth—travels through the global undersea networks. In fact, most descriptions of the Internet simply ignore this part of the new reality. We take this infrastructure for granted, yet there is no overarching assessment of the "as-is" state or its vulnerabilities, including constrained capacity, security threats, geopolitical risks, and exposure to natural and human-made disruptions.

Starosielski (2015) reminds us how the construction of the built undersea ecology has traditionally fueled powerful competition among major powers.

Today, the U.S. military relies heavily on undersea cables, and, according to one account, even all drone feeds go via undersea cables (Matis 2012). In short, relative to all other aspects of the Internet, undersea networks are the least understood in many ways, least of all with respect to security, safety, and sustainability. Figure 5.18 shows the worldwide undersea cable network.

Among the most notable features of this submerged infrastructure are the following: (1) undersea networks are built almost entirely by the private sector—today, even Google is building its own undersea cables; (2) policy-making communities are diverse, diffuse, and fragmented; (3) different facets of the undersea world are governed by different international agreements, such as the United Nations Convention on the Law of the Sea, the International Convention for the Protection of Undersea Submarine Cables, International Maritime Organization, the International Tribunal on the Law of the Sea, and the International Seabed Authority; (4) installation of cable systems includes protection mechanisms—notably when applied to the High Seas, to the Exclusive Economic Zone, or to the Continental Shelf; (5) the use of undersea cable systems for intelligence gathering; and (6) White Zones, beyond sovereignty, territorial waters, or jurisdiction. All of these factors obscure who controls *what, when, why*, and *how*.

All of the forgoing pertains to operations under normal conditions. The individual parts are well known. Their integration into a whole remains totally ambiguous at best, if not entirely unknown. The dearth of research is noteworthy. Also, very unclear are conditions at the landing points with respect to security, safety, and sustainability. Even the most cursory look at figure 5.18 allows for speculation, even inferences, about the potential implications of interruptions or damages at the end point locations. Especially unclear are implications of such potentials for the Internet exchange (IX) system starting with the IX entity closest to the landing point. It is fair to say that the undersea network system harbors many unknowns in operational terms for the layers of the Internet (chapter 2), in strategic terms for the levels of analysis in international relations (chapter 3), and for their intersection (chapter 4).

The fact remains that all traffic in undersea networks is expected to reach a landing point. This is where the location of IXs assumes new importance, and is relevant to almost all the issues covered in this chapter. Figure 5.19 presents the states with the largest number of IXs as of 2018. All this brings us back to situational factors and the physical layer of the Internet.

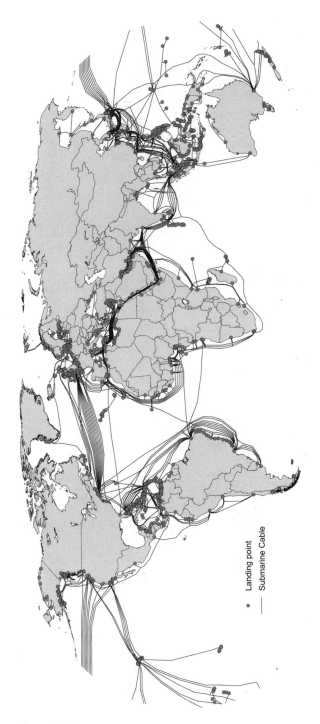

Figure 5.18
Undersea cable networks.
Source: TeleGeography (2017).

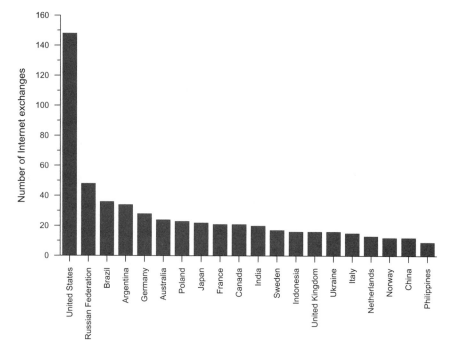

Figure 5.19
States with largest number of Internet exchanges (IXs), 2018.
Source: Based on CAIDA (2018b).

5.6   The Global System—Cyberspace and Sustainability

It is also helpful at this point to consider important similarities between cyberspace with its global reach and highly interconnected character, and environmental parameters—most notably climate change—with their fluidity and pervasive character as well as global scale and scope. We have already seen the politicization of both the natural and the man-made features of the "fourth image," and we expect a continued trend in that direction. Further, we also see the emergence of a global civil society whose concerns and interests transcend the traditional levels of analysis and address the global system and its contours.

These matters are especially relevant at a time characterized, on the one hand, by struggles over the management of cyberspace and, on the other hand, by the near universal recognition of the need to develop and implement a worldwide strategy in response to scientific evidence of climate change resulting from human actions. Although the fourth image is not a decision system, in the usual sense, it affects and is affected by human decisions at all levels of analysis. The globalization literature bears directly on these issues given its focus on flows of goods, services, people, and other factors across state boundaries. Especially notable, as we observed earlier, are the investigations in Pollins and Schweller (1999) on "linking the levels." These trends influence the nature of societies and economies and, under certain circumstances, may even alter them in fundamental ways. Inevitably, they also shape and reshape international exchanges and interactions.

Then, also, some new and somewhat compelling trends can be gleaned. On the one hand, cyber access and use can legitimately be characterized as chaotic, reinforcing global anarchy (as understood in international relations). No one is in control. On the other hand, the expansion of cyberspace and cyber participation may generate a demand for governance structures and processes that transcend territorial sovereignty and rein in the chaos of interaction.

In many ways cyberspace has been seen to assume properties that are characteristic of the global commons. There is a tendency to consider the cyber domain as an open grazing pasture, so to speak, subject to the same mechanism of protection devised in theory and in practice for the management of common spaces. At issue here is less the matter of equivalence than the query as to the potential for cyber "tragedy," if any, at this time or at any point in the future.[3] Far more important, as noted many times, is the fact that participation in the cyber arena has to date largely been led by private entities—through the provision of services, functions, applications, and the like. Today the state system is encroaching on many aspects of what could have been the "commons." This is already apparent in the environmental domain where one overarching indicator, such as CO_2 emissions, reflects various factors that threaten the stability of the social order worldwide, namely climate change. Recall the trends shown in chapter 3.

With the growth of international decision-making organizations and trends in the evolving global agenda (notably the *Millennium Development Goals*), institutional linkages within and across both state and nonstate bureaucracies and agencies have assumed increasingly greater complexity. In this connection, civil society, a cross-level social construct, is an aggregation of individuals with demands and capabilities distinct, even separate, from those of the state or organized nonstate actors.

Closely connected to the forgoing is the notion of *sustainability*—a relative newcomer to theory issues in international relations but a critical feature of contemporary political practice in many parts of the world— developed and developing (Choucri et al. 2007). We are beginning to think about the sustainability of cyber systems. By contrast, the concept of *resilience*, often used at other levels of analysis, tends to carry more active and potentially adaptive or creative possibilities. Implicit in both concepts is the role of innovation. It is salient and forefront in "resilience" more than it is for "sustainability." In many ways it has become a central feature of how we assess the viability of a state.[4]

Early in the twenty-first century, we saw the first evidence of the convergence of two, hitherto separate, policy issues in international forums; namely, the *salience of cyberspace* and the consolidation of a *sustainability agenda*. Later, in chapter 9, we shall note how this convergence became evident at the World Summit on the Information Society (WSIS) in its pursuit of two objectives: to enhance cyber participation and to support transitions toward sustainability. In so doing, WSIS effectively coupled two issues that were separate in their origin and development by pushing for uses of cyberspace for sustainability purposes.

Furthermore, when cyber venues are used to pursue global objectives via international institutions, added challenges emerge, each with competing supporters and contenders, depending on interests, influence, and leverage. This raises new challenges for the sustainability of the constructed domain and for its future.

5.7 Endnote: What Have We Learned?

By now, almost everyone appreciates the ubiquity of cyberspace and its challenges. Today, as is amply clear, the "virtual" and the "real" are no longer autonomous and separate; they are joint in powerful ways. What we may have once considered as parallel realities, the virtual and the physical, have become inextricably interconnected. Even the term used earlier, "entanglement," may not accurately reflect the pervasive joint influences with attendant system-changing effects. Increasingly we see more contentions among the diversity of actors and entities, notably, the private sector managing order in cyberspace and sovereign authority managing order in the traditional domain worldwide, as well as various entities seeking to shape emergent cyber norms and practices.

We have witnessed the increased density of actors/users in cyberspace as well as density of decision entities, in conjunction with the remarkable expansion of governance structures for the management of information and communication technologies and the support of development goals. Clearly, cyberspace has also accelerated the formation of new entities as well as consolidation of private and public interests that become influential entities in their own right, with goals and objectives, priorities, and problems. With such expansion comes the potential for contention and opportunities for conflict.

Early in this chapter, we argued that the state is increasingly burdened by new demands and pressures to ensure its overall security. The state must now protect the security of its own cyber systems and capabilities, as well as defend against uses of cyberspace to undermine its overall security, stability, safety, and sustainability—in addition to the protection of its border and variable concerns about the life-supporting properties of the natural environment.

Almost all international institutions have extended their reach and performance by using cyber tools and capabilities. Little in this trend is surprising, except perhaps the speed at which the use of cyber access is taking shape. Although states are the stockholders in international governance, nonstate actors and other stakeholders resort to cyber venues for interest articulation and aggregation decision forums. Various nonstate groups, for profit and not for profit, have been accorded observer status or otherwise allowed to participate in international forums, with no voting rights, but they may well influence the outcomes.

We extend the earlier logic defining the basic building blocks of the state—population, resources, technology—and argue that different combinations of the master variables yield different state cyber profiles. We find that many states exhibit different propensities for expansion in cyber and in real domains. It is too early to determine if these are robust differences or, alternatively, if they are transitional effects that reflect differing ways of adjusting to the cyber domain. Clearly, there could be a wide range of other possibilities.

Finally, we find that states with technology-dominant profiles demonstrate higher propensities for expansion in the *cyber* domain. Here we come full circle—as state actors expand beyond their territorial boundaries, they are likely to encounter others similarly engaged. Intersection among spheres of influence is thus the first step in the complex set of dynamics leading to conflict and violence.

Appendix 5.1
On Cyber Data

This appendix focuses on all data, indicators, metrics and sources used for the cyber domain, for the period 2000–2015, annually. See Choucri and Agarwal (2016, 2017) for details.

Indicators

Table 5.1 identifies the indicators for cyber master variables, cyber state profile, and cyber lateral pressure index.

Master Variables

Master variables of state i in year j, for *cyber state profile and cyber lateral pressure index* are defined as follows.

$$Cyber\ Population\ Index_{i,j} = \frac{ICT\ users_{i,j}}{\sum ICT\ users_{i,j}}$$

where $ICT\ users_{i,j}$ are the number of Internet users state i in year j, and $\sum ICT\ users_{i,j}$ is the *summed* total of Internet users in the world in year j. The cyber resource index consists of four indicators (see table 5.1). In the absence of compelling evidence to suggest otherwise, we assign equal weights to each indicator:

$$Cyber\ Resources\ Index_{i,j} = 0.25 \times \frac{Fixed\ telephone_{i,j}}{\sum Fixed\ telephone_{i,j}} +$$
$$0.25 \times \frac{Mobile\ telephone_{i,j}}{\sum Mobile\ telephone_{i,j}} +$$
$$0.25 \times \frac{Fixed\ broadband_{i,j}}{\sum Fixed\ broadband_{i,j}} +$$
$$0.25 \times \frac{Mobile\ broadband_{i,j}}{\sum Mobile\ broadband_{i,j}}$$

where $\sum Fixed\ telephone_{i,j}$, $\sum Mobile\ telephone_{i,j}$, $\sum Fixed\ broadband_{i,j}$, and $\sum Mobile\ broadband_{i,j}$ consist of the summed total of fixed-telephone, mobile-cellular telephone, fixed-broadband, and active mobile-broadband subscriptions in the world in year j respectively.

$$Cyber\ Technology\ Index_{i,j} = \frac{ICT\ exports_{i,j}}{\sum ICT\ exports_{i,j}}$$
$$ICT\ exports_{i,j} = ICT\ goods\ exports_{i,j} + ICT\ services\ exports_{i,j}$$

where $ICT\ good\ exports_{i,j}$ consist of exports of ICT goods from state i in year j, $ICT\ service\ exports_{i,j}$ include exports of computer and communication, and information services from state i in year j, $ICT\ exports_{i,j}$ consist of the *summed* total of ICT good and services exports from state i in year j, and $\sum ICT\ exports_{i,j}$ *consist* of the *summed* total of ICT goods and services exports from all states in year j.

Table 5.1
Indicators for cyber domain.

Master Variable	Indicator	Measures
Population	Internet users	State population with Internet access
Resources	Valued assets and enablers	Fixed-telephone subscriptions Mobile-telephone subscriptions Fixed-broadband subscriptions Mobile-broadband subscriptions
Technology	Technology exports	Exports of ICT goods Exports of ICT services

Prices in current local currency or current U.S. dollars converted to constant 2010 U.S. dollars (see World Bank 2017j, 2017k).

State Profiles
The definitions in table 3.1, chapter 3 hold for cyber state profiles.

Lateral Pressure Index
See section 3.4.2 in chapter 3 for specification.

Data and Sources
Cyber population master variable:
Internet users: Internet users (from any location) in the past three months via a computer, mobile phone, personal digital assistant, games machine, digital TV, and so forth. *See* World Bank (2017g, IT.NET.USER.ZS).

Population: Midyear estimates of *de facto* population. *See* World Bank (2017g, SP.POP.TOTL).

Cyber resources master variable:
Fixed-telephone subscriptions: The sum of active number of analog fixed-telephone lines, voice-over-IP subscriptions, fixed wireless local loop subscriptions, ISDN voice-channel equivalents, and fixed public payphones. For exclusions see International Telecommunication Union (2017a, i112).

Mobile-cellular telephone subscriptions: Subscriptions to a public mobile telephone service for access to the PSTN using cellular technology. For exclusions see International Telecommunication Union (2017a, i271).

Fixed-broadband subscriptions: Subscriptions to high-speed access to the public Internet (a TCP/IP connection), at downstream speeds equal to, or greater than, 256 kbit/s, and includes all cable modem, DSL, fiber-to-the-home/building and other fixed (wired)-broadband subscriptions—irrespective payment method. For exclusions see International Telecommunication Union (2017a, i4213tfbb).

Active mobile-broadband subscriptions: Sum of standard mobile-broadband and dedicated mobile-broadband subscriptions to the public Internet. For exclusions see International Telecommunication Union (2017a, i271mw).

Cyber technology master variable:
ICT goods exports: Defined as percentage of total goods exports, include telecommunications, audio and video, computer and related equipment; electronic components; and other information and communication technology goods. Software is excluded. *See* World Bank (2017c, TX.VAL.ICTG.ZS.UN).

ICT service exports (% of service exports, BoP): Defined as percentage of total service exports, include computer and communications services (telecommunications and postal and courier services) and information services (computer data and news-related service transactions). *See* World Bank (2017c, BX.GSR.CCIS.ZS).

Appendix 5.2
Distribution of States by Real and Cyber Profile Types

This appendix lists states with (a) *similar* cyber and real profile type (table 5.2), and (b) *different* cyber and real profile type (table 5.3 and table 5.4).

Missing data overall
British Virgin Islands; Cayman Islands; Channel Islands; Curacao; French Polynesia; Gibraltar; Korea, Dem. People's Rep.; New Caledonia; San Marino; Sint Maarten (Dutch part); Somalia; St. Martin (French part); Syrian Arab Republic; and Turks and Caicos Islands.

Missing data for cyber profiles. Parentheses refer to real profile type.
American Samoa (III[a]); Andorra (VI[c]); Aruba (VI[e]); Central African Republic (I); Chad (I); Congo, Rep. (I); Cuba (III[a]); Equatorial Guinea (IV); Eritrea (I[d]); Faroe Islands (V[e]); Gabon (I); Greenland (IV[a]); Guam (VI[a]); Iran, Islamic Rep. (I[a]); Isle of Man (VI[b]); Kosovo (III); Liechtenstein (VI[e]); Marshall Islands (III); Monaco (VI[e]); Nauru (III); Northern Mariana Islands (VI[a]); Palau (I); Puerto

Rico (VI^c); Turkmenistan (I); United Arab Emirates (VI); Uzbekistan (II); Virgin Islands (U.S.) (VI^a); and West Bank and Gaza (III).

Note: Real state profile, indicated in roman numerals within parenthesis, is for year 2016, unless noted by an identifier within parenthesis: ^a2015; ^b2014; ^c2013; ^d2011; ^e2010.

Table 5.2
States with *similar* real and cyber profiles.

R>P>T (I)	P>R>T (II)	P>T>R (III)	R>T>P (IV)	T>R>P (V)	T>P>R (VI)
Belarus	Albania	Mexico		Finland	Czech Rep.
Botswana	Armenia	Philippines		Sweden	Kuwait[a]
Congo, Dem. Rep.	Bosnia and Herzego.				Malaysia
Georgia	Cabo Verde				Poland
Guinea[2]	Comoros[3]				Seychelles
Guinea-Bissau[2]	Ecuador				Slovak Rep.
Lao PDR	Egypt, Arab Rep.				
Liberia[2]	Gambia, The[3]				
Libya[4(d)]	Guatemala				
Madagascar[2]	Haiti				
Mali[1]	Honduras				
Mauritania	Iraq				
Mongolia	Jordan				
Montenegro	Kenya[1]				
Mozambique	Kiribati[2]				
Namibia	Lesotho				
Nicaragua	Macedonia, FYR				
Niger[2]	Malaw				
Papua New Guinea[1(b)]	Micronesia[1]				

Solomon Islands	Morocco
Suriname	Myanmar
	Nigeria
	Pakistan
	Rwanda
	Samoa
	Sao Tome and Princ.
	Swaziland
	Tajikistan
	Timor-Leste[a]
	Tonga[2]
	Tunisia
	Uganda
	Ukraine

Notes: Cyber state profile for 2015, unless noted by an identifier: [1]2014; [2]2013; [3]2012; [4]2011. Real state profile for 2016, unless noted by an identifier: [a]2015; [b]2014; [d]2011.

Table 5.3
States with *different* real and cyber profiles—by cyber profile.

	Cyber State Profile (Real state profile in parenthesis)				
R>P>T (I)	P>R>T (II)	P>T>R (III)	R>T>P (IV)	T>R>P (V)	T>P>R (VI)
Australia (IV)	Afghanistan (I)	Vietnam (II)	Costa Rica (III)	Austria (VI)	Latvia (IV)
Bangladesh (III)	Algeria (I)		Italy (VI)	Barbados[2] (VI)	Norway (V)
Benin (II)	Angola (I)		Japan (VI)	Belgium (VI)	
Brazil (IV)	Antigua and Barb.[2] (VI)		Portugal (VI)	Bermuda[2] (VI[c])	
Bulgaria (II)	Argentina (I)		Spain (VI)	Canada (IV)	
Burkina Faso[1] (II)	Azerbaijan (III)		United States (V)	Denmark (VI)	
Burundi (II)	Bahamas, The (V)			Estonia (IV)	
Cambodia[1] (II)	Bahrain[1] (VI[a])			France (VI)	
China (III)	Belize (I)			Germany (VI)	
Cote d'Ivoire[2] (II)	Bhutan (I)			Hong Kong, China (VI)	
Croatia (VI)	Bolivia (I)			Hungary (VI)	
El Salvador (III)	Brunei Daruss. (VI)			Iceland (IV)	
Ethiopia[3] (II)	Cameroon (I)			Ireland (VI)	
Ghana[2] (II)	Chile (IV)			Israel (VI)	
Greece (VI)	Colombia (I)			Korea, Rep. (VI)	
Grenada[2] (III)	Cyprus (VI)			Luxembourg (VI)	
Indonesia (II)	Djibouti (I[a])			Malta (VI)	
Lithuania (V)	Dominica[2] (III)			Mauritius (III)	

Macao, China (VI)

Moldova (II)

Nepal (II)

New Zealand (V)

Romania (III)

Senegal[1] (II)

Serbia (II)

Sierra Leone[1] (II)

Sri Lanka (III)

Tanzania (II)

Togo (II)

Uruguay (IV)

Dominican Rep. (III)

Fiji (I)

Guyana (I)

India (III)

Jamaica (III)

Kazakhstan (IV)

Kyrgyz Republic (I)

Lebanon (III)

Maldives[5] (III)

Oman (IV[a])

Panama (V)

Paraguay (I)

Peru (I)

Qatar (VI)

Russian Fed. (IV)

Saudi Arabia (IV)

South Africa (I)

South Sudan[1] (I[a])

St. Kitts and Nev.[2] (VI)

St. Lucia[2] (III)

St. Vincent and
Grenadines[2] (III)

Netherlands (VI)

Singapore (VI)

Slovenia (VI)

Switzerland (VI)

Thailand (III)

United Kingdom (VI)

(continued)

Table 5.3 (continued)

	Cyber State Profile (Real state profile in parenthesis)				
R>P>T (I)	P>R>T (II)	P>T>R (III)	R>T>P (IV)	T>R>P (V)	T>P>R (VI)
	Sudan (I)				
	Trinidad and Tob. (VI)				
	Turkey (VI)				
	Tuvalu[2] (III)				
	Vanuatu (I)				
	Venezuela[2] (IV[c])				
	Yemen, Rep. (I)				
	Zambia (I)				
	Zimbabwe (I)				

Notes: Cyber state profile for 2015, unless noted by an identifier: [1]2014; [2]2013; [3]2012; [5]2010. Real state profile, indicated in roman numerals in parenthesis, for 2016, unless noted by an identifier: [a]2015; [c]2013.

Table 5.4

States with *different* real and cyber profiles—by real profile.

	Real State Profile (Cyber state profile in parenthesis)				
R > P > T (I)	P > R > T (II)	P > T > R (III)	R > T > P (IV)	T > R > P (V)	T > P > R (VI)
Afghanistan (II)	Benin (I)	Azerbaijan (II)	Australia (I)	Bahamas, The (II)	Antigua and Barb. (II²)
Algeria (II)	Bulgaria (I)	Bangladesh (I)	Brazil (I)	Lithuania (I)	Austria (V)
Angola (II)	Burkina Faso (I¹)	China (I)	Canada (V)	New Zealand (I)	Bahrain[a] (II¹)
Argentina (II)	Burundi (I)	Costa Rica (IV)	Chile (II)	Norway (VI)	Barbados (V²)
Belize (II)	Cambodia (I¹)	Dominica (II²)	Estonia (V)	Panama (II)	Belgium (V)
Bhutan (II)	Cote d'Ivoire (I²)	Dominican Rep. (II)	Iceland (V)	United States (IV)	Bermuda[c] (V²)
Bolivia (II)	Ethiopia (I³)	El Salvador (I)	Kazakhstan (II)		Brunei (II)
Cameroon (II)	Ghana (I²)	Grenada (I²)	Latvia (VI)		Croatia (I)
Colombia (II)	Indonesia (I)	India (II)	Oman[a] (II)		Cyprus (II)
Djibouti[a] (II)	Moldova (I)	Jamaica (II)	Russian Fed. (II)		Denmark (V)
Fiji (II)	Nepal (I)	Lebanon (II)	Saudi Arabia (II)		France (V)
Guyana (II)	Senegal (I¹)	Maldives (II⁵)	Uruguay (I)		Germany (V)
Kyrgyz Rep. (II)	Serbia (I)	Mauritius (V)	Venezuela[c] (II²)		Greece (I)
Paraguay (II)	Sierra Leone (I¹)	Romania (I)			Hong Kong, China (V)
Peru (II)	Tanzania (I)	Sri Lanka (I)			Hungary (V)
South Africa (II)	Togo (I)	St. Lucia (II²)			Ireland (V)
South Sudan[a] (II¹)	Vietnam (III)	St. Vincent and Grenadines (II²)			Israel (V)

(continued)

Table 5.4 (continued)

	Real State Profile (Cyber state profile in parenthesis)				
R>P>T (I)	P>R>T (II)	P>T>R (III)	R>T>P (IV)	T>R>P (V)	T>P>R (VI)
Sudan (II)		Thailand (V)			Italy (IV)
Vanuatu (II)		Tuvalu (II[2])			Japan (IV)
Yemen, Rep. (II)					Korea, Rep. (V)
Zambia (II)					Luxembourg (V)
Zimbabwe (II)					Macao, China (I)
					Malta (V)
					Netherlands (V)
					Portugal (IV)
					Qatar (II)
					Singapore (V)
					Slovenia (V)
					Spain (IV)
					St. Kitts and Nev. (II[2])
					Switzerland (V)
					Trinidad and Tobago (II)
					Turkey (II)
					United Kingd. (V)

Notes: Real state profile for 2016, unless noted by an identifier: [a]2015; [c]2013. Cyber state profile in parenthesis, or 2015, unless noted by an identifier: [1]2014; [2]2013; [3]2012; [5]2010.

II   Complexities of Co-Evolution

6 Control Point Analysis: Locating Power and Leverage

Building on the early chapters of this book, we now concentrate on core features of the joint cyber–international relations system that make the pieces hang together, namely power manifested in various forms of leverage and control. The review of the layers of the Internet in chapter 2 illustrated the critical structural features and the wide range of actors and entities that operate or interact within and across the layers. The review of the levels of analysis in international relations in chapter 3 illustrated structural features as well as salient actors at different levels of analysis. The integrated view of cyberspace and international relations in chapter 4 highlighted the diversity of actors and actions in the joint, combined, integrated, and interactive system. We must keep in mind that these reviews are rather stylistic in the sense that they centered on high-level features and not on the microlevel details of operations or activities.

Early on we considered different systems of authority—private and public as well as mixed—in an international relations context and in the cyber domain. The international system is anchored in public state-based authority. Cyberspace is almost entirely built on the power and practice of private authority. By now, it is clear that, from the perspective of international relations theory, policy, and practice, the salience of the private sector is inconsistent with the role assigned to it in traditional theory of international relations.

The early decades of private sector domination over the Internet and, by extension, the cyber domain broadly defined, may well become the exception not the rule in decades to come. All of this raises an important question: *who controls cyberspace?* This chapter addresses this question by putting forth a method of inquiry entitled *control point analysis* that is designed to capture and understand the power relationships created by specific design decisions surrounding the Internet.

6.1 Control Points

As the Internet becomes increasingly embedded in every sector of society, more and more actors have become concerned with its character, now and in the future. The private sector actors, such as Internet service providers (ISPs), are motivated by profits as they shape and influence the Internet. The public sector is driven by a range of objectives: access and uptake, competition policy, regime stability, policies with regard to controlling access to classes of content, and the like. Control points are points in a process.

The range of actions open to governments to shape the Internet are traditional and well understood, including law and regulation, procurement, investment in research and development, participation in the standards process, and more-diffuse forms of leadership. But, these actions do not *directly* shape the Internet. They bear on the actors that in turn have direct influence over the Internet and what happens there. Thus, as part of any inquiry about the shaping of the Internet, there is a narrower question that must be answered: given the Internet as it is today, who are the actors that can exercise direct control over how it works, what options for control do they actually have, and how can they, in turn, be influenced?

Addressing these questions requires an understanding of the Internet as a technology, in technical, operational, and organizational terms. A technical description of a system like the Internet usually begins with its modularity (e.g., layers and regions), and the functions and formats of its protocols. We have proceeded along those lines in chapter 2. But these sorts of descriptions are often not of much use when describing a system to a nontechnical listener—the mass of unfamiliar details masks any insights about the *implications* of the design with respect to issues such as economics or the relative power of various actors to influence the operation of the system. They are also not of much use to the political analyst who recognizes the connection between situational imperatives, capability, leverage points, and instruments used.

Control point analysis focuses on the question of finding the locus of power and control implied by the design—is power centralized (and if so, to what actor) or diffuse? Does the design create points of control or avoid them? A useful conversation across disciplines must begin with a method of extracting and cataloging the important implications of the design without first getting lost in the technical details of the design. Control point analysis is a possible method for doing this.

It is important to stress that we begin here with a design already developed and an architecture already in operation. We are not addressing the question of *why*, rather than *what*, *who*, and *how*.

Different architectures for the Internet and designs for cyberspace can have major implications for the balance of power among the various interested actors. This consequence may not be obvious to all network designers—and few, if any, analysts of international relations—but it has long been very clear, at least to some. At the same time, however, this clarity did not generate a framework for control.

In the 1970s, there was a substantial debate between advocates of two sorts of network, called "datagram" and "virtual circuit." Datagram networks have a simpler core, with more functions shifted to the hosts at the edge. Virtual circuit networks have more function in the core of the net, and thus more power and control shifted to the network operator. The Internet is a datagram network; the ARPAnet was more a virtual circuit network, and the data network standard developed by the telephone industry, Asynchronous Transfer Mode, is a virtual circuit network.

One of the vocal advocates of the datagram approach was Louis Pouzin, who was building a datagram network called Cyclades in France at the same time that the Internet was being first built. In 1976, he published a paper with the following conclusion (Pouzin 1976):

> The controversy DG vs. VC in public packet networks should be placed in its proper context.
>
> First, it is a technical issue, where each side has arguments. It is hard to tell objectively what a balanced opinion should be, since there is no unbiased expert. This paper argues in favor of DG's, but the author does not pretend being unbiased. Even if no compromise could be found, the implications would be limited to some additional cost in hardware and software at the network interface. So much resources are already wasted in computing and communications that the end result may not be affected dramatically.
>
> Second, the political significance of the controversy is much more fundamental, as it signals ambushes in a power struggle between carriers and computer industry. Everyone knows that in the end, it means IBM vs. Telecommunications,

through mercenaries. It may be tempting for some governments to let their carrier monopolize the data processing market, as a way to control IBM. What may happen, is that they fail in checking IBM but succeed in destroying smaller industries. Another possible outcome is underdevelopment, as for the telephone. It looks as if we may need some sort of peacemaker to draw up boundary lines before we all get in trouble.

In contrast to the Internet, Pouzin's Cyclades network was not ultimately successful. Its failure is often (if speculatively) attributed to the hostility and resistance of the state-run French telephone company.

We now turn to the current Internet.

6.2   Control Point Analysis of the Internet

Control point analysis is an approach developed to help think in a methodical way about the design of a system from a particular perspective—that of determining *which actors obtain power, economic or otherwise, by virtue of control over key components of the system.* The result or end point of this analysis is a catalog of all the relevant actors in the ecosystem, the locus of their control, and the forms of control and power that they exercise. This captures the nature of the architecture, the diversity of actors, the key roles and functions, and the structure of dependence.

A notable feature of control point analysis is its *user-based process.* It proceeds by listing the steps of common actions (for example, retrieving a Web page) and asking at each step if one has encountered a significant point of control.[1] One must be methodical and complete as one catalogs the steps, but in this way, one can identify control points in the ecosystem that might have been overlooked in the initial catalog of the technical system and its parts. Different functionalities involve different control points and control profiles, that is, locus, actors, actions, and outcomes.

6.2.1   Base Case: Retrieving a Web Page

Figure 6.1 illustrates the steps that lead up to the retrieval of a Web page. At this scale, it is perhaps most useful as an eye chart, and is presented in this form primarily to illustrate the scope and complexity of the process. For easier viewing, we break this figure down into three parts: (1) preparation of the computer, (2) preparation of the Web page, and (3) the actual retrieval

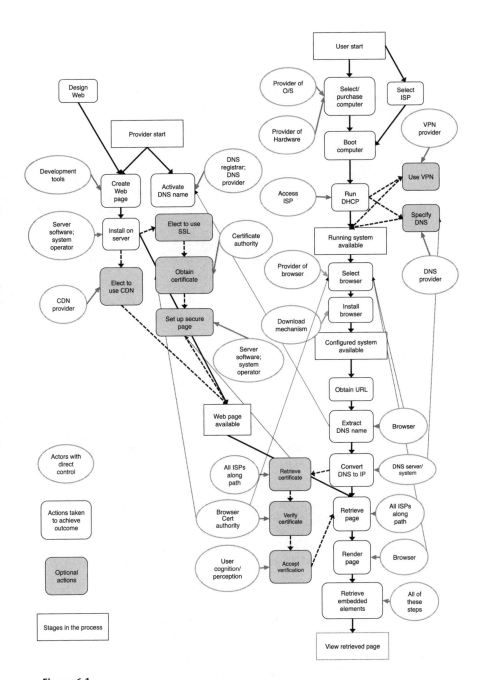

Figure 6.1

Steps in the retrieval and viewing of a Web page.

Note: Solid arrows indicate the normal sequence of steps. Dashed arrows indicate optional, alternative paths. Ovals catalog the actor(s) that has control of the outcome of each step. Lighter gray arrows capture dependencies on prior steps.

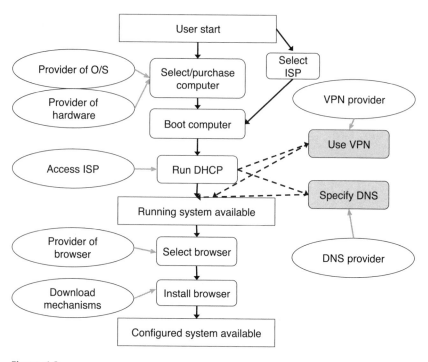

Figure 6.2
The initial steps that prepare the computer for use on the Internet.
Note: Optional steps (often taken to increase security) are in gray.

of the Web page. This breakdown allows for a more-detailed view of who controls what, when, and how.

6.2.1.1 Select a computer In figure 6.2, the reader will note that the sequence of steps has been taken back to the very beginning; step 1 is "select and purchase computer." This may seem extreme, but including this step helps to remind us that it is not just the technical features of the system that matter in determining whether we can successfully accomplish our goal or whether there are actors with the power to disrupt or manipulate what we are doing toward an undesirable outcome.

Each step in the process has been annotated (in an oval) with the actors that have influence over the action—actors that can cause it to be successful or disrupted. The picture is thus not just about identifying actors but is a map of security vulnerabilities—one sort of power that an actor can hold is the power to disrupt or attack. So one way to read the annotations is that at each step, success must either depend on the trustworthy nature of the actor or the constraints within which the actor sits that limit his ability or reduce his motivation to disrupt.

- Thus, the first step where the user purchases a computer reminds us that we depend both on the hardware and software to work as expected. Concerns about corruption of the hardware and software supply chain, which might lead to malicious hardware or preinstalled malware, are captured here.

- After a computer is booted and started up, it normally runs a protocol called Dynamic Host Configuration Protocol (DHCP). In this step, which happens automatically as the computer is connected to the Internet, the access ISP gives the computer its IP address, the address of a machine (a router) that is the computer's path into the Internet, and the address of a Domain Name System (DNS) server. The DNS is the system that translates names (for example, names like www.example.com) into actual IP addresses. The DNS server is the starting point for this conversion service. Since the DHCP protocol specifies the DNS server to be used, the user must trust the access ISP to provide a trustworthy DNS server, unless the user takes the optional steps of manually configuring a DNS server or opening a virtual private network (VPN) to effectively connect to a different access ISP.

- The user may optionally choose to download and install the browser of his choice, as opposed to using the browser that came with the system. Today there are open source browsers (Firefox), and more closed browsers, such as Internet Explorer.

6.2.1.2 Control for content provider Concurrently, the user expects to be able to retrieve content generated by others. This leads us to a different set of actors and activities.

Figure 6.3 captures the steps that a content provider takes to make a Web page available on the Web.

- The first (and obvious) step is to make the page. The correct outcome depends on the development tools, as well as (of course) on the skill and attention of the developer.

- The next step is to specify the uniform resource locator (URL) for the page, which requires that the domain name of the server be known and

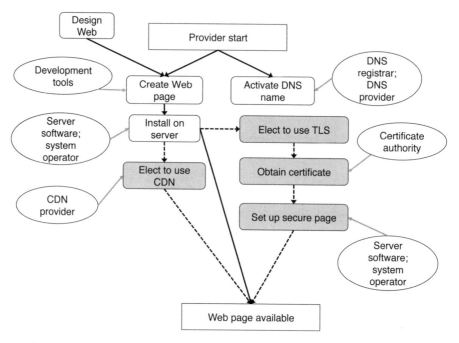

Figure 6.3
Steps taken by a content provider to ready a page for viewing on the Internet.

included in the URL. For example, if the URL were http://www.example
.com/really/cool/page, then the DNS name is www.example.com. This
requires that the DNS name (example.com) be obtained by purchasing it from one of the many providers of names, and also requires that
the relevant DNS servers be configured to "resolve" the name—that is,
return the address of the server when the name is looked up in the DNS.

• The final required step is to install the page on the selected server. Both
the software that implements the server and the human operators that
maintain the server have the ability to influence this step. In particular,
poor attention by human operators is the source of many security vulnerabilities and thus loss of control to attackers.

• In addition to these basic steps, the provider may choose to improve the
availability of the page by contracting with a content delivery network
(a CDN) to replicate the page at points across the Internet, which creates
a dependency on the CDN provider.

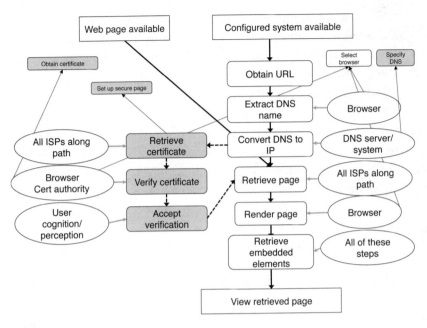

Figure 6.4
The steps that make up the actual retrieval and viewing of the page.
Note: Dotted arrows to smaller boxes (which are from previous figures) capture various dependencies on the prior steps.

- The provider may also choose to use secure Web protocols (Transport Layer Security, or TLS) to enhance the security of the anticipated downloads. To do this, the provider must obtain a *merchant certificate* from a *certificate authority* (a CA)—essentially a signed verification that the provider of the page is whom it claims to be. Encryption tools are used to create and validate these certificates.

6.2.1.3 Control of retrieval   Once the user has a running system, and once the provider of the Web page creates the page and makes it available on the Web, the actual steps of retrieving the page can occur, as illustrated in figure 6.4.

The retrieval process and the control actors engage as follows:

- The user acquires a URL by some means, perhaps from a search, by typing it in or by clicking on a link in another Web page. This action is carried out using the browser software that either came with the system or was selected as one of the steps in figure 6.2. The provider of the browser is a relevant actor with power in the ecosystem. There have been claims in the past that certain browsers would not allow the user to use certain URLs, but this does not seem to be a major concern today. The browser presents other options for control; see the following discussion.

- The DNS name in the URL must be extracted and translated into the IP address of a server, which requires the use of the DNS. As described earlier, the system begins the process of translation by connecting to the DNS server that was specified in the steps in figure 6.2, either provided by the access ISP or chosen by an optional action taken by the user. The DNS protocols and interfaces are specified in open Internet Engineering Task Force (IETF) standards, and for a long time were not seen as an important point of control. However, the DNS system itself is highly decentralized, with most ISPs operating a server for their clients. For this reason, each ISP (or other service provider, such as a hotel or hot spot) has a very high degree of control over what address is returned in response to a DNS lookup. Many misdirections occur in practice today using this point of control, and DNS servers have also been the target of attackers who install misdirections of their own. Secure DNS (DNSSEC) provides technical tools to prevent a benign server from being misled by a malicious server, and at best can allow a user to tell that he has received invalid information.

- Assuming that the DNS has returned an IP address, the browser opens a connection (in tech speak, a TCP connection) to that address. The routers at each hop along the path to the server look up the preferred path toward that address and forward the packet. They thus have absolute control over whether the client can reach the server. If the router has no route computed to that server, no connection can occur. (This outcome does not normally arise, but can during transient outages.) More significantly, if the router deliberately misdirects the packet, or changes the destination address in the packet, the packet will arrive at the wrong server.[2] A secure version of Border Gateway Protocol (BGP) is now being pushed for deployment, which provides tools to prevent a benign region of the net from being misled by a malicious region.[3]

- If the website uses secure protocols (signaled by the prefix HTTPS rather than HTTP at the beginning of the URL), the server will return to the browser a *certificate* attesting to the identity of the server. The certificate is signed or validated by one of a number of CAs, based on the steps shown in figure 6.3. There are a number of important points of control surrounding these CAs. Different CAs may exercise different degrees of care before signing a certificate. But more interesting, all browsers today have built into them a list of CAs that are deemed trustworthy, which gives the browser designers a significant measure of control.[4]

- The use of certificates can detect some of the forms of misdirection that occur at the DNS or router level. That is, if the DNS or router has misdirected the browser, this can be detected. The consequence is that the browser will raise some sort of alert or alarm to the user. However, most users have no idea what to make of these alarms and often proceed ("click through") to connect to the wrong server, to their peril.

- The website then finds the stored content associated with the URL (or prepares the content dynamically if this is what is required) and returns this content to the browser over the network. The content may have "embedded content": URLs of further pages that are to be retrieved by the browser and displayed as part of the page. This process requires the browser to repeat all of the aforementioned steps for each of those embedded content links. Each of them may be subjected to misdirection by the same points of control. Some of the embedded content may be hosted on other servers. The most common example of this is advertising. Advertising raises specific risks aside from annoyance, because malware can be hidden in innocent-looking Web pages. Any Web server that includes third-party ads on its website must trust that the site generating the ads is trustworthy and has not been infiltrated. There is no way for the original Web server to check.

- It might seem that the site hosting the content has (as one would expect) ultimate control over the format and content of the page. However, for a number of reasons, this is not correct. Since the ISPs along the path from the server to the browser control the routing, any of them can redirect the returning Web page to an intermediate node that performs arbitrary modifications to it before sending it on to the browser. Unless secure connections are used (TLS, as described previously), the power of the ISP to control routing gives it the ultimate control. Examples of modifications by ISPs that have occurred today include reformatting the page to fit onto the small display of a mobile device (which seems somewhat benign) and finding embedded content URLs and replacing them—for example, replacing the ads selected by the Web server with ads selected by the ISP. This behavior is not normally considered benign.

6.3 The Options for Control

The foregoing points to a number of processes—with structure, decision, actors, and outcomes—that are fundamental to the Internet. Control points are in large part defined by the architecture. They can be viewed as operational and organizational infrastructure, but their diversity and the location in the overall interaction in question also reflect different sources of legitimacy with different implications for behavior and modes of activity. *Who* controls *what* could be situational or a function of the entity in question, the political system, or the function examined.

The control point analysis of this type reveals that the Internet, although sometimes described by its creators as "simple," contains a rich mix of points of control and a range of design principles that different actors use to "blunt the instruments of control" by other actors. Encrypting content is an obvious example of an application-level design option to protect the content from control by others—an ISP cannot change what is signed and cannot see what is encrypted. Other approaches used to blunt the controls of the ISPs include the use of VPNs, a common tool for travelers using ISPs, hotels, and hot spots they do not trust. A VPN provides an encrypted path over which it then sends all traffic from the client host back to a trustworthy relay point (e.g., at the traveler's corporate headquarters), where the traffic is then injected into the Internet as if it originated there. The IP addresses that the client machine is trying to reach are encrypted until they reach the trustworthy relay site, so intermediate untrustworthy routers cannot see them.

Table 6.1 provides a summary of the control point analysis presented before. It consists of the actors from the three figures in this chapter with two further notations: (1) the sorts of failures and disruptions that the actor in question can inject, and (2) the range of constraints that limit the actions of this actor. These two additions highlight diversity—as noted earlier—but also variety in implications of "misbehavior."

Table 6.1 is about control points. As well, it is also about the processes involved in executing a particular task or calling for a specific function.

Table 6.1
List of steps that comprise the retrieval of a Web page.

Step	Optional Step	Controlling Actor(s)	Examples of Problems	Constraints on Abuse
		USER steps		
Purchase computer		Hardware designer/ manufacturer	Corrupted supply chain, DRM	Lost reputation and market share
		Software (OS) provider	Block third-party browser, block types of content, flawed code	Lost reputation and market share
Select ISP				
Boot computer				
Run DHCP		Access ISP	Use NAT, provide untrustworthy DNS	Variable—regulation, reputation, no constraints
	Initiate VPN	Access ISP, VPN provider	Access ISP can block VPN	VPN: Persistent relation-ship with provider
	Select alternative DNS server	Access ISP, DNS provider	Access ISP can block access to remote DNS	DNS provider: reputation
Running machine	Select/download preferred browser	OS, download steps (as described here), maker of original and preferred browser	Some browsers have refused to download other browsers (in past)	Loss of reputation
Configured machine				
		WEB PROVIDER steps		
Design Web		Standards bodies		Loss of reputation
Create Web page		Development tools		Loss of reputation,
Activate DNS name		Domain registrars, sellers	Name disputes, release of personal information	ICANN intervention (?)

(continued)

Table 6.1 (continued)

Step	Optional Step	Controlling Actor(s)	Examples of Problems	Constraints on Abuse
Install Web page on server		Server software (e.g., Apache), SysOps, Provider hosting server	Poor server configuration and lack of patches lead to penetration and installation of malware for subsequent download	
	Utilization of CDN Elect to use TLS	CDN provider		Persistent business relationship
	Obtain merchant cert	Certificate authority (CA)	Lax attention leads to penetration of CA and creation of false certs	Loss of reputation, business Lawsuits (?)
		USER steps		
Obtain URL		Depends on source	Phishing attacks	Cognition and perception of user
Extract DNS name		Browser		
Get IP address of server		DNS server selected/provided above	Misdirection to wrong IP address	Highly variable constraints depending on context
	If SSL, retrieve cert	All ISPs along path		
	Verify cert	Browser, CA	Corruption of CA	
	Accept result of verification	User downloading page	"Look-alike" names	Cognition and perception of user
Attempt to download page from server		All ISPs along path	Adverse outcomes Without SLL: delivery of wrong/malicious version of page With SSL: unambiguous failure if mechanisms run properly	
Render page **View page**		Browser		

Table 6.2
Summary of outcomes when a Web page is retrieved.

Primary Outcomes		Examples
Intended	Correct page viewed	
	Wrong certificate triggers failure	
	Benign delivery of wrong page	Hot spot login page
Unintended	Malicious delivery of wrong page	Phishing, ISP redirection, notification of blocked access
	Attacker in the middle	Modification of page; capture of user info
	No apparent response	ISP blocking, server down; network failure
Secondary Outcomes		Examples
	Intended side effects	Delivery of cookies; tracking by provider; release of behavioral information to third parties
	Unintended side effects	Delivery of malware; corruption of browser/system; theft of user information

6.3.1 Outcomes of User Action

Given the range of actors that can exercise control over the attempt to download a Web page, a variety of outcomes can occur in practice (and do occur) when a download is attempted. Table 6.2 summarizes the range of outcomes that a user can encounter in practice today. These are noted in terms of primary outcomes as well as secondary outcomes (intended or unintended). This differentiation points to the range of results that are generated within and beyond the control of the user.

6.4 Lessons and Observations

Much of the previous discussion should lead us to wonder: given all these potential points of control and disruption, why does the Internet work? There are many aspects of the environment that tend to constrain bad actors and actions, but in general, they are neither technical constraints nor law. The constraints are "soft." In the idiom of international relations, many of these soft features can be viewed as elements of "soft power." These constraints include, for example, the following.

6.4.1   Reputation

Looking down the right-hand column of table 6.1, one point that stands out is that the constraint that disciplines many of the actors is a fear of loss of reputation. For private sector actors, loss of reputation translates into loss of business and revenue. For public sector providers, the loss of reputation can have other consequences. For some actors, the loss of reputation because of disreputable Internet behavior is minimal. Very few people walk out of a hotel because of the manipulation of its Internet service, although there are some who do not return. Some of the constraints may be codified as law, so that legal retribution might result from misbehavior, but in many cases, the discipline is less formal. In fact, what this table reflects is that norms and expectations shape proper behavior by actors such as ISPs.

With the expansion of the user base and growth of cyber access—in all parts of the world—and with the development of performance-tracking tools and evaluation techniques, the proverbial "word of mouth" assumes more and more importance. The diffusion of reputations is done at unprecedented speed. And, little can be easily "suppressed" (we shall return to these issues later in this book).

6.4.2   The Role of Technical Mechanisms

The role of technology is very specific. Secure connections (TLS), secure BGP, or secure DNS do not ensure correct operation. They can't protect benign and trustworthy regions of the Internet from being controlled and disrupted by untrustworthy regions; the best they can do in general (if they work as desired) is to detect incorrect operation and give the user an unambiguous signal of failure. It is up to the user to avoid or bypass the misfunctioning (or malicious) component, or somehow demand proper behavior. Tools such as manual configuration of DNSs and VPNs serve as bypass tools to reduce the influence of an untrustworthy access ISP.

This analysis points us to a related issue that may not be central to this chapter—a more general principle for network design if the goal is operation in the presence of untrustworthy elements. What security protection mechanisms must do is translate arbitrary intervention by various actors into a clear signal to the user of a problem. What the network architecture should then do is give the user the ability to "route around" as many actors as possible. For example, multihoming and user selection of routes at a suitable level are means to bypass ISPs that are exercising undesired control. Of course, some secondary actors (e.g., nation states, rights holders, and the like) want to impose their controls on users, and their goal is to prevent bypass or "routing around." This is an essential tussle of control.

6.4.3 Norms

Many of the behaviors that we expect of the various actors—ISPs, DNS providers and so on—are not defined by precise standards or laws. The constraints are more often commonly held expectations—norms of behavior. Part of the struggle today with the future of the Internet is to come to an understanding of what these norms are. Attempts to codify what is generally understood are often failures.

The DNS provides a good example of a norms-based domain where attempting to codify the norms is very difficult. As a starting point, one might propose the following as the norm that should define the operation of the DNS:

> The owner of a DNS name should have sole control over what address is returned by the DNS system when that name is looked up.

In other words, Google, and no other actor, should be able to specify what address is returned when one queries a DNS name such as www.google.com.

This seems like a nice norm, and if everyone obeyed it, it would seem to eliminate many of the misdirections and abuses that occur today. However, if one were to try to codify this norm, it would almost certainly trigger great pushback. One reason has to do with what happens at hotels, hot spots, and the like. When one first connects and attempts to go to a Web page, the page that is actually returned is the login page (payment page) of the provider. This redirection is implemented by either modifying the result of the DNS lookup or modifying the routing. This sort of "messing with" the DNS would violate that norm. And, objections would not only come from those sorts of providers, it would come from governments. Governments, in their push to control access to illegal content (defined by the various laws of the various lands), have been looking for mechanisms of control, and the DNS system is an obvious target. Many governments, including the United States,[5] have considered mandating that the DNS service providers return the "wrong" answer for domains that have been found to host unacceptable content.

One could consider a modified form of the norm, as follows:

> The owner of a DNS name should have sole control over what address is returned by the DNS system when that name is looked up, *except to the extent that the law of the land specifies otherwise.*

This version of the norm would allow for at least the intervention of the state, as described before, but would probably make people very uncomfortable if it were actually written down and debated, because it would seem to legitimize the actions of more repressive states, which filter vast amounts of content, doing so, of course, consistent with the law of their land. Norms are tricky things.

One could have similar discussions about norms concerning the level of care to be expected of Web-hosting services, operators of the Internet routing system, the level of training and care to be expected of normal Internet users, under what circumstances Web pages can be modified as they transfer from the server to the user, or blocking of VPNs. To varying degrees, all these norms prove slippery if one tries to nail them down.

Concurrently, we have already seen the emergence of norms of user behavior, new shorthand forms of communication, a new vocabulary, and so forth—often supported by new applications that reinforce and help diversify new trends in norms and behaviors.

6.4.4   Control of Choice

This issue is perhaps less related to *why* than to *how*. If the user is to "route around" a misbehaving actor, the design of the system must give the user that degree of choice. The tussle of control is often thus over who controls the choice. Examples include which ISP to use, which DNS to use, which browser to use, and there are more subtle and complex choices that are embedded in the control picture. Different designs give control of these choices to different actors, so one must review the catalog of actors to see, in the context of a specific design option, which actors have control over which choices.

When we consider technical features and issues surrounding control of choice, we must recognize the underlying political dimensions defined by *who* choses, *how*, and *why*? Again, we shall return to these issues in a later chapter.

6.5 Highlighting Who Controls What

At this point, it is useful to take stock of the major entities whose actions and decisions provide management and coherence for the Internet as a whole—and by extension for cyberspace more broadly defined. We have encountered some of these earlier in chapter 2. Here we consider them in the context of control point analysis.

If we look at the major actors that manage and operate the Internet, we see that different actors hold different points of control with different powers—if there is engagement or tussle among these actors using their leverage and influence, it is generally an asymmetric engagement. The nature of the asymmetry is related to the role, function (or service), capability, degree of autonomy, and so forth. Among the first-order key actors are the following:

- *ISPs* build and operate regions of the network. Within their regions, they control topology and completion of connections (e.g., who talks to whom under what circumstances). There is no monolithic Internet, but different parts controlled by different ISPs that may be trusted (or not) to different extents. Examples of control include physical topology and routing (making sure traffic actually passes through a firewall or point of censorship). They exercise ultimate control; if they do not forward packets, the operation fails.

- *Internet exchange managers* operate physical facilities where ISPs position equipment and interconnect. Since these facilities exist inside some jurisdiction, they are an appealing point of control and surveillance. However, not all traffic flows through exchanges, and an exercise of power at this point will serve to drive the traffic flows elsewhere. So any undertaking to use Internet exchanges (IXs) as points of control must be done with restraint and sensitivity to the degrees of freedom held by the other actors.

- *Application designers*, by their decisions, define the available patterns of communication, and thus shape the consequences of intervention by various other actors. One could analyze a range of applications, just as we did the Web. One could diagram sending an email, a VoIP call, or a music-sharing protocol. In each case, what we would see is that the design of the application shapes the overall patterns of success and failure. For example, different placement of services and servers (and different degrees of decentralization) change the options for bypassing undesirable actors. Different uses of encryption determine what is revealed or concealed in the messages being communicated. Encryption can occur at different levels in the system (link, VPN, end-to-end, or application), but only the application level can discriminate among different parts of the communicated information, encrypting some but revealing other parts. For example, the design of email protocols reveals the headers of the email, even if the body is encrypted. This design decision actually reveals a great deal of information, but at the same time permits staged delivery, which in turn allows for the "outsourcing" of virus checking and spam filtering.

- *Users and their end-node computers* control the initiation of activity. To the extent they have choice in the selection of service providers, they can use that choice as a discipline to select for trustworthy providers. In many ways, users exercise their "demand" by manifesting behaviors throughout their Internet experience.

- *Operating system designers* provide the platform for execution of end-node software. While some platforms today are more open (Linux) and some are more controlled by their owners (e.g., Windows), most operating systems today are viewed as raising few fears of explicit exercise of control. However, some do exercise considerable control; the iPad operating system and browser, for example, will not render Flash elements in Web pages.

- The *DNS and the distributed servers* that implement it play a critical role in translating names (e.g., URLs) into IP addresses. The system is highly decentralized, with different regions operating under different constraints, and being more or less worthy of trust, as we demonstrate in chapter 9. DNSSEC can (if fully implemented and deployed) help ensure that the results of a DNS query are valid.

- The *certificate authorities* are the collection of mechanisms and institutions that have been created to govern this ecosystem, and try to assure its overall trustworthy character.

- *BGP* is a set of rules for exchanging routing information between gateway hosts in a network of autonomous systems.

This view of major actors is an operational one, that is, framed in terms of entities that users "encounter" almost immediately upon embarking on their Internet experience. It is not a view that readily translates into a market perspective of buyers and sellers of content and information, or a state-based view of government and constituencies. But it does remind us of the control entities.

6.6   Other Control-Related Actors

Control point analysis reminds us of the actors that can intervene directly in the operation of the network. There are tiers of actors supporting networks or behind them that can influence the behavior of this first tier of actors in many ways, from offering economic incentives to writing standards and supporting, even passing, laws and regulation (or encouraging the passing of such laws). The fact that they are indirect actors should not minimize their relevance.

6.6.1   Private Sector Actors—Profit Seeking

Some of the actors in this category are established industries that have been strongly affected by the Internet. In most cases, they do not exercise significant direct power over points of control in cyberspace, but many of them have demonstrated considerable ability to shape cyberspace indirectly, by shaping legislation, regulations, standards, and public policy. For the most part, in industrial societies these are profit-seeking entities. For example,

- Telephone companies and their suppliers
- The music industry
- Radio
- The video/movie/TV industry
- "Brick-and-mortar" merchants of various sorts, such as booksellers
- The "print media" industries: newspapers, magazines, and so forth
- Publishing (generally)
- The advertising industry
- Gambling, pornography, and other marginal social activities

Other actors (or activities) relevant here include those that have emerged as a result of the Internet enabling interactions in cyberspace: computer games, massive multiplayer games, virtual worlds, online auctions (eBay, etc.), and search providers (Google, etc.)

6.6.2   Governments

Governments, as the traditional instruments of the state in both domestic policy and international relations, are clearly important. In the early years of the worldwide Internet and the emergence of cyberspace, governments did not routinely exercise direct control over the cyber domain. Over time, governments have increasingly begun to influence cyber engagements. They exercise influence over actors using a wide range of tools, such as regulation, legislation, investment (procurement and research) and standards, for example. Governments can influence other states using diplomacy, inducements, and related tools. As we shall consider further along, the whole challenge of cyber governance has assumed major proportions in international arenas.

6.6.3   Not-for-Profit Entities for Cyber Management

This special class of nongovernmental organizations includes standards bodies, such as:

- IETF (standards)
- Institute of Electrical and Electronics Engineers
- World Wide Web Consortium (W3C)

These actors clearly exercise great power, and thus are the targets in turn of other actors that want to exercise indirect influence.

The category also includes actors concerned with governance and management of cyberspace as discussed later in chapter 9. These entities include but are not limited to:

- Internet Corporation for Assigned Names and Numbers (ICANN) (allocation of domain names and addresses)
- Internet Society
- North American Network Operators Group (management)

6.6.4   Illegitimates

This category includes classic types of crime such as confidence games, extortion, fraud, identity theft, and so forth. It also includes industrial and political espionage, as well as emerging state and nonstate actors using tools such as terrorism.

6.6.5   Innovators

These are innovators of new functions and services that reflect co-evolution and generativity.

From a levels of analysis perspective (chapter 3), it is increasingly apparent that the individual level is assuming greater relevance than is conventionally accorded. Nongovernmental actors are also more salient. But, as noted earlier, despite the importance of private sector entities in the construction and management of the Internet, they are not yet central in the fabric of world politics as conventionally viewed.

6.7   ISPs and IXs as Control Points—Roles and Functions

Earlier, in chapter 2, we introduced the ISPs and the IXs as major entities of the overall ecology, demography, and topography of cyberspace at this time. ISPs and IXs provide generic functions of connectivity and transport—without them the Internet would not exist. Given that centrality, it is notable that the ISPs and IXs are seldom the focus of attention in scholarly or policy-making circles—and certainly not in the context of international relations. So far, they remain firmly lodged in the realm of the apolitical, not even of "low politics."

The consensus is that they are carriers of packets, with no other appreciable value or influence of their own. But this consensus may be misleading. Given the great variability in their scale, scale, scope, position, and organization, they represent a wide range of different interests that are likely to grow and perhaps consolidate, rather than to decline and dissipate. Still in the realm of low politics, they are not likely to remain in this relatively low-visibility position much longer.

ISPs are in many lines of business, some broad and some specific, enabled by diverse technical strategies and mechanisms. At this point, these include retail wireline and wireless access, wholesale (transit) access, application-level service such as email, hosting and cloud services, and the like. Each of these different sorts of services provide different opportunities for control, and thus attention from other actors intent on exercising that control.

The politicization of the ISPs is already apparent. In many countries, ISPs have the obligation to assist law enforcement and intelligence agencies with surveillance, allowing them to gather both actual content being sent and the source and destination of the flows. The U.S. program known as PRISM provides for broad monitoring of Internet user traffic, raising questions about appropriate bounds on the power of government. It is not uncommon for ISPs to integrate diverse surveillance equipment into their networks, which then feeds the data to law-enforcement/intelligence networks.

These actors—ISPs and IXs—are going to come under increasing scrutiny because of this politicization. In this context, it is important to understand both the population of these actors and their functions. Since the ISPs carry the actual traffic, it is tempting to look to them as a point of control. However, this option has limitations. In the early days of the Internet, it seemed as if the Tier 1 providers might be a locus for control, because much of the traffic passed through them. However, with the emergence of peering at lower layers, the Tier 1 providers carry only a small part of the total Internet traffic.

An IX might seem to be a useful point of control, but again, only certain flows pass through the IX, and in the hybrid model, the high-volume flows may go over private peering paths, even though the IX is used for other connections. So any attempt to use a Tier 1 provider or an IX as a point of control will have only fragmentary results, unless the topology of the Internet is constrained as part of regulatory intervention.

For example, if an international organization sought to impose one or another sort of regulation on international traffic, they could propose a treaty that said that international interconnection among ISPs could only be done by a special class of provider, which then assumed the regulatory obligations. This pattern would somewhat resemble the earlier pattern of international telephone calls, in which international connections were only provided by a class of provider called an International Record Carrier (IRC). U.S. domestic telephone companies were not permitted themselves to carry traffic internationally or make direct connections to telephone companies overseas.

Were such a model to be imposed on the Internet, it would have a number of highly problematic consequences, from increased cost to (possibly) reduced diversity and resilience and degradation in performance. At the moment, however, there is no pressure to move in this direction, and the dense peering mesh among ISPs is implemented both domestically and internationally.

The remaining point of control, topologically, is at the edge, not in the interior, of the Internet. The class of ISPs called broadband access providers, who provide connections into homes and small businesses, sit between their users and the rest of the Internet. For this reason, they are seen as potential points of control.

We still have to address the matter of governance more broadly defined. We have yet to consider the role of jurisdiction and territoriality, contentions among sovereign states regarding the nature of the global system and its policy agenda, and the evolution of international law—a few of the constitutive features of the world in which we live. There are many entities that are involved in the management, governance, and control of the Internet. In chapter 9, we will discuss the institutional history of Internet governance.

6.8   Endnote: What Have We Learned?

Throughout this chapter, we have used control point analysis to identify leverage points and dominant actors. This process has many dimensions and can be used for different purposes—depending on the motives, goals, and preferences of the analyst.

Control point analysis can be used for *mapping* the domain of interaction, identifying junctions of decision and choice, and focusing on actors who control them. It can be used to explore options for active control— options for manipulation or modification of the intended task. It can be used for understanding the decision and organizational interface of technical architectures for information and communication systems.

This method can also be used to consider alternative designs and architectures. Other than the mapping motive, these are all interventionist uses. Taken together, we can consider the uses of control point analysis to range from sheer observation of system structure and process, on the one hand, to instrumental and interventionist purposes, on the other hand. Put simply, the dimensions of control are at a minimum dual in nature— (1) observation versus (2) manipulation—with varying degrees of intensity and detail.

We selected the term "control" initially because control is an act of deployment of leverage for active intervention. Presumably, it has visible and immediate consequences. However, passive observation—spying, monitoring, or whatever—does not manifest in immediate consequences. Its consequences are more diffuse and can occur later. They could include behavioral profiling, revelation of personal information, punishment for unacceptable usage, and the like—a broad range of outcomes.

For each point of control, one can construct a table similar to our control table, but focused on what is revealed, and what limits, if any, govern that revelation and its consequences. In addition, many of the methods that the user can use to thwart unwelcome control also serve to thwart unwelcome observation. VPNs, because they encrypt what is being sent, limit what can be observed. In fact, it is this obscuration that helps thwart control. Since the observer cannot see all the various things the user may be doing, his tools of control are blunted—all he can do is interfere indiscriminately, which would be an ineffective version of control in most (but not all) cases.

All of the contingencies noted in this chapter could be cast in political terms, without reference to technical system architecture and design or structure of process. But the lenses of politics, or political science, cannot capture the complexity at hand. As we have argued in chapter 4, the intersection of layers and levels provides a holistic view of cyberspace, and international relations is greater than the sum of its individual parts. Here we signal an important feature of complexity, namely that interactions among the various "pieces" contribute to shaping an emergent reality where the parts can no longer retain their separate autonomy.

Chapter 7 extends this analysis by applying control point analysis to four very different cases: the United States, private rights holders, Google, and China. Each is embedded in fundamentally different contexts and constraints, and each has enabled different control points.

7 The Power over Control Points: Cases in Context

Given the ecosystem of the Internet—and the dynamics of cyberspace—with multitudes of options for control, it might seem that an organized actor could find some way to exercise control if that were his or her intention. Given the logic of layers and levels, it might seem that the cyber ecosystem creates potentials for control. And given the diversity of power and influence of various traditional and cyber actors in international relations, it may appear almost impossible to map out who can control what, when, and how. These issues all pertain to the broad space of contention delineated as much by the architecture and manipulability of the Internet layers as by the distribution of power and capabilities across the levels of analysis in international relations.

This chapter seeks to illustrate the space of contention, its configuration, and the control options of key actors. In many ways, we can consider control as an operational manifestation and power and leverage. More specifically, we focus on points of influence exercised by five significant actors: (1) a typical U.S. Internet service provider (ISP), (2) the U.S. government, (3) owners of content who are concerned with piracy, (4) Google (a major player in the Internet ecosystem with many interests and potential points of control), and (5) the government of China.

7.1 A Typical U.S. ISP

The first case, the ISP, is illustrated in figure 7.1. The ISP was noted in an earlier chapter as an actor with direct access to control points in the flow of packets. The influence of an ISP is significant, but is concentrated in the steps where packets are being sent, or (because of the ISP's control of the domain

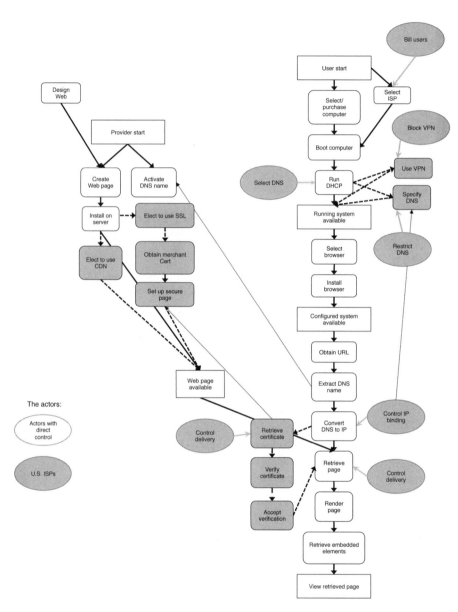

Figure 7.1
Points of control for a typical ISP in the United States.

name system (DNS) servers) when a name is resolved into an Internet protocol (IP) address. ISPs can block traffic selectively, the potential for which is at the center of the current disputes about "network neutrality." As well, because they have a relationship with the user as a customer, they can act at the people layer to identify what user is associated with certain actions.

7.2   The U.S. Government

In figure 7.2, the U.S. government is added as an actor. It does not act directly on the Internet but acts indirectly, by means of law and regulation bearing on other primary actors, such as ISPs and content-hosting sites. It also exercises a more long-term and indirect influence through its procurement, funding of research, and the like. These are not illustrated in the figure.

In particular, the figure illustrates the consequences of the U.S. law called the Digital Millennium Copyright Act (DMCA), which imposed obligations on ISPs to reveal the identity of their customers under specific circumstances, and provides protections and obligations on those who host content, if the content turns out to infringe on a copyright. The figure also illustrates the imposition of so-called "network neutrality" rules on ISPs, and the obligation of certain service providers to assist in carrying out wiretaps. The ongoing debate as we write this book about the widespread surveillance by the U.S. National Security Agency illustrates a broader intrusion of the state into the business of the ISPs.

7.3   Content Owners

The owners of content are fundamental players in the cyber domain. Their proven ability to protect their interests in the conventional economy is not readily portable to the cyber domain. The music and movie industries have been trying to control the flow of unauthorized (pirated) material over the Internet. Because they do not have direct access to any of these points of control, they have been forced to work indirectly, often using the instruments of the states—laws and related directives they negotiated for the purpose. Figure 7.3 illustrates their points of control in competitive contexts.

In general, content providers have only two options: (1) enlist the aid of an actor that has direct access to one of the points of control or (2) work to have the design of the system changed so that there are new options

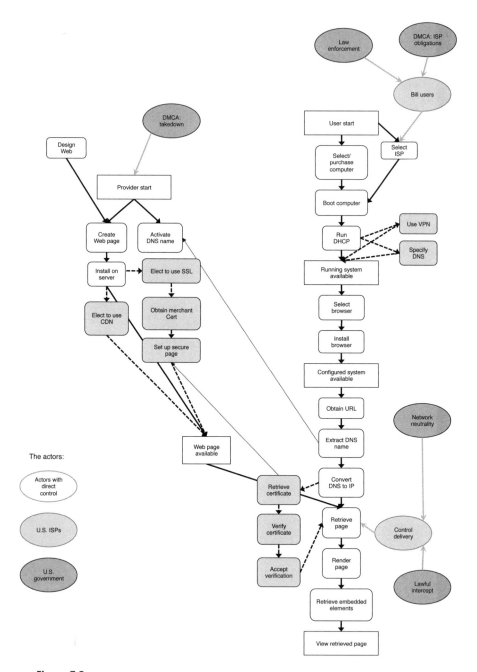

Figure 7.2
Points of control for the U.S. government, showing influence over ISPs and other primary actors.

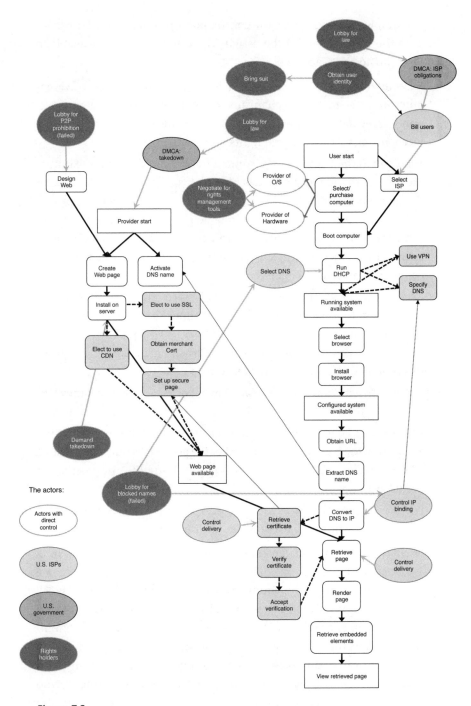

Figure 7.3
Points of control for a content owner trying to suppress piracy.

for control, in essence, redraw the control point picture. The latter is hard because they do not control the design. These are the actions available to content providers at each step:

- *Select/purchase computer:* Content owners have worked with the computer industry to add mechanisms to computers (hardware and software) to regulate how protected content can be used. In general, these mechanisms are called digital rights management.

- *Select ISP:* In the United States, content owners can demand of ISPs that they reveal the identity of a user at a particular IP address, because of the above-mentioned DMCA. The law gives them the right of private action. Of course, this law exists in large part because these industries can exercise influence over the government, for example, by lobbying to achieve their objectives. In some countries, they have persuaded ISPs to ban users that traffic in pirated material.

- *Convert DNS to IP:* The content owners worked with supporters in the government to propose a law (the Stop Online Piracy Act, SOPA), which would have authorized the government to order DNS providers to return the "wrong" address of sites hosting infringing material. (At this time, this proposal is not being pushed forward.)

- *Install on server:* Content owners can demand of hosting sites that they take down unauthorized copyright materials, under the terms of the DMCA.

- *Retrieve page*: They can become users of the system, observe which sites are hosting the content, and demand of the access ISPs that they disclose who the owner of the site is. (This option illustrates the "observation point" aspect of this paper.)

- *Provider start:* They can bring lawsuits against providers of infringing content, once the ISPs have provided their identity.

Several of these options illustrate conclusions that arise from the integrated system from chapter 4. The SOPA proposal stalled because some of the remedies were at the wrong layer (a lower layer). Trying to block the distribution of infringing content (an issue at the information layer) by blocking names at the DNS layer either has a "blunt instrument" outcome, it disrupts the security and coherence of the DNS, or it is so narrow that infringers can easily sidestep the barriers by creating new names. On the other hand, moving *up* in the layers and identifying infringers who are then targeted for lawsuits may be of some value. These options also illustrate that a problem of one scope (in this case, global) can over time be addressed by working within each jurisdiction for a domestic response. The rights holders seem to have concluded that although they work at the international scope (e.g., through the World Intellectual Property Organization), it is quicker to work in parallel within any domestic jurisdiction that is sympathetic to their concerns.

In this chapter, as in the previous one, we have looked at one application—downloading a Web page. But, every application has its own control point analysis, and the users interested in sharing unauthorized content try to deflect intervention by designing new applications (specifically peer-to-peer systems) that try to avoid points of control.

7.4 Google

Figure 7.4 singles out Google as an example of an important and powerful private-sector player, specifically because of the many actions it has taken to shape the Internet experience.

Google is a distinctively powerful private sector actor, with many direct means to control the experience of using the Internet. In the Google case, the key actions at each step are:

- *Select/purchase computer:* Google has developed and made available to smartphone manufacturers the Android operating system, in order to increase choice in the consumer marketplace.
- *Select browser:* Google has developed a browser called Chrome, which is available for free download. Chrome attempts to offer enhanced features for Web browsing and enhanced security for Google downloads.
- *Obtain uniform resource locator (URL):* Google, of course, is the major search engine in many parts of the world. As a point of control, they customize and in some cases filter search results in various parts of the world.
- *Specify DNS:* Google makes available a DNS server that anyone can connect to, in order to avoid servers that may be returning inappropriate answers.
- *Create Web page:* Not only does Google return search results but it is a provider of YouTube, one of the most popular sites on the Web.
- *Elect to use content delivery network (CDN):* Google has built its own CDN, with global reach and direct connection to many consumer-facing ISPs.

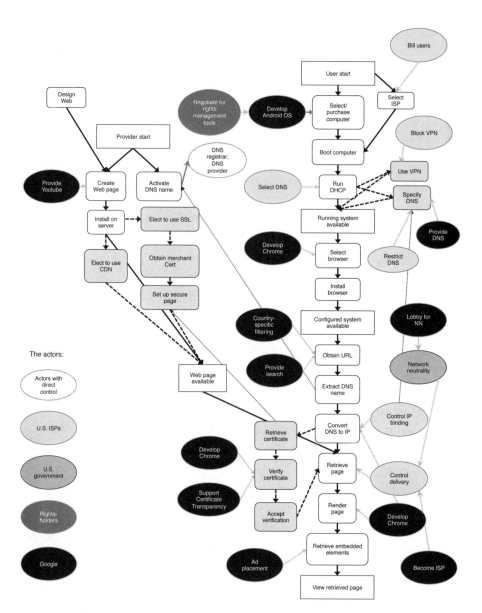

Figure 7.4
Points of control for Google.

- *Retrieve page*: Because Google has its own network with global reach, in many cases content downloaded from Google crosses only two ISPs, the access ISP of the consumer and the Google network. This configuration reduces the number of ISPs that might otherwise be in a position to manipulate the transfer.

At this writing, Google is a global enterprise—in every sense of the term. Its reach is global in scale and scope, and its provision of goods and services has become legendary and promises to expand further. From an international relations perspective, there are no obvious precedents for Google as an entity.

7.5   The Government of China

Typically, governments do not have direct access to most of the control points in the diagram and must act indirectly. However, in China the government's leverage over some of those actors is considerable, through ownership or substantial regulation. Figure 7.5 shows the China case.

Given the power, leverage, and reach of the Chinese government, its role seems almost that of a direct controller.

- *User start:* China controls user behavior. It has arrested users who are sources of unacceptable content on the net.
- *Select O/S*: China developed filtering software (Green Dam) that was to be installed in all Windows systems. This effort only partially succeeded; for a period the software was installed on computers in Internet cafes but not necessarily on personal computers. The project has now failed.
- *Select ISP*: China requires that all ISPs, including mobile hot spots, obtain and retain the identity of each user.
- *Use virtual private network (VPN)*: China regularly blocks protocols such as VPNs and more sophisticated bypass software such as TOR, either by blocking the protocol or the destination port number.
- *Run Dynamic Host Configuration Protocol*: China can impose restrictions on which DNS server is used.
- *Obtain URL*: China imposes requirement on providers of search tools to remove unacceptable content from the search results.
- *Convert DNS to IP*: By their control of the DNS system, they can return incorrect IP addresses for blocked content, or return no answer at all.

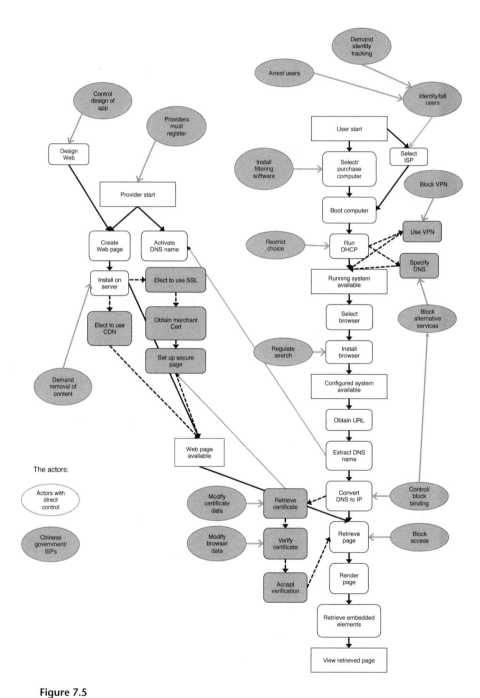

Figure 7.5
Points of control as used by the government of China.
Note: Distinction between primary actor (e.g., the ISP) and the state is not illustrated.

- *Retrieve page*: China instructs its ISPs to control routes, especially at their borders, block access to certain applications (e.g., Facebook, Google, Twitter, and so on), block access to specific websites, block circumvention protocols, and use deep packet inspection to look for specific keywords in the packets and terminate the connection. Attempts to reach an IP address that returned a sensitive keyword may be blocked for some period.

- *Design applications*: China has blocked many popular Web applications such as Facebook, Twitter, Google, eBay, PayPal, Skype, and YouTube. They have been replaced by Chinese alternatives, which are designed consistent with Chinese language and culture but that also allow nuanced control of content.

- *Provider start*: Providers of certain sorts of Web content, such as online forums or audio and video services, must register with the government.

- *Install on server*: China has constructed a complex sociotechnical framework to detect unacceptable content and mandate its removal or modification.

7.6   Control Point Analysis and Illegitimates

Our discussion of control points provides a guide as to how actors that want to shape the behavior of users on the Internet can attempt to exercise control. In this respect, it is a guide to the practice of conflict. Lurking in the control point diagrams are examples of how different actors try to blunt the options for control by other actors. Both through design decisions and operational decisions, different actors try to preserve their options to control (either protect or disrupt) the actions of others. ISPs normally try to preserve the ability of users to carry out their objectives (e.g., to retrieve a Web page) but on occasion try to disrupt these activities (perhaps justified by the demands of security or less-well justified by the objectives of profit maximization).

As a further example of how control point analysis can illustrate the process of conflict, one can reverse what we did in chapter 6, where we diagramed a benign and expected action (getting a Web page), and instead diagram the actions of an actor attempting to carry out an unwelcome action. In this case, the labels of "good guy" and "bad guy" are reversed, but the structure is just the same. We draw a diagram of the sequence of steps necessary to carry out the action (by the "bad guy") and then look for points of control (in this case available to the "good guy").

The case we use is derived from a research project designed to disrupt the selling of "knock-off" drugs on the Internet, for example, unbranded Viagra (Franklin et al. 2007 and McCoy et al. 2012). Spam advertising of these drugs was quite prevalent but has become much less common in the last few years. This is the result of an extensive research campaign to understand the method of the sellers (in our language, to construct the control point diagram) and then find the best point of control.

Figure 7.6 illustrates, among other things, that a range of "bad guy" actors must cooperate to achieve this objective. In fact, to use the language of the business schools, there is a rich value chain for the production of illegal activities. The marketing channel for these drugs was unsolicited bulk email ("spam"). The way spam is sent today involves exploiting a large number of computers attached to the Internet that have been previously compromised. These machines are called "bots," and a collection a "bot-net," controlled by a "bot-master." So, the sequence of steps begins on the left side of the diagram where the bot-master builds a bot-net, which the seller of the drug then rents to send the spam. The seller must also set up a website where interested purchasers can place orders. Assuming that willing purchasers respond to the spam email advertising and place an order on the website, then the seller must fulfill the purchase. The seller must have access to a pharmaceutical manufacturer that can provide the drug wholesale (it appears that the drugs shipped are chemically correct—the sellers are interested in repeat sales). Once the seller has the drug in hand, it must be shipped to the purchaser (usually overseas) and the payment must be received.

In this picture, we have not drawn the ovals that illustrate the options for control, but the team trying to disrupt this sequence did the equivalent, as they describe in their papers. They considered trying to disrupt the bot-net, but the bot-master had too many options for creating it, and the seller might have devised other options to advertise. They considered disabling the website by disabling the domain name that pointed to it (similar to the approach that was considered by copyright holders to block access to servers hosting infringing content), but the sellers were able to create new domain names faster than they could be blocked. They considered trying to block the delivery of the physical product, but this was too complex— there were too many possible shippers, and the product could too easily be disguised. This sort of control, in our layered model, is going "down" the layers to the physical layer, and as we observed in other examples, using

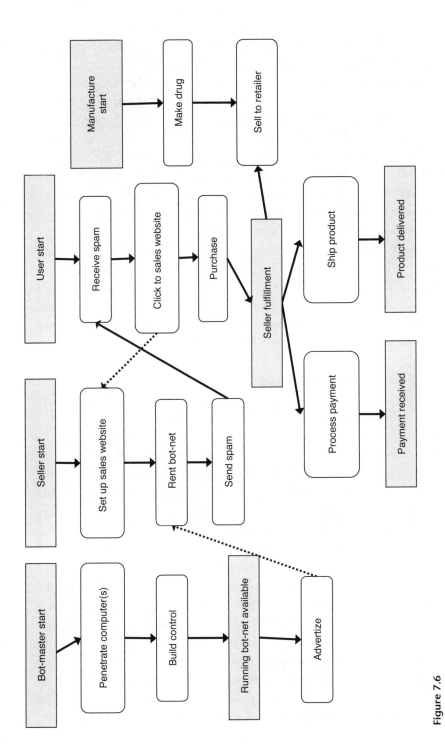

Figure 7.6
The sequence of steps to market and sell knockoff drugs.

lower layer controls is often ineffective, because the generality of the lower layer service (in this case, physical shipping) makes it hard to single out the offending behavior. After some analysis, they concluded that the step in the process that was most vulnerable to intervention was the payment system, which depended on the seller being able to contract with a bank to process suspect credit card transactions. It turned out that there were only three banks that were being used by the sellers, and a threat from the credit card networks to cut the banks off from the credit card system persuaded them to stop payment processing for the sellers. For this step, the sellers had no alternative, and they were essentially driven out of business.

One could look at this last step as going "up" the layers, toward the people. Credit card transactions are easy to identify and classify at the time they are placed, so long as the detection is done by the processing actor (the merchant bank). Another way to look at this intervention is in terms of time constants—the sellers could not move to a new bank as fast as the credit card network could force the bank to drop them as customers. Therefore, they had no recourse to this intervention.

7.7   Endnote: What Have We Learned?

One of the themes of this book is to look at technical architecture from the perspective of options for control: which actors have affordances to monitor or control what happens on the Internet? Despite the conventional perspective that the Internet carries no political implications—other than the respect for openness—its very architecture carries differentiated roles and functions, and necessarily requires the services of a range of actors to support a range of fundamental activities or operations. The traditional definition of politics in terms of *who gets what, when,* and *how* becomes simply a function of *who does what, when,* and *how.*

In each of these examples, the illustrated actors contend to shape the Internet experience as they would prefer. It would seem that the tussle over control is ongoing, with no lasting victory for any side. One actor designs an application, other actors hunt for points of control, others design mitigations to the controls, and so on. The assessment should not be a surprise.

Actors that lack direct control over any part of the Internet and the experience it delivers to users can still exercise influence, using a diverse set of tools specific to their capabilities. But they can only exercise influence to the extent that there is some direct point of control that can accomplish their goals, and the direct points of control are created by the technical features of the system.

Different nations seem to have different access to points of control, based in part on legal frameworks and customary limits on their powers. However, the actor with the richest set of control points is not a state (although China has many points of control) but Google, which is an example of a powerful, private-sector actor with global influence.

8 Cybersecurity and International Complexities

This chapter presents several somewhat countervailing perspectives on threats to cybersecurity—modes, mechanisms, and manifestations. The first is a brief note on perennial predicaments in the cyber domain, some "state-of-the-art" views. The second is a look at well-known modes of cyber threat. The third focuses on seventeen cases of cyber conflicts for insights these might yield. We ask: what systematic inferences, if any, can be drawn from a set of cases reported in narrative form? Without foreshadowing the nature of the evidence or the reliability of prevailing assessments, we then turn to the fourth perspective and ask: what is the international community doing, if anything, in response to contentions the cyber domain? Invariably, in each of these lines of inquiry we are constrained by the nature of the evidence, the type of methods used, the diversity of damage—to note only a few of the most salient factors. Our purpose overall is to signal, "*reader, beware, uncertainties abound.*"

8.1 Perennial Predicaments

Earlier in part I we consider cybersecurity largely from a technical perspective. Traditionally, the notion of security in international relations is about state-based interactions. Different theories focus on different aspects of causes as well as consequences. The actors are well defined, the actions observable and often measurable in terms of type, intensity of hostility, and impact. Even when the logic of the situation involves nonstate actors, the same general approach holds. However, such features seldom hold in the cyber domain. The identity of the initiating actor usually involves the "attribution problem." The very initiation can be obscure, usually by inference based on what is observed and often long after the fact. The intended

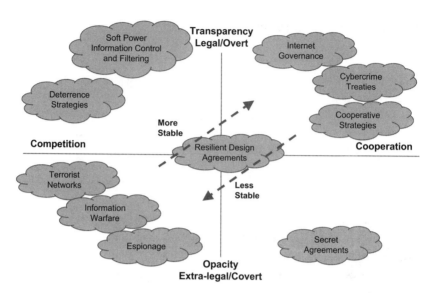

Figure 8.1
Dimensions of contentions.
Source: Choucri, Hurwitz, and Mallery (2013).

damage is not always apparent, the instruments used are often new, and there are considerable difficulties in constructing a cumulative view of the type, scale, scope, and damage due to unauthorized intrusion. Cyberspace also draws attention, perhaps more than ever before, to the complexities generated by differences between overt and covert activities. Figure 8.1 illustrates, but hardly does justice, to such complexities.

Given that competition for power and influence is a common feature of politics among nations, we know that in the "real" domain, *intersections* among spheres of influences inevitably fuel prevailing hostilities. Intersections of this sort reinforce military competition. This is the root for the well-known phenomenon of an arms race that we have seen repeatedly. It is not at all clear if similar dynamics prevail in the cyber domain. What would intersections in spheres of influence mean in the "virtual" world? As yet, there is little systematic accounting of the sources and consequences of cyber threats from state or nonstate entities. Nonetheless, many instances of system-threatening cyber behaviors on issues ranging from conflicts over the control of rules and regulations for managing cyber interactions, to a wide range of antagonizing activities, are already apparent.

Clearly, we are in the early stages of understanding the sources, manifestations, and consequences of conflict conducted with significant resort to, or use of, cyberspace. Concepts of common currency in traditional international relations find resonance and are often used with the presumption that they are just as relevant to cyber-based interactions. In the geopolitics of international relations, threats involve *intent* to inflict damage as well as *capability* to do so. And capability is usually framed in terms of various forms of physical leverage.

The temptation is strong to assume that conflict and contention for the cyber domain follow the same well-understood logics of traditional international relations. However convenient that might be, it is important that we not make such an assumption without sustained investigation. Also, important, and perhaps even creating added ambiguity, are the changing features of the cyber arena itself in response to greater user access, changing patterns of access, new opportunities, and innovative activities—as well as an expansion of motives and intents on both sides of the ledger, system threats and system supports.

All this seems reasonable enough. Less appreciated, however, is the impact of a powerful paradox that impedes our understanding of the challenges at hand, let alone effective responses. On the one hand, a large number of institutions and research initiatives—private and public—are devoted to identifying and metricizing cyber threat incidents. Metricizing security threats is already generating a large "industry" of cybersecurity firms, national and international, each with its individual products. On the other hand, there is little advance toward a consensus about the nature, let alone the specifics, of the overall evidence. There are no agreed upon ways of combining metrics based on different principles, different labels, different categories and so forth, which prevents the effective use of this seemingly "data-rich" situation. In sum, we are hardly "data poor," but we are remarkably short of analytical foundations and inquiries, and almost overwhelmed by the growth and availability of observations, even "metrics." By necessity, we must take these realities into account.

In an earlier inquiry, we suggested that cyber conflicts tend to fall into three overarching modes, ranging from least to most conflictual. These are (1) contentions over management of cyberspace, (2) conflict for strategic advantage, and (3) cyber threats to national security.[1] Each mode is manifested in various ways, and we provide examples of cases that seem to fit each mode.

In the absence of robust data, this approach seemed reasonable enough, especially when supported by specific cases. The sections that follow are devoted to some empirical observations of different types of threats to cybersecurity. Our purpose is to recognize and illustrate the increasing diversity and complexity of cyber threats and manifestations of conflict dynamics.

8.2   Modes of Cyber Threat

A large and diverse literature has evolved over the past decades surrounding different aspects of cyber threat, based on different assumptions, arguments, and assessment of implications. But we have yet to develop and converge on measures of scale, scope, duration, and intensity—to note the most obvious. Many of the inferences or conclusions drawn in public debates, in the press, or in the scholarly community to date reflect a cyber "ambiance" dominated by unauthorized intrusions using diverse modes and methods for which we have as yet no ready defense. Much of the evidence at hand is not cumulative, is not critically analyzed, and barely passes the most limited standards of scientific inquiry. However, the sheer power of the message—conveyed in many different forms—is compelling, alarming, and difficult to ignore.

We can argue but cannot assume that there is a degree of consistency of definitions *within* a particular investigation supported by an organization or reporting source, even if we cannot assume consistency *across* initiatives or institutions. That said, figure 8.2 presents the monthly cumulative threat alerts over four years.

The attention given to cybersecurity in recent years is subject to most, if not all, of the concerns associated with the paradox noted before—plus it remains in search of pragmatic perspective and operational definition. Whereas there is an increasing awareness of cybersecurity breaches in general terms, the details are often unclear, and much is still to be learned about intents, instruments, and impacts associated with different forms of unauthorized access. To complicate matters, the entire ecology of cyber intrusions is becoming increasingly complicated.

Cybersecurity continues to be an issue area in search of ontology—or organization of meaning—in terms of concepts, dimensions, metrics, and facets, to name the most obvious. This is true for the cyber arena broadly defined and is especially relevant for cybersecurity given its salience in all

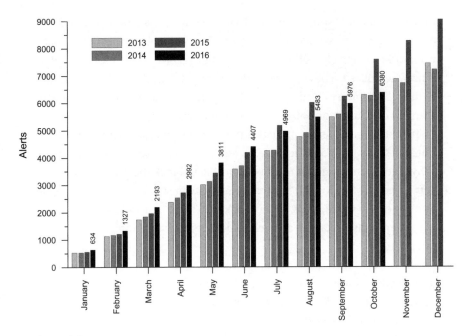

Figure 8.2
Cumulative annual alert totals, 2013–2016.
Source: Based on Cisco Systems Inc. (2017, 42).
Note: Alerts defined as vendor-reported vulnerabilities.

contexts, private and public. It seems reasonable to consider cybersecurity in a dual context of managing risk and creating resilience, thus calling attention to risk assessments, on the one hand, and decisions, on the other (Collier et al. 2014). By necessity, this requires attention to the empirical as well as the subjective, and the observable as well as the inferred.

8.2.1 Malicious Acts, Cybercrime, and Espionage
The increasing evidence of *cyber threats* to national security reinforces the politicization of cyberspace and its salience in emergent policy discourse, with terms like militarization, weaponization, damages to critical infrastructures, various types of cybercrimes, and other broad issues. These are generally labeled after their manifestations in the physical domain (termed "real" in contrast to "virtual") despite the fundamental differences in action, transmission mechanisms, and overall configuration.

We do not as yet have agreed upon ways to quantify cyber risk, assess levels of vulnerability and observe attack at the time of execution, or anticipate the cost of different sorts of failures. In most countries, an individual or group can circulate its message in cyberspace with a reasonable expectation that it will not be effectively—or at least not completely—regulated, controlled, or otherwise policed. These create loads on the state and stress its capabilities. In this simple ratio of loads to capabilities, the numerator can become greater than the denominator, with potential system-wide ramifications.

Turning to commercial or market domains, we must ask: why is it that the Internet seems to make attack (e.g., espionage) easy and prevention hard? Why, at the same time, has China been able to block the use within its borders of most of the popular applications that shape the user experience today in most of the world, such as Facebook, YouTube, and Twitter? When does the Internet favor control and when does it favor the unregulated flow of information?

Rhetorical as such questions might seem, the fact remains that we are confronted with growing complexity and multiplicity in the facets and dimensions of co-evolution. For the most part, the dynamic processes underlying market and commercial dysfunctions appear to be driven by low politics (such as population dynamics, resource uses, technological developments, and environmental changes), as well as by high politics (such as strategic competition, conflict and warfare, and contentions over "right" and "wrong").

An interesting insight into this complexity is provided by the risk level associated with the top targets of cyberattacks to applications used by industry. Figure 8.3 shows the risk levels in different industries. Figure 8.4 shows the risk levels in different regions. The message is obvious, but important: uses of applications vary as do the associated risks.

It should come as no surprise that cyber-based financial crimes are increasingly reported. The patterns and details in figure 8.5 are noteworthy and somewhat puzzling. Why, for instance, do we see a remarkable rise in the record of stolen payments reported for 2013 followed by a decline in 2014?

At this point, cybersecurity is assuming center stage in the calculus of many governments. Increasingly, states seek to control access to cyber venues and, when possible, to prosecute presumed offenders. Some go to great lengths to limit the exposure of their citizens to messages deemed as undesirable. Governments try to use cyber venues to exert their power and influence and extend their reach as well as their instruments of sanction and leverage—and pursue their own security by increasing the insecurity of their critics or detractors.

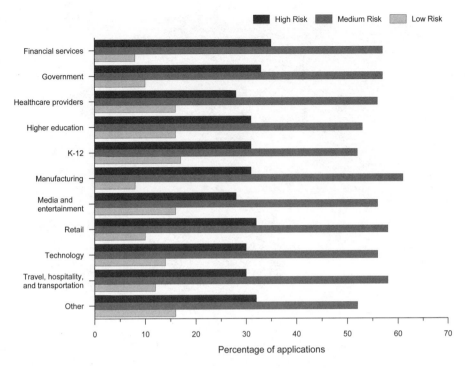

Figure 8.3
Level of risk to applications used, by industry.
Source: Based on Cisco Systems Inc. (2017, 18).

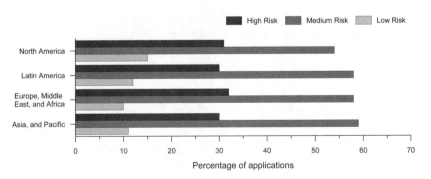

Figure 8.4
Level of risk to applications used, by region.
Source: Based on Cisco Systems Inc. (2017, 18).

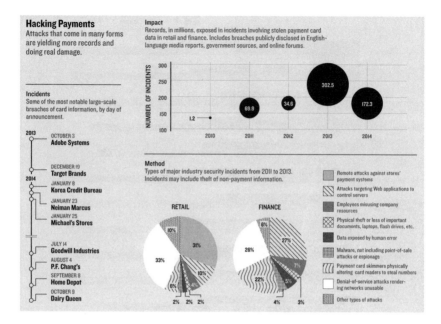

Figure 8.5
Analysis of cyber-based financial crimes.
Source: MIT *Technology Review* (2015).

Many states have not been reluctant to request user and transactions data. The legal forms differ as do their effectiveness. In figure 8.6 we illustrate these emerging dynamics by showing the count of individual requests received by Google from states to remove data, as well as the total number of removal (2009–2016).

Espionage is undoubtedly one of the earliest forms of advanced "undetected intelligence." Traditionally, state-sourced espionage has been for political purposes, with the intent to obtain information about motives and capabilities of adversaries. Theft of industrial or intellectual property and the like—through whatever means—violates generally accepted practice pursued for economic gain. There are many terms for this practice, and none of them are complimentary.

Using system dynamics for a multilevel analysis of the effects of cyber-crime on the financial sector, Lagazio, Sherif, and Cushman (2014) employ targeted surveys to help inform the model and shape its logic as well as its basic structural features. They distinguish between cybercrime and fraud—an apparently well-understood difference among financial analysts—and then show how strong dynamic relationships between the tangible and

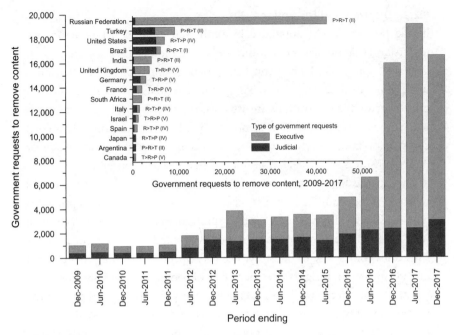

Figure 8.6
Total removal requests received by Google, 2009–2017.
Inset: States with cyber profiles, 2015.
Source: Based on data from Google Inc. (2018).

the intangible factors of the financial sector affect the cost of cybercrime. One conclusion is that the cost of cybercrime is driven less by the actual losses (as costs) than by the ways in which financial firms seek to protect their business, given the prevalence of cybercrime. It is difficult to ignore the combination of two chronic features—common underreporting and notable overspending on security. In addition, the conjunction of what the authors note as weak policing and jurisdictional arbitrage, along with limited coordinated international responses, all but assure the increasing cost of cybercrime.

A recurrent theme in both the media and more scholarly analyses—in metric, narrative, case, or other form—points to China as a major practitioner with a wide range of attacks on targets worldwide. The government of China is suspected of utilizing national hackers to engage in international attacks. In May 2014, the United States formally accused several government officials in China of targeting American firms in a sustained and organized way (Rayman 2014). Other such accusations were not unusual.

8.2.2 Disputes and Disruptions

In the physical world populated by both states and nonstate actors, we understand that incidents of conflict and contention lie on a spectrum, with large scale wars at the far end and a range of behaviors along that spectrum—using different tools and motivated by different goals. For the profit-driven private sector, the motivations are usually economic, and critical contentions may converge on cooperation or on conflict. In Western economic theory, competition is a core driver of progress and change, and thus firms in similar lines of business are by default positioned in a space of conflict.

Due to the highly interconnected character of cyberspace, competitors must often cooperate. The term "coopetition" has been coined to capture this bimodal state of affairs. There is again a spectrum of cooperation and conflict, with different modes of interaction, but the bimodal character of relationships adds complexity to the story. The very operations of the cyber domain provide important insights into the nature of contentions and disputes.

For the Internet to work and to enable cyberspace, the various parts of the network must be interconnected, as we discussed in chapter 2. Without connection, there would not be a coherent cyberspace, but just islands of connectivity. Recall that the early approach to interconnection was for regional Internet service providers (ISPs) to pay a Tier 1 provider (the Internet equivalent of a long-distance phone company) to interconnect them. This structure resolved the ambivalence of the bimodal relationship—competing ISPs paid a third party to interconnect them—so they did not have to deal with each other directly. But as the Internet has matured, ISPs have realized that it would be less costly for them to interconnect directly (so-called "peering" connections) and avoid paying the Tier 1 middleman. This requires that competitors learn how to cooperate, to negotiate the terms under which they will interconnect.

In this context, what does the far end of the conflict spectrum look like? One extreme point is where two ISPs become so hostile to each other that they literally "pull the plug" and disconnect from each other. Under certain circumstances this can actually fragment the Internet, as happened in 2008 when Sprint and Cogent "de-peered" each other (Underwood 2008). Outcry normally causes issues like this to be resolved in a few days, but these disputes arise from time to time. However, "pulling the plug" is far from going to war in the conventional sense. But there are costs to such actions, and tradeoffs must be considered carefully.

Sometimes, these disputes end up in court. This path is particularly important when the interconnection is international, because the physical point of interconnection may determine the jurisdiction in which the litigation occurs. When Cogent and France Telecom were not able to resolve their dispute about interconnection in France, the French court declared that Cogent would have to pay France Telecom for the privilege of peering (Autorité de la concurrence 2012).

Such disputes seem to arise in only a small number of situations involving interconnection among competitors. Then, too, competitors are not "enemies" in the conventional understanding of the term. The Internet is highly connected today, and most of the interconnections are properly sized to carry the intended traffic. Perhaps the most manifest example of cooperation among competitors is the major Internet exchanges in Europe, most of which are created as partnerships among competitors to ensure cost-effective interconnection of the Internet.

So far we referred only to contentions among commercial competitors. We have not addressed cases in which the state develops a legal position to induce a change in the prevailing practices of a major private actor in cyberspace or to draw on public authority to override the practices introduced by private authority.

8.3   Cases in Cyber Conflict—Empirical Inferences

Given that we are at the early stages of addressing matters of concept and ontology—as well as metrics and measurement—for conflict in the cyber domain, there are few agreed-upon principles, if any, for differentiation among degrees of scale and scope, or facets of intent and action. For this reason, we begin with matters of method before turning to a set of cases that have been developed under a common framing.

All things considered, if we view cyber conflicts and contentions from different theoretical, political, technological, or pragmatic perspectives, then we would be likely to draw different inferences—much as the proverbial "blind men" signal different features of their "elephant."

If we focus on *state* and *nonstate actors* and activities, intents, motivations, and capabilities, then we can envisage drawing on insights from the conflict intensity approach so prevalent in quantitative analyses of international relations—dating back to the early days of metricized methods. For example, one could explore the use of scaling methods that capture that span from "normal" contentions, such as competitive behavior (in markets or politics), to overt low-level intrusions, extractive access (industrial espionage and/or intelligence gathering), and cybercrime, all the way to overt cyber warfare. Even in the abstract, it is evident that intensity levels must be contextualized, and that agreement on criteria for defining "context" as well as intensity are required.

If we consider cyber conflict as a form of *unconventional hostility* in international relations, then we might gain some insights from three traditional models, each of which is anchored in physical (kinetic) conditions. The *instrument* model focuses on the utility of the cyber tools relative to substitutable kinetic ones; the *effects* model focuses on the impact on the target; and the strict-*liability* model treats attacks against critical infrastructure automatically as armed attacks (Carr 2009, 59). These models rest on the known identity of the adversary. Nonetheless, they shed light on the remarkable diversity of instruments, threats, drivers of progress and change, and thus firms in similar lines of business are positioned by default in a space of conflict. Of these, the most developed approach, the "best" when dealing with cyberattacks, appears to be the effects-based model (Carr 2009, 61). This model focuses on severity, immediacy, directness, invasiveness, measurability, and presumptive legitimacy.

8.3.1   Framing an "Experiment"

We turn next to a set of cyber conflicts provided in narrative form by the Atlantic Council in their book called *A Fierce Domain* (Healey 2013) and highlight some notable conclusions based on a reanalysis of cases between 1985 and 2013 (Gamero-Garrido 2014). The cases ranged from low-level intrusions, such as petty crime to creating spam networks, to higher levels of conflict intensity and then all the way to high-scale, state-sponsored cyber warfare. Our purpose is to identify the individual layer of the Internet as used by the contenders in each of the cases. The "experiment" is about the utility of transforming narrative text into structured form through the use of filters to enable systematic cross-case investigation. The filters target specific features of the case studies, pertaining to the following:

- **Actors:** types of *contenders*, such as state versus state (Russia vs. Estonia, Russia vs. Georgia, and Stuxnet), state versus firm, (Google in China), and firm versus firm (Google vs. Apple), people versus government (Egypt, Iran), and government versus people (Syria)

- **Contention**: dominant *objective type* such as espionage (industrial or political secrets), and crime (of various sorts)
- **Power relations:** type of *leverage* or influence
- **Internet layers:** *four*-layer model
- **Mechanism:** *instrument*, intrusions, malware, and so forth
- **Impact:** observable *effects* or *outcomes*

Table 8.1 lists the original Atlantic Council cases in chronological order (plus the one case that we added), identifies the target layer(s), and notes the nature of the unauthorized intrusion and attendant damage. Of course, we cannot argue that these are randomly selected. They are largely United States centered. This could be due to the priorities and methodology of the Atlantic Council, or to their relative visibility, or to the fact that the United States remains at the frontier of all issues related to the cyber domain—or all of the above plus a few more.

8.3.2   What the Cases Show

In an early chapter, we argue that a large number of new players in world politics have been empowered by access to cyberspace, and this empowerment translated into political behavior. As a result, a large number of previously apolitical actors, or ones traditionally confined to "low politics," catapulted to "high politics," and joined the traditional state system as prime participants in international conflict via cyber venues. Here we find support for this proposition.

Although generalizations are always difficult to draw, nonetheless the reanalysis of the sixteen original cases plus the one we have added yields valuable insights. Here we consider these through the lenses of *levels* of analysis as well as *layers* of the Internet. This approach yields the following results:

1. Most of the cases in table 8.1 are related to a then-ongoing conflict or dispute in the physical domain, or they refer to policy moves on the ground. The apparent motivations for cyberattacks vary—these range from political or social activism, to stealing intellectual property, to for-profit crime, to state-sponsored warfare.

2. In these cases, the cyber domain is used as an extension of the traditional one, not an alternative. In many cases, the first move results in a set of common consequences. These include diffusion effects, expansion of participants, and escalation dynamics.

Table 8.1
Cases of cyberattacks.

Case		Target Layer	Description
1.	Cuckoo's Egg	Physical	Hess accessed data stored on hardware at the target installation.
2.	Morris Worm	Physical	The worm overloaded the infected hosts, resulting in disabled hardware.
		Application	The spread mechanism of the worm used applications such as SEND MAIL.
3.	Dutch Hackers and British Hackers	Information	Espionage operations that seemingly do not attack infrastructure (physical) or protocols and applications (logical) are classified as targeting the information layer.
4.	Operation Solar Sunrise	Logical and information	The first is due to the implantation of malware for espionage purposes, and the second is due to espionage operation.
5.	Moonlight Maze	Information	Espionage operations that seemingly do not attack infrastructure (physical) or protocols and applications (logical) are classified as targeting the information layer.
6.	Electronic Disturbance Theater	Physical and logical	Distributed denial of service (DDoS) attacks affected both the infrastructure (physical) and the ability to carry traffic (logical).
7.	ILOVEYOU	Information, logical, and physical	The first attacks of the virus destroyed files (information), and the secondary DDoS resulted in attack to both the physical (infrastructure) and logical (ability to carry traffic) layers.
8.	Patriotic Hackers	Physical, logical, information, and user	DDoS resulted in an attack to both the physical and logical layers. Altering data on hosts with malicious intent relates to the information layer. The attacks were targeted at actual groups, affecting the user layer.
9.	Chinese Cyber Espionage	Information*	Espionage operations that seemingly do not attack infrastructure (physical) or protocols and applications (logical) are classified as targeting the information layer.
10.	Estonia Receives Cyber attacks	Physical, logical, information, and user	DDoS resulted in an attack to both the physical and logical layers. Posting data on hosts (web-sites) relates to the information layer. The attacks targeted actual groups, affecting the user layer.
11.	Russo-Georgian War	Physical, logical, information, and user	DDoS resulted in an attack to both the physical and logical layers. Altering data on hosts (for defacement or otherwise) with malicious intent relates to the information layer. Finally, the attacks were targeted at actual groups, affecting the user layer.

Case		Target Layer	Description
12.	Operation Buckshot Yankee	Information	Espionage operations that seemingly do not attack infrastructure (physical) or protocols and applications (logical) are classified as targeting the information layer.
13.	Conficker	Physical, logical, and information	Conficker took part of the computing capabilities of its victims then using removable media for transmission, resulting in an attack to the physical layer. It modified the software of the host to prevent being detected (information), and spread through the Internet (logical).
14.	Stuxnet, Flame, and Duqu	Physical, logical, information, and user	DDoS on third parties resulted in an attack to both the physical and logical layers. Stuxnet also caused malfunction of hardware (physical). Altering data on hosts with malicious intent relates to the information layer. Attacks were also targeted at specific groups, affecting the user layer.
15.	WikiLeaks	Physical, logical, information, and user	The main operation of WikiLeaks was public release of information. Anonymous targeted DDoS attacked the remaining layers. Defensive measures dealt with users.
16.	Edward Snowden NSA leaks	Information and user	Snowden's actions were focused on releasing secret information, related to specific agencies in the United States and elsewhere (user layer).
17.	Hackers intrude into *New York Times*	Physical, information, and user	Installing malware tools resulted in an attack to the physical layer. The episode was targeted, affecting the user layer. Accessing nonpublic information resulted in an attack to the information layer.

Source: Based on Gamero-Garrido (2014), used with permission.
*The attack might have involved other layers, but there is considerable uncertainty to enable a good assessment.

3. Only about one-third of the cases (six out of seventeen) have "global reach." Most of the attacks are restricted to either one or a handful of jurisdictions. Although the cases are United States centered, nonetheless, twenty-three countries report to be involved in at least one case, either in attack or defense. Countries connected to two or more cases are (frequency in parenthesis): United States (sixteen), Russia (seven), China (three), Israel (three), the Netherlands (two), and Germany (two).

4. On the state-sponsored side, the incidents show an increasing level of sophistication, extent of impact, and consequences.

5. The involvement of the private sector is noteworthy. Sixteen out of the seventeen cases listed in table 8.1 show the private sector either as initiator or as target of cyber conflict.

6. Private citizens, who otherwise probably would not have a voice in international conflicts, have participated cyber conflicts.

7. The most dominant type of cyberattack involves distributed denial of service (DDoS). Other types include email-based malware, identity theft or defacement, to note the most obvious. Air-gapped networks, or networks not connected to the public Internet, have not been exempt from attacks, as Stuxnet and Buckshot Yankee show (Cases 12 and 14).

8. The sophistication of for-profit malware tools has been steadily increasing, as is shown by Conficker (Case 13). Hackers have used email, known or unknown vulnerabilities in operating systems, deception, and outsourcing of traffic attacks, among other attack tools.

9. The targets of the attacks vary significantly across the cases. These range from nuclear facilities, to military or classified networks, to random computers, and to bringing down the affected hosts or disconnecting them from the Internet—as well as counterattacks, software patches, and relocation of the servers in different countries, among others.

10. Some cases signal the physical layer as a target of attack. Although it may not be the logic used by the attackers, it could be explained by the fact that it is the most readily understood in geostrategic and traditional terms.

11. A new vocabulary is in the offing when some countries, such as Russia and China, are recognizing the importance of cyber skills and capabilities and are recruiting and organizing what we now call "cyber militia."

12. Taken together, these cases show that the individual, as the first level of analysis in international relations usually encompassed by the state, has demonstrated the capacity to engage in, or at least unleash dynamics of "high politics."

Finally, a necessary caveat is in order. The above consists of a rather modest set of inferences. We are well aware that these seventeen cases provide useful evidence and inferences, but they cannot be used for generalization to a broader "universe" of cyber conflicts.

8.3.3 "High Politics" in Cyberspace

For the most part, the cases in table 8.1 are largely motivated by political considerations. Some are intensely political at the onset. Given that the cases are diverse in key features and type of contenders, nonetheless, those most highly politicized are *state versus state* (i.e., Estonia-Russia, Russia-Georgia), or use diverse *capabilities and instruments* (i.e., Agent biz, Stuxnet); or cause damage by action of *individuals* (i.e., WikiLeaks)—to note the most obvious. But these features are only entry points, so to speak. They are elevated to the realm of high politics if they exacerbate existing social cleavages, or if the ramifications of the first moves are internationalized, or if new forms of organizations are deployed, or if they demonstrate coordinated capabilities. To illustrate, we turn to some examples from the set of cyber conflicts examined.

Of the entries in table 8.1, several cases have assumed near-legendary proportions of "classic cases" in ushering in the cyber conflict era, namely, the Estonia-Russia case and Russia-Georgia. Both cases involved actors other than the principal contenders, both involved all layers of the Internet, and both involved notable physical engagement. One case, Estonia-Russia, involved the distribution of ethnic populations, a defining feature of the context. Another, the Russia-Georgia cyber war, was embedded in a physical conflict that took place at the same time as the ongoing Russian operation on South Ossetia, a disputed region in the north of Georgia whose independence efforts are openly supported by the Kremlin. The original case narratives noted that forensic evidence pointed directly to the Kremlin. (The narratives also draw attention to the emergence of cyber militia. One consequence of the downtime of the banks' electronic systems was the loss of access to funds of cyber militias.)

Growing sophistication with targeted intrusions and attacks is apparent. Clearly, capabilities are increasing all around. The virus *Agent.btz* infected classified and unclassified networks in the U.S. military, reached air-gapped networks (not connected to the public Internet), and targeted the information layer of the Internet. Although the origins of this virus are unclear, the general tendency is to point to Russia.

The *joint* Stuxnet, Flame, and Duqu case refers to a cyber campaign led by the United States, several allies, and select firms, to disrupt the control systems in Iranian nuclear facilities. All layers of the Internet—physical, logical, information, and user—were affected. Analysts argue that the technical complexity and extension of the virus introduced, and the sophistication of knowledge needed to produce it, pointed to state agencies as the major actors.

Both WikiLeaks and Snowden are landmark cases. Their release of thousands of politically sensitive documents and diplomatic cables pertaining to the U.S. State Department and its missions abroad was unprecedented in scale and scope. WikiLeaks, a "transparency" organization founded by Julian Assange, released thousands of U.S. classified diplomatic cables. All the layers of the Internet were affected: physical, logical, information, and user. There was a near-predictable response evident in efforts to bring down sites hostile to WikiLeaks.

The international ramifications were vast. The United States had warned countries granting asylum to Snowden (most notably Venezuela) about the potential damage in diplomatic relations. The Organization of American States, United Nations, Union of South American Nations, and European diplomats all assumed a high moral posture by claiming invasion of privacy.

8.3.4 Caution or Countervailing Evidence?

If we consider evidence based on different assumptions, different methods, different data, and different coverage, we are invariably drawn to a different set of inferences. The evidence from state-centered cyber conflicts provides a different view. For example, Valeriano and Maness (2014) argue that current concerns over cyber conflict and cyber war are "...conjured through spectacular flights of the imagination" (p. 347) and that inquiry into these issues should be founded on robust social sciences theory and methods. Accordingly, they extended the initial study of Klein, Goertz, and Diehl (2006) by the addition of cyber interactions and developed a quantitative data set spanning 2001 to 2011. This set consists of 110 cyber incidents and 45 disputes among rival states between known and mutually acknowledged rivals. Framed in dyadic terms, each incident and dispute is coded in terms of scope, length, and damage of cyber incidents.

Valeriano and Maness (2014) found that only twenty of the 126 dyadic conflicts resorted to cyber venues, with an average of three incidents in each conflict that involved cyberspace. Not surprising, however, is the salience of the U.S.-China dyad that witnessed the most cyber conflict (a total of twenty-two incidents) grouped in five overall disputes. On this basis they argue that restraint is a better explanation for the patterns observed than is escalation. They posit that countries will not risk cyber war given the state of their own cyber capabilities. This logic is relevant only to state-based cyber conflicts given that the entire set is anchored in the state. One could argue that terrorists and other nonstate actors can be more reckless (and have less to lose).

The Valeriano and Maness study considers cyber activities within the broader range of international interaction. Their unit of analysis is the state-based dyadic conflict broadly defined, not the cyber conflict or dispute per se—as in the comparative case analysis discussed earlier. Anonymous actors are not included nor are multiparty rivalries that cannot be reduced to dyadic interactions. Their major contribution, in this connection, is that they focused on conventional conflicts within the quantitative conflict analysis tradition in international relations. As such, these are restricted to the traditional rivalries or enmities, and refrain from drawing inferences about cyber-based conflicts.

Also relevant is the growth and development of anonymity networks introduced in chapter 5. We note once more that they are especially important in co-evolution for cyberspace and international relations and are particularly significant generative processes in the cyber domain. These are mechanisms through which it is difficult to trace back to, or identify, the initial source of information transmitted. Here we must ask: do mechanisms like The Onion Router (Tor) create multiplier effects for conflict and contention in the cyber arena? The co-evolution of user access and Tor-like services reflect emergent responses to demands for privacy and protection of identity—with no concern with the goals of actors, potentials for threats, or engagement in cyber conflict. At this point it is reasonable to raise the question without going beyond *user beware*.

We now turn to the fourth question in the introduction to this chapter: what has been the international community's response to cyber threats and conditions that undermine cybersecurity? Clearly, all of the forgoing may well shape demand for new forms of international cooperation, even initiatives in which both public and private entities become necessary allies in efforts to combat the rapid growth of cyberattacks. The principle is easy to understand. But as is often said, "The devil is in the details."

8.4 The "New Normal"

The "new normal" in world politics in the cyber age involves a growing diversity of actors and actions. Many nonstate entities—known and unknown—operate in a highly dynamic and volatile international system. It is a context that places serious barriers on the efficacy of traditional approaches to the notion of deterrence—the concept and the practice—that assumes knowledge of the identity of the adversary.

The very nature of the activity in the "virtual" arena is distinct from that in the physical or kinetic arena, which can be problematic for high-salience issue areas. The problems here are twofold: First, the cyber and the traditional domains are now so interconnected that the foundations and assumptions of traditional international relations theory can no longer be relied upon to provide robust bases for empirical analysis or for policy, at any level of analysis. Second is the limited portability of traditional international relations theory (notably in relation to "deterrence," for example). There is a dearth of "relevant theory" and "robust methods" for understanding (or even inferring) the interconnections between "real" and "virtual" moves.

A product of the Cold War, deterrence theory and policy is based the assumption that the higher the costs of hostile action by an adversary, the lower will be the propensity to engage in hostility. Traditional deterrence theory assumes known actors as well as knowledge about potential actions and expected costs. The guiding principle is to make it too costly for an adversary to initiate overt hostility. At this writing there remains a general tendency in both academic and policy-making circles to consider deterrence theory portable "as is" to the twenty-first-century cyber realities.

For purposes of brevity, we show in table 8.2 two contexts or "environments" within which to consider deterrence theory, policy, and practice—in other words, the deterrence context *then* and *now*—and highlight some

Table 8.2
Deterrence—then and now.

Then	Now
Twentieth-century power politics	Twenty-first-century cyber politics
Major powers only	Anyone and everyone
International bipolarity	International diversity
Structural balance	Instability and volatility
Deterrence in power politics	Deterrence in diverse domains
Recognized symmetry	Uncertain symmetry
Known identity	Obscured identity
Shared aversions	Varied aversions
State dominance	Loss of state dominance
Known paths and outcomes	Unknown paths and outcomes

major differences between the two. It is highly unlikely that traditional deterrence (then) can be practiced in today's context (now). It may well be that we have yet to find or frame an appropriate deterrence posture. The "new normal" does not accommodate the basic requisites for effective deterrence developed during the Cold War era, framed mainly with reference to nuclear weapons.

Reasoning by analogy is often very useful. To date, however, there appears to be little consensus in the scholarly or the policy communities as to the direct relevance of deterrence in the nuclear competition ushered in by the Cold War. A more "customized" framing of deterrence may well be suitable for the "new normal." For example, Elliott (2011) suggests that, under certain conditions the notion of deterrence by denial works in the cyber domain. For example, if the cost of unauthorized penetration increases significantly, then the relative advantage shifts away from offense and improves defense. This is only one of the many arguments for the "best" way of framing deterrence in the cyber domain. They all remain in the domain of contingency, especially in light of the apparent success of a recent well-cited offense initiative, namely Stuxnet (to which we shall return later).

In short, the "new normal" is hardly consistent with the standard textbook of international politics anchored in a state system that has a monopoly over the use of force, where force is defined largely in military terms. The "new normal" for the state system is that the "old ways" no longer fit the current realities. Looking back, the "old days" appear now to be considerably less volatile than the cyber age. It should not be surprising that, to date, we are still struggling with ways to control cybercrime, espionage, and other forms of damage.

We now turn to international institutional responses to the "new normal." Most targeted institutional responses are new and emerging, established specifically in response to threats of the cyber age. But many responses are also framed by well-established institutions anchored in the "old order."

8.5   International Institutional Responses

Institutional responses to damaging cyber activities have evolved gradually—in different contexts and with different effects—yet threat behaviors have grown at much faster rates than have response initiatives. Prevailing responses can best be appreciated when viewed in the context of broader strategic imperatives. What follows is a brief look at four different forms of responses, each with distinctive features, reflecting different interests, priorities, and perspectives. Two are state based, and two are "mixed," involving states and nonstate entities. The state-based initiatives consist of (1) actions by traditional international and regional institutions, and (2) a formal international convention; the "mixed" responses consist of (3) a global security agenda and formal collaboration, and (4) national institutions focused on cybersecurity. We now turn to each of these responses and focus on their distinctive features.

8.5.1   Traditional International and Regional Institutions

We begin with the International Telecommunication Union (ITU), the oldest international institution devoted to international communication. Then we turn to more recent cyber-centered institutional initiatives.

It is not unusual for analysts of international relations to consider the ITU as the most legitimate international organization enfranchised to oversee the cyber domain. What "oversee" might mean remains highly unclear, as do the mechanisms, instruments, or overall responsibilities. By contrast, analysts of cyberspace carry little if any respect for the ITU and consider it superfluous at best. Our purpose is not to adjudicate the matter but to signal once more the fundamental differences in between state-based versus distributed principles of management.

In 2005, the ITU released a comparative analysis of cybersecurity initiatives worldwide (Dunn 2005). This report revealed a wide range of approaches with different degrees of development. Although the process of institutionalizing responses to cyber threats is at an early stage, it is conceivable to discern possible emergent trajectories via the use of (highly incomplete) quantitative data provided by national governments. Although it is unlikely that governments will publicly release data related to national security intrusions, information related to civilian criminal activities is available for select countries.

One of ITU's core missions is to standardize telecommunication technology and release statistics that can be used to track the Internet connectivity of nations (ITU 2009). Utilizing a group of high-level experts, ITU provides a variety of resources and toolkits addressing legislation, awareness, self-assessment, bot-nets, and Computer Emergency Response Teams (CERTs). Additionally, ITU publishes guides that educate developing nations on cybercrime and promote best practices and approaches. The ITU core competencies are mission specific, nonetheless, they have recently acted in a direct fashion by establishing an arm that will provide international threat response. Finally, we note that ITU was given the primary responsibility for coordinating the implementation of the World Summit on Information Society (WSIS) Action Line C5.

Despite or because of its long-standing status, or more appropriately by default, the Telecommunications Union is positioning itself as a clear contender for managing the cyber order. It represents the principle that the sovereign state is the ultimate and sole decision maker in the international system. As such, the state system in its multilateral form is the only legitimate basis for governance. Put simply, public authority dominates. This principle, by definition, runs counter to the primacy of private authority in the management of the Internet or to the legitimacy of its organizational activities. These contentions have taken on the form of "multilateral" versus "multistakeholder" governance. The apparently enhanced role of the ITU is resisted by those institutions that were created specifically for the management of cyberspace. Resistance of this sort is driven less by security concerns than by the perception that the ITU is increasingly seeking to encroach on the cyber-governance responsibilities of diverse entities that govern the cyber domain broadly defined.

Among the dominant organizations now "weighing in" with the emergent responses to growing insecurity of the cyber domain is the dominant security alliance among the Western states, namely, the North Atlantic Treaty Organization (NATO). Given the dramatic demonstration of cyberattacks against Estonia in 2007 (a NATO member), this intergovernmental organization established the Cooperative Cyber Defense Centre of Excellence (CCDCOE). It was given the responsibility for training NATO member states, conducting counterattack exercises, and supporting NATO in the event of an international cyberattack (European Parliament 2004).

Interestingly, not all NATO states have joined the CCDCOE program, with many countries opting to rely on their own traditional military cyber defense networks. To date there is no strong evidence to suggest that all members of NATO are willing to engage in a common approach to a shared problem, presumably because many states are developing their own strategies for cyber warfare. At the same time, however, the CCDCOE fills an important void for several European states, notably for those whose own cybersecurity capabilities remain to be developed.

The European Union has published numerous resolutions on cybercrime, and the European Police Office is actively engaged in investigation; to date however, the European Union's only substantive action thus far has been the creation of the European Network and Information Security Agency (ENISA). Tasked with the broad mandate of enhancing the capabilities of the European Union to prevent and manage problems of information security, ENISA largely focuses on awareness building, promoting Internet safety practices, and working with regional CERTs, and does not provide a comprehensive defense against regional cyber incidents.

8.5.2 Convention on Cybercrime

European organizations have taken the lead within the legislative area. By partnering with the United States, Japan, and others, the Council of Europe ratified the *Convention on Cybercrime* in 2004, which remains the only binding international legislation dealing with cybercrime. The convention defines the criminality of cybercrime, encourages law enforcement agencies to effectively investigate electronic crimes, and supports international cooperation and data sharing (Council of Europe 2001). As of October 2017, fifty-six countries had ratified the treaty, and an additional twenty countries had signed but not yet ratified (Council of Europe 2017a).

In support of the Convention, the Council of Europe implemented two distinct action plans to train law enforcement agencies and improve national legislation; it has also hosted biannual global conferences on cybercrime issues (Council of Europe 2017c). The Council of Europe maintains an extensive database on national cybercrime legislation (Council of Europe 2017b). At this point, it remains unclear whether the provisions of the Convention will keep pace with the rapid developments in this area. The true value of the Convention may thus lie in its capacity to "jump-start" national cybercrime legislation via its provision of an adaptive legal framework.

The United States is a signatory to the Convention on Cyber Crime, albeit with reservations. Its own responses to the threats of 2001—when the Federal Bureau of Investigation collaborated with the National White Collar Crime Center to form the Internet Crime Complaint Center (IC3)—is a notable case of organizational restructuring in response to cyber threats. Sharing some structural similarities with INTERPOL's 24/7 network, IC3 was established to provide a central contact point for reporting Internet crimes.

In many ways, the United States is simultaneously pursuing centralized and decentralized approaches to combating cybercrime. Critical to the success of either approach is the creation of a national culture that understands, recognizes, and reports cybercrime. Although statistics on the success of local efforts remain limited, it is important to recognize that initial investments in cultural change may not display immediate dividends. This process takes time.

8.5.3 Global Security Agenda—IMPACT

Rooted in its assignment as the lead entity to organize WSIS, the ITU launched the Global Cybersecurity Agenda in 2007, working with the *International Multilateral Partnership Against Cyber Threats* (IMPACT), a public-private venture headquartered in Malaysia (United Nations 2009). Among other services, IMPACT facilitates a real-time warning network to 191 member countries, 24/7 response centers, and the development of software that allows security organizations across the globe to pool resources and coordinate their defense efforts. IMPACT maintains a research division, hosts educational workshops, and conducts high-level security briefings with representatives of member states. These efforts are intended to make IMPACT a major center on cyber threat (Al Morshid 2009).

Its efforts to promote cybersecurity arose as a function of increasing threat rather than as part of its original mission. In this case, the international community chose to build upon existing organizational strengths rather than establishing a new institution. If this initiative were successful, an important precedent would be set for the proposition that an international organization can effectively perform a mission that lies beyond its initial cyber mandate, build upon its core competencies, and extend its regulatory domain in response to technological innovations.

8.5.4 CERTs

CERTs occupy a potentially powerful role in the cybersecurity landscape, one that remains to be realized. As defined by the CERT Coordination Center (CERT/CC), these teams organize responses to security emergencies, promote the use of valid security technology, and ensure network continuity (Software Engineering Institute [SEI] 2017). A general goal is to identify vulnerabilities and foster communication between security vendors, users, and private organizations. Although the majority of CERTs were founded as nonprofit organizations, many have transitioned toward public-private partnerships in recent years. At present, there are over 200 recognized CERTs, with widely different levels of organization, funding, and expertise (FIRST.org 2017b). Figure 8.7 shows the fifteen states with the largest number of CERTs and the "rest of the world."

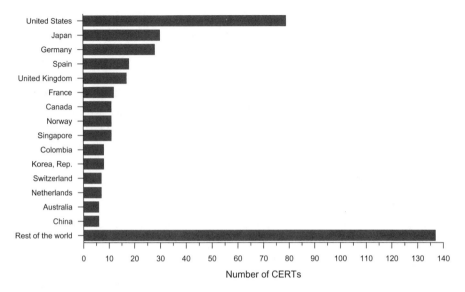

Figure 8.7
States with the largest number of CERTs globally, 2017.
Source: Based on the data from FIRST.org (2017c).

Established at Carnegie Mellon University in 1998 in response to a major Internet worm, CERT/CC was the first operational CERT, and defined many functions for this type of entity.[2] National CERTs occupy a first-line responder role in the event of attacks on national civilian networks, but lack the jurisdictional authority to shut down criminal networks and prosecute perpetrators. CERTs interact with parallel coordination networks, such as the *Forum of Incident Response and Security Teams* (FIRST). This body was established to enhance information sharing between disparate security groups (FIRST.org 2017a, 2017b). Now composed of more than 200 organizations, FIRST is notable for its influential annual conferences and its extensive integration of national, academic, and private CERT teams (FIRST.org 2017d).

In general, CERTs share a common structure. In principle, this should help coordination. In practice, however, there has been little effort to align or coordinate methods of data collection, thus availability and reliability of reported information varies widely across the CERT landscape. This means that the focus on organization has not yet extended to matters of performance and coordination. Figure 8.8 displays the distribution of CERTs by

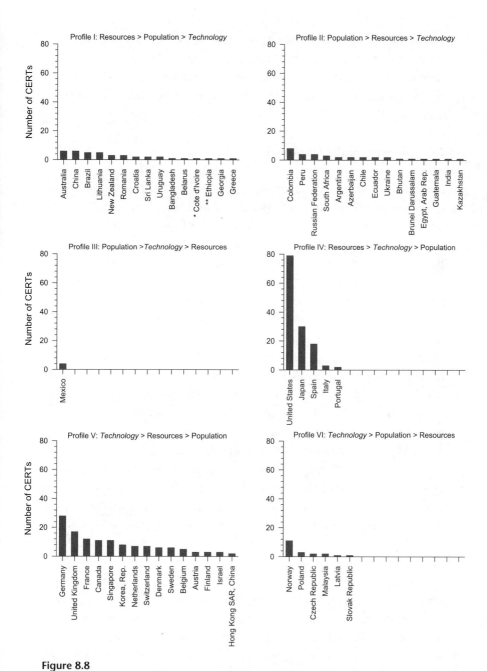

Figure 8.8

Number of CERTs for states in each cyber profile, 2017.

Source: Based on data from FIRST.org (2017c).

Note: Cyber state profiles for year 2015 unless indicated: *2013 data; ** 2012 data.

cyber state profile. The results are predictable in that the cyber resource dominant states as well as the cyber technology dominant ones have the highest number of CERTS. None of this, however, informs us about the quality and performance of CERTS or the extent to which the state relies on their capabilities.

8.6   Dilemmas of Data Provision

It is clear that we have no agreed-upon means of metricizing, testing, evaluating, and understanding the size, scale, and scope of unauthorized cyber intrusions. There are major uncertainties about how frequent these attacks are, who is attacked, and how dangerous are the attacks. We have many data points based on various firms and state agencies announcing that they have located "espionage" but few robust inferences beyond basic reporting on intrusions and damages. The CERT system illustrates much of the data-related dilemmas that must be addressed. Moreover, there are no efforts underway to formally align and standardize metrics.

In general, the lack of robust data can be traced to three underlying factors. First, it is inherently difficult to quantify cyber data due to uncertainties surrounding the nature, geographical location, and target of attacks. Second, many CERTs lack a compelling business reason to gather or verify the accuracy of their quantitative data. CERTs typically possess limited funding, and many organizations choose to allocate their resources to cyber response in lieu of robust data collection. Lastly, there is no central authority or volunteer organization tasked with disseminating, collecting, or verifying CERT data. If there is an impediment to effective data use it is to be found in the domain of motivation—the foundations and the data are in place, but there appears to be little incentive in taking the next steps to enhance the quality, coherence, or usability of information.

Although quantitative data are fragmented, the collaborative nature of the CERT network generates a significant amount of qualitative information. Useful insights can also be gleaned by viewing aggregate data at the regional level. In particular, AP-CERT and several other regional bodies publish statistics that cover the number of incidents handled and reported, attack vectors, counts of defaced websites, and other Web vulnerabilities.

Generally, these statistics are not as robust as those provided by the private sector; they are partitioned along national lines and provide country-specific information that is valuable for analyzing divergent responses to cyber threats. By coupling this information with widely available metrics such as Internet connectivity or arrest rates, and controlling for data quality, it may be possible to develop a statistical model to analyze the overall effectiveness of cyber defense across states.

Many organizations provide valuable qualitative data but few provide quantitative statistics required for robust analysis. As a result, it is difficult to objectively determine the overall performance of these organizations. This operational gap may gradually be mitigated as organizations move from a passive posture to an active and fully engaged role within the security landscape, as is evident with the establishment of IMPACT and CCD-COE. Until then, data provided by intergovernmental organizations can be most effectively used to trace the enactment of legislation, standards, and policies across member states. Utilizing stocktaking databases and ratification systems, it should be possible to determine which countries or regions are on the leading edge of enacting the necessary institutional frameworks to properly combat cybercrime.

Further, institutionalized data collection activities are always undertaken within a mission framework. In other words, collection of data is driven by the overall self-defined objectives and priorities of each organization. This reality is a major source of noncomparability across data sets. So far, at least, we have not seen efforts to standardize definitions, collection procedures, or reporting mechanisms. In one sense, this may be expected, as information standardization usually takes place only after widespread data provision and persistent demand for improvements.

8.7   Theory—Issues in Context

Given that much of what is presented in this book departs from convention in international relations, we now turn to traditional theory that signals some wisdom and explanatory power developed in earlier periods so very different from ours today. We must still ask: how would traditional theory—specifically realism, institutionalism, and constructivism—understand the challenges created by the joint cyber–international relations (IR) system or help us manage our current predicament?

Recall that traditional international relations theory is state-based, generally anchored in Westphalian principles, and many of the assumptions and the evolution of international relations theory are derived from the experience of the industrial West, and focused on sociopolitical, economic, and other forms of organized social interactions. In other words, attention is strictly on the human system. Recognition of environmental degradation as a serious matter in world politics led to an upsurge of empirical investigation and policy analyses.

8.7.1 Realism and Power

Realism (and all of its variants), as well as its sources and its developments, are rooted in the history of major powers. As a state-centered theory, the pursuit of power and wealth remain basic motivations even as traditional realist theory begins to refine its basic perspective. For example, the notion of physical or "hard" power is now enriched with notions of "soft" power and "smart" power. At issue are scale and scope of power, various motivations, and modes of leverage. The basic assumptions are Hobbesian in nature, for the individual, the state, and the international system.

Realists would be the first to question, then be alarmed by, the empirical evidence showing the greater propensity for expansion and dominance of China compared to the United States in both the cyber and the "real" arenas. And they might wish to consider the relevance of the Saudi Arabian case whose salience in the traditional international arena is well understood but whose propensity to expand into the cyber area is remarkably low. (These results persist even as we experiment with different metrics for the lateral pressure indices.)

With respect to the direct deployment of cyber power for purposes of creating damage (e.g. cyberattack), from a realist perspective there would be uncertainty about its effectiveness. Uncertainty can lead to instability, as actors misestimate their power in this space. In a traditional (kinetic) conflict, belligerents will almost certainly target the critical (military relevant) communications infrastructure of adversaries. The asymmetries in the "real" system are not necessarily reflected in the cyber domain. Realists may have to consider that the space of cyber power may be more symmetrical than other aspects of hard power. This fact, and as well the rise of China, could be seen as facets of power transition in traditional realism.

The anonymity of actors in the cyber domain is somewhat vexing for world politics. We now see efforts to eliminate anonymity by assigning the unknown actor to a sovereign state. In principle, realists would find that to be a fine response and encourage the state to proceed accordingly. Equally, if not more, important is understanding the limitations of kinetic power and the promise of traditional deterrence theory in the joint cyber-IR system. Clearly, matters of power and leverage will not go away; also clear are the new complexities that allow for multiple forms and manifestations of power, creating added challenges to already complex situations.

Given that both the cyber and "real" international systems are often seen as anarchic, can the state leverage its power over the private sector? The state "experimented" with use of force by private actors. Would private entities always follow the directives of the state? Would they pursue only their own commercial interests? Do they fit the category of privateers, mercenaries, or of munition manufacturers in the traditional world? What is the role of alliances in this context? Do such questions hold only for "open" societies? With respect to soft power, we see China wooing developing states in formal international organizations such as the ITU. But we have not yet seen a hard-power moment that illustrates what issues might arise in the context of alliance commitments. We can see hints, as in discussions about analogs between overflight rules and the use of third-country communications assets to conduct a cyberattack.

In sum, almost everyone everywhere appreciates how matters of power are central to world politics. The joint cyber-IR system of the twenty-first century is, in principle, all-inclusive. Dominant kinetic power provides little guarantee against cyber threats, nor can national security as a whole be considered without attention to cybersecurity. Sooner or later, realists will have to address the implications of this simple proposition.

8.7.2   Institutions and Organizations

The essence of institutional theories of international relations is that by cooperating, we can create a "better than zero-sum game" for the world, and thus we should work to find ways to cooperate. Although the system boundary is similar to that of realism, institutionalism rejects the Hobbesian image and prefers the Kantian one. Again, the key actors are states.

One important contribution of this tradition relates to institutional bargaining, that is, bargaining about the rules over which institutional mechanisms will be deployed. Aside from the matter of key actors, the thinking in this space seems to map onto, and possibly even contribute to, the discussions about cyber contention (and preferred outcomes) and is sensitive to consolidation of global civil society as a constituency that transcends the bounds of the state.

Traditional public sector institutions are generally heavily structured around deliberation, and based on legal precepts, they are ponderous and devoid of contingencies for managing rapid change. It is not difficult to understand how and why they have not kept pace with cyberspace. It seems reasonable to suggest that more informal, private organizations seem to be more effective and less ponderous than public sector entities. But we should consider their source of authority and bases for legitimacy and account-ability, at least in principle, when evaluating the private sector. Because the more-traditional organizations cannot "speed up" decision or action, so to the extent that they gain control over the future of cyberspace, it will be by slowing it down. Countries such as the United States, which see cyber-space as a source of innovation and economic growth, will put economic considerations first and will thus fight any actors who would threaten the rate of cyber access, hence of innovation. So one aspect of the institutional challenge may be a contention over the desirable rate of change.

There may be natural dynamics of organizational performance. We have seen international institutions "come and go," but on the whole the overall trend is upward—and at a notable trajectory as shown in chapter 5. Even those institutions that are no longer in operation are replaced by new ones often built on the earlier edifice and renamed to reflect changing condi-tions. Institutional theory and game theory provide us with the notion of renegotiation proof to help address such issues (see, for example, Shepsle 1989). In the broadest terms, renegotiation equilibria are norms or social conventions that continue to be beneficial. To the extent that prevailing norms are sufficiently agreeable and beneficial to all the relevant parties, they may agree to the current form of adaptation or accommodation. How-ever, as needs and aspirations evolve, actors may defect from the institution or call for new ones.

Traditional state-centered organizations in the international arena may strive for consensus, but voting is the formal mechanism of decision and choice. By definition, private sector organizations pursue private ends (at least in principle). Not-for-profit entities can allow dissenting voices to go elsewhere as long as they can pursue their objectives—be these tied to pri-vate or public goals. Then, too, for profit versus not for profit remains a notable cleavage in the international private sector institutional landscape.

Institutionalism in international relations theory will certainly remain part of the conceptual corpus for the twenty-first century. We expect greater rather than lesser attention in the years to come.

8.7.3   Social Construction

Constructivism stresses the social narrative. This mode of thinking seems to be on target to understand cyberspace, as shown in the literature review in chapter 3. Focusing on the role of social construction, this perspective rejects the premises and views of realism and its underlying assumptions, as it does those of institutionalism. For constructivists, the structures and practices in international relations are based not on anarchy and its management but on norms, on the historical experience as interpreted by society, and on the ways developed over time for managing current conditions.

The causal logic flows from situation and context to social interpretation, to consolidation of an agreed-upon reality, and to mode of operation. It explicitly rejects the anarchy view of international relations and its Hobbesian underpinnings, and it seeks to reframe how we approach international institutions and how we construct them. Central to this perspective is a rejection of materialism and of the "objectively derived" calculations and assessments of power and power relations. To simplify, international relations is seen in the eye of the societal beholder with its interpretation and assignment of meaning.

A constructivist theory of international relations could argue that legitimacy of governance, a social construct, is realized as a function of the societal context. It is not a function of power politics or of existing institutional arrangement. By the same token, the legitimacy of governance, itself a social construct, derives from the prior conditions in place. It is not clear at all if the constructivist perspective provides added value—greater than the institutional one—for consensus-based emergence and support of governance mechanisms. The construction and operation of cyberspace is undertaken by actors whose legitimacy and influence is defined, not by delegation from some authority, but by performance, mutual dependence, and joint appreciation. Constructivism would argue that this situation is natural and proper, and should be respected and nurtured.

The rapid rate of change around all aspects of cyberspace—and all tools and technologies pertaining to the cyber domain—leaves society with uncertainty about the norms that should shape our behavior there. Some have argued that what happens in cyberspace is not some distinct and unique experience but a range of experiences many of which can be mapped back to analogs in the "off-line" world. But our investigations in earlier chapters show that the attributes and behaviors of actors in the "real" and the "virtual" are not mirror images of each other. The norms from those analogs should act as guideposts in shaping our expectations in cyberspace. None of these issues, however, relates to a salient feature of both the "real" and the cyber worlds, namely the pervasive sociopolitical, cultural, economic and other features of the local and global social systems that increasingly politicize deliberations over cyberspace and the "proper" norms and forms of behavior.

8.8 Endnote: What Have We Learned?

We began this chapter with a cautionary note, in the nature of "reader, beware." Early on, we pointed to ambiguities of concepts and categories as well as barriers to the development of reliable metrics and construction of cumulative databases. At this writing, we have as yet no established method for defining, tracking, and analyzing cyber conflicts—all in stark contrast to well-established methods in the analysis of conflict in traditional world politics.

8.8.1 Views of Cyber Conflicts

This chapter demonstrates some key features of what is known about threats to cybersecurity from a relatively limited database that is structured in internally consistent ways. This "landscape" resembles a security patchwork that covers critical areas rather than an umbrella that spans all of the known modes and sources of cyber threat. Among key features of these conflicts are diversity, asymmetry, autonomy, and a wide range of other ways that reflect lack of coordination.

Nonetheless, we are able to highlight some of the contentions surrounding the framing of authority conflicts around a range of issues in the cyber system, the "tussles" among actors, and the role of powerful entities based initially in the domain of "low politics" but rapidly converging on to "high politics." At this point in time, we may well be early into a process of transformation in the structure of global authority over the deployment of cyber-based large-scale information systems.

Concurrently, we see the growing use of cyber venues by nonstate groups whose objectives are to undermine the security of the state or to alter its very foundations. Recent WikiLeaks episodes showed in unambiguous ways the politicization and disruptiveness of cyberspace. Responses varied across the international landscape, but in general most, if not all, countries viewed this episode as a threat to their sovereignty and to their security, and are becoming more and more aware of their own vulnerabilities.

We can now anticipate the expansion of new features of world politics, each creating new concerns for the state and the state system—and there are surely many more. For example, the WikiLeaks type of incidents and the Snowden saga signal a potentially powerful role of individual action with direct state-level and international ramifications. The increased role of nonstate actors at the level of "high politics" undermines the "diplomacy behind closed doors" model of state-to-state interactions.

An immediate follow-up challenge pertains to the rules for institutional development that are required to meet these new conditions. The challenge will be greater if the nature of the cyber-based participation in global deliberations influences significantly the shaping of national positions in international forums, or alternatively, if cyber participation undermines the established processes and leads to a transformation of state-centric exclusivity in international decision-making arenas.

If there is one categorical observation to be made, it is that the conduct of conflict, violence, and warfare in the cyber domain is significantly different from tradition in international relations. The salience of nonstate actors, the potential influence of the individual, and the role of group activity are all clearly significant. Yet, in almost all conflicts that seemingly involve private actors, we see still see a strong role for the state. At the same time, however, as we have discussed in previous chapters, the state remains the dominant entity in world politics, but it no longer holds monopoly over the use of force. Nonetheless, all evidence suggests that it is seeking to assert (or reassert) its dominance. By necessity, we must revisit data-related issues, imperatives for research, and policy implications.

8.8.2   Research Essentials

Overall, this chapter signals three essential imperatives for research, with potential gains for policy.

The first is to build on the bits and pieces we now have and develop a meta-level view of current data on intrusions and instances of "espionage." This will help us combine seemingly idiosyncratic observations into more aggregate, even generic, types—a common practice in most areas of scientific inquiry. It is done in other contexts and on other issues, and it is fundamental for knowledge development. If we had a generic meta-level data framework, then we could situate the individual intrusions (and efforts to protect) in a context that would allow for generalization.

The second imperative, a potential extension of the first, is to examine the data on malware currently available and organize these in terms of their damage capabilities in general, as well as by damage targeted to specific situations or contexts. Simply put, this means that we must exploit existing knowledge and information about diverse types of intrusion tools, instruments, targets, impacts, and so forth. Various ways have been developed to garner such information, some of which involve constructing somewhat controlled markets for malware (as does Microsoft), but little is known about their effectiveness.

The third imperative is to strengthen analytical capabilities for cyber threat assessment. We know that rates of cyber threats are growing faster than our ability to understand, respond, or manage these undesirables. Whatever might be the preferred analytical tools at hand, it is especially useful to: (1) identify system-wide changes overall as well as those derived from subsystem elements (i.e., bottom-up), (2) explore the cross-level feedback (i.e., the "top-down" and "bottom-up"), (3) construct a system representation that allows us to address and to model the diverse "realities" as well as the dynamics of change therein, and (4) explore systematically the potential effects of intrusions and examine various "what if" contingencies.

Initiatives of this sort are undoubtedly being undertaken in both private and public settings, but with little cumulative knowledge that serves neither the individual entity nor the common welfare. Further, such information is valued for enhancing the capability of the firm or entity, but carries little incentive for disclosure, sharing, or common pooling. Under the best of circumstances, all of this takes time. Eventually these imperatives will be addressed in a collective context. Meanwhile we can share insights about the advantages of exploring different short-term strategies to help manage the many threats to safety and security.

8.8.3 Policy: What Can Be Done?

At least three relatively well-known practices have useful potential if they become more widespread.

One is to concentrate on the *impact* side, not the source of the offending action. It is important to develop *profiles of impacts*, rather than concentrate on singular incidents or on aggregate numbers at the source. There are few positive incentives associated with admitting, let alone profiling, damages. It is likely that the potential insights, if not outright gains, could make the inevitable less unpleasant.

Two is to *reverse engineer* the intrusion pathway, and do so using control point analysis as discussed in the previous chapters. Although we do not always find traces of the specific intrusive access or espionage moves, segments of the pathways are generally understood. Clearly, anonymity networks do not help in this respect, but control point analysis could at least assist to concentrate the mind and potentially strengthen the arsenal of protection.

Three is to *prioritize* for protection. Already many institutions engage in such practice. All enterprises—private or public, for profit or not for profit— are faced with the need to differentiate among their "valued" elements. In principle, everything has value to someone, somewhere in the system. However, setting priorities for cybersecurity can seldom, if ever, be avoided.

In sum, our purpose in this chapter is to signal key features of an evolving cyber ecology of conflict and contention. It is not clear if we should best refer to ecology, topography, demography, or other features of a familiar nature. In so doing, we highlight key characteristics of the overall "ambiance" for the cyber domain at this point in time. The cyber "ambiance" is manifested by behavior shaped by institutional understandings of the collective good, driven by diverse motivations and objectives, possibly with eventual convergence on institutional response at all levels of analysis and on the general "rules of the road."

9   Distributed Internet Governance: Private Authority and International Order

At this writing, the international community is going through a set of debates over distributed governance of the Internet and its future management. At the same time, there are emergent contentions over norms governing use of cyber venues in international relations. This chapter is about governance matters, based on recent collaboration.[1]

We begin with a brief note on governance. Then we turn to the foundational features of governance for the Internet, followed by a mapping of its operational order. Drawing on the idiom of *ecosystem* as an organizing device, we focus on the entry point to each segment of the ecosystem. In this way, we are able to capture many critical features of governance. These involve (and often accommodate) a wide variety of operational modes. Then we consider the broader international institutional context and global priorities that intersect with the management of cyberspace. After that, we shall turn to the challenging issue of international law and cyberspace.

9.1   Governance Matters

Governance refers to the mechanisms—principles and norms, structures and processes—through which social activities are ordered, managed, and routinized over time. For the most part, governance systems are formal, institutionalized in some manner, rather than entirely informal based on norms and mutual expectations. Often the starting point for accord among the participants is the mechanism known as a *memorandum of understanding* (MOU), an articulation of a shared mode of interaction that could evolve into norms or other institutional mechanisms. This mechanism reflects initial shared intents and goodwill in the pursuit of common goals, often with the implication that this could evolve more formally if needed.

The governance of large-scale systems is generally anchored in some form of centralized authority. The governance of political systems involves organized structures and processes, legitimacy and authority, as well as mechanisms for enforcement. This is true only for individual states. By contrast, the international system as a whole—a system of states—is generally characterized as anarchic, conflict prone, dominated by "self-help" strategies and activities, and comparatively devoid of order—let alone enforceable law. It is in this context that the cyber domain took shape as more and more people began to use the Internet.

The proverbial "textbook" may well separate governance from government, but for the most part, it concentrates on traditional features of governments as a way of addressing matters of governance. The conventional well-known model of government is one in which vertical hierarchy dominates both in the conduct of activities to meet responsibilities as well as in modes and directions of accountability. The conventional model is also endowed with official status and responsibilities assigned to various actors in the overall governance system.

It should come as no surprise that there is a long and distinguished tradition of governance embedded in institutional theories of international relations. The classical literature in this field focused on the United Nations as the "solution" to the obvious failure of the League of Nations. Although this literature was largely descriptive, highlighting structure and function, it served as an important feature of theory for the remainder of the twentieth century. With the evolution of European integration, the conceptual frame of reference shifted to the demand for formal coordination and to the gradual supply of institutional mechanisms for governance in international relations.

9.1.1 Theory Once More

Earlier, we refer to three of the major theoretical orientations in the study of international relations: realism, institutionalism, and constructivism. Of these, institutionalism is clearly the most relevant to the concerns of this chapter, but the others cannot be ignored entirely, as we shall point out.

P. A. Hall and Taylor (1996) argue that the contemporary "new institutionalism" is actually an amalgam of three theoretical considerations rather than one single theory, namely, historical institutionalism, rational choice institutionalism, and sociological institutionalism. The first focuses largely on constitutional issues, bureaucratic arrangements, and operating procedures of interaction. The second concentrates on the value of reduced transaction costs, the relationship between principals and agents, and strategic interaction, all based on the underlying logic of rational choice. Sociological institutionalism, the third variant, centers largely on why organizations adopt particular sets of institutional forms, and why some procedures and symbols are selected. Transcending matters of theory is the proposition that context and conditions dictate "best practices" or "most favorable" institutional forms, thus placing the empirical factors in the forefront and matters of theory in a derivative position.

Informed by regime theory, a variant of institutionalism, the literature tends to argue that consensus on norms precedes the formation of institution. This perspective fits well the policy imperatives created by the cyber domain as framed by Nye (2014), who proposed the notion of a "global cyber regime complex." Drawing on existing institutional approaches to international collaboration, Nye defined a regime complex as a cluster of shared norms and expectations around a set of issues (or issue areas) all with common properties related to cyberspace. Each of the clusters considered intersects directly or indirectly with the management of the cyber domain. With "regime" as the overarching concept, Nye's approach to the cyber domain yields an informative overview of governance.

Today it is nearly impossible to consider any facet of governance anywhere without reference to sovereign authority, directly or indirectly. That is simply a fact of contemporary realities. However, as we noted previously, the state system is a latecomer to the management of cyber matters in general and to governance of cyberspace in particular. This leaves us with the complexities associated with the core structures and functions for management of the cyber domain. If the international system is generally regarded as anarchic, given the absence of central authority, the cyber domain is perhaps "ultra-anarchic" given its distributed management that seemed to bypass the state system and its authority almost entirely.

Although we acknowledge the centrality of institutionalism to this chapter, we cannot dismiss realism as irrelevant, especially during the early foundational years of the Internet. Realism is generally framed in the context of great power politics, and it is notable that the construction of cyberspace emerged from the scientific and technological communities in the United

States, the dominant power then as now. Cyberspace emerged from investments by the public sector, but was then built, managed, and developed further by the private sector. At the same time, we cannot dismiss constructivism, given the inevitable gap between perceptions and the views of the world as it "should be," on the one hand, and the empirical "realities" as we recognize them, on the other. Furthermore, constructivism draws attention to the implicit, if not explicit, role of "open-society" values and beliefs in the architecture and operation of the Internet.

9.1.2 From *Then* to *Now*

This brief note is on foundation and consolidation. We begin with a foundational consideration of core principles and architecture for Internet governance and, by extension, basic order for the cyber domain. It is relevant largely for contextual purposes and underlines the power of legacy. The Internet was conceived and constructed during the Cold War, and was part of the overall arsenal for use by the U.S. government. The U.S. Department of Defense (DoD) and the Advanced Research Project Agency (ARPA) investigated techniques and technologies for interlinking packet networks of various kinds. The goal was to develop protocols that would allow networked computers to communicate transparently across multiple, linked packet networks, building on earlier work developing specific packet networks such as ARPANET.

The early years were devoted to the design and construction of the new technology—the architecture and core principles—and its related governance system. By the late 1980s, the population of Internet users and network constituents began to include global institutions and academic actors, as well as commercial constituents. Toward the beginning of the 1990s, the Internet had grown to include some five thousand networks in thirty-six countries, with approximately four million people online.

A key element of early Internet governance was the allocation of Internet protocol (IP) addresses to organizations and the allocation of user-friendly names to the machines attached to the Internet. The U.S. Department of Defense contracted with computer scientist Jon Postel, through the University of Southern California's Information Sciences Institute, to allocate IP addresses and manage the Domain Name System (DNS). At the start there were two or three people, not a formal entity, responsible for what became the Internet Assigned Numbers Authority (IANA).

The DNS, critical to the operation and growth of the Internet, provides a highly decentralized means to associate human-friendly names with the hosts attached to the Internet. IANA was responsible for the creation and control of the top-level names. In 1992, the U.S. government established Network Solutions, Inc., now known as VeriSign. Subsequently, the government orchestrated the creation of the Internet Corporation for Assigned Names and Numbers (ICANN), a California nonprofit public-benefit corporation, which assumed responsibility for names and numbers in 1998. Established by contract with the U.S. Department of Commerce, National Telecommunications & Information Administration (NTIA), it was agreed early on that the ICANN contract would run out in 2016, initiating a transition period. By all counts the plan was fully realized.

Although ICANN may seem to be an example of a centralized authority, the authority enabling this "centralization" is highly distributed. It is based on the activity, authority, and performance of a large number of institutions—each with its constituents and support systems. The key point is that the interdependent nature of the technology's infrastructure is reflected in its management and coordination. Invariably, the most influential stakeholders or constituencies are also the most active, increasing the gap between them and the less-involved ones or newcomers.

There are many ways of viewing the development of the Internet, the key steps, and the defining features. Table 9.1 presents a notional view of structure and process in the evolution of the Internet, and the key entities involved in decision or guidance. This table is for illustrative purposes only. Jointly the features noted in table 9.1 reflect situational realities that shape the distributed governance system. (The ICANN transition in 2016, envisaged early on, is not included in table 9.1.) At this time, the entire Internet-centered community is facing daunting challenges of management. The following section focuses on structure and process of governance, mapping out core features, and architectural underpinnings. Then, too, we must acknowledge that legitimacy for the distributed model of Internet governance rests on *authority derived from performance*.

9.2   Mapping Internet Governance

Our purpose here is to highlight the features of Internet governance, from the early days to the end of the ICANN contract in 2016. There remains

Table 9.1
Illustrating structure and process.

Mechanisms	Major Entities
Foundations: Architecture and Principles	ARPA, IAB, research community, IANA
Standards: Definitions and Norms	IETF
Deployment: Construction and Operations	ARPA, NSF, and individual ISPs
Distribution: Geographical Diffusion	RIRs, local university researchers, local ISPs, certificate authorities
Evolution: Politicization	WSIS, IGF, WCIT, NETmundial
Formalization: International Institutions, non-Governmental Actors and Treaties	ITU, ISOC, Convention on Cyber Crime

some question as to whether the term "governance" is appropriate for the way in which various entities, formal and informal, are involved in making the IANA functions "work." For this reason, it may be more appropriate to consider such issues as forms of institutional mechanisms, forming an overall institutional ecology—with the understanding that both actors and activities are routinized by the support and involvement of the participants. The IANA functions are probably the only centralized elements in an overall distributed and highly decentralized system. Put differently, it is the singular "top-down" feature of an ecology that, buttressed by lateral or regional anchors, is overwhelmingly "bottom-up" in its operational manifestations.

At its origin, ICANN's role was largely one of housing the IANA functions, all of which predated it. Managing the IANA functions is a form of cyber power—contingent almost entirely on the support, participation, and cooperation of a network of collaborative institutions. Over time, ICANN's internal organization and external relations provided the basis for taking on more of a political rather than technical stance in worldwide debates on Internet governance. In addition, or perhaps as a result, it has become the touchstone for other organizations and actors in developing new coordination policies over the management of Internet resources.

9.2.1 Mapping Parameters

The parameters framing our mapping initiative, shown in table 9.2, consist of: (1) three core built ecosystems, (2) geographical scope and scale, and (3) key functions systemwide. Our purpose is to illustrate key features of distributed governance.

The *core built ecosystems* are the essential components of the Internet's architecture—Internet Technical Standards and Protocols (IP), Number Resources (autonomous system numbers and IP addresses), and the DNS. The notion of "ecosystem" helps capture (1) the operational functions (2) embedded in specific institutional relationships (3) that cohere around specific products or processes. The individual pieces are distinctive in their own right. With respect to *scale and scope*, we begin at the global level, and then proceed to international and regional processes, with the understanding that the national is contingent on the regional. However, we do not delve into the details of the state level of analysis. Finally, for *key functions*, we focus on institutional actors that directly performed the three major functions: technical standards, deployment, and implementation.

We covered the "usual literature" by way of establishing the prevailing context and the critical constructs that best represent the building of structure and process. The records upon which we have developed the figures

Table 9.2
Mapping parameters, 1998–2016.

Core Ecosystems	Internet Protocol Ecosystem
	Number Resources Ecosystem
	Domain Name System; Root-Server Infrastructure Ecosystem
Scope and Scale	Global level
	Regional Level
	National Level
Key Functions	Technical Standards
	Deployment
	Implementation

in this chapter, and the narrative that supports them, consist mainly of two primary sources. First are the MOUs recorded in their original form as well as their evolution over time. These focus on *principles* and are very useful to establish relationships, but they do not offer insights into *who does what, where*—and *why*. The second source consists of *Network Working Groups* and the Internet Engineering Task Force (IETF) *Request for Comments* (RFCs), a proactive mechanism institutionalized during the early days of the Internet.[2] These focus on *practice*. In many ways, the RFCs are "primary materials" in that there are few "sanitizing" steps between the events that are being reported upon and the actual reports. When they are edited or changed over time, they reflect the Internet community's evolving ideas and reactions.

9.2.2 Entry Points

The entry point for our inquiry is usually provided by an entity that aligns closely to, or is responsible for, the function at hand. As a result, our narrative shifts depending on the specific ecosystem of interest and the institutions of governance in that ecosystem.

For *the IP ecosystem*, the segment that dictates the behavior of data packets across networks, we focus on institutions that govern or standardize behavior and their construction. The entry point is the IETF, the entity responsible for Internet standards.

For the *Internet Number Resources ecosystem*, which manages the numbers that serve as addresses for the attachment points to the Internet, the focus is on institutions that govern the deployment and distribution processes. The entry point is at the initial process of distribution. It begins with IANA that provides blocks of addresses to the regional Internet registries (RIRs), after which all assignment to Internet service providers (ISPs) and end organizations is done by the RIRs.

For the *Domain Name System Root-Server Infrastructure*, an ecosystem consisting of highly decentralized hierarchical servers that translate domain names into Internet addresses, IANA manages the list of top-level domains database in the root servers. All other databases are managed by the individual institutions, as we describe below.

We now turn to each of these built ecosystems for a more detailed representation of characteristic features and functions, beginning with the IP system.

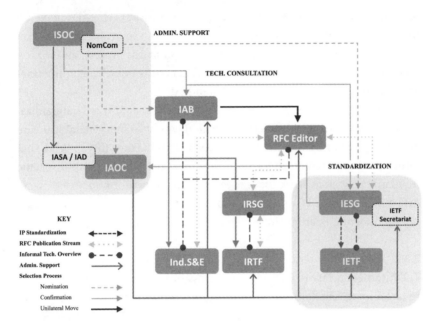

Figure 9.1
Overview of Internet protocol ecosystem.
Source: Cheung (2016).

9.3   Internet Protocol Ecosystem

The IP ecosystem consists of all elements for managing norms evolving over time and, only rarely, standards for operations. It provides three important functionalities: (1) standardization, (2) administration and technical support, and (3) selection of its own leadership. The final product is the standard for any function in the operation of the Internet. Figure 9.1 shows the key features of the IP ecosystem, the key actors, and the institutional context—with the IETF as the entry point depicted in the lower-right side of the figure.

We now turn to each of the functional components of the IP ecosystem, beginning with the standards process.

9.3.1   Standards Process

Founded in 1986, the IETF is responsible for the creation of Internet standards. The work is done by a collective community made up of designers, operators, vendors, and researchers. It consists of working groups organized into areas, each with one to three area directors (ADs). The ADs make up the Internet Engineering Steering Group, which is responsible for technical management of IETF activities, the Internet standards process, and for the process of movement along the Internet "standards track," including final approval of specifications as Internet standards.

Work with a longer horizon—more applied research than standardization—is carried out in a parallel organization with the same general structure of working groups called the Internet Research Task Force (IRTF). Work that relates to the overall architecture of the Internet (as opposed to a specific standard), as well as work that relates to architectural or policy (e.g., security) guidance for IETF working groups to consider is discussed in the Internet Architecture Board (IAB), which can also publish RFCs.

9.3.2 Technical and Administration Support

The Internet Society (ISOC) was formed by Vint Cerf and Bob Kahn in 1992 to be an internationally recognized neutral body devoted to the support of Internet standards process and for the general advocacy of the Internet, its founding concepts, and its deployment. ISOC is a global collective of volunteers and professionals from the engineering and standards community that provides services or support that enables the work of the IETF.

In a complex interlocking structure between the IETF and ISOC, the IETF delegates to the ISOC the financial and administrative infrastructure of the standards-setting process. A group called the IETF Administrative Oversight Committee (IAOC) directs and oversees the administrative functions. The IAOC consists of volunteers, all chosen directly or indirectly by the IETF community, as well as appropriate ex officio members from ISOC and IETF leadership.

9.3.3 Bottom-Up Logic

Because these organizations are essentially bottom-up communities, the process of electing leadership has been carefully crafted to maintain stability and competence. The ISOC president appoints a nonvoting chair for the IETF nominating committee, that person calls for volunteers from the IETF community, and then, using a random process, selects members of a nominating committee. The nominating committee nominates individual members of the IAB (only half of the seats are in play each year) and selects area directors and some members of the IAOC.

To the outside observer, such arrangements look suspiciously like an "interlocking directorate" of obscure acronyms. It is difficult to discern the checks and balances for such closely knit arrangements given the absence of central authority for overall oversight, as is usually the case in traditional governance systems. All is managed by the core entities themselves. These mechanisms reflect truly bottom-up organization. At the same time, it is generally agreed that this community has put considerable effort into the evolution of these processes to ensure that they are both effective and accepted by the community itself. There is no attempt to organize a vote of the larger community (for which, in fact, there is no membership criterion or definition), but every selected nominee is confirmed by a group that is not the target of the nomination. If there is one obvious inference from the forgoing it is the remarkable absence of hierarchical, coupled modes of coordination and the pursuit of consensus, for example, by seeking public comment on nominations rather than a vote.

9.4   Number Resource Ecosystem

The Number Resource Ecosystem focuses on the assignment of IP addresses and autonomous system numbers (ASNs), used to identify physical networks and individual hosts of the (e.g., ISPs). For the most part, any policy innovation is done largely to accommodate local conditions. All policies are developed within the individual RIRs and only when a policy directly impacts IANA (e.g., tells IANA how to allocate big blocks of addresses) does a policy become global—after all the RIRs agree on a common text and ICANN approves it.

Parenthetically, the last global policy was quite a while ago and it directed IANA how to allocate the last segments of IPv4 address space as they ran out. There have only been three or four global policies since ICANN was set up and there have been hundreds of RIR-local polices developed within the individual RIRs—each of those polices only applies to the RIR that developed the policy. As such, the Number Resource Ecosystem is a major supporting mechanism for the globally designed distributed governance system. Figure 9.2 depicts this ecosystem.

Early in the history of the Internet, address assignment was delegated from the IANA (originally by Jon Postel) to RIRs representing the interests of different regions. Réseaux IP Européens began in 1989, and took over

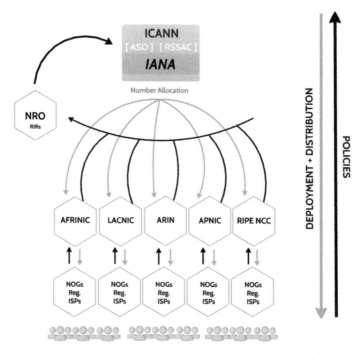

Figure 9.2
Overview of number resource ecosystem.
Source: Cheung (2016).

number allocation for the region in 1992.[3] The Asia-Pacific Network Information Centre (APNIC) was also organized starting in 1992. The American Registry for Internet Numbers (ARIN) was incorporated in 1997 (prior to this time, address allocation for the Americas was handled by Network Solutions, Inc.),[4] and the Latin America and Caribbean Network Information Centre (LACNIC) and the African Network Information Centre (AFRINIC) were subsequently formed. These organizations are the current regional Internet registries. When ICANN was subsequently created in 1998, there was a top-down/bottom-up negotiation as to how the preexisting organizations would agree to be folded into the new ICANN. On its part, ICANN, defined a group called the Address Supporting Organization (ASO) as part of its own organization.

In 2003, the four then-existing RIRs signed a bottom-up memorandum of understanding to create a group called the Number Resource Organization (NRO), with a council made up of one member selected by each

RIR. Then, in negotiation with ICANN, the latter agreed that this bottom-up organization (the NRO) would serve as the ASO for ICANN.

In this way, ICANN accepted the bottom-up authority of the RIRs to individually develop their own alignment policies, which function as part of ICANN. The major purpose of the NRO is to preserve and protect the Internet number resource pool that remains unallocated, support and pursue "the bottom-up policy development process," and serve as a "focal point for Internet community input into the RIR system."[5]

RIRs are membership organizations composed of networking operating groups, ISPs, and National Internet Registries. Some RIRs, such as AFRINIC, are mostly made up of Local Internet Registries,[6] whereas others, such as ARIN, are mostly made up of ISPs.[7] Each RIR has its own independent distribution process at a regional-to-national/local level. Thus, as each chain of distribution moves further down, the more distinct and separate policies and distribution procedures become.[8] Presently, all RIRs are distributing IPv6 address blocks as well as Autonomous System numbers to their members.

9.5   Domain Name System (DNS)

The ecosystem of the DNS is hierarchical in its operations, not in its decision making. Our analysis will focus on the root server infrastructure (RSI), illustrated in figure 9.3. However, as context we provide a brief description of how the overall DNS operates.

9.5.1   DNS Basics

Domain names are hierarchical, of the form "www.example.com." The rightmost component, "com," is an illustration of a top-level or root domain name. There is a service for the "com" domain that can be queried for information about the "example.com" domain, and a service for the "example.com" domain that can be queried to find information about the name "www.example.com." Each of these services is operated independently; the organization that owns the name "something.com," for example, would normally operate (or delegate to a specific service provider) the server for that name, and would have exclusive control over what subnames are used and any policies concerning the operation of the domain and who can register within the domain. There could be subdomains called "www.something.com," as well as "info.example.com," and so on. In this respect, we say that the DNS

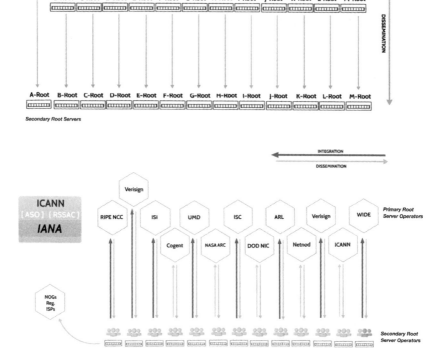

Figure 9.3
Overview of DNS root-server infrastructure ecosystem.
Source: Cheung (2016).

is hierarchical in organization but not in decision making. Each level is responsible for registrations at that level within the specific domain.

Starting with the servers that support the top-level domains (the root servers), your computer sends a query to a domain name server responsible for a level in the hierarchy to find out addresses for DNSs that support the next lower level domain, until the query is sent to the DNS that includes the specific host (e.g., www) that you are looking for. Although the DNS protocols and database information are standardized, as is the general configuration of the servers, all policies about *who* can register within a domain are defined by the domain manager, not by any other entity.

9.5.2 Management of Root Name and Server

The root level of the DNS is critical to its overall operation, because conceptually it is the first step is the resolution of any DNS name to an IP address. Oversight over root-server management lies with IANA. As stated by one of the primary root operators, IANA is an accepted authoritative source of the root zone data for the general Internet root name server, and further, the integrity of its data is fundamental for the root name server system (Cogent Communications, 2014).

The root name servers and their operation predate ICANN but are now generally considered to operate under its influence, if not control. Thirteen different organizations (for convenience given the shorthand names "A" through "M") operate root servers for the Internet as a whole. Many of these provide multiple physical servers that can be queried, so there is much redundancy in this system. Among these, only one possesses the master version of the root name database.

The privileged service, known as Service A, was operated by VeriSign, Inc., then contracted by the U.S. Department of Commerce (DoC). The rest of the services all extract copies of the original root name file from Service A. Verisign, Inc., possesses the technical capacity to make adjustments to the file; an arm of the DoC, NTIA, approves such changes before they are made. This technical coordination is dependent on the rest of the Internet community, particularly with ICANN's Root Server System Advisory Committee.

Presently there are twelve primary root server operators, each with their own distinct network of root server network that they manage over. In contrast, there are thousands of secondary root servers. Each of the root server operators may work out arrangements to operate copies of that root server (appearing in the same IP address) if they want a decision local to that operator.

9.6 System-Wide View of Internet Governance

At this point we pull the pieces together and combine the three ecosystems into an integrated whole system. Rendered in simplified form, the integrated view is shown in figure 9.4. What we see is a loosely connected ecosystem of ecosystems. The individual pieces of the overall system in the figure are distinctive in their own right.

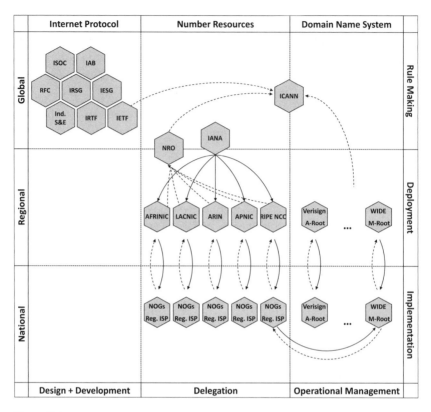

Figure 9.4

Overview of distributed Internet governance system—integrating core ecosystems. *Source*: Cheung (2016).

The system-wide view is designed to (1) show the connections among the three ecosystems and their interactions, (2) identify their key characteristics, (3) focus on key functionalities, and (4) highlight the operational level of analysis. If we proceed from left to right, we first encounter the IP Internet standards ecosystem, rendered in highly stylized form. The center segment shows the Internet Numbers Resources ecosystem; and the right side shows the DNS-RSI ecosystem.

The conjunction of mutual dependencies, the salience of consensus, and absence of coercive mechanisms—all in the course of managing and running a large-scale, cross-jurisdiction, distributed system—is very new. In addition, this figure signals two important connective features of the overall ecosystem. One, is about the flow of authority, namely *delegation* (top to bottom) and *localization* (bottom up) shown by the lines of communication depicted by the straight arrows on the right. The other consists of the *linkage points* across the ecosystems.

9.7 Matters of Trust

The global and highly decentralized character of cyberspace implies that cyberspace itself as well as its governance structures are made up of actors with a range of interests and motivations, some of which may be misaligned with respect to each other. Some actors may be incompetent, malicious, or have adversarial motivations. With respect to technology specifically, experience has shown that technical design seldom can coerce a set of actors into harmonious behavior against their wishes. The pressures that can push actors toward harmonious behavior will arise in the larger context—conformance to laws or norms, loss of reputation, or shunning. Both stable operation of the systems of cyberspace as well as stable governance must depend on the ability to detect which of the relevant actors in the ecosystem are behaving in a trustworthy fashion and which are not, and the ability to avoid dependency on actors deemed untrustworthy.

The operation of the Certificate Authority (CA) system provides a rich example of the role of trust, and the management of untrustworthy actors. When a user invokes a browser to contact a Web server, the connection may optionally be secured using a protocol called Transport Layer Security (TLS). TLS, if used, provides cryptographic assurance against unauthorized disclosure and modification of the data being communicated. However, to initiate a connection using TLS, the client (e.g., the browser) needs to know the cryptographic key of the Web server. This key is provided to the client using what is known as a *certificate*. Certificates are issued by actors known as certificate authorities. A CA is responsible for verifying (with due care) that the key they provide is the key of the actual Web server, as opposed to a rogue site impersonating that Web server. Assuming that the CA has done its job properly, the certificate it provides to the client assures the client that it is talking to the intended Web server. But how does the overall CA system ensure that an individual CA is actually trustworthy, and not providing the wrong keys for a specific Web server? In practice, CAs have been known to issue false certificates, either because they have been penetrated by malicious actors or because they are themselves corrupt or malicious. How does the user get assurance that the CA issuing the certificate is itself not a fraudulent imposter?

The initial framework for trust was laid out in 1999 by the IETF in RFC 2527 (Chokhani and Ford 1999). The RFC asserts that a user should only trust a certificate from an authority with a suitable policy. This discussion hints at the absolute bottom-up structure of this system—any entity can declare itself a certificate authority and start issuing certificates. But how can an individual user make a judgment as to which CAs to trust? That is an unrealistic burden to place on naïve users. To address this challenge, for a CA to be accepted into the system, it must persuade a higher-level CA to vouch for it. The CAs are organized into hierarchies, with higher-level CAs vouching for lower-level CAs, and so-called *root* CAs vouching for those higher-level CAs. A client (the Web browser) must know the identity of the various root CAs as a way to get started. For this purpose, a list of certificates for root CAs is included when a user downloads a browser.

The root CAs are supposed to be the "root of trust" for the system, but what if one of the root servers is itself misbehaving (as has happened in practice)? There is no way that an individual user can make a determination of which root CAs are actually trustworthy. To address this problem, the major top-level CAs and browser manufacturers established the Certification Authority Browser Forum[9] in 2005. But the final decision as to which top-level CAs will be included in a browser is made by the developer of the browser, and this list can differ from browser to browser. So individual users are putting their trust in the provider of their browser, whether or not they even know they are doing so, to provide them with certificates only for trustworthy root CAs.

The system also suffers from the weakness that if an actor is in a position to add a new CA to the list of trusted root CAs in the browser, that actor can then issue any certificate desired (with whatever potentially false information desired). This capability has been exploited by employers to observe the encrypted communication of their employees and by network operators to intercept the encrypted communication of their customers. As we write this book, there is much discussion in the security community as to how to make a bottom-up scheme like this more robust against operational manipulation.

So, as the CA system has matured, we see an evolution from an initial simple but unrealistic statement—a user should only trust a certificate from an authority with a suitable policy—to a complex web of expected trust, in which a set of actors, disciplined mostly by potential loss of reputation but as well by risk of shunning and exclusion from the system, cooperate to some degree to produce an overall system that usually works well enough but that does at times fail with serious consequences. Part of the definition of trust is that it can be betrayed. Today we see further evolution of the system, with new actors asserting that they should be the ones trusted to provide overall assurance that the system is working properly.

9.8 Distributed Internet Governance—Theoretical Synthesis

So far, we have presented an overview of the distributed governance system of the Internet, the overall ecosystem, and the ecosystems of its individual parts. In so doing, we referred only to the functions at the core of the Internet, the entities designed for their management, and the networks that sustain them. When we consider all of these features jointly, they are hardly consistent with conventional modes of governance in international relations. More specifically, there are no known precedents for the conjunction of these governance features. They constitute, in both conceptual and operational terms, a new model of governance in international contexts. What follows is a theoretical synthesis, beginning with general principles, then moving to more behavioral and operational matters.

9.8.1 Principles of Culture and "Constitution"

Much has been written about the culture of the early Internet architects and the prevailing ambiance. It goes without saying that the culture was one of "low politics" driven by core values of innovation, decentralization, individualism in teamwork, and respect for operation. This was an "epistemic community" in the starkest form, but with one important exception. Traditional epistemic communities are knowledge-generation centered, but not operational or technical entities; they focus on the creation and to some extent the diffusion of ideas, old and new, but they do not cohere around particular products or processes; they are innovators in the world of ideas, but they are not driven by the burdens of implementation. By contrast, the construction and management of the Internet was driven by the pursuit of new knowledge but, above all, by its implementation in operational terms and on a worldwide scale.

The principles of distributed management were understood—framed and implemented early on, implicitly agreed upon rather than rendered through an explicit formal process. Little time was lost in addressing the management challenges and creating the operational principles and rules. Thus, the Internet governance functions, such as they were—and attendant operational entities—were put in place concurrently with the construction of the cyber domain. These included various forms of consultation for consensus that were developed to retain cohesion and install operational accountability.

Of the many ways of describing the "constitution" of distributed governance, three "articles" or principles are especially noteworthy in shaping operations.

First is *self-organization and adaptation*, common features in knowledge communities but not necessarily in operational ones. In self-organizing systems, decision making is based on consensus and is agreed upon on a voluntary basis. These notions stand in sharp contrast with most other known forms of governance.

Second is the salience of *freedom values*, manifested in the conception and construction of the Internet. The broader values of open societies served as anchors for technical decisions. If there is politics in the architecture of the Internet, it is to support an open "virtual" experience and expression on the Internet for individuals, groups, and all forms of aggregates. This is also the politics of empowerment for individuals and entities with the capacity to *create their own ecosystems*, their own worlds.

Third, and closely connected, is the sustained quest for innovation *toward new frontiers*—of theory and practice most broadly conceived. Matters of "right" or "wrong," "good" or "bad" were subsumed under the above.

Closely aligned with the community culture, these powerful features of constitution shaped the architecture and construction of the Internet and its governance. Overall, the focus was on connectivity not on cybersecurity. We now turn to the more operational features consistent with, and reinforcing, the general directives noted therein.

9.8.2 Fundamentals of Distributed Governance

Based on, and extending the previous discussion, the operational features of distributed governance can be consolidated to provide an overarching view as follows:

One: The system is designed, built, and operated by the private sector, based on *private authority*. The state system and the principles of sovereignty are of limited relevance for such purpose, if any.

Two: The conception, design, and implementation phases all converge around a common principle of *decentralization* and are manifested in distributed diffusion.

Three: This decentralization principle governs the overall "ecosystem" composed of loosely coupled specialized ecologies—functions, structures, and process—constructed entities connected to each other by *distinct linkages* all reinforcing the common normative and operational core.

Four: Central to the distributed model is *top-to-bottom* and *bottom-to-top* design and decision. Basic architecture, the three core features, is in large part top to bottom. Policies, feedback, expansion, correctives, and the like are usually bottom to top.

Five: *Feedback loops* operate within and across ecosystems, depending on functions at hand (for example, operation vs. information, or implementation vs. outreach), reflecting the consultative processes valued by the community, the apparent "division of labor" among the key entities, and the creation of new ones.

Six: The technocratic operation of the overall ecosystem and its constituent parts is dominated by a *protective ethos* manifested by operational efforts to retain the integrity of vision, design, and architecture for all core functions (standardization, distribution, and deployment).

Seven: Often overlooked are the *power of legacy*—and the attendant salience of legacy entities, notably the IAB, part of IETF, and others—and the cumulative effects on the development of distributed governance.

Eight: New *institutional and behavioral innovations* are created (such as ISOC) to bypass the power of emergent constraints or to protect basic principles of constitution.

Nine: Although in principle a voice in the process is open to all, in practice governance is subject to the "*inclusion-exclusion paradox*," and the fact that at the core, technocratic actors operate as powerful "gatekeepers," protecting the principles and its political culture.

The level of technical expertise required to participate is high, thus effectively excluding a broader community and the general public.

Ten: Implicit in principle, and explicit in the operations of the collective community concerned with "making the Internet work better," is the role of trust pervading the entire ecosystem—this role might be considered somewhat analogous to using *"trust as currency."* In other words, it is not power or wealth that provides the foundation for interaction and exchange but the authority of performance based in trust.

So far in the chapter, we have made little, if any, reference to the state system or to its salience at national, international, and global levels. There is simply no need to do so. We refer to the state at one key junction, namely, when we review the early days in the construction of the Internet and the role of the U.S. government. Remarkably absent were any of the elements that shape the nature of international politics. But now we must return to the state system.

9.9   The State System and Major International Initiatives

Much of the narrative in this chapter focused on the global networking system that was constructed and rendered operational entirely within the domain of low politics. All of this took place long before the Internet became politicized and catapulted to high politics at both national and global levels. The shift to high politics inevitably also shifted the context of the narrative (in theory, in policy, and in practice) at a time of increasing coupling of the cyber and the traditional domains. At this point in time, the "new normal" is one of co-evolution reinforced by the reality of mutually intrusive interdependence. We now turn to major developments resulting from, and contributing to, increasing politicization of the cyber domain. Inevitably, all of this leads to even greater coupling of the cyber and the traditional worlds.

9.9.1   Critical Convergence

During roughly the same time frame covered so far, a concurrent "parallel track" of worldwide policy development was taking shape through the venue of preparations for, and the conduct of, global conferences. In this connection, as we note earlier, one of the most important such events took place in 1990, the United Nations Conference on Environment and Development (UNCED), also known as the Rio conference. Among its key products is *Agenda 21*, which summarized the global consensus for policies and priorities to facilitate transitions to sustainable development. Shortly thereafter, comes the *Millennium Development Goals* (MDGs), along with a process to track the international community's progress toward each of the goals.

Agenda 21 devoted one chapter to matters of information and communication. Considerably more attention to these issues was given in the course of framing MDGs. But it is not until the next set of global conferences that the entire focus centers on information and communication, technologies and policies, and the power of the Internet. Here we consider three seminal global conferences to date, each with its motivation and message, as well as products and outcomes, namely: (1) *World Summit on the Information Society* (WSIS), a new intergovernmental initiative, organized in two phases, to pursue a global agenda; (2) *World Conference on International Telecommunications* (WCIT-12), a formal conference convened to update an operational treaty; and (3) *NETmundial*, a notable and unexpected initiative that came at a time marked by a convergence of surprising events, including the Snowden revelations and their aftermath, and the U.S. announcement of its "separation" from ICANN, a driver for consensus-building around plans for managing this transition.

Of importance throughout are more the processes at hand rather than the specific results. Together these processes illustrate the broad differences in entities, institutions, and legal status and statutory status of actors in an increasingly complex intergovernmental maneuvering on issues managed to date by nongovernmental entities. Further, all interactions, contentions, tussles, and the like were now well entrenched in the realm of high politics.

We now turn briefly to each of these global initiatives. The first and second of these conferences were of a multilateral character, that is organized and managed by state-based entities. The third was explicitly framed as a multistakeholder initiative, recognizing the state as one, but not the only or even the most dominant, entity. Early on, notable cross-cutting contentions took shape, most of which could be viewed as debates between the two principles of authority—public versus private. However, this seemingly simple framing obscures a set of major policy and strategic issues.

9.9.2 World Summit on the Information Society

Convened by the Secretary General of the United Nations, WSIS is the first comprehensive response to the emergent "virtual" global society increasingly concerned with the dilemmas of sustainable development. The ITU was given the organizational lead, in collaboration with the United Nations Educational, Scientific and Cultural Organization (UNESCO) and the United Nations Development Programme (UNDP). As a UN-based initiative, all stakeholders wishing to participate in the overall process—from agenda setting to various forms and forums of deliberations—were encouraged to do so. This practice dates back to the UNCED in 1990, a major landmark in the history of international collaboration. And finally, most important of all, was the active engagement and participation by a range of nonstate actors whose influence could not be ignored. They had no voting power. But, they were "in the room."

The WSIS intergovernmental initiative is a milestone in its own right in that it sought to combine several distinct aspects of the UN's twentieth-century development agenda with emergent implications of information technology. As a UN-based initiative, WSIS decisions are made at the state level, and only sovereign states serve as decision makers. Again, all stakeholders wishing to participate in the overall process are encouraged to do so.

Operationally, the WSIS was organized into two phases, each standing as a global conference in its own right. The first phase, held in Geneva in 2003, had representatives from over 175 countries committed to a wide-ranging action plan. Action Line C5 focused on "building confidence and security," and committed member countries to increasing security awareness, enacting legislation, and cooperating more extensively with the private sector (ITU 2006). These goals expanded in 2005 at the second phase in Tunis, when member organizations reaffirmed their Geneva commitments and agreed upon a collective stocktaking method to track action line implementation.

A distinctive feature of WSIS is its position as a "follow-up" for the Rio process that created *Agenda 21* (United Nations 1992) and the subsequent framing of the *Millennium Development Goals* (United Nations 2017b). This, in effect, contributes to the integration of cyberspace and international relations by providing a powerful force for their co-evolution centering on development priorities. Since 2005, meetings known as "WSIS Forums" are held in a variety of countries on an annual basis (WSIS 2006). Each of the major multilateral organizations assumed specific responsibilities at WSIS. UNESCO represents the management of knowledge; the United Nations Conference on Trade and Development (UNCTAD) focuses on international trade; and UNDP concentrates on the world's development agenda.

The political implications of this combination of host and co-conveners illustrate the trajectory-shaping agenda of these major international institutions. Important is the shift from a multilateral to a *multistakeholder* approach. The Internet Governance Forum (IGF), a major product of WSIS (Tunis), represents an institutional manifestation of this shift.

9.9.3   World Conference on International Telecommunication

In December 2012, the International Telecommunications Union (ITU) convened WCIT-12 in Dubai, United Arab Emirates. The purpose was to revise the International Telecommunication Regulations (ITRs), the 1988 treaty that define the ITU's scope and role agreed upon by 178 countries and had not been updated since then. The ITRs frame the general principles for smooth and efficient telephone network connectivity with fair access (International Telecommunication Union 2012). Many of the preparatory events, international conferences in their own right, provide insights into the position of various countries and the polarities that emerge as a result. But that political ecosystem is still fluid and may remain so for a long time to come. WCIT-12 will continue to be about "the tussle" over the control of cyberspace.

WCIT consists of a mix of discussions, much of which is embedded in broader issues such as human rights, environment, climate change, energy, and others. The communication-centered concerns included interconnection and interoperability and telecommunication origin identification, for example, in the context of international mobile roaming, mostly discussed in the context of the telephone world. Especially salient were matters related to quality of service and "net neutrality," salience of critical national infrastructure, and the broader issue of cybersecurity. Not to be ignored were matters of taxation.

Overall, little noticeable progress was made in terms of revising the ITRs to address these issues. Some (largely symbolic) provisions were added to the ITRs on communication as a human right, international mobile roaming, environment and climate change, and making information and communications technology accessible to people with disabilities. At this writing, eighty-nine countries signed the ITRs treaty. The United States and a large number of other countries did not sign because they felt that the changes bring the ITU into the area of management of the Internet.

9.9.4 NETmundial

Future historians may point to NETmundial 2014 as an event of note in the evolution of global discourse. Narratives about NETmundial, its roots and its implications, undoubtedly vary, as do the various underlying causal logics. It is difficult to untangle the empirical from the meaning assigned to it (shades of constructivism), and changes in the relative power influence of states from their operational implications. In retrospect, it is not entirely clear whether an opportunity was seized or was created. The outcome is a decision to convene a global conference, known as NETmundial.

The largest group of actors that submitted documents for consideration at NETmundial were governments. Almost all countries attending submitted documents about their country's principles regarding Internet governance. This speaks to and reflects *multilateral* principles. Organizations dedicated to addressing the challenges of Internet governance issues—such as the Internet Governance Project and the IGF—distributed a set of documents that presented their own positions on the issues.[10] This speaks to and reflects consolidation of *multistakeholder* principles. (Additionally, a number of papers on Internet governance were submitted by academics associated with universities all over the world.)

The politics of NETmundial are more important than its results. But even the latter set in motion a set of initiatives with powerful consensus-building effects. It is at this historical moment that the two starkly different principles of authority—*state-based* versus *stakeholder authority*—are consolidated, thus further legitimizing the stakeholders.

At this point, it is difficult to define the "old" and "new" international orders in terms of their supporting states. Invariably, support for a "new order" intersects with various facets of a changing international structure (power relations in the state system), a contentious world order (public systems and private authority), and an evolving global agenda (Rio+20 and its aftermath). More important, however, is that the protectors of the "old order" are likely to strengthen their resolve to fend off serious threats and impede efforts toward change. As long as the process remains only a tussle, the international community may be spared a potentially disruptive set of inter-actions. The possibility remains, however, that prevailing contentions may become more heated and evolve into various shades of conflict and with possibilities of kinetic expression.

9.10 International Law and Cyberspace

Despite major innovations in the construction and management of the Internet, the core of cyberspace—or perhaps because of the obvious suc-cess of distributed governance—the international community is now on the verge of a new challenge, namely, how to frame the relationship between international law and cyberspace. One analyst observes that there is a "simple choice," that is, between "[m]ore global law and a less global internet" (Kohl 2007, 28–30). The fact of the matter is that states have started to develop national laws for their management of cyber-based interactions, but this does not address the challenge or its impli-cations. More fundamental, however, are the implications of the basic reality that the physical layer of the Internet, by definition, is embedded in the territoriality of a state. That simple fact creates the inviolate con-nection between the *physical layer* of the Internet, the foundational layer, and *state sovereignty*, a defining feature of the international system. At this point we consider two competing perspectives on international law and cyberspace, by way of framing the parameters of what will become an emerging discourse.

On the one hand is the view that cyberspace requires a set of rules that are different from those that regulate interactions in the physical territorial domain, as argued for example by D. R. Johnson and Post (1997). This view recognizes that rules are needed, but not those that govern the traditional order defined by state boundaries. Cyberspace is not bounded by physical or geographical markers.

On the other hand is the view that cyberspace enables cross-border inter-actions and therefore international law is applicable to the cyber arena. This view is well developed and articulated in *Tallinn Manual 2.0 on the International Law Applicable to Cyber Operations* (Schmitt 2017), the result of a large-scale initiative undertaken by a group of experts convened—in their personal capacity—by the NATO Cooperative Cyber Defense Center of Excellence.

The *Manual* consists of four parts. It should come as no surprise that state sovereignty serves as anchor and entry point for the entire initiative. Part I is on general international law and cyberspace, and begins with chapter 1 on sovereignty. Part II focuses on specialized regimes of international law and cyberspace. Part III is on international peace and security and cyber activities, and part IV on the law of armed conflict. Each part is divided into chapters (some of which are further divided into sections), and each chapter consists of specific rules. It is at the level of rules that the substantive materials are framed as explicit directives—points of law. The chapters are labeled in ways that facilitate the location of, and transition to, a total of 154 rules. This effort is designed as an explicit application of traditional international law to cyberspace.

This highly structured approach, presented in the traditional linear sequential text form, records the text of each rule, rule by rule, and its connections to other rules. A document of nearly 600 pages, reading the *Manual* amounts to a daunting task for anyone who wishes to comprehend it in its entirety, or even in its parts. It is difficult to track salient relationships, mutual dependencies, or reciprocal linkages among directives presented as rules. Further, the text as conduit imposes a form of sequential order in a complex and interconnected set of directives. More importantly, it may not do justice to what is clearly a major effort. For these reasons, among others, our purpose in the remainder of this section is to present the content of the *Manual* in several different visual representations that are literally derived from the text and highlight initial implications.

We begin with a representation of the *Tallinn Manual 2.0* in a structured-model form. This representation is created by converting the text into a domain structure matrix (DSM). A DSM is generally a square matrix that represents the elements of a system identified in the rows (on the left of the matrix), in the columns (above the top row), and the linkages among them (the off-diagonal cells). The essence of the 154 rules is presented in appendix 9.1.

If we view the *Manual*-DSM at the chapter level, we obtain a 20 by 20 matrix (segmented into four parts), as shown in table 9.3. In this table, we signal the number of times that an individual column-rule is mentioned in any of the row-rules. The entries in the diagonal cells show the number of times rules within a chapter refer to rules within the *same* chapter. For example, the rules in chapter 1 on sovereignty occur ten times in that same chapter 1. We interpret this occurrence as a form of concentrated or

Table 9.3

Number of references to an individual rule in a column-chapter by rules in an individual row-chapter.

	Part I					Part II						Part III				Part IV				
	1	2	3	4	5	6	7	8	9	10	11	12	13	14	15	16	17	18	19	20
Part I 1. State Sovereignty	10	1	9	8	1	3	4	3	1		2		5	4	1		2			1
2. State Due Diligence	2	2	2	6	1	1							1	2		1			4	2
3. Principles of Jurisdiction	8	2	9	3		3	9	13	1	3					1	2	1			1
4. International Responsibility	10	13		64	3	4	3	1		1	1		5	13	5	5	11			
5. Unregulated Cyber Activities	3	2		9	1		2	1					2	5		2	1			
Part II 6. Human Rights			1	2	1	13					1			1						
7. Diplomatic Matters		2	3	5	1	1	10									2				
8. Law of the Sea Issues	8		2	5				14	1		3		2	3		2	2			
9. Air Matters	2		4		1			2	2		2		1	4		2	2			
10. Space Matters			1	17				1	1	2	3				1		9			
11. International Telecommunication	3		3	1	1	1		4	3	1	3					2				
Part III 12. Dispute Settlement	1		1	4	1	1					1	0	1	1		1				
13. Nonintervention in other States	4		1	6	1	1					1	2	2	1						
14. Cyber Force	2	3	1	17	1	1	1					1	1	15	4	1				
15. Matters of Collective Security			1	2		1		1				1	8	8	7	2	5			1
Part IV 16. Law of Armed Conflict	3			1									1			7	14	1		
17. Cyber Actions															2	3	226	7		11
18. Status of Select Actors																	34	4	5	
19. Cyber Actions in Occupied Territories																		2	3	
20. Neutrality of Cyber Assets	1			2													2			6

Part I: International Law

Part II: Legal Principles for Cyberspace in Specialized Areas

Part III: Cyber Activities, Peace, and Security

Part IV: Law of Armed Conflict

Source: Choucri and Agarwal (2018), based on text in Schmitt (2017).

Note: Cells signal the number of references to rules in a column-chapter by rules in an individual row-chapter.

centered reinforcement that serves to stress the salience of the principle and its situational features.

Especially noteworthy in table 9.3 is the entry of 226 on the diagonal at the intersection of row and column in chapter 17, a chapter devoted to conduct of hostilities. This entry refers to the number of times that rules 86–130 are self-referenced within that chapter. This case is the *highest incidence of self-references* in the entire system. Note, for example, that chapter 17 rules are referred to only three times in chapter 1. We consider this a rather loose dependency that may signal conceptual or operational disconnects.

Clearly, all rules do not carry the same significance when viewed in a system-wide context. Table 9.4 identifies the rules with greatest centrality.

Table 9.4
Rules in *Tallinn Manual 2.0* with most centrality.

Rule and Essence		Chapter and Essence	
4	Violation of sovereignty via cyber venues is prohibited.	1	State Sovereignty
15	State is responsible for cyber actions of all its agencies.	4	International Responsibility
17	Nonstate cyber acts attributed to state when acknowledged by state.	4	International Responsibility
18	States must not coordinate with other states for wrongful cyber acts.	4	International Responsibility
20	When state is entitled to engage in countermeasures.	4	International Responsibility
66	State intervention in other state by any means is prohibited.	13	Nonintervention in Other States
68	State use of cyber force against another state is unlawful.	14	Cyber Force
71	State self-defense is permissible.	14	Cyber Force
76	United Nations priority is to use nonforce measures.	15	Matters of Collective Security
92	Cyberattack is defined as cyber action that causes injury or death.	17	Cyber Activities in International Conflict

Source: Based on text in Schmitt (2017). See *Tallinn Manual 2.0* for authoritative wording, analysis, and commentary for each rule. See appendix 9.1 on general meaning (not text) of *Manual*.

We fully appreciate that this differentiation is not related to the mission of the *Manual*, nonetheless, but is a notable feature of the application of international law articulated therein.

We now turn to a network view of *Tallinn Manual 2.0*, which we derive from the structural DSM model. Figure 9.5 shows all of the linkages among rules within and across the four parts of the *Manual*. This figure also shows the specific rules (represented as nodes) that are of high centrality. The centrality feature is defined by location of an individual node in the network based on the relationship to other high-ranking neighboring nodes (known as eigenvalue centrality). In other words, the centrality of other nodes, in relation to an individual node, defines the centrality, or salience, of that node.

In chapter 1 of this book, we noted key features of cyberspace that challenge the state system. These features reflect powerful disconnects between the imperatives put forth in *Tallinn Manual 2.0*, on the one hand, and the "new realities" shaped by the cyber domain, on the other. At the same time, the ubiquity of cyberspace and its near total permeation in almost all aspects of the traditional order—at all levels of analysis—makes it difficult to isolate cyber-specific elements. Given that the physical layer of the Internet, anchored in territoriality, creates an unavoidable connection to the international system, it is especially difficult to retain a view of international relations that is devoid of the virtual. At the same time, although states are increasingly able to control Internet access and content transmitted, the cyber system as a whole relies on private nonstate entities for the effective operation of the global network.

9.11   Endnote: What Have We Learned?

In this chapter, we highlight the complexity of the institutional mechanisms managing the core Internet functions, and most importantly, the very distinctive features that create the model of *distributed governance*. We have learned that the governance of the Internet, since its very early days, was conceived, designed, and developed along principles of decentralization. The foundational concepts were neither anchored nor derived from international or national law. As we look to the future, it is unlikely that the governance principles will be revoked or redesigned. If there is a routinization of governance in

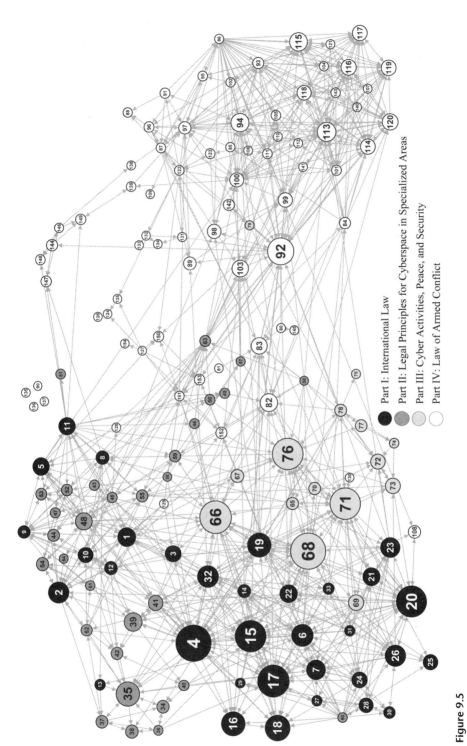

Figure 9.5
Network view of *Tallinn Manual 2.0*. *Source*: Choucri and Agarwal (2017a); based on Schmitt (2017). *Note*: Each node is a rule; shade identifies *Manual* part; size signals eigenvector centrality.[11]

Part I: International Law
Part II: Legal Principles for Cyberspace in Specialized Areas
Part III: Cyber Activities, Peace, and Security
Part IV: Law of Armed Conflict

the cyber domain, it is framed in normative and operational terms rather than in organizational terms framed in formal institutional contexts.

Recall that the salience of the private sector has been evident since the founding years, despite the driving role of the United States early on. But, the United States was an outlier. Until very recently cyberspace had been a matter of low politics for the state system as a whole. This is no longer the case, clearly. Not only is the cyber domain highly politicized but the increased coupling with international relations reinforces the dynamics of co-evolution that we introduced earlier.

We also learn how the state system gradually responds to the new arena of interaction by embarking on several large scale, system-wide international conferences. In each case, the preparatory process is as important as the event itself, thus reinforcing the politicization of cyberspace and its salience in high politics.

This chapter also provides a formal representation of *Tallinn Manual 2.0* by converting the text to a design structure matrix and, based on the matrix, creating a network view of the content and concepts in the text. The results show how the principle of sovereignty pervades and dominates all aspects of international law for cyber operations, thus eliminating any significant difference between the structure of the international system and its legal principles, on the one hand, and the networked construction of cyberspace and its operational principles, on the other.

Now that cyberspace has been catapulted to the highest levels of high politics, the international community as a whole is faced with a common dilemma—how to manage the cyber domain in a world dominated by diversity and contention, rather than cooperation and cohesion. Although the state system is increasingly engaged in this dilemma, the principle of sovereignty is yet to be reconciled with the realities of global communication networks and information flows.

Appendix 9.1
Essence of Rules in *Tallinn Manual 2.0*

This appendix presents the general meaning, the essence, of the rules— by chapter and part—in terms of general meaning in *Tallinn Manual 2.0* (Schmitt 2017). Our purpose is to help contextualize the visual representation in this chapter. See *Tallinn Manual 2.0* for authoritative wording, commentaries, and analysis of each rule.

Part I International Law

Rule	Rule Essence

Chapter 1: State Sovereignty

Rule 1   Sovereignty applies to cyberspace.
Rule 2   Internal cyber sovereignty is subject to international commitments.
Rule 3   External cyber sovereignty is subject to international law.
Rule 4   Violation of sovereignty via cyber venues is prohibited.
Rule 5   Prohibited intervention in cyber venues with sovereign immunity.

Chapter 2: State Due Diligence

Rule 6   Due diligence must be exercised to prevent cyber harm.
Rule 7   State compliance with rule 6 must not create harm.

Chapter 3: Principles of Jurisdiction

Rule 8   State can exercise control over cyber activities under its jurisdiction.
Rule 9   States can exercise internal jurisdiction over its cyber acts.
Rule 10   State has external jurisdiction to protect its cyber and interests.
Rule 11   Conditions for enforcing extraterritorial jurisdiction.
Rule 12   State cannot control cyber actors that enjoy immunity.
Rule 13   State must enforce international accord as required.

Chapter 4: International Responsibility

Rule 14   State is responsible for wrongful cyber acts.
Rule 15   State is responsible for cyber actions of all its agencies.
Rule 16   Nonstate cyber acts are attributed to states that assist.
Rule 17   Nonstate cyber acts are attributed to state when acknowledged by state.
Rule 18   States must not coordinate with other states for wrongful cyber acts.
Rule 19   When state cyber activities are not deemed wrongful.
Rule 20   When state is entitled to engage in countermeasures.
Rule 21   Countermeasure goals.
Rule 22   Constraints on countermeasures.
Rule 23   Pursuit of proportional countermeasures is required.
Rule 24   Injured state alone is allowed to pursue countermeasures.
Rule 25   Prohibition of countermeasures that violate legal obligations.
Rule 26   State responses may be necessary to protect its interests.
Rule 27   State obligated to termination and not repeat wrongful cyber acts.
Rule 28   State required to make reparation for wrongful cyber acts.
Rule 29   Diverse methods can be used for reparation.

Part I (continued)

Rule	Rule Essence
Rule 30	State may have obligations owed to all (*ergo omnes*).
Rule 31	International organization is responsible for attributed cyber breaches.

Chapter 5: Unregulated Cyber Activities

Rule 32	Methods of cyber espionage in peacetime may be unlawful.
Rule 33	Nonstate actors are subject to limited regulation.

Part II Legal Principles for Cyberspace in Specialized Areas

Rule	Rule Essence

Chapter 6: Human Rights

Rule 34	Human rights law applies to cyberspace.
Rule 35	Individual cyber rights are also applicable.
Rule 36	State obligations to support cyber rights.
Rule 37	Select constraints on protection of human rights.
Rule 38	State can cancel commitments as allowed under the treaty.

Chapter 7: Diplomatic Matters

Rule 39	Inviolability of cyber infrastructure in consular space.
Rule 40	Host state must protect consular cyber infrastructure.
Rule 41	Inviolability of official records and diplomatic correspondence.
Rule 42	Host state is responsible for enabling cyber communications.
Rule 43	Use of premises for cyber activities deemed not allowable.
Rule 44	Immunities of diplomatic and consular officers.

Chapter 8: Law of the Sea Issues

Rule 45	Only peaceful cyber conduct is allowed on the high seas.
Rule 46	Clarifications on right to visit to vessel.
Rule 47	Respectful cyber conduct is required in exclusive economic zone.
Rule 48	Respectful cyber conduct is required in territorial sea.
Rule 49	Cyber conduct during armed conflict.
Rule 50	State jurisdiction in territorial sea.
Rule 51	Cyber actions in contiguous zones.
Rule 52	Cyber actions in international straits.
Rule 53	Cyber actions in archipelagic areas.
Rule 54	Submarine laws apply to communication cables.

(continued)

Part II (continued)

Rule	Rule Essence

Chapter 9: Air Matters

Rule 55   State controls cyber activities in aerial jurisdiction.

Rule 56   State cyber air activities are subject to international law.

Rule 57   State is forbidden to undermine international civil aviation safety.

Chapter 10: Space Matters

Rule 58   Cyber activities must be peace driven.

Rule 59   State is required to respect all cyber items in its registry.

Rule 60   Cyber activities are subject to space law.

Chapter 11: International Telecommunication

Rule 61   States are responsible for telecommunication infrastructure.

Rule 62   Conditions for lawful suspension of cyber communication.

Rule 63   Prohibition of harm due to state use of radio frequencies.

Rule 64   State exercises control over its military radio installations.

Part III Cyber Activities, Peace, and Security

Rule	Rule Essence

Chapter 12: Dispute Settlement

Rule 65   State must exert efforts to settle cyber disputes.

Chapter 13: Nonintervention in other States

Rule 66   State intervention in other states by any means is prohibited.

Rule 67   United Nations intervention requires Security Council authorization.

Chapter 14: Cyber Force

Rule 68   State use of cyber force against another state is unlawful.

Rule 69   Cyber force is framed as commensurate with noncyber force.

Rule 70   Cyber threats are lawful if they are deemed so when undertaken.

Rule 71   State self-defense is permissible.

Rule 72   Use of cyber force is lawful if proportionate and in self-defense.

Rule 73   Cyber force for self-defense requires threat immediacy.

Rule 74   Collective cyber force is lawful only with request of victim state.

Rule 75   States must report acts of self-defense to UN Security Council.

Part III (continued)

Rule	Rule Essence

Chapter 15: Matters of Collective Security

Rule 76	United Nations priority is to use nonforce measures.
Rule 77	UN Security Council authorization action by international entities.
Rule 78	States must comply with prevailing mandate for peace.
Rule 79	UN personnel and assets are protected by law of armed conflict.

Part IV Law of Armed Conflict

Rule	Rule Essence

Chapter 16: Law of Armed Conflict

Rule 80	Law of armed conflict applies to cyber equivalence of armed conflict.
Rule 81	Scale and scope of cyber acts are subject to law of armed conflict.
Rule 82	International conflict refers to hostilities between two or more states.
Rule 83	Noninternational conflict refers to hostilities below a certain intensity.
Rule 84	Cyber acts deemed war crimes may lead to individual accountability.
Rule 85	Military personnel and agents are responsible for cyber war crimes.

Chapter 17: Cyber Actions in International Conflict

Rule 86	Law of armed conflict does not prevent cyber activities.
Rule 87	Compliance with prisoner of war (PoW) status is required.
Rule 88	Combatant immunity is accorded to PoW status
Rule 89	Military staff involved in cyber espionage lose PoW status.
Rule 90	Mercenaries do not have combatant immunity and PoW status.
Rule 91	Civilians involved in cyber acts lose protection from cyberattacks.
Rule 92	Cyberattack is defined as cyber action that causes injury or death.
Rule 93	Principle of distinction applies to cyberattacks.
Rule 94	Civilians are protected against cyberattacks.
Rule 95	The status of civilian dominates under conditions of uncertainty.
Rule 96	Military and other participants in conflict can be targets of cyberattack.
Rule 97	Unless involved in conflict, civilians are protected against cyberattack.
Rule 98	Cyberattacks designed to create civilian terror are prohibited.
Rule 99	Civilian objects are not to be the target of cyberattacks.
Rule 100	Objects that are not military targets are defined as civilian.

(continued)

Part IV (continued)

Rule	Rule Essence
Rule 101	Dual-purpose cyber infrastructure is defined as military.
Rule 102	Uncertain status of object requires careful assessment.
Rule 103	Means and methods of cyber warfare refer to cyber weapons and tactics.
Rule 104	Cyber warfare used for causing superfluous suffering is prohibited.
Rule 105	Indiscriminate use of cyber weapons is prohibited.
Rule 106	Cyber booby traps are prohibited, per law of armed conflict.
Rule 107	Use of cyber venues to induce civilian starvation is prohibited.
Rule 108	Cyber mechanisms for belligerent reprisals are prohibited.
Rule 109	Cyber force deployed for reprisal purposes is forbidden.
Rule 110	Compliance of cyber activity with law of armed conflict is required.
Rule 111	Cyberattacks must discriminate between civilian and military targets.
Rule 112	Cyberattacks against potential civilian infrastructure are forbidden.
Rule 113	Cyberattacks must adhere to proportionality.
Rule 114	Efforts are required to spare civilians during conflicts.
Rule 115	Verification of target must be done before cyberattack.
Rule 116	Use of cyber mechanisms must minimize loss to civilians.
Rule 117	Proportionality must be used as a form of precaution.
Rule 118	Selection of military objectives must minimize loss to civilians.
Rule 119	Cyberattack must end if civilian loss exceeds military gains.
Rule 120	Adversary must be warned of cyber action that impacts civilians.
Rule 121	Precautions are needed to protect civilians from effects of cyberattacks.
Rule 122	Use of cyber mechanisms for *perfidy* is prohibited.
Rule 123	Use of cyber operations for *ruses* is permitted.
Rule 124	Improper use of protective identifiers is prohibited.
Rule 125	Unauthorized use of United Nations identifiers is prohibited.
Rule 126	Improper use of military identifiers is prohibited.
Rule 127	Improper use of neutral indicators/identifiers is prohibited
Rule 128	Use of cyber methods for aerial/naval blockades is permitted.
Rule 129	Cyber methods used for blockades must not affect a neutral party.
Rule 130	States can engage in cyber activities to establish and control zones.

Chapter 18: Status of Select Actors

Rule 131	Medical and religious personal are protected.
Rule 132	Medical IT materials should not be object of cyberattacks.
Rule 133	Provisions for identification of protected medical infrastructure.

Part IV (continued)

Rule	Rule Essence
Rule 134	Medical infrastructures are protected only for humanitarian functions.
Rule 135	Protection of prisoners of war and others against cyber harms is required.
Rule 136	Rights of PoW access to select correspondence are protected.
Rule 137	Prohibited use of PoW for cyber acts against their own country.
Rule 138	Use of children in cyber operations/attacks is prohibited.
Rule 139	Civilian journalists working in war zone are protected.
Rule 140	Avoid release of toxins from dams, dykes, and nuclear power plants.
Rule 141	Destruction of factors indispensable for survival of citizens is prohibited.
Rule 142	Cultural items are protected against cyber actions as civilian objects.
Rule 143	Protection of natural environment from cyber destruction is essential.
Rule 144	Prohibition of collective punishment by cyber methods.
Rule 145	Cyber activities should not interfere with humanitarian support.

Chapter 19: Cyber Actions in Occupied Territories

Rule 146	Persons in occupied territories are protected from cyber activities.
Rule 147	Occupying power must respect national, including cyber, law.
Rule 148	Occupying power can pursue security and control of its cyber systems.
Rule 149	Law of occupation allows permitted control of cyber infrastructure.

Chapter 20: Neutrality of Cyber Assets

Rule 150	Cyberattacks on cyber infrastructure in neutral territory are prohibited.
Rule 151	Cyber operations in neutral areas are prohibited.
Rule 152	Neutral state cannot use its cyber assets for belligerent purposes.
Rule 153	Neutral state is punished if it cannot stop cyberattacks from its territory.
Rule 154	Neutrality principles cannot be used simply to justify state actions.

10 The Co-Evolution Dilemma: Complexity of Transformation and Change

Early in chapter 1 we introduced the co-evolution dilemma and stressed its implications for the state and the state system. We now take on a more challenging task, namely to focus on overall dynamics of transformation and change—the sources and the consequences—and the drivers shaping the co-evolution of the twenty-first-century system, as we know it. The "co-evolution dilemma" may well include the state system, but it most surely transcends all matters related to sovereignty. The dilemma is multifaceted, with diverse time constants, authority systems, operational mechanisms, formal and informal rule, actors and entities—with all of the contentions therein—creating sustained challenges for all actors, formal and informal, established or emerging.[1]

10.1 Gaps in Theory

It is fair to say that international relations theory of any kind does not address issues of change head on. For the most part, alternative inferences are based on different assumptions. In chapter 3 we introduced the propositions developed by Robert Gilpin from a realist perspective,[2] namely that: (1) the distribution of power in the international system shapes the framework of international interactions, and (2) the dominant power forges the rules and regulations that govern relations among states, but (3) over time, ascending powers threaten the dominant state and will seek to undermine the prevailing principles of governance. In other words, the direction and form of transformation and change reflect the emergent power relations in the international system. Generally, these propositions—based on the historical record of the industrial west—carry considerable weight in the context of the traditional international system. But can we generalize to the cyber domain? Or to the joint cyber-international relations (IR) system?

We noted in chapter 5 some convergence between traditional indicators of state attributes in the international system and the new cyber-based indicators, and that patterns of cyber access are not always consistent with the power distribution in the international system. Further, we have already seen that the rapid diffusion of cyber access and participation worldwide created new patterns of power and leverage, new interests and new opportunities, and this occurred far more rapidly than would have been anticipated by the conventional view of world politics. The new patterns of power have now begun to challenge the prevailing, based on the efficiency of the private sector, not only from ascending states as traditionally defined but from civil society.

Considering both realist theory and emergent reality, if we follow the logic of change introduced by Robert Gilpin (1987) summarized herein, we would expect that, in the short run, the diffusion of cyber capabilities would be commensurate with the distribution of power; but over time, cyber access worldwide would tend to expand political participation, enhance politicization of both idiom and action, and increase competition for influence and control over the management of cyberspace. In the long run, these pressures will shape new ways of exerting power and leverage in the cyber and the traditional domains, create new structures and processes, and frame new demands for cyber norms—all of which will reflect the demography, capability, and values of the emergent cyber constituencies, to note the most obvious.

By the same token, technological innovations in the United States— the major power at this time—led to the construction of cyberspace, so invariably U.S. values, norms, and general principles dominated the initial design, implementation, and early applications. This we have already seen. But with the emergence of new forms of structure and of process, we fully expect the growth of contestation over the character of cyberspace as states driven by different values compete with the power in place.

Recognizing the complexities at hand, we focus on some of the more fundamental changes with potential system-wide effects. More specifically, some of the drivers of change are new *products* or *processes* that induce change, others consist of the *actions* of aggregate *actors* whose decisions are *transformational*, in contrast to actors whose interaction and *equilibrium-seeking* dynamics may be system changing.

In this chapter, we highlight the dynamics of technology change, the pivotal role of standards, the salience of the private sector, the state system and international relations, the influence of civil society worldwide, as well as international institutions and imperatives of global governance. We then turn to the search for "stable points." This chapter concludes on the familiar theme of "what have we learned?" For the most part, we shall focus on aggregate and macro-level processes rather than on singular or micro-level factors—noting the latter only if relevant.

10.2   The Red Queen's Hypothesis

As a way to frame the dynamics of co-evolution, we begin with "the Red Queen's hypothesis," a simple proposition with complex implications that frames the potential power of *transformations* in the co-evolution dilemma. This framing was proposed by Van Valen (1973).[3] His work focuses on the extinction of species, but the hypothesis is relevant to other systems of interacting and interdependent entities. In summary, his thesis is that: "For an evolutionary system, continuing development by each component is needed just in order to maintain its fitness relative to the systems it is co-evolving with" (Heylighen 1993).

The various elements of the ecosystem—technology, standards, the private sector, the state, civil society, and international institutions—are each challenged to "maintain their fitness." The point we will make in this chapter is that different parts of this ecosystem have very different natural rates of change, a fact that leads to major structural problems within the system. To illustrate, we quickly focus on the state and the differentials in the rates of change inherent in the cyber and in the state system. The institution of the state is anchored in continuity and stability, shaped by bureaucratic logic, the legal system, participatory mechanisms, accounting imperatives, authorization requirements, and so forth. In addition, all of these factors may vary across contexts, states, regions, issue areas, and so on.

In contrast, as this chapter will discuss, the technology of cyberspace can and does evolve rapidly, much faster than we normally expect the state system to evolve. When we see an actor like the state that is challenged to co-evolve to remain fit for purpose in the context of another actor that can naturally evolve much more rapidly, we can see several potential outcomes.

- Under "normal" conditions, the controls of the state are constantly being "out-evolved" by the dynamics of cyberspace and, in the language of the hypothesis, will "not be fit for purpose." This outcome is going to be less and less tolerable to the state, as more and more issues emerge that call for intervention and potential regulation.

- The speed of government intervention accelerates to match the pace of the evolution of technology and business practice in competitive economies. Such a speedup may be possible in specific cases, but this speed must be supported by routinization and attendant infrastructure supports. Such speedup is very difficult and is not likely, in general, given the nature of bureaucratic entities and state processes. Such accelerations invariably generate disturbance, if not dysfunction, especially if they involve bypassing basic protections for social well-being.

- The pace of transformation and change in cyberspace is slowed down (e.g., by regulation) to the rate at which the state controls can evolve. Transformation becomes a formally sanctioned process. Slowing down the pace of evolution of cyberspace is an option that governments, to date, have resisted because they see cyberspace as a powerful engine of economic growth in open economies, and as well in controlled economies to the extent possible.[4] Invariably, all states are confronted with the challenge of retaining advantage rather than stagnating and losing capabilities.

- The states find stable points in the operational architecture of cyberspace onto which they can exercise control. By attaching regulation to these stable points, the state can exert the influence it deems necessary, while allowing other aspects of cyberspace to retain their evolutionary potential. We will return to this final option later.

As we explore the drivers of change and the interacting dynamics of this system, it is useful to look at the behavior of various actors through the lens of these four outcomes. We pose these frames to indicate potential trajectories of the co-evolution dilemma, not to predict what will happen. The state is the most assertive actor in world politics, in that it can take decisions and proceed accordingly. However, its power to take decisions does not imply its ability to maintain fitness for purpose.

In the next sections of this chapter, we examine the various sectors of the cyber ecosystem, looking to understand their natural rates of change and the drivers of these dynamics. Since this chapter addresses diverse sources of change, it will signal, directly or indirectly, the potential power of the Red Queen's hypothesis.

10.3   Technological Change

One of the most cited drivers of change in cyberspace is Moore's law (Moore 1965), which is not a "law of nature" but a behaviorally derived prediction as to the rate of investment in innovation that will yield the best return. Moore's law asserts that the best return will result if the performance of information technology doubles about every eighteen months.[5] This sort of growth, a doubling in every period, is called *exponential* growth. Like compound interest, it just keeps multiplying. A doubling in eighteen months grows by a factor of 10 every five years, 100 every ten years, 1000 every fifteen years, and so on. This rate of change has profound implications for the technology of cyberspace.

The speed of processors, the speed of communication links (e.g., fibers), and the size of disks are all on a performance curve with exponential shape. While the rates of growth may differ, the result is the same. What engineers could only contemplate ten or fifteen years ago is now practical at low cost. Then we could only imagine (or perhaps prototype at high cost) tablets and cheap smartphones, watching video on a computer or mobile device, storing all of our data "in the cloud," real-time navigation systems, and so on. Fifteen years ago, Internet access was dial-up, with broadband an emerging aspiration. Today we have consumer devices with amazing capabilities—capabilities that sometime seem to outrun need. We not only have digital cameras, we have cameras that can recognize whether there is a face in a picture.

Moore's law can be exploited by technologists in two ways: more performance for constant cost or constant performance for shrinking cost. For constant performance, the cost may drop at the same rate, by ten every five years. So improving performance first brought us mobile devices like tablets and smartphones, and once performance is adequate for a range of useful tasks, Moore's law has been turned to reducing costs, to the point that inexpensive smartphones can be made overseas for less than $50 and essentially given away in the developing world. (Costs for a device like that will not continue to decline indefinitely—there are some components that do not follow an exponential improvement curve.) Therefore, it is Moore's law that has allowed the developing world to come online in the recent years.

At the high end of the performance curve, we can now imagine computers that can scan a video feed of a large number of people (e.g., a protest rally or sports event) and match the face of every known person in the crowd. We can imagine a system that can record and "understand" all speech it can capture. We can imagine enough storage to make a record of our whole lives—everything we see and hear, everyone we meet, and so on. We see hints of the future—imagine a future in which we can look at the real world and see, in real time, the "cyber manifestation" of every object there. We see the beginnings of digital money, and the implantation of cyber technology inside us—the vision of the "cyborg." At the low end, the space of shrinking costs, we see the embedding of information technology (IT) into "everything," sometimes called the "Internet of Things." Light bulbs and light switches, thermostats and toasters—all of these exist in an online form today. In ten years, they will be commonplace.

What are the implications of these trends? Even if the exact predictions are wrong, we will see the increasing penetration of cyber technology into "everything," both physically and in terms of every aspect of our lives. We see more and more aspects of society going online, from money to war to discourse. We have already become increasingly dependent on this technology, and thus increasingly threatened by its complexity, its opacity, and the possibility of failure. At this writing, cybersecurity, variously defined, has already become an issue of major concern for both public and private actors and entities at all layers of the Internet and levels of international relations.

10.4   Standards and Standards Organizations

As discussed earlier in chapter 9, standard setting is fundamental to the entire process of technological change. Good standards define well-understood interfaces, and thus well-defined industry boundaries. A standard constrains the behavior at the point of interaction among the parts, but equally decouples the innovation that is internal to each part. So well-defined system modularity with well-defined standards is key to innovation and evolution.

In dynamic markets, there is a tension (in fact, a competition) between organizations to produce standards that are most "fit for purpose." In most of cyberspace there has been little success imposing standards from a "state legitimized" body; private sector standards bodies, such as the Internet Engineering Task Force (IETF), have been more nimble and effective than state-centered bodies such as International Telecommunication Union (ITU) in setting standards that are fit. In fact, industry players sometimes see the IETF itself as moving too slowly, and create industry consortia (with limited agenda and limited membership) to allow them to move more rapidly. Once again, we see the ability of an organization to "out-evolve" its competitors and survive in the space of rapid co-evolution as key to success.

Standards are critical to the state, the market, the users, and the international system. From a control point perspective, standards are a path, perhaps *the* path, to the creation of points of control for the state in cyberspace. Given the growing tendency of all states to exert control over cyber-based interactions, an important, practical question for the state system is how it can exercise influence over the standards process to achieve its goals. Of course, standards are not the only venues for state control. A story may illustrate this process in action.

The tool of "lawful intercept" or "wiretapping" is a part of police and intelligence procedures in most countries. In the late 1990s, the U.S. government became concerned with its ability to carry out lawful intercept (e.g., wiretap) on phone calls over the Internet. The U.S. Communications Assistance for Law Enforcement Act (CALEA), passed in 1994, required that manufacturers of telecommunications equipment design their equipment so that it had built-in surveillance capabilities, but that law did not apply to Internet equipment. So the U.S. government went to the IETF and requested it develop standards for lawful intercept over the Internet. The IETF, as a private sector, international institution, politely refused, saying that one country (the United States) should not presume to direct an international group, and that the IETF did not work on issues that relate to policy (IAB and IESG 2000).

One interesting aspect of the position taken by the IETF is that they consider themselves an international body. Lawful intercept is an international concern, so a possible response by the U.S. government would have been to find an international venue to push for the creation of international regulations. In fact, the Convention on Cybercrime, a European treaty drawn up in 2001, refers to lawful intercept. However, this approach might well have bogged down in disagreements about the specifics of the regulation and the jurisdiction to regulate.

Instead, governments proceeded more informally. The history is not well documented, but we can deduce the following events. First, perhaps as a result of informal discussion across law enforcement agencies in different countries, several European countries encouraged their equipment vendors to push for standards for lawful intercept, working with a more compliant standards body: the European Telecommunications Standards Institute

(ETSI). ETSI produced a series of standards, starting with a requirements document in 2001.[6] In 2005 and 2006, the U.S. Federal Communications Commission (FCC), under their authority to impose regulation pursuant to CALEA, released Report and Orders that clarified that CALEA applied to carrier-based voice over Internet protocol (VoIP) and VoIP interconnected to the PSTN.[7] While the IETF position continued to be that they would not standardize methods and interfaces for lawful intercept, the IETF did publish in 2004 an informational document from Cisco, the largest manufacturer of Internet routers and related equipment, describing their architecture for lawful intercept (Baker et al. 2004). While not a standard, this document offered a possible approach that other vendors might follow.

By 2013, the revelations of massive National Security Agency surveillance make clear that the government had in place widespread and effective tools for interception of Internet traffic. One could argue whether moving from initial rebuff in 2000 to a massive, installed surveillance infrastructure by 2013 is evidence of rapid or slow progress. However, an important factor in this case is that although the government did try to regulate compliance by industry, they also expended substantial public funds to build their own technology. When the government uses its own funds, it can proceed closer to the pace of technology and less at the pace of regulation.

It remains to be determined if this case is portable. But there is a broader implication of this story. Standards are largely set by equipment makers. Operators (e.g., the Internet service providers, ISPs) can push their suppliers to deliver one or another sort of device, but only the large operators have the power to exercise this influence. Most operators are "standards takers," not "standards makers." The previous story shows that countries can align to influence their equipment makers to desired outcomes, but only countries with a significant IT equipment industry can participate in this game.

Countries with no IT industry, including essentially the entire developing world (with the exception of China, India, and perhaps others), thus become "standards takers" as well, with no ability to influence the creation (or not) of control points. Some of the pressure from the developing world to empower the ITU seems to come from a sense that this is the only way they can get a seat at the table, but the problem with this approach is that it invokes an institution with a tradition of very slow evolution. The fear of many parties is that if the ITU actually acquired power in this space, the outcome would be the option we listed before of slowing the rate of innovation to the pace of ITU evolution.

There is a cleavage worldwide regarding the ITU and its operations. On the one hand are China and most developing countries, which see the ITU as a useful venue to shape cyberspace. On the other hand is the United States, the European states, and select others, who prefer a less-state-centered approach. The debates over the role of the ITU can be seen as a proxy for an underlying contest, namely whose principles, norms, and values will dominate cyberspace in decades to come?

A related aspect of this situation is the emergence of competing technology, often embodying different standards, from which countries can pick to effect their preferred approach to control. The Chinese have developed a large IT industry, typified by the Chinese router company Huawei, and are now selling this equipment aggressively to the developing world. They compete on price (often using pricing strategies that regulated American and European firms cannot match), but to some extent the competition may be driven by different capabilities for domestic control embedded in the equipment.[8] For China, however, this type of situation follows a long-standing strategy to penetrate deep into the markets of developing countries, including the less affluent.

10.5   Business and the Private Sector

As the previous discussion illustrates, the rapid pace of innovation enabled by Moore's law causes the landscape of the private sector to evolve rapidly. There is an aphorism from business schools: "all advantage is temporary." Nowhere is this more true than in the IT sector, where competitive advantage (in competitive economies) can be gained and lost in only a few years, if not months. As we look at the rise and fall and reincarnation of old and traditional firms like IBM, and newer firms like Microsoft, we have to imagine that our giants of today—Google, Facebook, or Twitter, for example—will also suffer this emergent and, as we understand it, inevitable fate. Yesterday Blackberry, today the iPhone. Like the Red Queen, firms have to run hard just to stay in place.

10.5.1   The Layers Model

Our layer model in chapter 2 is a useful framework through which to understand the character of change in business and the private sector.

10.5.1.1   The physical layer   At the *physical* layer, we see a massive rebuilding of the world's communications infrastructure, replacing our old "telephone wires" with fiber and radio. We see investment to push this new technology into essentially all the world, a trend gated by the fact that labor and sources of capital do not follow a Moore's law cost function. Nevertheless, in ten or twenty years, we will be done in most parts of the world. In addition, because of the massive capacity of fiber optics, this effort will pay returns for several decades. This undertaking is transient in that, although it may take two or more decades, it will eventually take us to a new, stable place.

However, capital does not grow at a Moore's law pace, so the rate of evolution is gated in part by the need for capital expenditures, contingent on access to financial and other resources. The physical layer is tangible—it is fibers, towers, racks of hardware, and so on. Companies that have invested in physical assets, like fibers to the home, have a stable place in the ecosystem through that investment unless they have made a bad technology bet. The concept of "stranded investment" captures that risk, but we see firms such as Verizon, AT&T, or Comcast with a powerful and (apparently) relatively durable place in the market. Firms that grow based on an idea rather than on massive capital, like Facebook, can come (and perhaps go) quickly. A recurring tension in the commercial ecosystem is the constant pressure from the application innovators to seek new capabilities from the physical layer (e.g., more capacity to the home), whereas the investment in those capabilities must be made by a different set of firms.

Another physical manifestation of Moore's law is "the cloud." The emergence of the cloud is a current phenomenon of considerable importance. Despite the term, which suggests something of indefinite form and structure, the cloud is very physical—it is large data centers, drawing large amounts of power. The cloud allows the movement of storage and processing from smaller computers at the edge to these larger computers in these centers. For small firms, there are cost advantages to this move—firms no longer have to have as much expertise in running their own data systems. However, in order for them to make this move, the cloud industry must build up a framework of trust and dependability that companies can accept. The tensions that arise between the cost advantages on the one hand and the loss of control (or the transfer of trust into the cloud) on the other hand, are gating the move to the cloud.

10.5.1.2 The platform layer Within the platform layer, we see a wide range of dynamics. At the *Internet* sublayer, we see the durability of some key specifications (e.g., the specifications of the Internet itself) providing a stable foundation for rapid innovation at other layers. The specifications of the

Internet do evolve, as we see with the current effort, as we write this book, to convert the Internet to a new version that supports more addresses, but they evolve slowly, at the pace of human debate and capital deployment. Firms that operate at this layer, ISPs, face a tension in their business structure. The service that they offer, which is basic Internet transport service, is constrained and defined by that stable standard, so they can evolve their service offering only by improvements in those aspects of the Internet service that are not defined by that standard. However, if they try to evolve that service platform in ways that are unique to their particular firm, this effort disrupts the uniformity of the platform to the application sublayer that sits on top of this one. So they face a challenge in distinguishing themselves competitively, and run the risk of becoming providers of a commodity service.

In contrast, in the *application* sublayer, we see the process of innovation driven at almost frantic rates by the potential of a ten times improvement in the underlying technology every five years. Innovators dream, wait, and move when the technology permits, to try out ever new and surprising concepts.

10.5.1.3 The information layer At the *information* layer, we see the creation, storage, search, and retrieval of essentially all forms of data—information, content, knowledge, and so on—moving online. There seems to be no end to the explosion of information because the costs of storage decline on a Moore's law basis, and because we now realize that perhaps the most valuable forms of information are information about other pieces of information—sometimes called meta-data. Meta-data records things like the format, provenance, ownership, veracity of data, and abstract representations of data, such as a list of the identity of every person in a picture. We now record all transactions online—every purchase, every query, every interaction. We bemoan the loss of privacy, which will be a pivotal debate in society in the next decade. But the data is being recorded, and it is hard to imagine this trend will be reversed.

The combination of moving data online and massive computation suggests a future in which each individual gets a unique, tailored view of the stored information. The daily paper, the results of searches, and even more persistent information may look different to every person who sees it.

At the same time as we see this massive explosion of information enabled by the exponential growth in storage capacity, we also see this layer anchored in a need for deep stability. Formats for data must be stable or yesterday's stored information will be unreadable tomorrow. Any time we store information online, we are making an implicit assumption that the standards that define how that information was stored will be stable.

10.5.1.4 The people layer At the *people* level, on the one hand we see a transformative empowerment from the deployment of technology in the hands of users, and on the other hand, we see human capabilities that do not grow on a Moore's law curve. We do not get twice as smart, or twice as capable of processing information, every eighteen months. So we drown in "information overload" and call for even more technology to control the flood, which makes us even more dependent on the trustworthy operation of cyberspace. Issues of trust—its formation, its abuse, and its role as the basis of living in cyberspace—will be central to the next decade.

10.5.2 The Diverse Scope of Firms

One of the dimensions that distinguishes different layers in the private sector is the scope—domestic or international—of the firms. Firms at the physical layer, with their fibers and towers, are fixed "on the face of the earth" by those investments, cannot easily move, and are to a large extent domestic. Firms at the higher layers are more easily international. The global uniformity of the platform layer of the Internet (the key specifications that make it stable) means that an application running on this layer can be invoked or provided anywhere. The firm that creates the application may have a location in just one country or many at the same time that its application is used globally.

To some extent, the same consideration is true at the information layer, but there are both technical and jurisdictional issues that shape the scope of firms at the information layer. At the present time (and this is probably a temporary advantage, like all advantages), the United States has many of the large data centers or "cloud" facilities. Data from abroad is coming into the United States for storage and manipulation. This raises concerns about inconsistent privacy policies and the accessibility of this data to our intelligence services.

The easy fluidity of economic activity at these higher layers, the easy portability of data, global homogeneity, and the relative stability (to some extent) of the lower layers provide a powerful driver for globalization, as we defined in chapter 1. In cyberspace, the barriers to access in a global market, although still substantial, are lower than in spaces that are more physical.

And even when physical goods have to be shipped globally, improvements in the cost and efficiency of shipping have made global marketing in cyberspace effective, even for physical goods.

While there are many firms that populate the different layers at different scopes and jurisdictions, they are all driven by a similar set of motives—economic survival, profitability and growth, and competitive advantage. In general, firms have a uniform challenge—produce products that are preferred by their customers (perhaps shaping customer preference in the process)—initially in their home markets but eventually and often very rapidly in the international market. For this reason, to the extent there is an emergent homogeneity in customer demand, there will be a convergence to products that meet that demand, which may favor the emergence of global firms. When divergence and diversity emerge, then market conditions will allow more opportunity for market entry.

Of course, all of this is contingent on rules, regulations, legal regimes, and the like. In general, the role of the state is a powerful determinant, not only about the nature of the private sector but also of the drivers of innovation in the IT sector as well as in all productive activity more broadly defined. States differ widely in their relations with, and management of, the firm or the degree of management or control of the private sector. Even the most laissez faire economies are expected to recognize and operate within the laws of the state. This variation may help shape both structure and process of the international political economy and the distribution (and redistribution) of power and of wealth. Especially at the higher layers, which are less capital intensive and more dependent on imagination and innovative thinking, the opportunities for the developing world may be substantial.

10.6 The State and the International System

While private sector profit-seeking firms have a common motivation (economic survival, profitability, and growth), the state has a range of objectives, which are sometimes unrelated, sometimes in tension, and sometimes highly variable across different states. In chapter 1 and later in chapter 3, we signaled the general elements in states' strategic calculations. Here we review briefly some salient considerations.

States differ in the dominance of individual master variables relative to the others. This is true for the absolute levels as well as for the rates of change. These differences go a long way in explaining modes of behavior in international relations. When the state extends its activities beyond its borders, then its interests and activities can intersect with those of other states. Such intersections are near inevitable in world politics and are often features of competitive markets. They do not necessarily lead to hostilities, but they mark a first step, an important threshold, in the dynamics of conflict and violence. Similarly, firms and corporations are also driven by different factors in their propensities for expansion, both in direction and form. All evidence suggests a relatively close coupling between the growth and expansion of the home states, on the one hand, and the firm or corporate entities, on the other. For empirical support of this observation see Choucri (1993a). While differential change is at the root of lateral pressure, the consequences are far from deterministic. There are pathways and trajectories other than overt violence.

To date, the user population for access to cyberspace is and continues to be driven by the same core master variables, i.e., interactions among *technology*, (the applications of knowledge in various forms, and the manifestation of Moore's law), *population* (that is the size, skills, organization and capabilities of people) in conjunction with *resources* in various forms (economic, financial, and other assets that facilitate, even enhance, the user experience). It is not clear if these expectations will persist. The direct innovations associated with cyberspace (a version of the "IT revolution") have been the driver of much economic performance and indirectly the driver of anticipated improvements in productivity across the economy. This outcome is more likely to be the case in advanced industrial economies than in developing ones. However, we have seen cases in which adoption of advanced information technologies among the less-developed countries has been at rapid rates. For example, we wrote in chapter 5 that the growth of Chinese access to cyberspace is noteworthy, as is the increased use of the Chinese language. (So, too, the most rapid rate of increase in a non-English language is for Arabic.)

As states respond to many of their cyber-related concerns, they inject their own objectives and dynamics into the evolution of cyberspace. These may be more structured than the incoherent evolution we see, for example, in the rampant innovation of the application layer, but at the same time some may be in tension with each other, which both slows and, at worst, confounds the pursuit of the goals.

10.6.1   Security and Stability

As noted in earlier in this book, national security in all its dimensions and manifestations is always a central goal of the state—in the Western model or otherwise. All states are defined by territoriality and sovereignty and, in theory at least, seek to protect these attributes (and in some cases to expand as well). As we have discussed previously, security of cyberspace is now rising to the level of other dimensions of security. This goal would seem to call for regulation and control of cyberspace, to shape it so that prevention, detection, and deterrence can be effective.

This goal is related to another key feature of overall national security, namely that of internal order—the ability to carry out policing, enforce laws, and sustain a stable regime. Different states take different views about the role of cyberspace in a stable regime of governance, whether it is to allow all voices to be heard or to regulate speech to control unacceptable points of view. In stable pluralistic societies, the desire to enforce laws tends to call for accountability, by mapping from action to actor, whereas unfettered speech may call for the right of anonymity and private assembly. In the United States, much of the effort of the government to control behavior (and regulate content) on the Internet has centered on the protection of the private rights of copyright holders. In other countries, other values dominate. In still others, the effective regulation of behavior and content is often related to regime stability.

10.6.2   Power and Prosperity

In principle, economic growth and prosperity is a central matter for the state system. In practice, the salience of this goal differs from case to case. In recent years, there has been a subtle reassessment and shift in some countries of both the principle and practice, from an emphasis on growth to one of sustainable development, from material prosperity to overall human well-being.

So far, much of the innovation in cyberspace has been "made in the USA," but as capabilities expand and propensities for innovation diffuse worldwide, we are likely to see "made elsewhere." While it took decades for us to observe the trend in "made in Japan" and then "made in China," it is unlikely that the same time frame will hold in the IT sector or in the derivatives for the cyber domain. We would expect much more rapid entry of competitors and innovators than we have seen in the traditional economy.

In this connection, it is difficult to address these issues in a cultural or politically neutral venue or vocabulary. For example, the very issue of "liberalization" is intensely political, defined differently in economic versus political arenas, as defined by norms of the Western world and its historical experience. Its portability to other states and cultures and other parts of the world is limited in its relevance and propriety. The same may be said of concepts such as efficiency and equity. To simplify, some societies assign greater value to efficiency than equity, others value equity more than efficiency. Underlying these observations is a persistent struggle, a tussle, over shaping the future of global values.

10.6.3 "Network Neutrality"

The regulatory goal referred to as "network neutrality"—in the United States, Europe, Japan, and select other states—is an attempt to intervene in the private sector Internet ecosystem to balance the power of different sets of actors, the access ISPs versus the higher-level providers of applications and content.

The term network neutrality refers to the expectation that ISPs will not exercise unreasonable discrimination in the treatment of traffic from different sources. ISPs will not favor their own content, for example, over that of a competitor. It is an attempt to balance innovation at the application layer with investment at the physical layer. It is also a good example of different outcomes of the Red Queen's hypothesis in the co-evolution of regulation and business practice. In the United States, the FCC has promulgated three sets of rules with respect to neutrality, the third after the first two were challenged and overturned in the courts. The third attempt has not been overturned by the courts, but the FCC under the current Republican administration has voted to undo that third set of rules. This is a clear example of a case where the law as it shapes regulation seems not "fit for purpose" and has been out-evolved by the shape of technology. Other countries have taken very different and aggressive stances in imposing constraints on their ISP sector, including, for example, the approach in the United Kingdom of imposing structural separation on their incumbent telecoms provider, and splitting it into two firms, one at the physical layer and one at the platform layer.

10.6.4 Cyber Access

Many states have taken the view that the population should be able (and encouraged) to partake of the cyber experience (e.g., get onto the Internet) and have used both regulation and direct investment to encourage the build-out of broadband access. Many, if not most, have also invested in e-government capabilities. In parts of the developing world, the focus has been on wireless access, and the typical access device is a smartphone. Many others have taken the view that "denial of service" is necessary to protect critical social values. Almost all states have selected a denial of service posture at one point or another over one issue or other, as we have shown in chapter 8.

This assessment is necessarily incomplete—the concerns of the state are many and varied—as we have noted in chapter 5. In general, given the broad range of concerns, there can often be emergent tensions. More controls or fewer? More accountability or less? How much priority to give to direct investment versus regulation of the private sector? And so on.

While we recognize that social rates of change do not and cannot match the technological rates, we must also highlight the differentials in rates of change across different facets of society and institutions. By definition, institutions are expected to retain a certain degree of stability and robustness, on the one hand, but we also recognize the potential inertia that prevents adaptation to changing conditions and requires some form of institutional resilience, on the other hand.

In each of these contingencies, and all others, there are effects on the extent to which the state is a driver of change, a manager of transformation, or a controller of emergent trajectories. Even in competitive states, where the market shapes winners and losers, we have seen large-scale innovations initially supported and financed by the state. Thus, it would be superficial, even erroneous, to consider the state and the public sector versus the private sector and the economy as two mutually exclusive drivers of change for the integrated cyber-IR system. An equally, if not more salient distinction, may well be between the internal drivers as sources of innovation, on the one hand, and the external drivers as recipients or reactive sources of innovation, on the other.

10.7 Civil Society—Local and Global

Here we note briefly the consolidation and eventual politicization of civil society—as distinct from the public sector or the private for-profit sector—and its relevance to the co-evolution processes. Civil society at any level consists of diverse interests with different degrees of power and influence.

Diversity itself allows for coalition and alliance formation and, clearly, for efficient uses of information exchanges. Because of the many segments of civil society, it is useful to distinguish between those that operate within some legal framework and those that would generally be considered nonlegitimate. Each may have notable effects on co-evolution.

Civil society is at once an aggregate constituency and an aggregate consumer. Its activities and influences cross borders and are often difficult to contain by the state. In addition, recent tendencies to invite nonstate groups to participate in international deliberations (as nonvoting entities) reflect a form of legitimization by the state system. Alternatively, the traditional institutions may consider it less costly to include than to exclude their involvement in deliberations. Again, this reflects the new "voicing" enabled by cyber access.

Civil society has a "bottom-up" institutional form, even if its emergence results from the sanction of the state. Groups of people, acting in common interest, have shown a high degree of creativity and innovation in adapting the tools of cyberspace as they emerge, such as social networking, blogging, and cyber protest. Generally, this "learning" also involves increased politicization and greater mobilization and organization in the pursuit of stated goals. Since this organization is generally voluntary, it is always contingent on the role of individuals in the process of aggregation and articulation of interests.

When these behaviors run counter to the interests of the state, the result is a co-evolution race between the nimble features of a small group and the more deliberative but often more powerful forces of the state. In an earlier chapter, we pointed to the Arab Spring in Egypt, its "eruption," the speed with which the government adopted coercive measures, and resulting efforts to bypass the Internet and use more traditional means of communication. And in chapter 5 we noted examples of denial of service by a large number of states, including democracies. Clearly, the state system demonstrates increasing mastery of the means to infiltrate the tools of activists and opponents. If we look at the methods of censorship that we see in China, it would seem that the state is developing the ability to evolve its tools at a rate that keeps them fit for purpose.

10.8 Illegitimates and Criminality

If we turn to the illegitimates—criminals, terrorists, banned movements, illegal immigrants, and the like—it is easy to see that they play a special role in the co-evolution of cyberspace. It is not the illegitimates that change the character of cyberspace but the response to them in terms of new tools and mechanisms for detection and elimination. One of the lessons of cybercrime is that cybercriminals have learned the power of rapid evolution and have developed (or can purchase) the necessary skills to "out-evolve" the police. The response of law enforcement, not surprisingly, is to deemphasize fighting crime in the parts of cyberspace where evolution can occur rapidly and concentrate on those regions that evolve less quickly (such as money laundering). Some of the crimes that seem the hardest to combat (such as the sharing of child pornography) are those that also seem to lack a stable point of control. (Much child pornography is not bought and sold, but traded, in which case there is no money flow to track.)

The desire for enforcement and deterrence may lead to calls for better accountability, restrictions on patterns of use, and the like, which overall may imply a loss of potential for innovation. If we encourage only innovations that cannot have "bad uses," then we greatly limit the options for innovation, because there are few useful tools that have that character. Alternatively, as noted earlier, the growth of illegitimates is already framing new demand for technological and organizational responses. While the idiom of an arms race is not entirely appropriate here, the escalatory dynamic is particularly apt.

This leads us to a related, seemingly minor, issue, but one with potentially important implications. We do not know the extent of collusion and cooperation among different types of illegitimates or within one type. But we do know that law enforcement agencies do seek to cooperate, despite the often-overwhelming difficulties, and we should consider that fact in a favorable light. By contrast, however, there is inconsistent evidence of great cooperation among private sector actors who have been the victim of illegal cyber activities. On face value at least, we can see how different actors could influence such co-evolution trajectories.

There is an added issue that is increasingly problematic, namely understanding the extent to which "illegitimates" and "criminals" are state-based—that is, supported directly or indirectly by the state. Some may actually operate as instruments of the state.

10.9   Evolution of Governance and International Institutions

The previous discussion of the role of the state as a driver of change (and associated impediments) centered on issues that were largely internal. Given the
structure of the state system and the gradual emergence of a global agenda,
it is not surprising that internal responses to the salience of cyberspace lead
to or intersect with concerted international responses. International institutions found an important role in connecting the cyber domain to a growing
interest in information and communication technologies in the context of
the discourse on the global agenda as we noted in chapter 9.

For domestic issues, where the deliberation is local to the state, a single
state can use its sovereign powers in largely unilateral terms to shape its domestic policy, and it is likely to adopt a more homogeneous view of its priorities.
As discussed earlier, the formation of a shared perspective in international
contexts requires consensus building across states and related interests, sustained deliberation, and accommodation—all in the absence of overarching authority to manage the process, regulate the outcomes, and facilitate
implementation. Nonetheless, international institutions have become a
critical arena for framing the operational responses of co-evolution and
even seeking to forge new directions. All of this takes place in a context for
cooperation that invariably involves a degree of conflict and contention.
Invariably, the nature of the process itself becomes a fundamental requisite
for increasing propensity toward agreement.

The ecosystem of international organizations itself is evolving rapidly,
but there are a few generalizations that we can hazard at this moment.
The practical business of international negotiation and deliberation
around cyberspace is increasingly complex. Different facets are managed
by different entities and often in different contexts. The major traditional
international organization focused on information and communications
technology, the ITU, is increasingly seeking more influence in the cyber
arena. To date, its operational influence in quite limited.

The traditional state-centered institutions like the ITU embody the traditional pace of international deliberation. While they are challenged to
increase their speed to the pace of cyberspace evolution, they have shown
limited success in efforts to influence or shape the evolving "rules of the
road." As noted earlier, institutions by their very nature are designed to

regularize and routinize behavior; they are not intended to be optimally responsive to change.

This all stands in sharp contrast to the highly distributed and decentralized governance of the Internet, discussed in chapter 9, a system based on voluntary principles, not on the state or the state system. We have characterized this mode as less formal, less rigidly institutionalized, highly "bottom-up" arrangements that literally bypass state regulation, with its instruments and mechanisms.[9] It is also more adaptive and responsive than normal international mechanisms.

The nature of international institutions raises an important question, perhaps leading to a generalization for policy, technology, and society nationally and internationally. Should the primary goal of institutional performance be the speed of cyberspace? Should it be intermediation that is accommodating to the simultaneous salience of cyber speed and social speed? Should goals and principles guide the co-evolution of either or both of the cyber and the social domains, specifically international relations? And where does the creation of consensus among contending views and principles—actors and actions—fit in?

We noted earlier that one outcome in this co-evolutionary system is that the pace of evolution is slowed to the pace of state-centered deliberation and policy making. Transferring key control to an institution such as the ITU might have that effect, whether explicitly desired or not. Perhaps the preference that some states have for the ITU as a venue to resolve cyber issues is exactly to slow the pace of change to a rate they can internalize and comprehend. Or perhaps such preferences are driven by the desire to establish state control over the private sector in this domain.

Another issue, perhaps a generalization as well, comes from a study of how these different institutions acquire and maintain their authority and legitimacy. State-centered organizations claim their legitimacy by virtue of international treaty, and thus from the power of the collective sovereign states. Bottom-up private sector organizations have no such claim. To the extent they have authority, it is operational in nature. It is because they are immediately responsive to situations that can develop almost overnight, and they are effective. They have been "born" with the cyber era and live in a competitive region of the ecosystem where they themselves must "out-evolve" other organizations.

Many of these organizations take the business of evolution of their domain-specific responsibilities very seriously and explicitly. They are sensitive to their own constituencies. To the extent that they remain effective, they will facilitate the overarching trajectory of the common goals that are being articulated. Are state-based ISPs less, more, or as effective than those managed by the private sector? So we have another articulation of our co-evolution dilemma. The state system and international institutions are not likely to leave cyber management or the governance of cyberspace entirely to the private sector, however efficient or effective. Is the authority in this area based on legal mandate, or is it established as a function of performance?

Given what we know about the Westphalian system, at the highest level of generalization, it will force security to dominate efficiency. However, there is no theory or framework to clarify how this high-level imperative will interact with all of the ongoing, private sector activities that are driving change.

10.10   The Search for Stable Points[10]

In the previous sections, we have considered various sectors that make up the cyber ecosystem, with a focus on their rates of change and the drivers of that change. In doing so, we have referenced several outcomes that we deduced from our application of the Red Queen's hypothesis—an actor slow in adaptation and responsive to change, as are most states, may be out-evolved and not remain fit for purpose. But a slow actor may try to speed up to the rate of the faster actor, or slow the faster actor to the natural rate of the slower one. There is yet another possibility, which is that a slower actor finds stable points in the operational architecture of cyberspace onto which they can exercise control.

The consideration of stable points (or points of system stability) that can provide points of government control without impeding innovation and evolution is a substantial effort that is beyond the scope of this book. However, our work on control point analysis, discussed in chapter 6, provides one approach to this exercise, as does a careful, technology-centered study of the layer structure.

There are different stable points in cyberspace today. Stable points are constraints that the ecosystem has settled on in order to allow other parts of the ecosystem to be unconstrained. In some cases, these are specifically and intentionally designed with this goal in mind; in other cases they emerge organically. But they are deeply technical at their roots. For example, many stable points exist because they define interfaces between components.

Some examples of stable points (and their potential for control) may help to make the previous discussion more concrete.

- The basic specifications of the Internet have not changed since the beginning of the 1980s. They provide a fixed anchor that allows the technology below them (the physical transmission technologies) to evolve independently of the applications above them. So long as both the transmission technology and the application conform to the interface specification that links them, innovation is freed in both spaces.

- The instruction set of a processor (the set of basic steps a computer can execute) is a somewhat stable point. Since processors (hardware) and software are usually not all replaced at once, a new processor must be able to run the same programs (e.g., execute the same instructions) as the old one. A move from one "instruction set" to another is a major transition, although not as major as replacing the specifications of the Internet.

- The formats of information are a stable point. Information is usually intended to be long lasting. If formats are replaced and the software to process old formats is lost, information itself becomes unreadable and is lost. Data formats (for example, Portable Document Format or PDF) are long lasting.

Each of these examples provides options for integrating controls into the architecture of cyberspace. But each also signals the potential trade-offs associated with a decision.

- If a requirement for identity had been included in the specifications of the Internet, we would have more accountability but no anonymity. The current design choice is an explicit one, and in fact one of us has argued that embedding accountability and identity into the specification of the Internet would both be ineffective and contrary to many important societal needs (Clark and Landau 2010).

- If tools for protection of copyright material were built into the instruction set of a processor (a proposal that is called digital rights management or DRM hardware) the architecture of content control would become more durable. Again, this idea is contentious—there are arguments that this approach would not meet the needs of the copyright holders but would have very high economic and public costs.

- If document formats such as PDF included, in an unforgeable way, the identity of the creator, one could verify the provenance and validity of a piece of information without having to confirm where it came from. This idea is actually not highly contentious, and its lack is probably a serious error in design.

In sum, if the state attaches regulations to stable points, then it targets its influence without interfering with the evolutionary potential of other parts of cyberspace. If the concerns of the state can be addressed by exercise of influence over these stable points, the slower rate of adaptation by the state becomes less of a concern. This may also hold true with respect to state control of the physical layer, including exchange points, for example.

The complexities surrounding stable points and their potential role as points of control are daunting. The challenge of how to position stable control points into the fabric of cyberspace is complex, highly technical, highly political, and subtle, sometimes with unanticipated consequences. But there is always a decision, a set of actors, and underlying interests.

The discourse that has not happened (and indeed to which there is a bit of resistance) is whether stable points should be put into the architecture of cyberspace specifically to facilitate certain forms of state control. A conversation around this point would require a combination of technologists and experts in law and the concerns of governments. At the moment, there is no call for this conversation and no venue in which it could occur. Today, when governments meet (as with the ITU), the technologists are not typically at center stage. In addition, all "rational" actors in this or other ecosystems—be they technologists, educators, or governments—pursue their own interests first and foremost, and second tend to the viability of the ecosystem as a whole.

Increasingly, however, it is commonplace for governments to include scientists and technologists in their national delegations at international meetings. We have seen this in nuclear weapons negotiations, deliberations over the terms of environmental treaties, discussions of international health policies and standards, and so forth. At this point, there is no forum today where these issues around cyberspace are discussed in depth, and there is no way to identify larger social or state requirements and "throw them over the fence" into the hands of technologists, stakeholders, lawyers, or other groups. Among the many reasons is that the state has interests that are not always entirely consonant with one another; the tensions among the interests of the state impede the clear articulation of any design requirements. Therefore, the process of understanding how the relatively participatory state can exercise control over cyberspace proceeds in incremental and sometimes fragmentary ways, but such a process is perhaps all we could expect of the real world.

10.11   Endnote: What Have We Learned?

As we have said, the twenty-first-century reality is one in which the cyber domain and the social system—in all layers of the Internet and at all levels of analysis—are interconnected and so mutually interdependent. The two systems, which were once parallel and then gradually become joined, have generated a new "whole" whose features, dynamics, and overall "sum" are greater than what were once its individual parts.

10.11.1   The Enduring Anchor

The international decision context may have changed, but the high-level characteristics of the state and its objectives are not altered by the emergence of cyberspace, yet they may be seriously challenged. Even at the definitional level, when we consider sovereignty and territoriality as basic features of the state, interactions in the cyber domain are hardly designed to respect these requisites. Almost all states are responding to these realities by seeking to exert control "at the border" or at relevant junctures in network architecture. Few states, if any, have adopted a "hands-off" approach to infringements on sovereignty and territoriality.

Already many states are attempting to regulate cyber access. Here the domain of control is defined by the principle of jurisdiction. At the regional level, a set of institutions have been developed to facilitate coordinate and transition from global governance to state implementation, as discussed in chapter 9. At the global level, the entire cyber system is, to date, managed and dominated by the private sector. But it is at the international level that the contentions are unfolding over control and governance.

These requisites of statehood—the Westphalia design—relate to the state and its external environment. However, we cannot ignore the internal features that challenge the state, the regime, and the government, most notably the increased autonomy of action available to individuals via cyber access. This is generally true for all states regardless of regime type or form of government. However, as we have seen in chapter 7, the United States and China demonstrate two very different models of state control over the cyber domain.

The concerns of the state we list in section 10.5 are persistent and foundational. What seems to have changed is the power of the state to effect control, and the time constants of the co-evolution will be a challenge to the traditional deliberative tools of the state. Ironically, or perhaps by necessity, states appear to state the adoption of e-government in their own operations and in communication with its citizens (and people within its borders). "Electronic filing" is now part of our common vocabulary, as is "distance learning," and a host of related initiatives that can be seen as the state seeking to improve its performance.

The state can use the tools of cyberspace directly—it can mine data and monitor communication, even without the engineering of new points of control. The control point analysis of China, in chapter 7, demonstrates a streamlined structure that facilitates control (Hung 2012). China is the case of a state redefining the points of control in its cyberspace to implement its goals. But it does so in a platform designed for greater control when compared to the United States. In China it appears that several outcomes are happening at the same time—the Chinese Internet is far more controlled, based on explicit changes imposed on its design and operation (Yangyue 2015). It is also a venue for personal expression of opinion and a force for liberalization of the norms of acceptable speech. This seeming duality in China can be generalized across all states in the sense that controlling individual voicing is becoming increasingly difficult and in some cases near impossible. In some cases, it takes the action of only one individual to demonstrate the vulnerability of the state.

The question for the United States, or for any country, is how active, organized, and coherent a role it can or wants to play in this evolution. For the United States this question is particularly relevant given that the cyber domain evolved out of initial investments and research support provided by the government. It is often tempting to emphasize the role of the private sector in the operation and routinization of innovation—and in augmenting innovative applications and capabilities—but we cannot ignore, let alone forget, the origins of the cyber domain. All this took place at a time when the United States was arguably the only power in world politics, and the only state with financial resources supported by a tradition of investments in research and development. The world today is not that of the mid-twentieth century.

10.11.2   Co-Evolution and Emergent Order

Much of the forgoing is a precursor to an overarching challenge, namely the management of co-evolution in the context of global governance. At this point, the co-evolution of cyberspace and international relations has reached a degree of convergence that in all likelihood will not, or cannot, be reversed. Some states are able to manage the internal effects of convergence; most others will accommodate or adapt as conditions allow.

Concurrently, but also related to the forgoing, is the remarkable growth of nonstate international entities and the expansion of cross-border organizations intent on influencing the global agenda in both deliberations and resulting outcomes. At this writing, we are witnessing a worldwide "tussle" of authority over the control of access to the cyber domain at the national level. In chapter 9, we briefly reviewed the development of major international conferences designed to address cyber governance. The clear evidence is that the cyber and the real or traditional international relations domain can no longer remain separable.

At this point, there are multiple, diverse, and variable centers of power that interact to eventually shape emergent trajectories of global policies of priorities. The state system is losing its monopoly over control of who participates in deliberations over *who gets what, when,* and *how.* Recall that what began more as a basic mantra, namely the term "stakeholders," is now acknowledged as a formal status in the international deliberations. One important outcome of the forgoing is the increased density of entities that are involved in one way or another in some facet of international decision making.

The salient dynamics are already apparent—the international community is now trying to grapple with a new international system, one that requires new forms of international relations and a reassessment of "who counts" and "how" as well as "why"—and what to do about all of this.

Especially important in this connection is the growing scale and scope of discourse around global governance. Earlier, in chapter 5, we signaled the consolidation of the three domains of human interaction recognized early in the twenty-first century: society, nature, and cyberspace. Figure 5.1

illustrated the potential spillover effects across all three domains. And in chapter 9, we noted that with WSIS and NETmundial we see a clear interdependence, even coupling of governance for the social and cyber systems. The linkages to the third system, the natural environment, are made through efforts to manage strategies for sustainability. In principle, sustainable development now spans all three domains; in practice, the governance principles and practices remain somewhat uneven in their coverage.

Earlier in chapter 5, too, we made brief reference to sustainability of the cyber system. To date, however, the focus on sustainability in both scholarly and policy circles centers on society and environment, and we have as yet hardly any discourse on the sustainability of the cyber domain or on challenges to its viability. The recent interjection of threat to cybersecurity, a powerful fact of daily life in modern societies, signals a critical difference between the world before construction of the Internet and the world today with connectivity assumed to be the rule rather than the exception.

When we discuss the evolution of the Internet early in chapter 9—its origins and early years—we make little reference if any to matters of cybersecurity. This was not an omission on our part, rather a faithful adherence to the idiom and reality of the time. This is an idiom dominated by innovation and exploration, not by fear of threat or potentials of insecurity. At this point, we suggest that, in the best of all possible worlds, the next phase of co-evolution and of global governance must address threats to cybersecurity.

11 Alternative Futures: Trends and Contingencies

Drawing on what we have developed to this point, what can we infer about the future of cyberspace? In this chapter, we paint a number of pictures of possible futures for this co-evolving system. We draw on the earlier chapters and use the models and frameworks developed there to offer some inferences—clearly speculations—about the future. We do not *predict* the future—the drivers of change are too diverse and their interactions too unpredictable. But we can identify *critical drivers* and make some claims about likely directions.

We will draw on several of our lenses to map out possible futures:

1. the layer model
2. our levels of analysis model
3. our control point analysis model
4. our analysis of the governance of cyberspace.

These lenses are closely related, but very distinct in their perspectives and implications.

11.1 Change through the Lens of Layers

The layered model is particularly useful as a tool to study technology and policy futures, because the forces that drive the different layers are, as we have discussed, different in character.

11.1.1 The Physical Layer

At the physical layer, we see a number of important trends. The first is the change from a U.S.-centric pattern of wide area connectivity to a more mesh-like structure. In the early days of the Internet, most of the users and most of the information (e.g., Web pages) were in the United States. Undersea cables tended to run from the United States to other countries, as there was often a lack of direct paths between countries (or regulatory or economic barriers to the use of these paths). It was often cheaper to move data between two countries in Europe by sending it to the United States and back rather than utilizing a path directly between those countries.

A much more interconnected and decentralized mesh of interconnections has now displaced this pattern. What we see today is a natural shift to direct paths hooking nations together, both transoceanic (e. g., Brazil and Portugal) and overland. Construction of these paths is gated by the cost of construction, and as well, in some cases, by the need for international negotiation, but this trend seems like a natural consequence of the maturation of the physical global infrastructure. The emergence of Internet exchanges (IXs or IXPs as they are known) as physical points where inexpensive interconnection can be arranged among Internet service provider (ISPs) means that most traffic among ISPs today is exchanged directly, in what is sometimes called a "peering" interconnection—two networks that view themselves as peers in the ecosystem interconnect to exchange traffic.

11.1.2 The Platform Layer

The core definition of the Internet protocols has not changed. This stability, as we noted in chapter 10, is critical to the success of the Internet as a platform. However, there are many other ways in which the platform layer representing the Internet is changing.

The changes in the physical layer, described before, have led to dramatic reductions in the cost of sending traffic into the Internet. Costs for what is called "transit service"—a connection that gives access to the entire Internet—have dropped by orders of magnitude over the last two decades. In locations that are well supplied with connectivity and inexpensive exchange points, the cost may be as low as $1/month for each mb/s of connectivity, or, translating that into different terms, a cost of less than a penny to send a gigabyte of data. However, there is still wide variation in these costs across the globe. In parts of the developing world, the costs may be more than 10 times higher; in some places the costs are almost 100 times higher. This disparity greatly shapes variation in the Internet experience in different parts of the globe.

The low cost of technology based on the Internet protocols has led to the construction of other networks using that technology—not every network that runs the Internet protocols is "the Internet." There are corporate networks that span the globe, military networks that (one hopes) are separate from the Internet for security reasons, and so on. The economic benefits of moving all networking to this common technology is motivating a transition where the old "copper wire" circuit-switched telephone system will be decommissioned in favor of a voice over IP (VoIP) telephone system. Television transmission will move to an encoding based on IP. These networks may share the same physical resources as "the Internet" but are logically separate. However, the dependency on a common physical infrastructure and a common technology may lead to concerns about resilience and reliability. There might be common-mode failures that could bring down several of these networks at once.

The growth of capacity at the physical layer has enabled new sorts of applications to emerge, which for many users have led to a reconceptualization of what the Internet is. In the early days of the Internet, users equated the Internet to email. Later, they equated it to the Web. Now, many users equate the Internet to social networking and (in many parts of the world) Facebook in particular. To others, the Internet is now their source of video, with one firm (Netflix) responsible for over one-third of all the peak-hour residential traffic in the United States. Together with YouTube and some smaller providers, almost 60 percent of all residential traffic is streaming media, coming from only a handful of powerful companies. While there may be thousands of ISPs providing service around the globe, there are only a few powerful providers of services at the application layer.

11.1.3 The Application Layer

The application layer is marked by low barriers to entry and a rich potential for unexpected innovation. The generality of the platform layer invites a wide range of creative ideas to take root and try for success. In the current language of the users, whatever the problem, there is probably "an app for that." The platform ecosystem for application development is not just the Internet, as was the story only perhaps ten or fifteen years ago; it includes the cheap and ubiquitous computing and storage of cloud computing, global deployment of critical application components on content delivery networks, and the rich set of application development tools available for the Web and for the popular mobile platforms iPhone and Android. It is beyond the scope of this book to explore all the hints we can see about where the application experience might go, but there are some obvious trends, such as the merger of social networking, which is a rich form of communication among people, and video creation and delivery, an activity that is within reach of essentially anyone today. The blurring of prior boundaries (many of which were seen to exist only as an accident of prior cycles of innovation) raises challenges for governments who would regulate and seek stable points in the ecosystem as a point of control. Is Facebook in any way like a telephone company? Is it like a media company? Is the question even relevant?

A term that has recently entered the vocabulary of cyberspace is "Internet of Things" (IoT). The term is as much marketing and hype as reality—there is no homogeneous class of device that typifies IoT. In general terms, a "thing" is a device carrying out some fixed function, capable of communicating over the Internet and without the immediate direction of a human user. A thermostat, a fitness tracker, an Internet-enabled light switch and light bulb— these are all "things," as are devices in the context of industrial control, health care, the monitoring of public spaces, or the components of a self-driving car. The term "thing" was not a felicitous choice because it suggests a piece of hardware, which might cause us to position IoT as a physical layer concept. But it is the function of the device that is interesting—not that it is hardware but that it can control a furnace. In this respect, a better way to think about a "thing" is that it is an application (or a component of an application) embodied directly in dedicated hardware, as opposed to running on a general-purpose platform like a smartphone. Thus, we put consideration of IoT at the application layer.

What are the potential implications of IoT? First, it is a manifestation of a dominant trend in information and communication technology, a trend much older than the term IoT. As Moore's law makes computing, storage, and communication ever cheaper, there is a drive to exploit the potential benefit of putting those capabilities into more and more spaces. People have used examples such as a "smart brick" to make the point. What possible use could be made of putting computing (or sensing, more specifically) into a brick? The potential answer is that it could detect (and report) if it is failing, subjected to too much load, and so on. Sometimes putting the word "smart" in front of arbitrary nouns can stimulate thinking, as in "what might smart paint be?"

There are several broader implications about IoT, aside from speculation about the future of applications. These devices are inexpensive, which means that it is even harder in this context than in the traditional context of computers and smartphones to justify investment in good security. When a security vulnerability is detected in an application or operating system, we expect that the vendor will release a "patch" to correct the problem. Few devices classified as IoT have any capability for a software upgrade. Many of them have no real user interface—they cannot signal if they detect a problem, even if they can detect it.

At the same time, as we put computing into "everything" we become more and more dependent on its correct operation. There is thus the potential of a malicious attack targeting some class of IoT for some purpose. Although such an attack might end up as a "weapon of mass irritation," it could conceivably have serious consequences. As well, we have seen today that there are classes of IoT devices that have such poor security that they can be turned into attack devices themselves, in order to disrupt the larger Internet. One question that society will have to consider is whether we should impose on the designers of IoT devices any required standard of care to ensure that their devices cannot cause harm to the Internet itself.

Given that many of these devices are manufactured overseas, often in countries that on the one hand have low cost of production and on the other hand do not always have our best interests in mind, regulation of IoT might manifest as regulation of international trade.

11.1.4 The Information Layer

The changing pattern of information management is following the changing pattern at the physical layer. Most of the large centers of data storage and manipulation were initially in the United States, built by U.S. firms like Google and Amazon. The rest of the world came to the United States to retrieve information. Now, for a variety of reasons, we see the storage and management moving overseas, into a more decentralized model.

One reason for this trend is simple economics; it is cheaper to retrieve data if it is close by. A lot of high-volume data like video is replicated and cached around the globe to make retrieval cheap and efficient. Another reason is regulation—countries are demanding that data about their citizens be retained within the jurisdictional boundaries of that country. This requirement raises an interesting question as to whether data stored physically in one country can be deemed to be logically within another country, as with an embassy. However, with the recent revelations about National

Security Agency surveillance, many countries have doubts that data is adequately protected from observation by sophisticated intelligence services like those of the United States unless it is at least physically removed from U.S. jurisdiction.

Finally, we see the emergence of non-U.S.-centered firms and activities at the information layer. This internationalization of the information layer is only to be expected, as the rest of the world comes up to speed in the Internet. In some cases, countries have driven the creation of domestic firms, as with China, which has blocked access to Facebook and limited the activities of Google, while nurturing their domestic equivalents. Nonetheless, firms like Facebook have a strong global presence as of 2018, but there are important pressures for the Facebook data itself to be migrated out of a centralized U.S. placement into a distributed global placement that tracks jurisdictional requirements.

Of course, these sorts of considerations are not unique to the Internet. Transnational organizations such as credit card networks have been dealing with the need to respect jurisdictional requirements for some time. They have evolved models to deal with these issues while maintaining adequate efficiency and control of fraud.

11.1.5 The User Layer

As we noted in chapter 2, one of the drivers of the character of cyberspace has been the U.S. predilection for innovation and investment in new ideas. A brief look at the history of the Internet illustrates this particularly powerful feature of some U.S. core values. While the record has been extensively analyzed, nonetheless, we note here some key features that illustrate these processes. Our tolerance for risk-taking and for failure, our admiration for inventors, our education system, the availability of funding for innovation, and federal funding for advanced R&D all lead to a culture where new ideas are born and take root quickly. In the past, it has been hard for other nations to "out-innovate" us.

But the globalization process of the twentieth century and the added impetus and acceleration enabled by the Internet is itself leading (at least to some degree) to a globalization of the incentives to innovate. We already see other states launch down this path, whether as a result of top-down undertaking by governments or bottom-up inspiration of innovators in other countries that are exposed to the outcomes of successful innovation in cyberspace. Especially relevant here is the phenomenon we call technology leapfrogging—the innovations in different parts of the world do not recapitulate each other but can each build off the latest that has emerged elsewhere. In this way, states that may seem behind can accelerate their catching up and, to the extent they wish, avoid well-known environmental damages and dislocation effects.[1]

We have stressed a number of times in this volume the potential of the Internet to empower the individual. This empowerment is manifested along a number of dimensions. The access to global information and the ability to have a voice with global reach is surely transformative. As well, the mobile online world can bring finance to the unbanked citizen in the developing world, and the Web combined with a global credit card network and global shipping can bring a global market to an artisan in a remote village. Cyberspace has greatly extended the ability of ordinary citizens everywhere to be "citizens of the world."

However, at the same time that the Internet empowers the citizen, it empowers the state to observe and intervene in the activities of the citizen. Cyberspace has shifted the playing field for both the citizen and the state, and we are now in a period where the state, perhaps slower moving than the individual but nonetheless capable of moving, is using the tools of cyberspace to reassert its rights of control and regulation. How these shifts will play out is not clear, and how diverse the outcomes will be in different countries is not clear, but we are now in a time where the pendulum of empowerment, which swung toward the individual, is now swinging back toward the state.

11.1.6 The Blurring of the Layers?

The Internet of today is based on capital-intensive physical infrastructure. Governments that fret over the lack of universal broadband access have become painfully aware of this fact. Governments can regulate access providers, but it is very difficult to compel them to invest, and some of the strategies designed to offer them incentives have unacceptable consequences. Much of the infrastructure on which society depends—roads, water, and so forth—has been provided by the public sector and funded through taxes. In the past in most countries, the telephone system was itself provided by the government as a critical service. Other examples, such as power or natural gas, are paid for by those who benefit from them. Consumers generally pay for electricity, and the funds flow (perhaps imperfectly) through the power generation and distribution system to compensate the providers.

But use of the Internet is distinctively different. There is an added economic "dislocation" with the cyber functionalities of cyberspace, one that comes into focus through a layered lens. The physical layer is capital intensive—it involves construction and installation of wires, fibers, cell towers, undersea cables, and so on. However, these physical assets become valuable only as they support the higher layers—applications, information, and the like. The investment in physical infrastructure usually comes from the providers of the basic Internet service, the platform layer directly on top of the physical layer in our model. The strong, open interface between the platform layer of the Internet and the application services that run on top of it means that, in general, ISPs do not have an easy way to tap into the value that is being generated by these high-level services. Rather, ISPs are just paid to move bytes from source to destination. Generally, they find themselves in a business that is capital intensive, because they have to finance their use of physical resources, and at the same time essentially a commodity, given that the movement of bytes across these circuits is actually a simple task. So the money gets spent at the lower physical and platform layer, and is made at the application and information layer.

An obvious consequence of this is that ISPs are motivated to "move up the layers" and themselves get into the business of offering their own applications and content. Many ISPs (in particular those with a history of being cable TV providers) have always been in the business of delivering content as well as owning physical facilities. But in the context of the Internet, with a prior history of a clean interface that separates the ISP from the higher-level providers, the entry of the ISPs into this space, which the business schools would call *vertical integration*, can threaten the open character of the Internet, because ISPs that control the infrastructure may be motivated to discriminate against third-party applications and content if it competes with their own offerings.

At this writing, there is a vociferous debate, both in the United States and in other parts of the world, about the need to impose *neutrality* regulations on the ISPs to protect the open character of the network in the face of the desire of ISPs to extract revenues related to the value that is being created at the higher levels.

It is difficult to generalize about trends in ISP investment in different parts of the world given the different ways they are (or can be) controlled by the state. It is not unusual to find that the state in many countries controls the ISPs directly or indirectly, or even exercises outright ownership.

11.1.7 Centralization and Decentralization

When we look at higher layers—at the application and information layer—we see interesting patterns. The first important application of the Internet was email, and email is a highly decentralized system with a mesh structure. There is no central email server. The same is true of the Web—anyone can bring up and operate a Web server, and any client (browser) can connect directly to any server. But the more recent applications, which arose in a more commercial context, have a more centralized structure. Consider applications such as Facebook or Twitter, which are dominant applications as we write this book. The Facebook application is under the control of the eponymous company that designed and operates the service. The same is true of Twitter. The trend seems to have moved toward centralized control at the higher levels. Can we at least speculate as to why this pattern exists?

One answer is obvious—centralized control is a mechanism that leads to centralized revenue generation by the controlling entity. But another answer is that decentralized architectures are harder to design, due to the complexity of multiway negotiation and agreement. The easiest action is one that can be taken unilaterally, a slightly more difficult action involves bilateral agreement, and the most complex is a multiway agreement involving many parties. This pattern certainly holds at the state level; it is easiest for one nation to act alone, somewhat harder to negotiate a bilateral agreement, and harder still to negotiate a global treaty.

The early applications, email and the Web, have this multiway distributed structure. So given this observation, why did the Internet even emerge, or email, or the Web? The answer is that they are defined by standards, which in particular define the basis for interaction among the actors. There is a standards document that defines how two ISPs interconnect, how two mail servers interact, and how a browser and a Web server interact. If all parties agree to these standards, then interaction among the parties may require no advanced negotiation (as with the Web or email) or a bilateral negotiation that is constrained by the affordances of the standard. Standards are the result of multilateral negotiation and reduce the resulting complexity to (at most) bilateral negotiation.

So why, in turn, did the standards for the Internet, and for email and the Web, succeed? An important component of the answer is that they were written by actors who were not motivated by competition so much as by cooperation around a shared vision. The early standards for the Internet were devised mostly by researchers funded by government grants, and their motivation was exactly to build a decentralized system. In contrast, applications such as Facebook and Twitter emerged in an era more motivated by competition than by cooperation. There is usually no motivation for a dominant actor like a Facebook or a Twitter to develop open standards that allow other actors to enter their space. It is not clear that a cyberspace that resembles today's Internet would have emerged if the development had been driven by the private sector.

The shaping of the early Internet by a shared vision is one distinctive aspect of its development. In the international arena, we anticipate a general trend toward cooperation as a process, but not necessarily cooperation motivated by a common vision. Participation in international conferences is, in itself, a mode of cooperation. Evolving efforts to develop a shared vision among states over transitions toward sustainability is the most important development of the twentieth century and central to the agenda of the twenty-first century. Recent agreement over a shared vision for responding to climate change is certainly as important as that of sustainable development. Especially critical in this context is the nascent focus on cyberspace for sustainability (Choucri 2012). This refers to the use of cyber venues for facilitating transitions toward sustainability and eliminating barriers toward a more sustainable future.

Less ambiguous by far is a critical technical trend—the move to mobility. As we discussed in previous chapters, the consequences of Moore's law have allowed mobile devices to be created that are cheap enough to deploy in the developing world. We now see the shape of the Internet in the developing world, and it is based on the small screen and mobile connectivity, a reality that shows the adaptation and adaptability of the original vision for the Internet.

In the mobile context, what we call the "Internet experience" can be shaped anew, and it is up for grabs. Not surprisingly, it is the powerful commercial actors who are moving to shape the experience and thus dominate the market. A recent example is a variant of Facebook called 0.facebook. That first character is a zero, and it refers to cost. This application, which is targeting the mobile world, and in particular the developing world, is given to new users "for free," and in particular, for zero usage charges. That is, if the user buys a service plan with a monthly usage quota, the usage associated with 0.facebook does not count against that quota. While the business plans of Facebook are not trumpeted publicly, their goal seems clear. For this next cohort of users, they want the "Internet experience" to be Facebook. They want the user to think that Facebook is the portal to cyberspace.[2]

We have speculated that the deployment of devices and ready access to the Internet will be a force for user empowerment. We are optimistic and hopeful. But at the same time, we note the power of the commercial world that seems to dominate the forces of evolution today. Should we look at the users of tomorrow as broadly empowered or as users focused on their online network of friends?

11.2 Changes through the Lens of Levels of Analysis

The levels of analysis model from chapter 3 brings a focus on the interplay between the individual, the sovereign state as an entity, the international system of states and nonstate private actors, and the global system.

11.2.1 The Private Sector

We have stressed in this book the distinctive, if not unique, importance of the private sector in creating cyberspace and defining its character. It is not restricted to one level of analysis in international relations, but cuts across or pervades all levels. The Internet grew up in the context of U.S. government funding and users from the academic and research communities. Some of its surviving norms persist from this era. However, as we have discussed at length throughout this book, the Internet of today is largely shaped by large commercial interests. For some observers, this transition is so extreme that they can only hope that the applications that support noncommercial activities and the prospect of a strong and viable civil society can somehow survive by riding the trends of commercialization.

Many of the actors at the higher levels are large and powerful. The producers of commercial content—music, videos, and the like—fiercely protect their property. This has led to major actions by some states, with the United

States in the lead, to create laws and other forms of control to protect these interests. Additionally, the movement of video to the Internet has been the major driver of traffic growth (and thus cost for the infrastructure providers) over the last few years.

There is no reason to think that this trend toward commercialization will be reversed. States can encourage the creation of noncommercial content, spaces for civic engagement, and the like, but they will more or less be forced to do this in the context of a cyberspace that is mostly shaped by commercial interests. The engineering of the Internet for video has created enough capacity that any application other than video will generate comparatively negligible traffic. Even for video, the commercial success of sites like YouTube mean that creators of noncommercial content have a platform for dissemination that is literally free.

So far, the rate of commercialization has outpaced the rate of regulation. As a general statement, this holds across the board. But we must keep in mind the discussion in earlier chapters about the increasing propensity of the state system to intervene in the cyber domain, at least in so far as it pertains to national jurisdictions. Concurrently, we can expect that various forms of follow-up from NETmundial will involve support for as well as resistance to commercial domination. Even in the most abstract terms, it is not clear at this time what a balance between commercial and noncommercial might look like.

Clearly, the increasingly commercial aspect of the Internet is at odds with the original vision of the Internet as a commons where the citizen could participate in civic dialog. As we noted earlier, many of the important applications that facilitate communication among people—applications such as Facebook and Twitter—are designed by large commercial firms, with their primary motivation being profit, not the creation of a commons or a space of civic dialog. Today, the Internet may offer the illusion of a commons, but it is created by actors for whom this is not the primary motivation.

At the same time, we recognize that there is an underlying ethos in parts of the user community, as well as the providers or various services, to support the notion of "commons" especially given its global connotation—and the implied muting of state power. And the government delegations that participate in international human rights conferences often support the same type of "open vision."

11.2.2   States and Governments

Another theme on which we have touched several times is that although governments may have been slow to realize the importance of cyberspace to their priorities, they are now acting to exercise control over cyberspace in ways they consider necessary. In contrast to the private sector, which has a single high-level goal, economic success, governments have a range of diverse goals, which differ among countries. These include security of cyberspace from external disruption, regulation of the cyber domain to support internal stability, protection of private sector actors and their priorities (e.g., assistance in protection of copyright or prevention of industrial espionage), encouraging innovation and economic growth, generation of revenues (taxation), protection of the rights of the citizenry, protecting their own regimes, and so on.

While the trends worldwide are not yet fully consolidated, it stands to reason that some governments will encourage private-public cyber initiatives. The relatively stark distinction we have made throughout this book between the two domains is accompanied by the distinction between profit-oriented activities and those that are largely not for profit, in both the public and the private sectors.

Whatever the motivation, the consequence for cyberspace is often the same—to impose controls on it in order to limit and monitor what is done. Whether it is to block unacceptable content or to tax commerce, the means to the goal involves making what the users are doing visible and controllable. States with specific conceptions of how their domestic Internet should operate are demonstrating their ability to achieve such goals as control of access to unwelcome content.

In his book *Code: And Other Laws of Cyberspace*, Lawrence Lessig (1999) observed that the interests of the commercial sector and the governments are aligned—neither of them has an incentive to make cyberspace a region of unregulated and free interaction. Rather, both of these actors have a motivation to observe, regulate, and monetize the experience, which suggests that absent a countervailing force, the future of cyberspace may be less open and more regulated. That prediction about motivation and consequence seems, if anything, more compelling today than it was when first published.

11.2.2.1   The emergence of jurisdictional boundaries   How will these local experiences be shaped? One answer is that the drive for innovation in different regions of the world will lead to the introduction of localized applications; in other words, the driver could be the private sector, motivated in turn by an understanding of local conditions. Alternatively, the driver could be the public sector motivated by state policy to control content or shape the Internet. China, Saudi Arabia, and other Gulf states are prime examples for public sector dominance, even if the executing entity is defined as private. These are cases where the driver for diversification is the emerging interests of the state, as we have discussed.

We think of the United States and it Western counterparts as accepting a norm of free speech, but even among these nations we see localized concerns that relate to regulation of content. France bans the sale of Nazi memorabilia, some nations ban hate speech, and so on. Unless these forms of speech are going to be blocked globally (in other words, unless the Internet descends to the least common denominator of accepted speech), we will see the continued rise of country-specific blocking of content. Another variant in law that will lead to jurisdictional variation is the law of libel. Speech that is acceptable in one country may be libelous in another. Again, to avoid global blocking, the path of least resistance may be to block the distribution of this content on a country-specific basis.

Jurisdictional boundaries will also harden as a result of commercial pressures. Much commercial content today is licensed on a per-country basis. The ability of a consumer to download commercial content may be gated by the country that he is coming from. Consumers well understand this today, and sophisticated users use what are called "tunnels" or virtual private networks that route their traffic to another region of the network, where it then emerges in a jurisdiction where the content is available.

Looking at how content control is being achieved today, it will not happen by having "content police" monitoring the paths into different countries. The states of the world (with a few exceptions) are not putting technology into the network to filter and block. It will happen by using the power of the state to coerce the providers of content to do the filtering for them. In chapter 5, we illustrated such tendencies, with Google as a prime example. A large firm with a global footprint cannot afford to ignore demands for country-specific tailoring of the experience, for fear of being banned totally. We have seen, for example, YouTube being outright banned in certain countries because of an offensive (to that country) video. That sort of coarse-grained ban can indeed be implemented "at the border" by a determined country, again by using its ISPs as agents of the state. States will use this sort of "blunt-instrument" blocking to coerce the content providers to do more selective country-specific blocking at the source.

On the other hand, states will have little power over small actors who can evade these pressures. WikiLeaks is much more prepared (and organized) to resist pressure to refrain and block than a Google. This illustrates the paradox of the power of weakness. Given the volumes of traffic on the Internet, and the diverse (and rapidly evolving) set of applications that can be globally deployed, it is not likely that governments will be able to control the transfer of content from a willing sender to a willing receiver, except by means that cause collateral damage due to overreach (e.g., blocking all encrypted communication). It is when the communicator is large enough so that it can be found and coerced that control can be exercised.

Even though we predict that many of these controls will be applied "at the edges" rather than "in the network," there are still requirements for jurisdictional boundaries that must be supplied by the infrastructure. In particular, if a sender is blocking content on a country-specific basis, he must be able to tell from which country the potential receiver is coming. There have been a number of proposals for adding control mechanisms to support this requirement, ranging from allocating network addresses on a country-specific basis to requiring that users obtain from their country a "country of residence" certificate that can be included in the transborder request. Needless to say, all of these proposals are contested, based on different perceptions of benefits and costs to the domestic and global society. And again, although there is no effective venue for these issues to be debated, and for the voices of governments, the private sector, advocates for civil society, and so on all to be heard, such venues may be "under construction." The general trajectory of global discourse that led to WSIS and then to NETmundial could, if sustained, provide venues of this sort.

11.2.2.2   The move to universal surveillance and the power of the state   As we speculate on the empowerment of the future user, we see today the state empowered by the existing tools of cyberspace. As recent flaps about surveillance indicate, powerful and wealthy states like the United States have used their money and influence to build systems that give them wide-ranging opportunities for surveillance. In states where there is active protest and

opposition to the government, we see the activists using cyberspace to organize, but we increasingly see the state using its tools to track and disrupt the
activists. This is a space where there will be active and rapid co-evolution of
tools of dissent and tools of repression. It is unclear how this will work out,
but in general, the rules that apply in the real world will apply here—small
groups can maintain a social network that is private and hard to detect,
large groups become visible (and can be infiltrated by informers) and will
be betrayed.

The tracking of users by the state today is nothing compared to the tracking of users by the private sector, in pursuit of revenues, in particular advertising revenues. A fear that has already surfaced is that these companies may be
coerced into being agents of the state and sharing this information for purposes of intelligence and policing.[3] This is both a domestic and international
issue, in that interactions among people of different states may be tracked at
both ends, and different laws and norms may apply at those points.

Countries that value unregulated speech (and may be interested in foreign regime change) are now developing applications specifically for the use
of dissidents and activists. Systems such as the Onion Router (Tor) that we
discussed in chapter 5, which attempt to preserve the anonymity of users as
they run applications over the Internet, illustrate both an effort by a powerful state to try to shape the international character of the Internet (Tor was
initially designed by the U.S. Department of Defense) and the power of a
small group of individuals (who currently guide the deployment of Tor) to
confront the power of the state. Obviously, if the providers of systems such
as Tor are to be successful at this and protect these activists from retaliation
from the states in question, they must develop and operate these tools in a
way that can co-evolve at the required rate. Because the opponent state may
be using its intelligence service to break these tools, the tools must be of
high quality and evolve at high rates. Casual play in this space can cost lives.

An important development in this broad arena is the expansion of the
players and the increasing diversity in their goals, capabilities, intents, and
so forth. In addition, as we have shown in chapter 5, states do not always
operate or behave in the cyber domain the way they do in the traditional
arena of international relations. Already we see evidence of rapid enablement and expansion in the cyber domain that is not consistent, or commensurate, with their state profile of land-based capabilities, as shown in

chapter 3 and chapter 5. In notable cases, these are greater in the cyber domain than the territorial arena.

11.2.2.3 The international level—cross-level coordination The previous discussions hint at our predictions about modes of cyber governance. Individual states are showing increasing facility and competence in shaping their domestic Internet. The domestic actions that are available to different states will depend on the affordances of that state: Does it have a technology industry? How effectively can it control the owners of the physical infrastructure in its country?

At the international level, we conclude that state-centered institutions will play a role, but the complexity of negotiation over goals and the pace at which they can evolve will limit their effectiveness. Moreover, the effectiveness of the distributed governance of the cyber domain, discussed in considerable detail in chapter 9, remains sufficiently robust as to preclude any serious dislocation at the international level, including the regional areas.

The early governance principles have fully been institutionalized by the participating entities. The task now is to respond effectively to new challenges as they arise. Especially important is the role of entities like the Internet Engineering Task Force and processes like the Request for Comments, among others, noted in chapter 9. The policy formation versus delegation functions that shape the space in which these entities function appear well institutionalized, with regional entities diffusing global management principles to the state level.

We noted in several chapters the important role of the private sector—for profit and not for profit—in management of the Internet. It is difficult to identify another global infrastructure system that can be characterized thusly. Clearly, there are numerous infrastructure systems with worldwide reach based on private sector management and governance, but none with the global to local reach of the Internet, and none with the enabling functions that create a new domain of interaction like cyberspace.

11.2.2.4 State-centered international organizations As we write, we have seen a movement to empower the International Telecommunication Union (ITU) to have some authority to regulate the international character of the Internet. We discussed this in chapters 9 and 10. Recall that the World Conference on International Telecommunications 2012 was an attempt by a number of states to band together to try to establish a forum where they could shape and control the norms and methods for international inter-connection among ISPs. While that effort did not succeed, we can expect to see a recurring effort to establish this control—or at least to forge some form of control. We can also see sustained cooperation to participate in interna-tional forums (as noted earlier) specifically for the purpose of altering the current vision underlying the Internet.

In this respect, we see nation states, with the leadership of powerful ones, even aspiring to dominance (for example, China), acting in ways that are not that different from the corporate response to a regime that does not favor their interests. The behavior is generic—challenging to status and norms and institutions established by the dominant actors—but the context differs and so do the implications. In several chapters of this book we referred to this form of challenge, a well-document trajectory of power politics.

Informal conversation among interested states, translated into domestic actions in each of those states, may well be nimbler when the trade-offs are clear and not overly burdensome, and when visions of "win-win" can be framed effectively. Governments are gradually seeking to become more familiar with the role of the cyber-centered private sector, both technically (as is revealed in our control point diagrams) as well as the cyber-based busi-ness motivations and strategies, which are traditionally held secret. The private sector—providers of products, services, content, and so forth—may well have to respond to government directives perhaps more than has been done so far. Relevant to this powerful duality—business and the state—is the potential power and evolving position of various constituencies, voters as well as consumers.

A future with which we should concern ourselves is that either govern-ments or private sector actors will try to set up "tollbooths" on the Internet, in an attempt to extract revenues from the flows based on their perceived value. At the international level, this objective would require the authority of an international organization armed with legitimacy and the power, for example, by extending the authority of the ITU, as mentioned earlier. Any such attempt to impose a "value tax" on the Internet will drive all noncom-mercial content from the space. It will also create fault lines with supporters and detractors taking to the trenches, so to speak. None of this will serve to support common norms.

We expect that we will see increasing attempts to engineer this sort of revenue extraction from the Internet, as the providers of physical infrastructure attempt to recover their costs so they can evolve more rapidly in the commercial space. States may need to deploy regulation to prevent this, but the states may be motivated to encourage the behavior, if they can tax the resulting revenues. States as well as the private sector are motivated by economic concerns.

We have seen many instances in previous chapters of what we labeled "the paradox of the power of weakness." In chapter 5, we showed the expansion of access in the cyber domain that is greater than expansion in the traditional international arena. In other words, it seems that states are able to expand their strategic assets, even compensate, for relative vulnerabilities or weakness when we observe their behavior in both the cyber and the traditional arenas at the same time. China is a prime example, but as shown in chapter 5, there are others as well. This line of reasoning is empirically based, but it is far too early to tell if the logic is situational or if it allows for framing relatively robust conjectures.

The important question for international relations is whether there are joint or common motivations around which countries will come together to manage a common good, or whether issues that divide governments will lead to the further divergence in the character of the Internet in different parts of the world. The comparison with cooperation on environment management is only partly relevant at this point. Despite broad-based accord among many states that environmental policy is important and that no one state can solve the problem, domestic constituencies in the most powerful country, the United States, are still questioning the science and the necessity for strong international accords. Note that the nonstate entities and civil society at all levels of analysis were fundamental drivers of the environmental movement and the resulting global treaties. The same may well evolve for management of the cyber domain.

11.2.2.5 The increasingly diverse Internet The Internet, as a platform for moving bytes from one place to another, is globally uniform except where governments have intervened. Any set of willing machines can exchange data. And in the beginning, the applications that ran on top of this data transport platform, such as email, were also uniform. They were very "English centric," and used the Roman alphabet, but they were available (and used) around the globe. This state of affairs, which we now see as a transient in the growth of the Internet, led to hopes that the Internet might be a universal platform for global discourse.

We now see that the experience that users have on the Internet is much more diverse and to a large extent much more localized. One driver for this diversification is language. We have shown in chapter 5 the rapid expansion of non-Western languages observable on the Internet. The expansion of capability worldwide is a powerful push for diversity in languages, and that in turn attracts speakers of those languages, who gravitate to that version of the Internet. Another reason, closely related, is effective "localization" of competing applications to the needs of different cultures. Many applications, for example, auction sites, recommendation services, or job postings, can be tailored to the expectations and needs of different regions and thrive there. Diversity will be driven as well by the demands of the state, as is most obvious in China, which has blocked access to global applications such as Facebook and Twitter but encouraged the growth of domestic alternatives.

The trend that we see, which is likely to continue, is that people in different parts of the world are likely to see (and to gravitate toward) very different content-based Internet experiences. In many places, the global applications will be available and will be used by a part of the population. Some applications may gain and hold a strong global presence (but as we said earlier, all advantage is temporary). The pressures are toward diversity, not toward convergence. We should ask whether this diversification is an extreme case of what we see in print when the same magazine, for example, is published in different languages and in different cultures or countries.

This trend will not, as some have said, lead to the "Balkanization" of the Internet. The Internet will not splinter into disconnected fragments, except in a few countries with extreme concerns about content control and local regulation. For most countries, we will see a blending of a local experience with the option of a more cosmopolitan experience for those that want to partake. But even such "cosmopolitanism" need not necessarily be global in scale and scope. It could simply be viewed in terms of degree of departure from the local mean.

11.2.3   The Global Level of Analysis

What we see at all layers is that the U.S.-centric character of the Internet, which arose in part because of the early leadership of the United States and U.S. industry in bringing the Internet into existence, is now being replaced with a more global, more decentralized, and more localized version of the

Internet. But the core architecture and the global-level operations remain consistent with the original view of the dominant state.

Some might argue that this type of issue reflects the loss of power for the United States. The retort might be that the architecture of an Internet that mirrors U.S. values is in itself a major "win"—one that is good for the United States and, creating a trend, would seem to be good for the global society. The impact of the Internet signals the recognition in all parts of the globe of the transformative potential of cyberspace, and there is no way that this potential was ever going to remain controlled preferentially within and by the United States. A major policy issue that will become salient in short order is how the United States can best leverage its innovator advantages to continue to benefit preferentially from the Internet while pushing for opening up the globe to this new order. The globalization of the Internet is a near fact of life. The "openness" of its management is retained at the global level but may well be eroding at the state level.

So in scoping the range of futures for cyberspace (or more specifically the Internet), we see the interplay of two forces: the forces of decentralization, which seem a natural response to the globalization of the Internet, and which are facilitated by the standards that allow bilateral interconnection arrangements; and the forces of centralization within powerful and dominant actors, which are driven by classic competitive pressures and the dictates of power politics.

One way this force of centralization could be diffused would be to encourage the resilience and sustainability of the institutional mechanisms that defined the early Internet. So far, all evidence suggests that on a global scale the U.S. vision remains strong. At this point in time, the absence of state entities in the management of the Internet (discussed in chapter 9) is in itself powerful evidence of success for the core U.S. vision.

At the same time, however, once the Internet became commercially viable in the United States, the government stepped away from funding its development and governance, leaving it to the commercial sector, which was driven more by competition than by cooperation.

The pattern of interconnection (hierarchical, centralized, or mesh) and the degree of global uniformity may differ across different layers. The Internet may be globally connected in a rich mesh at the layer that forwards packets, and still offer a regional or localized set of user-facing services, and these themselves may be more centralized or decentralized based on the actors that drive their creation—those more motivated by competition, cooperation, or "coopetition." At the global level, the distributed model of Internet governance, discussed in chapter 9, provides a robust basis for envisaging a wide range of contingencies.

11.2.3.1 The future of cyberspace in the developing world At the present, the technology that is opening up cyberspace to the developing world is the inexpensive smartphone. For many, the mobile device *is* the Internet. And here again, we see the tension between commercialization and empowerment, as illustrated by the earlier example of 0.facebook, which has the potential of making its application synonymous with the Internet for beginning users in the developing world.

There is always something of a race going on in the provision of goods and services to developing countries. This clearly is the case with respect to expansion of access. Some of the most visible initiatives are connected to very low-cost hardware, others are based on simplified software, multilingual applications, or uses of visual rather than text bases. TARAHaat, one of the most effective initiatives of cyber literacy in developing societies—well known in India and in the worldwide sustainable development community—is a development strategy using telecenters in rural areas to introduce information and communication technologies. In that respect it is at the technology frontier for social conditions as defined by the developing countries rather than imported from the industrial countries and defined by their own market conditions. In addition, the United Nations, the dominant state-based international institution, supports a wide range of national initiatives that are undoubtedly broadening cyber access in remote areas.

The issues noted herein are closely related to transitions toward sustainability, an issue of importance for the international community and supported by almost all countries, as noted in chapter 5 and later in chapter 9. There is a growing awareness of the potential contributions of cyber venues to pathways toward sustainable development of social and natural systems, on the one hand, and the potential challenges related to the sustainability of the cyber domain and its development, on the other.

11.2.4 Individual Level of Analysis

In the cyber domain, individuals and aggregates are sometimes called the "users" of cyberspace, but this term, although easily understood, is misleading. People are not just users but creators. By their actions they jointly create the experience of cyberspace. Social networking would not exist if people were not motivated to capture their connections to other people in cyberspace. Wikipedia would not exist if people were not motivated to capture their knowledge in cyberspace. Perhaps the best antidote to the motivations of governments and corporations is the motivations of the people that make cyberspace. However, people need help in this act. People can contribute to Wikipedia or to the building of a social network only because there were others with technical skills and vision who built the framework or context in which ordinary people could then contribute. And perhaps one of the most unpredictable factors that will shape the future is whether, and in what way, people with technical skills and vision will create new frameworks or contexts into which ordinary people, the so-called "users," can act to create new experiences in cyberspace.

A recent innovation on the Internet is a fascinating example of the power of a small group of people to challenge a core institution of the state. We refer to the phenomenon of "cryptocurrency," of which the most well-known example is *Bitcoin*. The term cryptocurrency refers to a currency system in which advanced techniques of cryptography are used to create an anonymous but trustworthy digital medium of financial exchange. These forms of currency are not fiat currency—no state backs them or assures their value. Nor are they any form of commodity currency, in which there is some physical item of value standing behind the currency. The Bitcoin system was described in a paper by a pseudonymous author (Nakamoto, n.d.), and its utility is assured by the clever use of cryptography to create a public record of all Bitcoin transactions, where the record clearly indicates that a transaction has occurred, without showing who the parties to the transaction are.

To the extent that there is a mechanism to allow exchange between Bitcoins and other currencies (e.g., fiat currency), and the collective users believe in the validity of the mechanisms, Bitcoin can support the digital equivalent of cash, which permits an anonymous but trustworthy transaction between individuals. As we write this book, the Bitcoin system seems to be under the leadership of a group of five people (successors to the "author" of the original Bitcoin paper) and is being used around the world for online payments.

The decentralized basis for this digital equivalent for cash could very well evolve into a parallel medium, coexisting with the dominant institutional modes of exchange. We anticipate such innovations to establish themselves in a coexistent frame, thus facilitating provision to the core service, without seriously undermining the established mechanisms. But even on that limited scale, one could imagine conditions under which the virtual option could be viewed as threatening to the established one.

11.3   Change through the Lens of Control Point Analysis

The Internet is so much a part of our lives that we tend to take it as a fixed and stable infrastructure. But perhaps in the future a different version of the Internet might emerge, with different implications for the balance of power and options for control among different actors. In both the United States and in Europe, there have been long-range research projects funded to consider what the Internet of fifteen years from now might be, and these projects have produced some interesting alternative visions of a future Internet. Although it is not likely that there will be any wholesale replacement of the Internet in the future—it is too deeply embedded to imagine a complete replacement— these projects suggest possible directions along which the Internet might evolve.

Whereas the technical details of these alternative proposals are interesting to the networking research community, in this discussion we will use the lens of control points to bring out some of the salient features of these alternatives, allowing us to discuss shifts in power rather than shifts in technology. As we noted earlier, in political analysis, *who* controls is likely to determine, even shape, *who get what, when,* and *how*—the core issues for the social order, as introduced in chapter 1.

In theory, at least, the state has control over its sovereign territory. It is therefore in a position to control all control points on its jurisdiction. That said, the social contract, the political system, and the social order overall provide the operational parameters for permissible behavior. This means, for example, that it is difficult, if not impossible under current conditions, to consider that the U.S. government will directly control the Internet points on its territory. But, can we envisage conditions under which the government would increase its control more and more? This question itself signals the difference between the control points per se and the extent to which they can be subject to different controllers. The U.S. case is simple in that the government may have the capability to engage in such control. Only a few states, such as China, have the capabilities for realizing such a future.

11.3.1   Separating Location from Identity

In the current Internet, the address of the end nodes plays a dual role—
it serves both to identify the end node and specify its location. This linkage has led to some rather subtle but important consequences. The address
serves as an identifier, in that a query to the Domain Name System (DNS)
takes a name and returns an address, with the implication that a packet sent
to that address will reach the machine associated with the name. But at the
same time, the address specifies the location of the machine, in that the routing protocols of the Internet compute forwarding information so that packets can be routed using these addresses. If a service moves from one location
on the Internet to another, it may have to get a new address, which means
that the information stored in the DNS has to be changed, and any program
that has stored that address will somehow have to obtain a new one.

The problem with this dual use of the address becomes obvious when we
consider mobile devices, which may constantly change their location on the
Internet but which want to maintain a consistent identity. For this reason,
a future Internet might replace the single address field with two values: an
end point identifier and an end point locator. The locator would be used in
the interior of the Internet to forward the packet. It could be changed as the
end point moved. If the end point was moving, the identifier would provide
a persistent basis to look up the new location.

The consequence of this idea, from the perspective of control, is that this
new mobility management service itself becomes a potentially potent point
of control. What actor would build and operate this service? Why would
they be trustworthy? Is there the possibility of having competing services
operated by different actors, and if so, how would the router trying to forward the packet know which service to query?

The alternative to having a mobility management service is to assign to
the mobile end node itself the responsibility for telling its communicants if
it moves. For a mobile device talking to a fixed service, this can be straight-
forward. When the mobile device moves, it finds out what its new location
is and then sends a signed message to the fixed service with its identifier and
new location. In this approach, there needs to be no third-party mobility
management service, which seems like a preferred approach if the designers are worried about creating new points of control. But this scheme does
not work well if two mobile devices are talking to each other. What if they
both change their location at once? How then can each tell the other where

they are? It seems as if there has to be some fixed service in the network, a rendezvous point where each can send a message about its current location. A rendezvous point might be a lighter-weight mechanism than a mobility management service, and might provide more flexibility to the end points in avoiding untrustworthy elements disrupting their communication. But the downside of this is that the network itself has no way to forward a packet to an end point that has moved. If the packet reaches the specified location and the end point is no longer there, it has no option but to discard the packets and presume that the end points can somehow get together again.

The trade-off seems fundamental. If one wants the network to deliver a more sophisticated (and perhaps more efficient or dynamic) service, one must be prepared to trust that the network will do it in a reliable and trustworthy way.

11.3.1.1 The role of identifiers One can generalize the previous discussion as follows. A basic requirement for secure communication is that the communicating end points be able to verify that they are indeed communicating with the intended entities. So there has to be some shared concept of identity and means to verify it. But at one extreme, this matter can be strictly private to the end points. They can use arbitrary means to identify and validate each other, and no other parties need be involved in the process, which reduces the options for third-party intervention and control. All that would be visible in the packets as they flow through the interior of the network would be the locator. However, this approach puts a very high burden on the end nodes. A malicious third party could try to "highjack" the connection by observing the passing packets and then injecting packets that would seem to the recipient as being legitimate, so the process of validation would have to be a part of each packet transfer, not just a confirmation at the beginning of the connection that each end was as intended. This validation would probably have to take the form of some encryption scheme, so all communication would have to involve encryption.

If the only information visible in the packet is the locator, and the identifier is private to the end points (perhaps encrypted), this also shifts the balance of power with respect to surveillance. A lot of surveillance today is not focused on the content of the messages but on tracking who talks to whom, an objective sometimes called traffic analysis. If law enforcement has found a person of interest, they can use traffic analysis to discover linkages from that person to others, who may then also become persons of interest. But if the locator in the packets can change often, and has no robust linkage to any identifier, it becomes much harder for law enforcement to carry out traffic analysis. Of course, the schemes for creating and managing locators have to be designed with care if the goal is to thwart traffic analysis, and the design process itself can thus become a point of tussle over control and balance of power. Should the design goal of the network be to thwart traffic analysis, or should users who want this sort of protection have to resort to higher-level means of obfuscation, which in turn draws attention to their actions?

11.3.1.2 What do identifiers identify? In the previous discussion, it was assumed that what an identifier identified was an end node, a device attached to the network. This is how the current Internet works—the address in the packet allows the packet to be forwarded to a physical point on some piece of network equipment, where some computer is attached. But what if identifiers did not identify physical end points but some other sort of entity, such as a service or a piece of information?

What would it mean for an identifier to be associated with a service rather than a physical end point? The service might be replicated at many points around the network, and the network could forward the packet to the version that was closest, or perhaps a version that was currently under-utilized, or perhaps just to a version of the service that was running. In the current Internet, the DNS is sometimes used in this way—when the user presents a name to the DNS to be converted into an address, a potentially complicated algorithm can be run to pick the "best" address to return, based on locality, load, availability, and so on. Since the DNS is a highly decentralized system, this algorithm can be local to the server responsible for these specific names, so the trust assumption is aligned—the service that resolves these particular names to an address is run by the owner of the names, so presumably can be trusted to reflect the preferences of the owner.

This arrangement is perhaps as close as the Internet of today gets to a "locator-identity split," in that the name is mapped to potentially many locators, which may change over time as copies of the service are added or removed. One must think carefully about the implications for security and the potential for a malicious part of the DNS not to query the actual server responsible for these names but to give an invalid locator. As discussed earlier, the end nodes should have some ability to verify among themselves that a locator actually took them to a valid copy of the service. Of course, the implications differ based on the context—being sent to the "wrong" source of a movie has different consequences than being sent to a bogus version of a banking service.

From the perspective of understanding the options for control, the question to ask is which actor has control over the binding of the service identifier to the location to which the packet is actually directed. Is this control a part of a naming system like the DNS, a part of the network itself (e.g., under the control of the ISPs that operate the routers), a service that is somehow provided by competing operators, among whom the communicants can pick based on assumptions of trust, or some other option?

Alternatively, instead of naming a service, an identifier might name an object to be retrieved—a piece of information, content, or whatever. Collectively, these proposals are called information-centric networks. This approach is indeed radical; in the extreme this approach attempts to remove from the design all together any knowledge of the location of an "end point", and changes the routing and forwarding mechanisms so that they compute routes that do not target devices but content. One consequence of this approach is that it imposes complex demands on the routing system, because there are presumably many more pieces of content on the network than end points, and content itself may be mobile and highly replicated.

Again, the questions for control (and surveillance) relate to what is revealed in the packet and which actors control the steps that lead to the actual forwarding of the packet and its reply. In the scheme called Named Data Networking (NDN) (Zhang et al. 2014), the routers have control of the decisions that route the data requests to a source that can provide it. One must of necessity trust the network to perform a rather complex forwarding function. In a scheme called PURSUIT (Trossen and Parisis 2012), one of many competitive "rendezvous" services is used to find the actual location of the requested content. The content provider can, in principle, pick among competing rendezvous services to find one that functions in a trustworthy manner.

Designs in which the identifier is associated with content would seem to raise real concerns with respect to traffic analysis, because the packet would reveal both the location (but perhaps not the identity) of the requestor and what is being requested. This degree of revelation is much greater than happens in today's network and would seem to work to the advantage of a censor. However, NDN uses a novel design that mitigates this issue. In the Internet of today, and in most proposals for a future Internet, when a router forwards a packet it records no history of the packet. The current Internet is described as "stateless" or "forward and forget." In contrast, NDN requires every router that forwards a packet to make a record of the packet, including the incoming port from which the packet was received. A request for a data object leaves a conceptual trail of "bread crumbs" in every router it goes through, and the data itself, as it returns, follows that trail back to the requestor. The location or identity of the requestor is not revealed in the packet. So a third party, unless they have access to the dynamic information stored in every router, can only tell that "someone" requested a piece of information, not who that someone is.

11.3.1.3 Implications of different identity schemes The process of communication across any network involves a sequence of steps that start with a high-level representation of the desired interaction (the name of an end point, service, object to be retrieved, etc.) and through a series of conversions and computations, ends up with a sequence of packets flowing across the network. Different designs can have a different number of conversions (e.g., is the translation from high-level name to address in one step, or from name to identifier to address?), and these steps can differ with respect to dynamics and rate of change (is the goal to deal with information that may move slowly as it is archived, or mobile devices that move over seconds?). Each of these conversions is a potential point of control. Different designs can result in a single actor managing that point of control, a distributed and decentralized system where no one actor has control, to schemes that try to limit the actors that have control to the communicating parties themselves.

The latter schemes are more robust against the interventions of actors with adverse interests, but may be harder to design and implement, put responsibilities on the end nodes that are hard for nontechnical users to manage, and may be less efficient and flexible. Allowing the network (or other third parties) to provide more-complex services can lead to a network that is easier to use and more powerful under normal circumstances but less resistant to adverse control. One outcome might be a network where the end points can control the balance of power—whether they choose to depend on in-network or third-party services or depend as little as possible on actors other than themselves. One scheme that has this outcome is called Extensible Internet Architecture (Anand et al. 2011), where a packet header can contain many sorts of information: a physical end point locator, a service identifier, a content identifier, and so on. It is the choice of the communicating end points which to use.

These observations are designed to help stimulate framing visions of the future. These highlight directions of contingencies along with their salience and potential trajectories. They might also suggest that what we now have is an Internet that is "in transition."

11.3.2   Internet as the Core of Cyberspace

Early on in chapter 1, we defined the cyber arena as a domain of interaction, with the Internet as a mechanism of connectivity. In many chapters of this book, we have used the Internet as the manifest example of the connectivity that creates cyberspace. In chapter 2, for example, we focused on the Internet and its connectivity. In other chapters, we have used cyberspace in its overarching frame as a domain of interaction where dynamics of power, expansion, influence, and control prevail, as we have done in chapter 5. Clearly these views are interconnected, but given that they are not identical it is not difficult to appreciate that that the issues and the actors, although overlapping, are not necessarily identical.

It is highly unlikely that the Internet of the first decade of the twenty-first century will remain as is, sustained over time. In the future, we may see other forms of interconnection that parallel the Internet and lead to new forms of fragmentation and diversity. We might see a more-diversified connectivity system at national or regional levels, or even at the international level, coexisting with the Internet that we have at this point.

It may seem that the Internet is so dominant today that it would not easily be displaced, but this view misses an important distinction—between networks built out of Internet *technology* (in particular, based on the Internet protocol or IP) and the Internet itself. By definition, it also misses the potentials for conflict and competition over connections as well as connectivity. There are many networks today based on IP technology that are *not* the global Internet. The most obvious examples are the global internal networks of large corporations or militaries. For reasons of cost and compatibility, it is convenient to build these out of IP technology, but they may not be connected to the global Internet at all, or if connected, only in a weak way that imposes many more restrictions on traffic flows than can be found at any jurisdictional border. These are the "balkanized" networks, not the regions of the global Internet.

The ISPs of the world have each built networks based on these Internet standards. They hook them together to make the global Internet. They could also hook them together in other ways to make other global networks, networks based on the same standards but not the same business objectives. This sort of interconnection is happening today as part of the transition of our telephone networks from circuit switching to packet switching. Telephone calls today are more and more being carried using VoIP. Voice over IP is *not* necessarily voice over the Internet, a point many regulators have missed as they try to apply Internet regulation to voice. Commercial VoIP provided by ISPs is carried over a separately connected mesh of IP technology.

Given that these alternative IP networks are happening today, it is reasonable to predict that they will proliferate in the future in one form or another, unless they are blocked by regulation. We see today that some of these alternative networks seem more secure and thus a preferred platform for critical activities. This would leave the current Internet as a place for commercial content and casual amusements. This set of futures is still young enough to be shaped, and governments should be thinking about the implications of different outcomes and whether they want to play an active role in this space.

Underlying all of these contingencies is the rapid diffusion of technical capabilities. Early on, only a few entities could control architecture, design, and connectivity. Today technological "leapfrogging" along with greater diffusion of knowledge and skills creates greater possibilities for diversity in potential such future.

Recall also, that despite the above generalizations and contingencies, the fact remains that in very few countries in the world are the ISPs devoid of government control and regulation. The United States, and a handful of other states, have adopted a hands-off approach to the ISPs, but even there governments impose regulation such as network neutrality. In many European states, in Latin America, Africa, Asia, and the Middle East, the influence, control, or ownership of the state is the rule rather than the exception. So, the question arises: will we see an increased divergence or a growing convergence in the ways in which these states relate to or manage their ISPs? The same issues may arise with respect to certificate authorities.

So far, little attention has been given to either ISPs or certificate authorities at international deliberations such as WSIS or NETmundial. They are seen as derivative, rather than core, to the overall contentions we have referred to earlier. If there is to be a next round of global deliberations, and some accord reached, then it is more likely that such features of the overall governance system will be given greater attention.

11.4   Change through the Lenses of Global Governance

Of the many recurrent themes in the earlier chapters of this book, two are especially noteworthy as they may well hold the key to the future not only of cyberspace and its governance but also of the global order as a whole. We consider these as themes, but they also signal potentially powerful cleavages. One pertains to the private-public relationship, which, in many parts of the world, can be highly contentious. The other is about conflict versus cooperation.

If we consider the first of these themes, then at this writing, the private sector dominates in management of the global cyber connectivities and the standards that have been developed and continue to develop. But we do see in some countries, at the national level, the powerful hand of the state with its oversight and regulatory mechanisms. While it is unlikely that we shall see a receding role for the private sector in the United States, we can envisage conditions under which we will see more of government presence, if not active intervention. One that comes immediately to mind is with respect to cybersecurity. Without reviewing the recent policy developments and emergent frames and directives, there will be no retreat of the state from security-related issues.

If we turn to China, the government role is hardly subtle, and the new cybersecurity law is indicative of emergent trajectories. None of this is surprising. If we consider the rich developing countries, such as the states in the Gulf region of the Middle East, there is a general tendency for communication and information systems to be under the purview of the government. Under "normal" circumstances, we would have expected the Gulf countries that try to foster their private sector to encourage management of access at the national level. Current conditions are hardly "normal" given precarious security conditions in the region and increasing awareness of threats to cybersecurity.

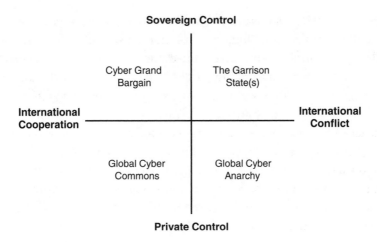

Figure 11.1
Potential futures of cyber politics in international relations.
Source: Choucri (2012, 235).

There is no need to review potential future trajectories, region by region, beyond the observations made in earlier chapters. This is clearly a highly fluid area, and states are more likely to conform to familiar practices of culture and policy than to explore the unknown—in policy or in practice.

When we turn to the second theme, that of conflict and cooperation, it is useful to remind ourselves that these are not pure concepts or conditions. The conduct of conflict generally entails implicit, if not explicit, cooperation among contenders. Cooperation is seldom if ever devoid of conflict. And, of course, there are varying degrees of intensity for both conflict and cooperation. With considerations in mind, we now turn to a set of models for alternative futures for the cyber domain that we had introduced briefly in the first book of the *ECIR* Project in 2012, *Cyberpolitics in International Relations*, which we referred to earlier in chapter 1.

These models were constructed at the intersection of (1) private versus public control and (2) conflict versus cooperation, yielding a two-by-two matrix, as shown in figure 11.1.

These are ideal types in the sense that they highlight the pure core of each quadrant. Without engaging in undue simplification, we suggest that if the U.S. vision of the Internet, in the very early years, had come to fruition in all of the ways hoped for, then the global cyber order could be moving more toward a *global cyber commons* (with private sector salience) or toward a *cyber grand bargain* (via accord among sovereign states). By contrast, if we consider the China case, it is not too difficult to suggest that a China that controls Internet access and traffic in a world of conflict may be closer to *the garrison state* so insightfully framed by Lasswell (1941). If the sovereign state "withdraws" and allows the private sector free rein, with the pursuit of profit unrestricted by regulation or the imposition of larger societal aspirations, then we can envisage something of *global cyber anarchy*.

Because these are ideal types, any attempt to operationalize these futures in more detail requires explicit reference to elements salient in other models. For example, even the most stark form of *global cyber anarchy* requires some cooperation—at least to enable the desired connectivity—and expectations that some coordination will always prevail.

The important point here is this—these future models were intellectual constructs based largely on the levels of analysis view with only limited attention to the layers of the Internet. In other words, they were built on only one part of the joint cyber–international relations (IR) system that we developed in earlier chapters and highlighted in chapter 4. By turning once more to two salient features of today's world (private vs. public and conflict vs. cooperation), we are signaling some fundamental parameters that will not change on short order. We conclude, therefore, that a review of the original four models of the future, given what we now know about the joint cyber-IR system, will put these visions to the test, but more importantly, we would be able to anticipate enabling conditions already in place.

11.5   Endnote: What Have We Learned?

Our inferences about the future are shaped by some general presumptions. Individuals and small groups of people can be very nimble at inventing unexpected and unpredictable innovations that may come to shape the future, for example, Bitcoin. The private sector can as well move quickly in certain circumstances (e.g., where capital is not the gating factor) and will continue to be a powerful driver of the future.

Individual states are proving that they can be effective at shaping their domestic Internet, whereas the state-centered international system, hampered by inconsistent goals and the complexity of negotiation, will be less effective at shaping the future—in the language of chapter 9, the state-centered international system may not prove fit for purpose. Informal transnational mechanisms will be more nimble than formal ones and can generate preferred paths for collective action, facilitating nations to achieve common goals.

But we must remember that if and as the adaptive and "nimble" arrangements are recognized as effective, then they are often converted into more formal arrangements. The conversion frees the global policy agenda and allows attention to be given to other seemingly more salient issues. So, too, even the most nimble arrangements are often supported by institutionalized mechanisms, such as insurance policies or conflict resolution techniques.

These factors suggest that the future will be a more diverse Internet, especially at the level that the user perceives it; what we have been calling the "Internet experience" will become more diverse. Especially relevant here are the affordances generated by the Internet experience and the potentials for innovations as well as departures from conventional modes of interaction in markets as well as politics. Users experience the Internet through the applications, and the lower layers that move packets are hidden. But so long as that lower layer remains globally coherent, and so long as states do not block the ability of their users to partake of the global experience to the extent that they choose to, the future of the Internet may be both a national experience for most of its users and a vector for globalization. This is the optimistic story of the future that we hope will prevail.

This book is about the emergence of cyberspace as a fundamental, unavoidable, and defining feature of contemporary international relations. Driven by technological change, human motivations, creative capabilities, and enabling conditions, cyberspace and the international system are increasingly interconnected. As a result, the views of the international system—in terms of the theories, conventional policies, and prevailing practices that dominated the twentieth century—are seldom consistent with the realities of the twenty-first century.

Cyberspace creates new conditions in world politics that require adjustment to traditional conceptions of the international system, on the one hand, and an understanding of how international relations affects and is affected by cyberspace, on the other. As we noted early on, the rate of cyber access has grown faster than our ability to respond effectively to new trends and emergent consequences. In chapter 1, we introduced the co-evolution dilemma, with figure 1.1 framing the overall question at hand.

The dilemma is shaped by the differential rates of change of two systems, cyberspace and international relations, as well as differentials in rates of change for their constitutive elements—thereby creating realities and uncertainties that are particularly difficult to anticipate and especially difficult to regulate. The dilemma is also multifaceted, with diverse time constants, authority systems, operational mechanisms, and formal and informal rules, actors and entities—with all of the contentions therein—creating sustained challenges for all actors, formal and informal, established or emerging.

In this book, we take on the challenge of developing a framework integrating both domains, one that allows us to examine their interconnections across different issues and in various contexts. We do so by presenting a

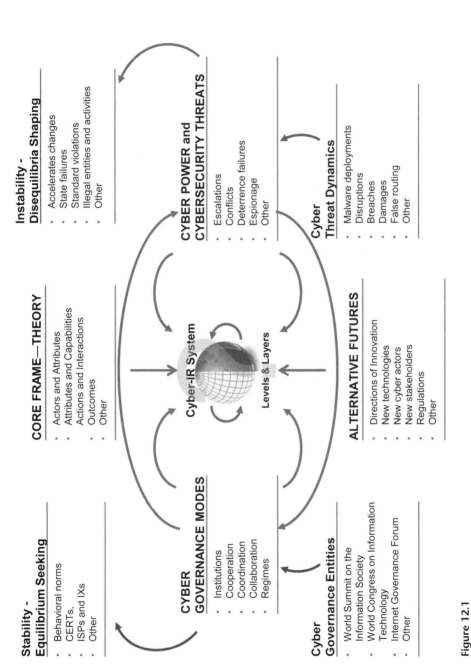

Stability -
Equilibrium Seeking

· Behavioral norms
· CERTs,
· ISPs and IXs
· Other

CORE FRAME—THEORY

· Actors and Attributes
· Attributes and Capabilities
· Actions and Interactions
· Outcomes
· Other

Instability -
Disequilibria Shaping

· Accelerates changes
· State failures
· Standard violations
· Illegal entities and activities
· Other

CYBER POWER and
CYBERSECURITY THREATS

· Escalations
· Conflicts
· Deterrence failures
· Espionage
· Other

Cyber-IR System

Levels & Layers

Cyber
Threat Dynamics

· Malware deployments
· Disruptions
· Breaches
· Damages
· False routing
· Other

ALTERNATIVE FUTURES

· Directions of Innovation
· New technologies
· New cyber actors
· New stakeholders
· Regulations
· Other

CYBER
GOVERNANCE MODES

· Institutions
· Cooperation
· Coordination
· Collaboration
· Regimes

Cyber
Governance Entities

· World Summit on the
  Information Society
· World Congress on Information
  Technology
· Internet Governance Forum
· Other

Figure 12.1
Select highlights of emergent cyber-IR theory. *Note:* All entries are illustrative. See figure 1.1 for reference.

series of models that are intended to clarify the character of cyberspace, and relate cyberspace to prevailing theory in international relations, to the spectrum of cooperation and conflict, as well as to the different modes of leverage, influence, and power by various actors, governance mechanisms, and management systems.

This last chapter begins with a review of process, focusing on the sequence of analysis and the diversity of methods and perspectives, with only few observations on results.[1] This tour highlights key elements of our approach, our methods and the underlying logic that enables us to frame, understand, represent, and, to some extent, anticipate impacts of co-evolution for cyberspace and international relations. By way of orientation, we represent in figure 12.1 the logic we develop as we proceed to address the question mark of figure 1.1.

Early on, we signal that the features of cyberspace (table 1.1) individually and collectively undermine the order established by the Treaty of West-phalia. None of these are usually considered particularly relevant from a technological or computer science perspective. But these features undermine the power and sovereignty of states and the traditional norms of the international system. The cyber system, a constructed arena of interaction, is here to stay. We must find ways of accommodating international relations theory, policy, and practice to its pervasive reality.

12.1   Systems of Interaction

Part I of this book focuses on the structures and processes of cyberspace (with the Internet at its core) and the international system (anchored in state and sovereignty). The first chapters are foundational. We construct a framework that enables us to the combine the distinct domains into one integrated system. The co-evolution dilemma is manifested in different ways, at different times, and in different contexts.

We begin by presenting a layered model of the Internet. The Internet and the applications that run on it are built artifacts. To the extent that designers can understand the constraints and tools that can stabilize a global association of willing individuals, those tools can be engineered into the applications that the Internet provides. We show that the layered structure induces a layered-industry structure, so not just technology but several classes of actors show a layered structure. As we get further from the technology itself (e.g., when we look at social interactions or government activities) the lay-ered structure is less pronounced, but it shapes operators, providers, stan-dards bodies, and some governance organizations. We also see certain cyber actors easily fitting into different scopes.

We distinguish between the physical layer, where resources are costly and where the actors that control these resources tend to be localized to a particular region, and the virtual layers above the physical (those we referred to as the Internet, services, application, and information layers) where the actors are more likely to be global, transnational, or in distant jurisdictions. Service providers at the lower layers (physical and Internet) are often associated with physical infrastructure. Ownership of capital-intensive physical assets (e.g., fibers, towers, etc.) tends to bind a provider to a location, and thus to a jurisdiction. So providers at this layer seem to fit naturally into the "state" scope. Actors at higher layers (e.g., a player such as Google), although they may have major infrastructure investments in one or another country, are more international in scope. Exceptions to the "state" physicality we associate with lower layer providers include satel-lite and undersea cable providers. These are more international in nature, which reflects the fact that they connect states together. We noted that the structure of the virtual layers makes enforcement of jurisdictional concerns difficult and, at the same time, the requirements and consequences of these layers can have effects on physical layers.

The layers model is a useful device to (1) locate cyber actors and activities, (2) signal changes in strategies or orientations, (3) identify the conditions under which actors operate across layers or, alternatively, chose to concen-trate their activities within a layer, and thus (4) help track and represent the processes of transformation and change in each of the layers of the Internet.

Then we turn to the international system and present an extended levels of analysis model. This view consists of four levels—the individual, the state (and nonstate actors), the international system and the overarching global system—and their interconnections. All are embedded in three distinct domains, that is, the social system, the natural environment, and cyberspace.

Unlike the layers structure, the permeability of influences across levels of analysis is the rule, not the exception. The extent to which conditions and behaviors at one level influence structure and process across others varies considerably and, despite evidence of increasing cyber access worldwide, the operational norms and practices vary considerably within levels and across jurisdictions.

At this point, cyberspace cannot be seen as separate and insulated from the traditional "real" international system; nor can we consider much of what happens in the cyber arena as a mirror image of, or equivalent to, behaviors in the off-line world. Their increasing interconnections call into question the extent to which we can continue to refer to these two domains as different "realities." We find that some states exhibit a similar profile type in the cyber as in the traditional arenas, but others exhibit a different profile type. These may even be important when viewed in geopolitical terms. So far we have focused on empirical analysis and hazarded only situational explanations for the similarities or the differences.

12.2   The Joint Cyber-IR System

By focusing on the *intersection* of the layers of the Internet and the levels of analysis in international relations (IR) we develop an alignment strategy to generate the integrated joint cyber-IR system. The integrated model is then used to make the point that many issues of importance—contentious or otherwise—can be positioned in the matrix formed by the combination of levels and layers, and that by locating an issue within that matrix, one can better understand the fundamental features of *who does what, when,* and *how.* We can infer the interests of the actors and then draw tentative conclusions as to possible approaches to dealing with the issues.

At the state level, our joint cyber-IR model should remind us that different states see their posture with respect to cyberspace at different scopes. The United States seems to view cyberspace as a global phenomenon, as signaled by former Secretary of State Hillary Clinton and her call for a global open Internet.[2] Other states, notably China, seem to see cyberspace at the scope of the state, with their more internal-facing concerns leading them to control the Internet that they want.

The integrated framework, presented in matrix form, provides an important first step, a useful baseline to help (1) track changes in actors, functions, situations, standards, and other critical factors shaping current realities, altering these realities, or taking on new significance over time; (2) identify, explore, and anticipate the potential futures—in conceptual, empirical, and perhaps even strategic terms; (3) signal emergent conflicts of interest or intersections in spheres of influence; and, especially important, (4) frame policy and practice on sound normative and empirical principles. For example, a wide range of recent political events demonstrate how aggregated activities at the individual level and the user layer (aggregated protest) impact the state level (threats to stability), which in turn, leads the state to control cyber access through denial of service or other policies.

As we identify specific problems and position them within this matrix, we conclude that an effective solution to a problem is best positioned at or above the layer at which the problem is located. With respect to the positioning of a problem within a level of analysis, a solution may arise at different levels; an effective solution depends on the existence of operational institutional mechanisms at that level.

Extending the lateral pressure model, we explore the extent to which the distribution of states by profile type in the international system is replicated in the cyber arena. We find that technology-dominant states tend to demonstrate tendencies for expansion—in both domains. We also find that the propensity of a state to expand behavior—power and influence—in the cyber domain does not necessarily mirror the propensity to expand in the "real" system. (It is tempting to infer that conscious policy choices are being made—even at early stages of development.) One consistent result is that China exhibits the greatest propensity for expansion in both real and cyber domains. The United States ranks second, and India is third. When we come to the ranking of states situated from the fourth position onward, we find notable differences in cross-domain postures. For example, Vietnam shows a clear propensity for expansion in cyberspace; by contrast Iran and Saudi Arabia show almost none. Further, it should come as no surprise that technology appears to be the dominant master variable for states with notable cyber lateral pressure.

Of the many features of the joint cyber-IR system that are distinct departures from tradition, two are especially relevant at this point: one is the increased autonomy (and vulnerability) of the individual empowered by access to cyber venues; the other is the growth (and salience) of civil society at all levels of analysis. Both of these shape new forms of interest aggregation and articulation, and are becoming important elements in politics, nationally and internationally. As we proceed, we see more departures from tradition. We do not dismiss the imperatives of power politics; we continue to expect all actors in the joint cyber-IR system to pursue and protect their own interests, expand their influence in ways other than deemed necessary, and shape rules and regulations in ways that are advantageous to them. But we do observe some revealing behavioral propensities. Clearly, as we noted early on, jurisdiction matters—and matters a lot—in international relations.

We then turn to the question, *who* controls access to the cyber arena and how? We ask, *why* is it that the Internet seems to make attack easy and prevention hard? *When* does the Internet favor control and when does it favor the unregulated flow of information?

12.3   Control Points

We introduce an approach we call control point analysis as a means to represent, and thus reason about, how different actors can exercise control over the operation of cyberspace. In contrast to the layers and levels, which is a static model, control point analysis provides a more dynamic picture of the flow of activity that sustains the cyber domain, as one set of actors try to carry out a task, and another set of actors potentially try to shape, regulate, or hinder that task. We use examples both of expected tasks (e.g., looking at a Web page or reading mail) and tasks that are considered inappropriate (e.g., using spam to market knockoff products).

Control point analysis is best described as a focus on a sequence along the structure-actor-process-decision-outcome chain, customized to the requirements of a particular task on the Internet. Once we have diagrammed a particular task and identified potential control points, we can then associate a specific control point with the actors that can exercise that control, and situate these control points within/or across the matrix of layers and levels. In some ways, this approach carries features in common with supply chain analysis in engineering, or process tracing in international relations. In short, control point analysis is about locational control of user access when users are distributed worldwide.

A central theme in our research is the interplay between private sector actors (who have specified, built, and operated cyberspace) and public sector actors (as states, actors, and international organizations) who assert traditional rights to shape, even regulate, the character of their respective states and the citizens therein. We have used a number of methods to compare and contrast the power and influence these two classes of entities.

Our linking of actors to control points allows us to show how the policies and practices of different actors and entities in the cyber domain are anchored in, or enabled by, the leverage of, and over, different control points. Especially important in this respect are the differences among actors in their own internal structuration for management of the Internet, and efforts to influence the cyber domain more broadly defined. We demonstrate in some detail how exercise of control points differs across jurisdictions, shaped by national values and institutional capacity.

Different countries (with different traditions and limitations) will push for more specific controls at different layers. China and the United States (with first amendment concerns) show very different willingness to intervene to shape or regulate information-layer activities. At the moment, the information layer of cyberspace is less shaped by open common standards and more shaped by the economic motivations of specific private sector actors (e.g., Facebook). The interplay between public and private sector actors around the character of the information layer is an emerging phenomenon and should be examined systematically, exploring the extent that we see state involvement with the private sector players at the information layer.

Cyber contention tends to focus on the layers of most relevance to the issue of concern, typically the application and information layers. For this reason, debates about the open nature of the Internet layer itself will become less central. Blocking at that level will be used only to determine which applications will be made available to users. Thus, China blocks Facebook (at the Internet layer), which has the consequence that Chinese users adopt the domestic alternatives such as Renren and WeChat, which seem to have more tools built in for censorship and control of content.

By comparing the United States and China, we demonstrate how states can use the various control points in the Internet structure to shape or influence the user experience, and illustrate how states manage the Internet in ways consistent with their political values and along principles congruent with those it uses to manage their political system. Then, by focusing on Google, we show how a global firm manages its uses of the Internet. These examples help us to better understand and appreciate some basic features of structure and process and the points at which the cyber experience is contingent on decisions and actions made by actors and entities that are entirely unknown in the traditional domain of international relations.

Both theory and methods pertaining to control point analysis are at early stages of development. We do not have an integrated perspective policy view of technical control, nor of the technical controls for policy implementation. Foundations are most certainly in place, given initiatives in diverse fields and disciplines. But coherence—in theory and method, policy and practice—is yet to be consolidated.

12.4 Complexities of Co-Evolution

Part II focuses on the complexities of co-evolution and the countervailing threats and supports that press upon the joint cyber-IR system. We highlight contentions of various forms, with the full appreciation of conceptual ambiguities, data problems, and the absence of standards for both concepts and metrics. We also draw attention to the institutions and mechanisms whose mission is to find ways of reducing conflicts and disturbances in the cyber arena. We then turn to the ways in which the international system and its member states begin to address the salience of cyberspace, the emergence of new forms of contention, and at times even converge on a trajectory of international collaboration.

Central to such complexities is the growth of threats to cybersecurity. We explore available evidence pertaining to cyberattacks and various forms of threat to cybersecurity. We present some broad sketches by way of capturing dominant trends in the evolution of the threats to cyber interactions, notably the increased sophistication of attacks. We then review the case-based evidence, where the case is a recognized cyber conflict (involving mainly nonstate entities) as well as statistical analysis (involving only individual states). In so doing, we illustrate the differences as well as similarities in the nature of interactions among contending actors, their use of cyber venues at, or across, different levels of analysis, and their resort to anonymity networks (such as Tor, a system that uses a transjurisdiction forwarding overlay to provide anonymity).

These investigations reveal a "new normal" for world politics in the cyber age that is shaped by, and contingent on, the activities of wide range of nonstate entities—known and unknown—who operate in a highly dynamic and volatile international context. If the traditional international system is considered "anarchic," then how can the joint cyber-IR system be less anarchic?

We then explore the governance mechanisms of the Internet and its implications for cyberspace, broadly defined. We rely largely on information provided in the memoranda of understanding, and then we focus on the Requests for Comments and attendant details. Our investigations indicate that the cyber domain, fully constitutive and operational, is itself governed in ways that are almost entirely separate from the rules and operations of, and in, traditional international relations. The governance model derived from these sources is distributed and decentralized in structure and process. This model is based entirely on private authority and managed via processes of self-organization and adaptation.

Governance of the Internet is based on consensus and managed by mutual expectations, rather than on formal mechanisms of traditional regulation. We show how authority is rendered to the operating entities and how legitimacy derives from performance. This means that management of the joint cyber-IR system today involves highly innovative and decentralized mechanisms (for the cyber domain) in conjunction with the very traditional institutional mechanisms (for the international system).

It is not too much of a leap in logic to anticipate what is in fact taking place—the state system as a whole is "pushing back" in its efforts to reassert control over what it considers as an uncontrolled arena. With few exceptions, the formal members of the international system have been slow to recognize the salience of the cyber domain as well as its relative insulation from traditional governance mechanisms. But, as we trace the co-evolution of the two parts of the combined system, we show how these begin to converge around shared institutional concerns supporting sustainable development for the traditional international system as well as sustainability of the constructed system. The convergence platforms appear in global conferences, and the emergent political agenda begins to span both the cyber and the traditional domains.

12.5 Changes and Challenges

The co-evolution of the combined system reminds us that all parts of cyberspace evolve, some quite rapidly. States shift in profile type, with some showing greater propensity for expansion in cyberspace than others. Even our control point analysis evolves over time, as different actors compete in ways that alter the balance of power and control. At this point we recognize once more the important functions of institutions, namely to routinize behaviors, facilitate change, and, by definition, to reduce volatility and uncertainty as much as possible.

Indeed, almost every chapter of this book deals with change, directly or indirectly. In chapter 10 we signal that different parts of the joint cyber-"real" ecosystem evolves at different rates. The technology of cyberspace evolves much more rapidly than we expect the state system to evolve. Speed is seldom a characteristic feature of governance, regulation, or state behavior. In chapter 11 we explore the matter of change through several different "lenses"—via the layer model, the levels model, control point analysis, and governance of cyberspace. It should come as no surprise that each "lens" yields a different view. Interestingly, jointly these provide a multidimensional perspective rather than mutually exclusive views.

Clearly, it becomes increasingly challenging, near impossible, to consider cyberspace and the state system as separate and autonomous domains. The twenty-first-century reality is one in which the cyber domain and the social system—in all of its facets and at all levels of analysis—are interconnected and mutually interdependent. The two systems, that were once parallel and then gradually become joined, have generated a new "whole" whose overall "sum" is greater than what were once individual "parts."

Can we predict the outcome of cyber contention? There seem to be two alternative outcomes. One extreme is that we converge on global norms with respect to regulation of the information layer, which would probably not match the desires of any single party. The other is that we shape a world with more diversity/heterogeneity with respect to norms, regulations, and control. This more heterogeneous world will not involve disrupting the open character of the Internet layer more than it is currently disrupted. China demonstrates that the current tools of control (e.g., port blocking) are adequate to allow it to achieve the desired heterogeneity at the information layer. It is at that layer where divergence and heterogeneity will consolidate.

We can predict what shape this "more diverse" Internet will take. We can see the pattern today with respect to Facebook. Those regions that favor a more open and inclusive version of cyberspace will naturally interconnect in an open and homogeneous way. Those actors that favor a more closed and regulated alternative (from the point of view of connectivity or topology) will find themselves at the "edge." Thus, Facebook connects most of the world, but China is not in its world map. The Chinese alternative, Renren, sits by itself as an alternative used only in China. (We note that if population matters, the Chinese alternative is used by a large segment of Internet users.)

Thus, with all due caution, our prediction is that the "connectedness map" of the future Internet, at all layers, will feature an interconnected core of regions that favor a more open and inclusive cyber experience, and other regions that are distinguished by the imposition of more controls and more limits on activity and behavior. Those who favor more regulation will exert regulation within their jurisdiction. It is not clear at this point what this might do to the global network as a whole. By now almost all countries, democratic and nondemocratic, impose some form of control over the diffusion of content.

Then, too, given that international relations theory—in its various manifestations—does not yet address the implications of cyberspace for world politics at any level of analysis, we now must ask, what can we say about fundamentals for twenty-first-century international relations theory given the salience of cyberspace in an increasingly complicated world? We do not presume to put forth an operational theory, rather our purpose is to highlight some essential elements.

12.6 Imperatives for Twenty-First-Century IR—Theory, Policy, and Practice

Our basic proposition is that twenty-first-century international relations theory must, by necessity, be framed as a *theory of change*—in the context of existing and emergent structures and processes, as well as underling regularities of norms and expectations for the management of complexity. We cannot predict the future trajectory of the Internet, or the emergent configurations of cyberspace, or the future of the international system. But it is difficult to overlook the explosion of new products and processes such as the Internet of Things, the salience of mobility in all its forms, machine-machine interactions, enhanced human-facing experience, and so forth.

In this context, a compelling challenge for twenty-first-century theory is to generate a sufficiently compelling representation of international relations and its complexities to help understand prevailing realities and to serve as a map to facilitate the formulation of policy and the shaping of practice. For this purpose, we focus on some basic, if not pressing, imperatives drawn from our investigations. The term "imperatives" refers to the essential, even necessary, anchors for twenty-first-century theory—as well as policy and practice—grounded in the evolution of knowledge as well as evidence and experiences of the past decades and not on assumptions or premises of twentieth-century power and politics. As imperatives, we consider these to be foundational for our understanding and management of emergent realities.

What follows is a brief statement of notable, critical, even necessary, imperatives—reflecting dynamics of change and complexity of theory—to capture defining features of twenty-first-century world politics. Although they are interconnected, we consider each one individually, and address them sequentially.

12.6.1 Structure and Process—Cyber and "Real"

The first and probably most important imperative—an immediate challenge—is to recognize that the joint cyber-IR system provides a fundamental context, a platform, for addressing power and politics worldwide. Given that the layers of the Internet and the levels of analysis in international relations are critical coordinates for situating *who* does *what, how,* and *why*—and with effects—the joint system is a necessary, perhaps even sufficient, entry point into framing twenty-first-century international relations theory, policy, and practice. This approach provides a view of the "whole" and the "parts" and helps contextualize actors and entities, interests and activities, as well as sources of change and potential impacts.

The layers framework distinguishes between the physical infrastructure of the Internet and its role as a carrier of information. The international system is affected by the construction of the cyber domain. Sophisticated controls at the information layer are required to address emergent international contentions, whereas "blunt instrument" approaches (as we have seen in Egypt and elsewhere) are both ineffective and counterproductive. It is also difficult to overlook the obvious. The physical layer of the Internet is anchored in a territorial context. Although sovereign reach may not permeate all layers, it is operative at the foundations.

Cyberspace evolves rapidly. Its rate of evolution has been likened to that of fruit flies. This fact is a consequence of the private sector drivers of investment, competition, and innovation. It is also a function of users and uses. Also relevant is its open character despite various efforts by various states to create constraints. But all parties are swept along at the same pace, irrespective of their ability to cope.

Recall that traditional theories are remarkably silent on the matter of time, the issue of timescale, or differential and uneven rates of change. By contrast, far from tradition is lateral pressure theory, for which the matter of time and the differentials in rates of change play a fundamental, if not determinant, role in explaining power relations, shifts in power, and potential of consequences—in both real and cyber domains.

Matters of theory aside, recall also the speed of technological diffusion throughout the world, in general terms as well as cyber related. We know that traditional public sector institutions for governance—formalized by definition and often structured around debate and deliberation—have not kept pace with the cyber dynamics. In general, the rapid pace of change in cyberspace seems to favor the nimbler, less formally institutionalized private entities for the governance of cyberspace.

12.6.2 Sovereign States versus Private Actors—Modes of Leverage

The second imperative, also a major challenge, is to revisit the role of the state. The state is not in a danger of being crowded out of the cyber-IR system. But the state may not be able to retain the leverage on nonstate entities accorded to it by its presumed monopoly over the use of force—a presumption with little if any evidence on the ground or "in the clouds."

Our extension of the traditional levels of analysis recognizes the importance of nonstate actors. The legitimacy of the state remains a major anchor for theory and policy, but its privileged role is greatly constrained by the dominance of private authority in the operation and management of cyberspace. The private sector—for profit and not for profit—is recognized as a key anchor of structure and function along with emergent mixed private–public entities as situationally driven. Private actors, motivated by economic incentives, will display different behaviors than nation states. For state actors, cyber power may be more manipulable than any aspect of hard power. This fact, reinforced by the rise of China, could be seen as instrumental in a power transition and should be considered from that point of view.

Then, too, to the various motivations that drive state behavior we must add sustainability—the pursuit of well-being as a critical goal—for humans, their natural environment, and the constructed cyber domain. This goal appears relevant and has been adopted by many states and private entities. Less evident, however, is the extent to which sustainability has become important in the discourse on the future of the cyber domain.

Central to the concerns of the state are its rights of jurisdiction, but so far cyberspace transcends jurisdictional boundaries. Some states seek to control content, but the character of the Internet makes that difficult. Some see cyberspace as a benefit to their citizens, but not all citizens are positioned to exploit its benefits. Many are concerned with the flow of revenue across their borders. In sum, content has value, and states struggle to protect, capture, tax, and manage such value to their advantage.

The growth in the number of actors increases the density of decision entities—each with new interests and new capabilities—shaping increasing intersections in spheres of influence. Among the new nonstate actors are commercial entities, creators of new markets, proxies for state actors, cybercriminals (generally too varied to list and too anonymous to identify); and not-for-profit actors (faith groups, international interest groups, agenda setters, etc.); and the anonymous actors—"good" and "bad" as the case may be—whose anonymity itself conflicts with traditional principles of international interactions.

Further, to have an effective means to exert influence over cyberspace, an actor must be able to act at the layer at which the issue arises. Because many issues of importance to states arise at the information layer, countries (such as the United States) with strong biases against regulation of speech will be at a disadvantage compared to countries with no such hesitations, and compared to private actors that are more empowered to regulate content, speech, and the like.

At the same time, however, we see that private actors can provide the means to stabilize international interaction, association, and transaction. For example, Internet service providers (ISPs), generally private entities in many countries, are more effective than states in managing situational resources that are critical for creating shared value and common good. Invariably states are driven by a wide range of often divergent objectives and motivations. In the constructed cyber system, the ISPs share the same goal of providing a valued product. In the United States and other industrial states, the growing tensions between public and private in the cyber domain are increasingly apparent. Recall that, in many of these states, the computer industry and the content industries are all private sector activities.

Especially noteworthy is consolidation of civil society as a distinct constituency or constituencies. It is plausible to suggest that in the absence of explicit external barriers, civil society for the cyber arena will consolidate under two conditions: when individuals converge around common interests or common aversions, and when the barriers intrinsic to any self-regulated associations can be held in check. At the same time, however, it may well be the lack of shared understanding of tools for self-regulation, rather than the imposition of barriers, that threatens civil society worldwide.

Much of the forgoing leads us to the governance of the Internet, its distributed structure, and its operations—as well as the formal, state based, initiatives that it engenders. The challenge is to retain and strengthen its most salient and fundamental features and, to the extent possible, improve and strengthen the performance and accountability of some essential but less robust elements, such as the certificate authorities, for example. Given that the entire system of distributed governance is built on an authority system whose legitimacy is contingent on operational performance, this aspect of the second imperative is especially important now and in the future.

12.6.3 Governance and Government—Shaping Futures for Cyberspace

The third imperative is about control of the processes that sustain the cyber-IR system. These processes are contentious. They have the goal of shaping the character of cyberspace itself. What degree of regulation? How much "openness" should there be in cyberspace? Contention is often related to symbolic issues that are central to national identity, such as alphabetic character sets.

At the international level, cyber contentions are centered at the application and information layers and above, not the physical or Internet layers. Many of the moves and countermoves involve attempts to blunt the instruments of one's opponents. The goals of the actors are asymmetric. Different parties may have incomparable or opposite objectives. This makes the analysis of cyber contention more complex. (For example, the United States is concerned about espionage and theft of IP. China is concerned about destabilizing content. In both cases, the two parties seem to hold "opposite" views on the issues, but the two issues are not directly linked. This raises the potential for shared interest in the resolution of cyber contentions.)

Standard setting and governance of the Internet, carried out by organizations such as the Corporation for Internet Assigned Names and numbers (ICANN) and the Internet Engineering Task Force (IETF), are to some greater or lesser degree private actors. With Internet governance defined more by performance and responsibility, and less by traditional principles of sovereignty, these institutions assume considerable power derived from their unique and unprecedented functions and position in the overall cyber domain. At this point, the entire cyber system rests on the integrity and effectiveness of their performance—and thus of their legitimacy.

Signaled earlier is the notable pushback by the International Telecommunication Union (ITU), and other international organizations, who appear to undermine the legitimacy of the new institutions for the management of the Internet (specifically ICANN, IETF, and others). This posture leads to growing contestation of influence and control over cyber venues and new tensions of legitimacy and responsibility, which further complicates the already thorny issue of accountability.

All of this represents growing intersections of influence and struggles over the control of emergent cyber norms and practices. These struggles are between sovereign authority and international institutions managing traditional order, on the one hand, and powerful nonstate entities with private authority for managing the Internet, on the other. They are also struggles between states with different values and visions, varied instruments of influence and leverage, and diverse preferences for the future of cyberspace.

Notable among the state-based initiatives engendered by the Internet and its governance are, for example, the Computer Emergency Response Teams (CERTs), a loose network of organizations in different parts of the world seeking to take stock of, and reduce, breaches of cybersecurity. A more formal response is illustrated by the Convention on Cybercrime, also known as the Budapest Convention on Cybercrime or the Budapest Convention, the first international treaty seeking to harmonize national laws and increase cooperation among states. Because the Internet and the applications that run on it are built artifacts, we expect tools to enable self-governance of human association to be essential for consolidating global civil society. By the same token, we anticipate the management of identity to be fundamental in this toolkit. To the extent that we can understand the constraints and tools that can stabilize a global association of willing individuals, those tools can be engineered into the applications that the Internet provides. All of this hearkens back to the underlying principle of an "open Internet" and to the protection of this principle. At a deeper level, there are powerful conflicts over the value of the principle itself.

Transcending all of the above is a rather vexing matter. We have a *situation in search of equilibrium*—but we cannot, as yet, converge on the conditions or parameters of equilibrium. There are some things that only the state can do; there are others that only the private sector can do; and there are still others that only people can do.

12.6.4   Cybersecurity and Conflict Dynamics

The fourth imperative is about threats to cybersecurity, dynamics of conflict surrounding cyber-based interactions, and new vulnerabilities transmitted via cyber venues. The challenge is to understand the various modalities and the ways in which different actors seek to exert influence and shape their environment in the way that supports this quest. Clearly, cybersecurity is attaining top billing in policy contexts, nationally and internationally—in both the private and the public sectors. It is almost impossible to consider the future of international relations theory or reality, policy or practice without recognizing the importance of seriously rethinking conventional conceptions of security—for the state, for civil society, and for people—at any or all levels of aggregation.

The growing concerns over cyber threats to the security of the state reinforce the politicization of cyberspace and its salience in emergent policy discourses. Threats of this type include the militarization or weaponization of cyberspace, damages to critical infrastructures, various types of cybercrimes and espionage, and other broad issues. Invariably, they contaminate the traditional calculus of conflict and cooperation based on the historical experience of major powers. This calculus is anchored in the assumptions that the military instruments of power dominate, that the identity of the contenders are known, and that, in the last analysis, "might" can be relied upon to make "right."

At the same time, we see the growing use of cyber venues by nonstate groups whose objectives are to register protest, or undermine the security of the state, or alter its very foundations. For example, the WikiLeaks episodes showed in unambiguous ways the politicization and disruptiveness of cyberspace. Responses varied across the international landscape, but in general most, if not all, states view these moves as a threat to sovereignty and security. They are also more and more aware of their own vulnerabilities.

Especially notable are "reverse asymmetries," for example, when weaker actors can influence or even threaten stronger actors (such as press reports of anonymous penetration incidences of the U.S. government computer systems). Reverse asymmetries reflect a potentially powerful shift in the nature of international politics, especially in cases of nonstate entities versus state actors. The influence of the former begins to chip away at the power of sovereignty as the defining principle of world order.

Invariably, this fourth imperative calls for—and will lead to—innovative methods for analyzing increasingly complicated features of emergent and dynamic realities. Even the simple variable of time, a commonly assumed and utilized feature analysis in world politics—one that is standardized, well recognized, and metricized at equal and invariant increments—will have to be reconsidered as we begin to appreciate the characteristics of cyberspace, the potentials for variability in the cyber domain, and the implications of what is often described as near-instantaneous interactions.

Increasingly scholars and analysts of international politics will have to focus on threats to the security of the layers of the Internet, and devote time and effort to understanding the implications for theory, policy, and practice. The salience of cybersecurity has already led to the greater use of such concepts as resilience, vulnerability, safety, and others—in addition to the well-accepted notion of sustainability. Assuming conceptual clarification, attention to matters of measurement and metrics in international interactions will invariably follow—over and above what is already apparent in the proverbial marketplace or in the plethora of policy circles. International relations theory and methods are at early stages of developing effective metrics for cybersecurity or for any features of the cyber domain.

12.6.5 Systems of Interaction: Overarching "Spaces"

This fifth imperative transcends both cyberspace and international relations, but it is fundamental to each, and, more to the point, it bears on all forms and modes of human interactions—at all levels of analysis and layers of the Internet. It is derived from our recognition that we are embedded in closely interconnected or overlapping systems (domains or "spaces") sensitive to, and shaped by, our normal day-to-day activities. This imperative is generic and derives from our increased, evidence-based understanding of the world in which we live.

To state once more the obvious, we are situated in a *social system*, we are inevitably and invariably anchored in a *natural environment* for the provision of life-supporting properties, and, increasingly, we find ourselves engaged in *cyberspace*, the built environment. These systems constitute the overarching contexts within which are embedded not only with respect to the four imperatives just presented, but by extension, for all of the issues addressed in this book.

The fifth imperative is this: because we cannot extricate ourselves from these "spaces" nor can we chose to "opt out," it is essential that we devote considerable time and effort to better understand not only their interconnections but also how they affect and are affected by human actions, directly and indirectly. To date, our modes of inquiry and research practices concentrate on each of these systems individually. The challenge is that we must examine and understand the interconnections among them. We recognize the generativity thereof—as shown in figure 5.1—but usually in ad hoc form. Missing, however, is sustained engagement in scientific inquiry of linkages, change, transformations, and evolution.

12.7   The End

The joint cyber-IR system—anchored at the intersection of the layers of the Internet and the levels of analysis in international relations—is a valuable mapping model of structure and process, as well as a baseline to help capture the emergent features of the twenty-first century—with attendant actors, actions, policies, and impacts. It helps amplify, deepen, and unfold the levels of analysis and cross-level effects. It signals the implications of action and decision at each layer of the Internet, most notably the physical layer with its anchor in state sovereignty. It also points to the impacts of, and implications for, different levels of analysis.

These five imperatives require attention, development, and formal articulation. There are surely many more. These serve largely as important points of departure for reflecting on fundamentals of transformation and change. The fact is that every facet of the social order is subject to change, in different ways and at different rates. These imperatives are not about change per se. They are about sources and consequences, trajectories and manifestations, as well as assumptions, explicit or implicit, that help frame our understanding of causal logic and attendant dynamics.

Although the proverbial skeptic may argue that *plus ça change, plus c'est la même chose*, it is difficult to envisage a reversal of co-evolution for cyberspace and international relations. It may also be difficult to conceive of a world enabled by other than an integrated joint cyber-IR system. But it is near impossible to anticipate the full measure of the co-evolution dilemma throughout the twenty-first century—and beyond.

Notes

2 Cyberspace

1. The term was coined by a science fiction writer, William Gibson, and popularized in his book *Neuromancer* (Gibson 1984).

3 International Relations

1. Especially relevant are the contributions of Almond and Powell (1966), who defined government activities as extractive, distributive, responsive, regulative, and symbolic in nature. It is not difficult to see the connection between this view of capabilities and most of the variables in the state's national budget. Less obvious is the reconciliation of these capabilities with one of the most fundamental functions of government, not explicitly addressed by Almond and Powell, namely the provision of national security.

2. The theory recognizes that the master variables are highly interactive. In other words, they cannot be viewed or represented as entirely autonomous, devoid of any mutual influence, and any and all circumstances.

3. Clearly there are different ways of constructing any index, depending on the underlying logic. For the lateral pressure index, we use a geometric mean to signal the *interactive* nature of the master variables. Any linear or additive index force a departure from the core logic.

4. See Keohane and Nye (1972) for early essays on various types of transnational actors.

4 The Cyber–IR System

1. This imposition of neutrality rules by the FCC was subsequently reversed in 2018 by the new chairman.

5   Co-Evolution and Complexity in Twenty-First-Century International Relations

1. This view assumes that (1) ideas matter, (2) perceptions and cognition matter (3) material factors are derivative of social relations, (4) meaning is socially derived, and (5) all of the forging drive international exchanges.

2. It would not be surprising if the generative features of social networking, uses of social media, and various voicing venues create pathways for developing constructivism more rapidly than would otherwise have been the case.

3. The "tragedy of the commons," introduced by Garret Hardin, has become a commonplace reference in the social sciences. See Hardin (1968).

4. The extensive literature on state failure is not matched by commensurate studies on the conditions of, and propensities for, state sustainability, despite the reasonable expectation that the loss of sustainability must surely mean an erosion of security, hence of sustainability, and therefore a precursor to state failure. But international relations theory also has little to say about sustainability and the state.

6   Control Point Analysis

1. A similar sort of diagram can be found in Koponen et al. (2011), where it is called information flow mapping.

2. This sort of misdirection (or a related misdirection involving the DNS) may seem unlikely, but it happens all the time. It is a common experience to open a browser window in a hotel or "hot spot," and attempt a connection to some page, only to get a page instead inviting the user to pay a fee for access. This happens only because of some intentional, if mostly benign, misdirection occurring within the hotel/hot spot system.

3. Interdomain routing provides options for control, which we have not diagrammed. It is positioned inside the step we call "Retrieve page."

4. If a user encounters a certificate signed by a certificate authority that is not on the list included in the browser, inexplicable error messages arise, which many users ignore. This outcome degrades usability as security.

5. As illustrated by the proposed but contested Stop Online Piracy Act (SOPA).

8   Cybersecurity and International Complexities

1. See Choucri (2012, 125–153).

2. The Defense Advanced Research Projects Agency (DARPA) originally provided federal funding for the organization on the assumption that CERT/CC would serve as a center for direct threat assessment and response. However, as cyberspace expanded,

a single organization proved insufficient to handle the increasing volume of security incidents. CERT/CC was forced to reframe its activities and priorities. Rather than responding directly to emerging incidents, CERT/CC's renewed mission utilized the lessons learned to provide guidelines, coordination, and standards for other CERTs.

9 Distributed Internet Governance

1. Sections 9.1–9.6 are based on Cheung (2016), reviewed and corrected by Scott Bradner. See Cheung, Bradner, and Choucri (2018). Section 9.10 is based on Choucri and Agarwal (2018).

2. RFCs were actually requests for comment in the early days but evolved by the early 1990s into standards. "RFC" is a brand name not an invitation.

3. See history in Réseaux IP Européens (2017b).

4. See history in American Registry for Internet Numbers (2017b).

5. See the Network Resource Organization (2017a).

6. See AFRINIC (2017b).

7. See American Registry for Internet Numbers (2017b).

8. For a comparative overview of the governance frameworks for each of the RIRs, see Network Resource Organization (2017b).

9. See CA/Browser Forum (2017).

10. See, for example, NETmundial (2014).

11. Eigenvector centrality is about the relevance of nodes. The eigenvector centrality of one node is based on the eigenvector centrality of its neighbors. Thus, it is not only the centrality of an individual node that dominates but also the centrality of the nodes to which it is connected. Nodes with higher eigenvector centrality generally belong to high-density subnetworks; they may have many neighbors that are connected to many other nodes (Benedictis et al. 2013). Scores are generated using Gephi software v 0.9.2 (Bastian, Heymann, and Jacomy 2009).

10 The Co-Evolution Dilemma

1. This chapter is based in part on Clark and Claffy (2015).

2. See Gilpin (1987).

3. In Lewis Carroll's *Through the Looking-Glass and What Alice Found There*, the Red Queen observes: "Now, *here*, you see, it takes all the running *you* can do, to keep in the same place. If you want to get somewhere else, you must run at least twice as fast as that!" (1872, 42).

4. But see the discussion of wireless communication in Clark and Claffy (2015, 857) for a counterexample.

5. Different versions of Moore's law give eighteen or twnty-four months as the period of doubling. This difference is not material in this discussion.

6. See European Telecommunications Standards Institute (2017).

7. See Federal Communications Commission (2017) for an overview of Communications Assistance for Law Enforcement Act (CALEA).

8. See, for example, Mance (2013).

9. The North American Network Operators Group, or NANOG, is a good example of such an organization. Its membership is in fact not limited to North America— its name reflects its origin, not its scope. It is an important venue, if not the only venue, where the private sector actors gather to discuss issues and harmonize operations. The state is largely missing in this and similar contexts.

10. For an extended discussion of stable points, see Clark and Claffy (2015).

11 Alternative Futures

1. The literature on sustainable development covers many such cases. See, for example, Choucri et al. (2007).

2. Subsequent to the launch of 0.facebook, Facebook created an open platform called Free Basics that allows other websites similarly to offer for free a version of their site with reduced functionality.

3. Or, more directly, selling the data to governments as a profit-making undertaking.

12 Imperatives of Co-Evolution

1. Recall that, in each chapter, the results are highlighted in the last section.

2. See Clinton (2011).

References

Abramson, Bram D. 2000. "Internet Globalization Indicators." *Telecommunications Policy* 24 (1): 69–74.

Acquisti, Alessandro, Laura Brandimarte, and George Loewenstein. 2015. "Privacy and Human Behavior in the Age of Information." *Science* 347 (6221): 509–515.

AFRINIC. 2017a. "Delegated-Afrinic-Extended-Latest." Accessed November 25, 2017. ftp://ftp.afrinic.net/pub/stats/afrinic/delegated-afrinic-extended-latest.

AFRINIC. 2017b. "Our Members." https://www.afrinic.net/en/about/our-members.

Agnew, John, and Stuart Corbridge. 1995. *Mastering Space: Hegemony, Territory and International Political Economy*. New York: Routledge.

Akamai. 2017. "Internet Connection Speeds and Adoption Rates by Geography." *State of the Internet Connectivity Visualizations*. Accessed November 18, 2017. https://www.akamai.com/us/en/about/our-thinking/state-of-the-internet-report/state-of-the-internet-connectivity-visualization.jsp.

Al Morshid, Sami Al Basheer. 2009. "Deployment of Cybersecurity Capabilities—IMPACT Global Response Centre." Telefax Communication BDT/POL/CYB DM-136. Geneva: International Telecommunication Union.

Alker, Hayward R. 1996. *Rediscoveries and Reformulations: Humanistic Methodologies for International Studies*. Cambridge: Cambridge University Press.

Alker, Hayward R., and Thomas J. Biersteker. 1984. "The Dialectics of World Order: Notes for a Future Archeologist of International Savoir Faire." *International Studies Quarterly* 28 (2): 121–142.

Allenby, Braden R., and Deanna J. Richards, eds. 1994. *The Greening of Industrial Ecosystems*. Washington, DC: National Academy Press.

Almond, Gabriel A., and G. Bingham Powell, Jr. 1966. *Comparative Politics: A Developmental Approach*. Boston: Little, Brown.

Amazon, and Various sources (International Games Week Berlin). 2017. "Number of Available Apps in the Amazon App store from March 2011 to April 2016." Accessed May 18, 2017. https://www.statista.com/statistics/307330/number-of-available-apps -in-the-amazon-appstore/.

American Registry for Internet Numbers. 2017a. "Delegated-Arin-Extended-Latest." Accessed November 25, 2017. ftp://ftp.arin.net/pub/stats/arin/delegated-arin-extended -latest.

American Registry for Internet Numbers. 2017b. "History." https://www.arin.net /about_us/history.html.

American Registry for Internet Numbers. 2017c. "Membership." https://www.arin .net/public/memberList.xhtml.

Anand, Ashok, Fahad Dogar, Dongsu Han, Boyan Li, Hyeontaek Lim, Michel Machado, Wenfei Wu, et al. 2011. "XIA: An Architecture for an Evolvable and Trustworthy Internet." In *Proceedings of the 10th ACM Workshop on Hot Topics in Networks*, 2:1–2:6. New York: ACM.

Anderson, Jon W. 1998. *Arabizing the Internet.* The Emirates Occasional Papers, No. 30. The Emirates Center for Strategic Studies and Research.

Anderson, Ross, and Tyler Moore. 2006. "The Economics of Information Security." *Science* 314 (5799): 610–613.

APNIC. 2017. "Delegated-Apnic-Extended-Latest." Accessed November 25, 2017. ftp://ftp.apnic.net/pub/stats/apnic/delegated-apnic-extended-latest.

AppBrain. 2017. "Number of Available Applications in the Google Play Store from December 2009 to March 2017." Accessed May 18, 2017. https://www.statista .com/statistics/266210/number-of-available-applications-in-the-google-play -store/.

Apple, and AppleInsider. 2017. "Number of Available Apps in the Apple App Store from July 2008 to January 2017." Accessed May 18, 2017. https://www.statista.com /statistics/263795/number-of-available-apps-in-the-apple-app-store/.

Arens, Yigal, Yigal Arens, Chin Y. Chee, Chun-Nan Hsu, and Craig A. Knoblock. 1993. "Retrieving and Integrating Data from Multiple Information Sources." *International Journal of Intelligent and Cooperative Information Systems* 2: 127–158.

Arkko, Jari. 2016. "30 Years of Engineering the Internet." *IETF News*, January 13. https://www.ietf.org/blog/30-years-engineering-internet/.

Aronson, Jonathan. 2002. "Global Networks and Their Impact." In *Information Technologies and Global Politics: The Changing Scope of Power and Governance*, edited by James N. Rosenau and J. P. Singh, 39–62. Albany, NY: State University of New York Press.

Autorité de la concurrence. 2012. "Internet Traffic—Peering Agreements." Press release, September 20. http://www.autoritedelaconcurrence.fr/user/standard.php?id_rub=418&id_article=1971.

Axelrod, Robert, and Michael D. Cohen. 2000. *Harnessing Complexity Organizational Implications of a Scientific Frontier*. New York: Free Press.

Azar, Edward. 1970. "Peace Research Reviews." *Canadian Peace Research Reviews* 4 (1): 1–106.

Bailey, Joseph P., and Lee W. McKnight, eds. 1995. *Internet Economics*. Cambridge, MA: MIT Press.

Baker, F., B. Foster, C. Sharp, and Cisco Systems. 2004. "Cisco Architecture for Lawful Intercept in IP Networks." *Request for Comments* 3924. The Internet Engineering Task Force.

Baker, McKenzie. 2016. "Final Passage of China's Cybersecurity Law." http://www.bakermckenzie.com/en/insight/publications/2016/11/final-passage-of-chinas-cybersecurity-law/.

Balkin, Jack M., James Grimmelmamm, Eddan Katz, Nimrod Kozlovski, Shlomit Wagman, and Tal Zarsky, eds. 2007. *Cybercrime: Digital Cops in a Networked Environment*. New York: New York University Press.

Barrett, Neil. 1996. *The State of the Cybernation: Cultural, Political and Economic Implications of the Internet*. London: Kogan Page.

Barzel, Yoram. 1997. *Economic Analysis of Property Rights*. 2nd ed. Cambridge: Cambridge University Press.

Baskaran, Angathevar, and Mammo Muchie, eds. 2006. *Bridging the Digital Divide: Innovation Systems for ICT in Brazil, China, India, Thailand and Southern Africa*. London: Adonis & Abbey.

Bastian, Mathieu, Sebastien Heymann, and Mathieu Jacomy. 2009. "Gephi: An Open Source Software for Exploring and Manipulating Networks." In *Proceedings of the Third International Conference on Weblogs and Social Media*, edited by Eytan Adar, Matthew Hurst, Tim Finin, Natalie Glance, Nicolas Nicolov, and Belle Tseng, 361–362. Menlo Park, CA: AAAI Press.

Bates, Tony, Philip Smith, and Geoff Huston. 2017. "CIDR Report." http://www.cidr-report.org/as2.0/.

Bayuk, Jennifer L., Jason Healey, Paul Rohmeyer, Marcus H. Sachs, Jeffrey Schmidt, and Joseph Weiss. 2012. *Cyber Security Policy Guidebook*. Hoboken, NJ: Wiley.

Beagle, Donald. 1999. "Conceptualizing an Information Commons." *Journal of Academic Librarianship* 25 (2): 82–89.

Becker, Egon, and Thomas Jahn, eds. 1999. *Sustainability and the Social Sciences: A Cross-Disciplinary Approach to Integrating Environmental Considerations into Theoretical Reorientation*. London: Zed Books.

Benedictis, Luca De, Silvia Nenci, Gianluca Santoni, Lucia Tajoli, and Claudio Vicarelli. 2013. "Network Analysis of World Trade Using the BACI-CEPII Dataset." *CEPII Working Paper* 2013–24. Paris: CEPII.

Benedikt, Michael, ed. 1992a. *Cyberspace: First Steps*. Cambridge, MA: MIT Press.

Benedikt, Michael. 1992b. "Cyberspace: Some Proposals." In *Cyberspace: First Steps*, edited by Michael Benedikt, 119–224. Cambridge, MA: MIT Press.

Benkler, Yochai. 2006. *The Wealth of Networks: How Social Production Transforms Markets and Freedom*. New Haven, CT: Yale University Press.

Bergstein, Brian. 2011. "Going Offline." *MIT Technology Review* 114 (6): 30–31.

Berners-Lee, Tim, and James Hendler. 2001. "Publishing on the Semantic Web." *Nature* 410 (6832): 1023–1024.

Best, Samuel J., and Brian S. Krueger. 2008. "Political Conflict and Public Perceptions of Government Surveillance on the Internet: An Experiment of Online Search Terms." *Journal of Information Technology & Politics* 5 (2): 191–212.

"Beyond the PC." 2011. *The Economist* 401(8754): S.3–S.5.

Bisby, Frank A. 2000. "The Quiet Revolution: Biodiversity Informatics and the Internet." *Science* 289 (5488): 2309–2312.

Black, Richard, and Howard White, eds. 2004. *Targeting Development: Critical Perspectives on the Millennium Development Goals*. London: Routledge.

Blumenthal, Marjory S., and David D. Clark. 2001. "Rethinking the Internet: The End-to-End Arguments vs. the Brave New World." *ACM Transactions on Internet Technology* 1 (1): 70–109.

Bonacich, Phillip. 1972. "Factoring and Weighting Approaches to Status Scores and Clique Identification." *Journal of Mathematical Sociology* 2 (1): 113–120.

Borchgrave, Arnaud de, Frank J. Cilluffo, Sharon L. Cardash, and Michèle M. Ledgerwood. 2001. *Cyber Threats and Information Security: Meeting the 21st Century Challenge*. Washington, DC: CSIS Press.

Borgatti, Stephen P., Ajay Mehra, Daniel J. Brass, and Giuseppe Labianca. 2009. "Network Analysis in the Social Sciences." *Science* 323 (5916): 892–895.

Borgman, Christine L. 2000. *From Gutenberg to the Global Information Infrastructure: Access to Information in the Networked World*. Cambridge, MA: MIT Press.

Boulding, Kenneth E. 1956. *The Image: Knowledge in Life and Society*. Ann Arbor: University of Michigan Press.

Braman, Sandra. 2006. *Change of State: Information, Policy, and Power*. Cambridge, MA: MIT Press.

Bremmer, Ian. 2010. "Democracy in Cyberspace: What Information Technology Can and Cannot Do." *Foreign Affairs* 89 (6): 86–92.

Brenner, Garry D. 1993. "Environmental Challenges and Managerial Responses: A Decision Perspective." In *Global Accord: Environmental Challenges and International Responses*, edited by Nazli Choucri, 281–303. Cambridge, MA: MIT Press.

Brenner, Joel. 2011. *America the Vulnerable: Inside the New Threat Matrix of Digital Espionage, Crime, and Warfare*. New York: Penguin.

Bridges.org. 2005. "Comparison of E-Readiness Assessment Models and Tools." http://ictlogy.net/bibliography/reports/projects.php?idp=333.

Brodhag, Christian. 2000. "Information, Gouvernance et Développement Durable." *International Political Science Review* 21 (3): 311–327.

Brown, Ian, and Christopher T. Marsden. 2013. *Regulating Code: Good Governance and Better Regulation in the Information Age*. Cambridge, MA: MIT Press.

Brown, John S., and Paul Duguid. 2000. *The Social Life of Information*. Boston: Harvard Business School Press.

Brown, Karen. 2002. "Environmental Data: Water Scarcity: Forecasting the Future with Spotty Data." *Science* 297 (5583): 926–927.

Brunn, Sandley D. 2013. "The Intersecting Worlds of Sustainability and Cyberspace: Old or/and New Boundaries." *International Archives of the Photogrammetry, Remote Sensing and Spatial Information Sciences* XL-4/W3 (3): 9–13.

Bryant, William D. 2016. *International Conflict and Cyberspace Superiority Theory and Practice*. London: Routledge.

Brynjolfsson, Erik, and Brian Kahin, eds. 2000. *Understanding the Digital Economy: Data, Tools, and Research*. Cambridge, MA: MIT Press.

Buck, Susan J. 1998. *The Global Commons: An Introduction*. Washington, DC: Island Press.

Bulte, Erwin, Richard Damania, Lindsey Gillson, and Keith Lindsay. 2004. "Space— The Final Frontier for Economists and Elephants." *Science* 306 (5695): 420–421.

CA/Browser Forum. 2017. "Welcome to the CA/Browser Forum." https://cabforum.org.

CAIDA. 2018a. "The CAIDA UCSD IXPs Dataset," April 5. https://www.caida.org/data/ixps/.

CAIDA. 2018b. "ixs_201802.jsonl," April 5. https://www.caida.org/data/ixps/.

CAIDA. 2018c. "locations_201802.jsonl," April 5. https://www.caida.org/data/ixps/.

Camp, L. Jean. 2001. *Trust and Risk in Internet Commerce*. Cambridge, MA: MIT Press.

Capra, Fritjof. 2002. *The Hidden Connections: Integrating the Biological, Cognitive, and Social Dimensions of Life into a Science of Sustainability*. New York: Doubleday.

Carr, Jeffrey. 2009. *Inside Cyber Warfare: Mapping the Cyber Underworld*. Sebastopol, CA: O'Reilly.

Carroll, Lewis. 1872. *Through the Looking Glass: And What Alice Found There*. London: Macmillan.

Castells, Manuel. 2002. *The Internet Galaxy: Reflections on the Internet, Business, and Society*. New York: Oxford University Press.

Castells, Manuel. 2005. "Global Governance and Global Politics." *Political Science and Politics* 38 (5): 9–16.

Castells, Manuel, Mireia Fernandez-Ardevol, Jack L. Qiu, and Araba Sey. 2009. *Mobile Communication and Society: A Global Perspective*. Cambridge, MA: MIT Press.

Central Intelligence Agency. 2012. "Map of the World Oceans, October 2012." https://www.loc.gov/resource/g3201p.ct003999/.

Cerny, Philip G. 1995. "Globalization and the Changing Logic of Collective Action." *International Organization* 49 (4): 595–625.

Chadwick, Andrew, and Philip N. Howard, eds. 2009. *Routledge Handbook of Internet Politics*. New York: Routledge.

Cheung, Sinéad C. 2016. "Cartographing the Governance Architecture of Cyberspace and Its Institutional Ecology." Bachelor's Thesis, Wellesley College, Wellesley, MA.

Cheung, Sinéad C., Scott Bradner, and Nazli Choucri. 2018. "Governance of the Internet." ECIR Working Paper, Massachusetts Institute of Technology, Cambridge, MA.

Chokhani, S., and W. Ford. 1999. "Internet X.509 Public Key Infrastructure Certificate Policy and Certification Practices Framework." *Request for Comments* 2527. The Internet Engineering Task Force.

Choucri, Nazli, ed. 1993a. *Global Accord: Environmental Challenges and International Responses*. Cambridge, MA: MIT Press.

Choucri, Nazli. 1993b. "Introduction: Theoretical, Empirical and Policy Perspectives." *Global Accord: Environmental Challenges and International Responses*, edited by Nazli Choucri, 1–40. Cambridge, MA: MIT Press.

Choucri, Nazli. 1993c. "Multinational Corporations and the Global Environment." In *Global Accord: Environmental Challenges and International Responses*, edited by Nazli Choucri, 205–255. Cambridge, MA: MIT Press.

Choucri, Nazli. 1993d. "Political Economy of the Global Environment." *International Political Science Review* 14 (1): 103–116.

Choucri, Nazli, ed. 1994. *Innovative Strategies in Technology and Finance for Sustainable Development*. Prepared for Environment and Natural Resources Group of the UNDP as Input to the Commission on Sustainable Development. Cambridge, MA: Massachusetts Institute of Technology.

Choucri, Nazli. 1995. "Globalization of Eco-Efficiency: GSSD on the WWW." *UNEP Industry and Environment* October–December: 45–49.

Choucri, Nazli. 1999a. "Innovations in Use of Cyberspace." In *Sustainability and the Social Sciences: A Cross-Disciplinary Approach to Integrating Environmental Considerations into Theoretical Reorientation*, edited by Egon Becker and Thomas Jahn, 274–283. London: Zed Books.

Choucri, Nazli. 1999b. "Strategic Partnerships with Multilingual Functionality for Globalization and Localization." In *Exploring the Information Society—IST 99*. Helsinki, Finland: European Commission Directorate.

Choucri, Nazli. 1999c. "The Political Logic of Sustainability." In *Sustainability and the Social Sciences: A Cross-Disciplinary Approach to Integrating Environmental Considerations into Theoretical Reorientation*, edited by Egon Becker and Thomas Jahn, 143–161. London: Zed Books.

Choucri, Nazli. 2000. "Introduction: CyberPolitics in International Relations." *International Political Science Review* 21 (3): 243–263.

Choucri, Nazli. 2001a. "Environmentalism." In *The Oxford Companion to Politics of the World*, edited by Joel Krieger, 2nd ed., 253–255. New York: Oxford University Press.

Choucri, Nazli. 2001b. "Knowledge Networking for Global Sustainability: New Modes of Cyberpartnering." In *Information Systems and the Environment*, edited by Deanna J. Richards, Braden R. Allenby, and Dale W. Compton, 195–210. Washington, DC: National Academy Press.

Choucri, Nazli. 2012. *Cyberpolitics in International Relations*. Cambridge, MA: MIT Press.

Choucri, Nazli, and Gaurav Agarwal. 2016. "Cyber Lateral Pressure Methodology." ECIR Working Paper, Massachusetts Institute of Technology, Cambridge, MA.

Choucri, Nazli, and Gaurav Agarwal. 2017. "The Theory of Lateral Pressure: Highlights of Quantification and Empirical Analysis." In *Oxford Research Encyclopedia of Politics*, edited by William R. Thompson. New York: Oxford University Press.

Choucri, Nazli, and Gaurav Agarwal. 2018. "Cyberspace and International Law." MIT Department of Political Science Research Paper, Massachusetts Institute of Technology, Cambridge, MA.

Choucri, Nazli, Wallace R. Baker, Farnaz Haghseta, Toufic Mezher, Dinsha Mistree, and Carlos I. Ortiz, eds. 2007. *Mapping Sustainability: Knowledge E-Networking and the Value Chain*. Dordrecht, Netherlands: Springer.

Choucri, Nazli, Roger Hurwitz, and John Mallery. 2013. "Explorations in Cyber International Relations." ECIR Internal Note, Massachusetts Institute of Technology, Cambridge, MA.

Choucri, Nazli, and Dinsha Mistree. 2010. "On the Causal Logic of Lateral Pressure Theory." ECIR Working Paper, Massachusetts Institute of Technology, Cambridge, MA.

Choucri, Nazli, and Robert C. North. 1975. *Nations in Conflict: National Growth and International Violence*. San Francisco: W. H. Freeman.

Choucri, Nazli, and Robert C. North. 1989. "Lateral Pressure in International Relations: Concept and Theory." In *Handbook of War Studies*, edited by Manus I. Midlarsky, 289–326. Ann Arbor: University of Michigan Press.

Choucri, Nazli, and Robert C. North. 1993. "Growth, Development, and Environmental Sustainability: Profile and Paradox." In *Global Accord: Environmental Challenges and International Responses*, edited by Nazli Choucri, 67–132. Cambridge, MA: MIT Press.

Choucri, Nazli, Robert C. North, and Susumu Yamakage. 1992. *The Challenge of Japan Before World War II and After: A Study of National Growth and Expansion*. London: Routledge.

Choucri, Nazli, and Jan Sundgren. 1994. "Toward Sustainable Consumption." Prepared for Environment Directorate. Paris: OECD.

Choucri, Nazli, and Frank Tipton. 1995. "Corporate Contributions to Sustainability: 'Best Practice' in Business and Industry." In *Strategic Imperatives for Technology Advance in Lebanon*, edited by Nazli Choucri, Toufic M. Mezher, Ahmed Kreydieh, and Frank Tipton. Cambridge, MA: Technology and Development Program, Massachusetts Institute of Technology.

Christie, Ian, and Mark Hepworth. 2001. "Towards the Sustainable E-Region." In *Digital Futures: Living in a Dot-Com World*, edited by James Wilsdon, 140–162. London: Earthscan.

Cisco Systems Inc. 2017. "Cisco 2017 Annual Cybersecurity Report." https://engage2demand.cisco.com/en-us-annual-cybersecurity-report-2017.

Clark, David D. 2010. "Characterizing Cyberspace: Past, Present and Future." ECIR Working Paper, Massachusetts Institute of Technology, Cambridge, MA.

Clark, David D., and K. C. Claffy. 2015. "Anchoring Policy Development Around Stable Points: An Approach to Regulating the Co-evolving ICT Ecosystem." *Telecommunications Policy* 39 (10): 848–860.

Clark, David D., and Susan Landau. 2010. "Untangling Attribution." In *Proceedings of a Workshop on Deterring Cyberattacks: Informing Strategies and Developing Options for U.S. Policy,* edited by National Research Council, 25–40. Washington, DC: National Academies Press.

Clark, Robert C. 1992. "Why So Many Lawyers? Are They Good or Bad?" *Fordham Law Review* 61 (2): 275–302.

Clarke, Richard A., and Robert K. Knake. 2010. *Cyber War: The Next Threat to National Security and What to Do About It.* New York: HarperCollins.

Clausewitz, Carl von. 1908. *On War,* translated by J. J. Graham. London: Kegan Paul, Trench, Trübner.

Clinton, Hillary R. 2011. "Remarks on the Release of President Obama Administration's International Strategy for Cyberspace." *Remarks by Secretary Clinton: May 2011.* Washington, DC: White House. https://2009-2017.state.gov/secretary/20092013clinton/rm/2011/05/163523.htm.

Cogent Communications. 2014. "c.root-servers.net." http://c.root-servers.org.

Collier, Paul, V. L. Elliott, Håvard Hegre, Anke Hoeffler, Marta Reynal-Querol, and Nicholas Sambanis. 2003. *Breaking the Conflict Trap: Civil War and Development Policy.* Washington, DC: World Bank / Oxford University Press.

Collier, Zachary A., Daniel DiMase, Steve Walters, Mark M. Tehranipoor, James H. Lambert, and Igor Linkov. 2014. "Cybersecurity Standards: Managing Risk and Creating Resilience." *Computer* 47 (9): 70–76.

Council of Europe. 2001. "European Treaty Series—No. 185." *Convention on Cybercrime, Budapest, 23/11/2001* ETS No.185. Budapest: Council of Europe.

Council of Europe. 2017a. "Chart of Signatures and Ratifications of Treaty 185: Convention on Cybercrime (Status as of 21/09/2017)." http://www.coe.int/en/web/conventions/full-list/-/conventions/treaty/185/signatures?p_auth=pIZLOHtC.

Council of Europe. 2017b. "Cybercrime Convention Committee." https://www.coe.int/en/web/cybercrime/tcy.

Council of Europe. 2017c. "T-CY Plenaries." http://www.coe.int/en/web/cybercrime/t-cy-plenaries.

Crandall, Robert W., and James H. Alleman. 2002. *Broadband: Should We Regulate High-Speed Internet Access?* Washington, DC: Brookings Institution Press.

"Cyber Survival." 2016. *MIT Technology Review* 119 (2): 69.

Dainotti, Alberto, Claudio Squarcella, Emile Aben, Kimberly C. Claffy, Marco Chiesa, Michele Russo, and Antonio Pescapé. 2011. "Analysis of Country-Wide Internet Outages Caused by Censorship." In *IMC 2011: Proceedings of the 2011*

ACM SIGCOMM on Internet Measurement Conference, Berlin, Germany, November 2–4, 2011, edited by Patrick Thiran and Walter Willinger, 1–18. New York: ACM Press.

Data Center Map. 2018. "Internet Exchange Points." May 6. http://www.datacentermap.com/ixps.html.

David, Paul A. 2000. "Understanding Digital Technology's Evolution and The Path of Measured Productivity Growth: Present and Future in the Mirror of the Past." In *Understanding the Digital Economy: Data, Tools, and Research*, edited by Erik Brynjolfsson and Brian Kahin, 49–95. Cambridge, MA: MIT Press.

David, Paul A. 2006. "Towards a Cyberinfrastructure for Enhanced Scientific Collaboration: Providing Its 'Soft' Foundations May Be the Hardest Part." In *Advancing Knowledge and the Knowledge Economy*, edited by Brian Kahin and Dominique Forey, 431–453. Cambridge, MA: MIT Press.

Deibert, Ronald J. 1997. *Parchment, Printing, and Hypermedia: Communication and World Order Transformation*. New York: Columbia University Press.

D'Elia, Danilo. 2016. "The Economics of Cybersecurity: From the Public Good to the Revenge of the Industry." In *Security of Industrial Control Systems and Cyber Physical Systems: First Workshop, CyberICS 2015 and First Workshop, WOS-CPS 2015*, Vienna, Austria, September 21–22, 2015, Revised Selected Papers, edited by Adrien Bécue, Nora Cuppens-Boulahia, Frédéric Cuppens, Sokratis Katsikas, and Costas Lambrinoudakis, 3–15. New York: Springer.

Dertouzos, Michael L. 1997. *What Will Be: How the New World of Information Will Change Our Lives*. London: HarperCollins.

Deutsch, Karl W. 1963. *The Nerves of Government: Models of Political Communication and Control*. New York: Free Press.

Diamond, Jared M. 1997. *Guns, Germs, and Steel: The Fates of Human Societies*. New York: Norton.

Diamond, Jared M. 2001. "Unwritten Knowledge." *Nature* 410 (6828): 521.

Diamond, Jared M. 2005. *Collapse: How Societies Choose to Fail or Survive*. New York: Viking Penguin.

Dickson, David. 2001. "Weaving a Social Web." *Nature* 414 (6864): 587.

Ditz, Daryl W., Janet Ranganathan, and R. Darryl Banks, eds. 1995. *Green Ledgers: Case Studies in Corporate Environmental Accounting*. Baltimore: World Resources Institute.

Dodge, Martin, and Rob Kitchin. 2001. *Mapping Cyberspace*. London: Routledge.

Dolšak, Nives, and Elinor Ostrom, eds. 2003. *The Commons in the New Millennium: Challenges and Adaptation*. Cambridge, MA: MIT Press.

Dunn, Myriam. 2005. "A Comparative Analysis of Cybersecurity Initiatives Worldwide." In *WSIS Thematic Meeting on Cybersecurity*, June 28–July 1, 1–34. Geneva: International Telecommunication Union.

Dunning, John H., ed. 1999. *Governments, Globalization, and International Business.* New York: Oxford University Press.

Easterly, William R. 2002. *The Elusive Quest for Growth: Economists' Adventures and Misadventures in the Tropics.* Cambridge, MA: MIT Press.

Easton, David. 1953. "The Authoritative Allocation of Values for a Society." In *The Political System: An Inquiry into the State of Political Science,* 129–134. New York: Knopf.

Easton, David. 1965. *A Systems Analysis of Political Life.* New York: Wiley.

Ehrlich, Paul R., Anne H. Ehrlich, and John P. Holdren. 1977. *Ecoscience: Population, Resources, Environment.* San Francisco: W.H. Freeman.

Elkins, David J. 1997. "Globalization, Telecommunication, and Virtual Ethnic Communities." *International Political Science Review* 18 (2): 139–152.

Ellickson, Robert C. 1991. *Order without Law: How Neighbors Settle Disputes.* Cambridge, MA: Harvard University Press.

Elliott, David. 2011. "Deterring Strategic Cyberattack." *IEEE Security & Privacy* 9 (5): 36–40.

Ericsson AB. 2017. "Data Traffic-Application." *Ericsson Mobility Report 2017: Traffic Exploration Tool (Interim Update: June 2017).* Accessed November 18, 2017. https://www.ericsson.com/TET/trafficView/loadBasicEditor.ericsson.

Eriksson, Johan, and Giampiero Giacomello. 2004. "International Relations and Security in the Digital Age." Paper presented at ISA Annual Convention 2004: Hegemony and its Discontents: Power, Ideology, and Knowledge in the Study and Practice of International Relations, Montreal, Canada, March 17–20.

Eriksson, Johan, and Giampiero Giacomello. 2006. "The Information Revolution, Security, and International Relations: (IR) Relevant Theory?" *International Political Science Review* 27 (3): 221–244.

ESRI, Michael Horner, and Story Maps Team. 2013. "Global Shipping Routes." April 13, 2013. https://www.arcgis.com/home/item.html?id=12c0789207e64714b9545ad30fca1633.

European Communities. 1996. "Council Resolution of 17 January 1995 on the Lawful Interception of Telecommunications." *Official Journal of the European Communities* 39 (96/C 329/01): 1–7.

European Parliament. 2004. "Regulation (EC) No 460/2004: European Network and Information Security Agency (ENISA)." *Official Journal of the European Union* L 077 13.3.2004 (CELEX No. 32004R0460): 1–11.

European Telecommunications Standards Institute. 2017. "Lawful Interception." http://www.etsi.org/technologies-clusters/technologies/lawful-interception.

Evans, James A., and Jacob Reimer. 2009. "Open Access and Global Participation in Science." *Science* 323 (5917): 1025.

Evans, Philip, and Thomas S. Wurster. 2000. *Blown to Bits: How the New Economics of Information Transforms Strategy.* Boston: Harvard Business School Press.

Federal Communications Commission. 2017. "Communications Assistance for Law Enforcement Act." *Policy and Licensing Division.* https://www.fcc.gov/public-safety -and-homeland-security/policy-and-licensing-division/general/communications -assistance.

Feeny, David, Fikret Berkes, Bonnie J. McCay, and James M. Acheson. 1990. "The Tragedy of the Commons: Twenty-Two Years Later." *Human Ecology* 18 (1): 1–19.

Feller, Joseph, Brian Fitzgerald, Scott A. Hissam, and Karim R. Lakhani, eds. 2005. *Perspectives on Free and Open Source Software.* Cambridge, MA: MIT Press.

Fensel, Dieter. 2001. *Ontologies: A Silver Bullet for Knowledge Management and Electronic Commerce.* Berlin: Springer.

Ferguson, Niall. 2000. "A Powerful Leap from Chaos." *Nature* 408 (6808): 21–22.

FIRST.org. 2017a. "About FIRST." https://www.first.org/about/.

FIRST.org. 2017b. "FIRST History." https://www.first.org/about/history.

FIRST.org. 2017c. "FIRST Members Around the World." https://www.first.org /members/map.

FIRST.org. 2017d. "Global Initiatives." https://www.first.org/global/.

Fleury, Terry, Himanshu Khurana, and Von Welch. 2008. "Towards a Taxonomy of Attacks Against Energy Control Systems." In *Critical Infrastructure Protection II,* edited by Mauricio Papa and Sujeet Shenoi, 71–85. Boston: Springer.

Fligstein, Neil. 1990. *The Transformation of Corporate Control.* Cambridge, MA: Harvard University Press.

Foray, Dominique. 2004. *Economics of Knowledge.* Cambridge, MA: MIT Press.

Forrester, Jay W. 1971. "Counterintuitive Behavior of Social Systems." *Theory and Decision* 2 (2): 109–140.

Forrester, Jay W. 1973. *World Dynamics.* 2nd ed. Cambridge, MA: Wright-Allen Press.

Foster, Kenneth R., Paolo Vecchia, and Michael H. Repacholi. 2000. "Risk Management. Science and the Precautionary Principle." *Science* 288 (5468): 979–981.

Franklin, Jason, Vern Paxson, Adrian Perrig, and Stefan Savage. 2007. "An Inquiry into the Nature and Causes of the Wealth of Internet Miscreants." In *Proceedings of the 14th ACM Conference on Computer and Communications Security*, Alexandria, VA, October 29–November 2, 2007, 375–388. New York: ACM.

Frauenfelder, Mark. 2004. "Domain Master." *MIT Technology Review* 107 (2): 74–75.

Frederick, Howard H. 1993. *Global Communication & International Relations*. Belmont, CA: Wadsworth.

Fuentes-Camacho, Teresa, ed. 2000. *The International Dimensions of Cyberspace Law*. Aldershot, United Kingdom: UNESCO.

Gamero-Garrido, Alexander M. 2014. "Cyber Conflicts in International Relations: Framework and Case Studies." ECIR Working Paper. Massachusetts Institute of Technology. https://dx.doi.org/10.2139/ssrn.2427993.

Garber, Lee, ed. 2016. *Advancing the Internet of Things: Computing Edge*. New York: IEEE Computer Society.

Gaulier, G., G. Santoni, D. Taglioni, and S. Zignago. 2013. "In the Wake of the Global Crisis Evidence from a New Quarterly Database of Export Competitiveness." Policy Research Working Paper, No. 6733, World Bank, Washington, DC.

Gell-Mann, Murray. 1994. *The Quark and the Jaguar: Adventures in the Simple and the Complex*. New York: W.H. Freeman.

Gell-Mann, Murray. 1995. "What Is Complexity? Remarks on Simplicity and Complexity by the Nobel Prize-Winning Author of The Quark and the Jaguar." *Complexity* 1 (1): 16–19.

Geller, Daniel S., and David J. Singer. 1998. *Nations at War: A Scientific Study of International Conflict*. Cambridge: Cambridge University Press.

Gewin, Virginia. 2002. "Taxonomy: All Living Things, Online." *Nature* 418 (6896): 362–363.

Gibson, William. 1984. *Neuromancer*. New York: Berkley Publishing Group.

Giles, Jim. 2002. "Scientific Uncertainty: When Doubt Is a Sure Thing." *Nature* 418 (6897): 476–478.

Gilpin, Robert. 1987. *The Political Economy of International Relations*. Princeton, NJ: Princeton University Press.

Gilpin, Robert. 1996. "Economic Evolution of National Systems." *International Studies Quarterly* 40 (3): 411–431.

Gilpin, Robert. 2001. *Global Political Economy: Understanding the International Economic Order*. Princeton, NJ: Princeton University Press.

Gleick, Peter H. 2002. "Water Management: Soft Water Paths." *Nature* 418 (6896): 373.

Goldsmith, Jack L., and Tim Wu. 2006. *Who Controls the Internet? Illusions of a Borderless World.* New York: Oxford University Press.

Goodman, Seymour E., and Herbert S. Lin, eds. 2007. *Toward a Safer and More Secure Cyberspace.* Washington, DC: National Academies Press.

Google Inc. 2018. "Government Requests to Remove Content." *Transparency Report.* Accessed May 22, 2017. https://transparencyreport.google.com/government-removals/overview?hl=en.

Gosler, James R. 2005. "The Digital Dimension." In *Transforming US Intelligence,* edited by Jennifer E. Simms and Burton Gerber, 96–114. Washington, DC: Georgetown University Press.

Gourevitch, Peter. 1978. "The Second Image Reversed: The International Sources of Domestic Politics." *International Organization* 32 (2): 881–912.

Gowdy, John. 1999. "Economic Concepts of Sustainability: Relocating Economic Activity Within Society and Environment." In *Sustainability and the Social Sciences: A Cross-Disciplinary Approach to Integrating Environmental Considerations into Theoretical Reorientation,* edited by Egon Becker and Thomas Jahn, 162–181. London: Zed Books.

Graham, Stephen. 2002. "FlowCity: Networked Mobilities and the Contemporary Metropolis." *Journal of Urban Technology* 9 (1): 1–20.

Grauwe, Paul de, and Filip Camerman. 2002. "How Big Are the Big Multinational Companies." *Review of Business and Economics/Tijdschrift voor Economie en Management* 47 (3): 311–326.

Greenstein, Ran, and Anriette Esterhuysen. 2006. "The Right to Development in the Information Society." In *Human Rights in the Global Information Society,* edited by Rikke F. Jørgensen, 281–302. Cambridge, MA: MIT Press.

Greenstein, Shane. 2000. "The Evolving Structure of Commercial Internet Markets." In *Understanding the Digital Economy: Data, Tools, and Research,* edited by Erik Brynjolfsson and Brian Kahin, 151–184. Cambridge, MA: MIT Press.

Gregory, Richard L. 2001. "Perceptions of Knowledge." *Nature* 410 (6824): 21.

Grieco, Joseph M. 1988. "Anarchy and the Limits of Cooperation: A Realist Critique of the Newest Liberal Institutionalism." *International Organization* 42 (3): 485–507.

Gross, Phillip. 1986. "Minutes of Fourth DARPA GADS Task Force Meeting." In *Proceedings of the 16–17 January 1986 DARPA Gateway Algorithms and Data Structures Task Force,* edited by Phillip Gross. McLean, VA: MITRE.

"Guidelines Agreed for New Social Contract." 1999. *Nature* 400 (6740): 100.

Guillén, Mauro F., and Sandra L. Suárez. 2001. "Developing the Internet: Entrepreneurship and Public Policy in Ireland, Singapore, Argentina, and Spain." *Telecommunications Policy* 25 (5): 349–371.

Haas, Ernst B. 1980. "Why Collaborate? Issue-Linkage and International Regimes." *World Politics* 32 (3): 357–405.

Haas, Ernst B. 1990. *When Knowledge Is Power: Three Models of Change in International Organizations.* Berkeley: University of California Press.

Haas, Ernst B., Mary P. Williams, and Don Babai. 1977. *Scientists and World Order: The Uses of Technical Knowledge in International Organizations.* Berkeley: University of California Press.

Haas, Peter M. 1989. "The Fourth Image Reversed: Epistemic Communities and Knowledge Based Bargaining as a Response to Uncertainty." Paper presented at the 1989 Annual Meeting of the American Political Science Association, August 20–September 3, Atlanta, GA.

Haas, Peter M., Robert O. Keohane, and Marc A. Levy, eds. 1993. *Institutions for the Earth: Sources of Effective International Environmental Protection.* Cambridge, MA: MIT Press.

Haas, Peter M., and Jan Sundgren. 1993. "Evolving International Environmental Law: Changing Practices of International Sovereignty." In *Global Accord: Environmental Challenges and International Responses*, edited by Nazli Choucri, 401–429. Cambridge, MA: MIT Press.

"Hacking Payments." 2015. *MIT Technology Review* 118 (2): 68.

Haghseta, Farnaz S. 2003. "Information Technology and Sustainable Development: Understanding Linkages in Theory and Practice." Master's Thesis, Massachusetts Institute of Technology, Cambridge, MA.

Hall, Peter A., and Rosemary C. R. Taylor. 1996. "Political Science and the Three New Institutionalisms." *Political Studies* 44: 936–957.

Hall, Rodney B., and Thomas J. Biersteker, eds. 2002. *The Emergence of Private Authority in Global Governance.* Cambridge: Cambridge University Press.

Halpern, Shanna L. 1993. *The United Nations Conference on Environment and Development: Process and Documentation.* Providence, RI: Academic Council on the United Nations System.

Hammond, Debora. 2003. *The Science of Synthesis: Exploring the Social Implications of General Systems Theory.* Boulder: University Press of Colorado.

Hardin, Garrett. 1968. "The Tragedy of the Commons." *Science* 162 (3859): 1243 LP–1248.

Hargittai, Eszter. 1999. "Weaving the Western Web: Explaining Differences in Internet Connectivity Among OECD Countries." *Telecommunications Policy* 23 (10): 701–718.

Hauben, Michael, and Ronda Hauben. 1997. *Netizens: On the History and Impact of Usenet and the Internet.* Los Alamitos, CA: IEEE Computer Society.

Hawkins, Jeff, and Sandra Blakeslee. 2004. *On Intelligence: How a New Understanding of the Brain Will Lead to the Creation of Truly Intelligent Machines.* New York: Times Books.

Healey, Jason. 2013. *A Fierce Domain: Conflict in Cyberspace, 1986 to 2012.* Vienna, VA: Cyber Conflict Studies Association.

Heater, Derek. 2004. *A Brief History of Citizenship.* New York: New York University Press.

Heflin, Jeff, and James A. Hendler. 2000. "Dynamic Ontologies on the Web." In *Proceedings of the Seventeenth National Conference on Artificial Intelligence and Twelfth Conference on Innovative Applications of Artificial Intelligence,* 443–449. Menlo Park, CA: AAAI Press.

Held, David, and Anthony McGrew. 2001. "Globalization." In *The Oxford Companion to Politics of the World,* edited by Joel Krieger, 324–327. New York: Oxford University Press.

Herz, John H. 1950. "Idealist Internationalism and the Security Dilemma." *World Politics* 2 (2): 157–180.

Heylighen, Francis. 1993. "The Red Queen Principle." In *Principia Cybernetica Web,* edited by Francis Heylighen, Cliff Joslyn, and Valentin Turchin. Brussels: Principia Cybernetica. http://cleamc11.vub.ac.be/REDQUEEN.html

Hoffman, Donna P., and Thomas P. Novak. 2000. "The Growing Digital Divide: Implications for an Open Research Agenda." In *Understanding the Digital Economy: Data, Tools, and Research,* edited by Erik Brynjolfsson and Brian Kahin, 245–260. Cambridge, MA: MIT Press.

Holling, C. S. 1995. "Sustainability: The Cross-Scale Dimension." In *Defining and Measuring Sustainability: The Biogeophysical Foundations,* edited by Mohan Munasinghe and Walter Shearer, 65–75. Washington, DC: World Bank.

Holm, Soren, and John Harris. 1999. "Precautionary Principle Stifles Discovery." *Nature* 400 (6743): 398.

Homer-Dixon, Thomas E. 1993. "Physical Dimensions of Global Change." In *Global Accord: Environmental Challenges and International Responses,* edited by Nazli Choucri, 43–66. Cambridge, MA: MIT Press.

Hovey, R., and S. Bradner. 1996. "The Organizations Involved in the IETF Standards Process." *Request for Comments* 2028. The Internet Engineering Task Force.

Huberman, Bernardo A. 2001. *The Laws of the Web: Patterns in the Ecology of Information.* Cambridge, MA: MIT Press.

Huberman, Bernardo A., and Rajan M. Lukose. 1997. "Social Dilemmas and Internet Congestion." *Science* 277 (5325): 535 LP–537.

Hung, Shirley. 2012. "The Chinese Internet: Control Through the Layers." ECIR Working Paper, Massachusetts Institute of Technology, Cambridge, MA.

IAB, and IESG. 2000. "IETF Policy on Wiretapping." *Request for Comments* 2804. The Internet Engineering Task Force.

Iacono, Suzanne C., and Peter A. Freeman. 2006. "Cyberinfrastructure-in-the-Making: Can We Get There from Here?" In *Advancing Knowledge and the Knowledge Economy*, edited by Brian Kahin and Dominique Foray, 455–78. Cambridge, MA: MIT Press.

ICANN. 2017. "Bylaws for Internet Corporation for Assigned Names and Numbers: A California Nonprofit Public-Benefit Corporation." https://www.icann.org/resources/pages/governance/bylaws-en/#article1.

IETF. 2017. "Request for Comments (RFC)." https://www.ietf.org/rfc.html.

Information Technologies Group. 2002. "Readiness for the Networked World: A Guide for Developing Countries." Center for International Development, Harvard University, Cambridge, MA.

International Telecommunication Union. 1998. "Telecommunications Regulatory Issues for Electronic Commerce." *ITU Regulatory Colloquium* 8. Geneva: ITU.

International Telecommunication Union. 2003. *ITU Internet Reports 2003: Birth of Broadband.* 5th ed. Geneva: ITU.

International Telecommunication Union. 2006. "Chairman's Report "Partnerships for Global Cybersecurity." C5 Report, Facilitation Meeting for WSIS Action Line C5: Building Confidence and Security in the Use of ICTs, Geneva, May 15–16. http://www.itu.int/osg/spu/cybersecurity/2006/chairmansreport.pdf.

International Telecommunication Union. 2009. *Measuring the Information Society: The ICT Development Index.* Geneva: ITU.

International Telecommunication Union. 2012. "What Are the International Telecommunication Regulations—and Why Do They Matter?" Background Brief 1, World Conference on International Telecommunications, Dubai, UAE.

International Telecommunication Union. 2017a. "Fixed-Telephone Subscriptions (i112); Fixed-Broadband Subscriptions (i4213tfbb); Mobile-Cellular Telephone Subscriptions, by Postpaid/Prepaid (i271); Active Mobile-Broadband Subscriptions (i271mw)." *World Telecommunication/ICT Indicators Database USB Key.* 21st Edition. Geneva: ITU. https://www.itu.int/pub/D-IND-WTID.OL-2017.

International Telecommunication Union. 2017b. "ITU Regions, and the UN M49 Developed/Developing Country Classification." http://www.itu.int/en/ITU-D/Statistics /Pages/definitions/regions.aspx.

International Telecommunication Union. 2017c. "Percentage of Individuals Using the Internet." *ICT Statistics: Country ICT Data (Until 2016)*. Accessed November 22, 2017. http://www.itu.int/en/ITU-D/Statistics/Pages/stat/default.aspx.

Internet Society. 2017. "The Internet Society and Internet History." https://www .internetsociety.org/history/.

Internet World Stats. 2017. "Internet World Users by Language: Top 10 Languages." Accessed December 01, 2017. https://www.internetworldstats.com/stats7.htm.

Iqbal, Asif. 2013. "Addressing Security Threats to Integrated Circuits." *SDM Pulse* 8 (3): 8–9. Cambridge, MA: Massachusetts Institute of Technology.

Jackson, Matthew O. 2008. *Social and Economic Networks*. Princeton, NJ: Princeton University Press.

James, Peter, and Peter Hopkinson. 2001. "Virtual Traffic: E-Commerce, Transport and Distribution." In *Digital Futures: Living in a Dot-Com World*, edited by James Wilsdon, 165–96. London: Earthscan.

Johnson, David R., and David G. Post. 1997. "The Rise of Law on the Global Network." In *Borders in Cyberspace: Information Policy and the Global Information Infrastructure*, edited by Brian Kahin and Charles R. Nesson, 3–47. Cambridge, MA: MIT Press.

Johnson, Loch K., and James J. Wirtz, eds. 2004. *Strategic Intelligence: Windows into a Secret World: An Anthology*. Los Angeles: Roxbury.

Johnson, Neil F. 2009. *Simply Complexity: A Clear Guide to Complexity Theory*. Oxford: Oneworld.

Jordan, Scott. 2007. "A Layered Network Approach to Net Neutrality (Special Section on Net Neutrality)." *International Journal of Communication* 1: 427–460.

Kahin, Brian, and Charles R. Nesson, eds. 1997. *Borders in Cyberspace: Information Policy and the Global Information Infrastructure*. Cambridge, MA: MIT Press.

Kahler, Miles, ed. 2015. *Networked Politics: Agency, Power, and Governance*. Ithaca, NY: Cornell University Press.

Kaplan, Morton A. 1957. *System and Process in International Politics*. New York: John Wiley.

Katz, Jerrold J. 2000. *Realistic Rationalism*. Cambridge, MA: MIT Press.

Kauffman, Stuart. 1996. *At Home in the Universe: The Search for Laws of Self-Organization and Complexity*. New York: Oxford University Press.

Kaufmann, Daniel, Aart Kraay, and Massimo Mastruzzi. 2006. "Governance Matters V: Aggregate and Individual Governance Indicators for 1996–2005." Policy Research Working Paper, No. 4012, World Bank, Washington, DC.

Kaufmann, Daniel, Aart Kraay, and Massimo Mastruzzi. 2007. "The Worldwide Governance Indicators Project: Answering the Critics." Policy Research Working Paper, No. 4149, World Bank, Washington, DC.

Keatley, Anne. 1983. "Knowledge as Real Estate." *Science* 222 (4625): 717 LP–717.

Kelly, Sanja, Mai Truong, Adrian Shahbaz, Madeline Earp, and Jessica White. 2017. "Overview of Score Changes." In *Freedom on the Net 2017: Manipulating Social Media to Undermine Democracy*, 32–33. Washington, DC: Freedom House.

Keohane, Robert O., and Joseph S. Nye, Jr., eds. 1972. *Transnational Relations and World Politics*. Cambridge, MA: Harvard University Press.

Keohane, Robert O., and Elinor Ostrom, eds. 1995. *Local Commons and Global Interdependence: Heterogeneity and Cooperation in Two Domains*. London: Sage.

Kindleberger, Charles P. 1970. *Power and Money: The Economics of International Politics and the Politics of International Economics*. London: Macmillan.

Klein, James P., Gary Goertz, and Paul F. Diehl. 2006. "The New Rivalry Dataset: Procedures and Patterns." *Journal of Peace Research* 43 (3): 331–348.

Koh, Harold H. 2012. "The State Department Legal Adviser's Office: Eight Decades in Peace and War." *The Georgetown Law Journals* 100 (5): 1747–1782.

Kohl, Uta. 2007. *Jurisdiction and the Internet: A Study of Regulatory Competence over Online Activity*. Cambridge: Cambridge University Press.

Koponen, Teemu, Scott Shenker, Hari Balakrishnan, Nick Feamster, Igor Ganichev, Ali Ghodsi, P Brighten Godfrey, et al. 2011. "Architecting for Innovation." *SIGCOMM Comput. Commun. Rev.* 41 (3): 24–36.

Korten, David C. 1995. *When Corporations Rule the World*. West Hartford, CT: Kumarian Press.

Koutsoukis, Nikitas-Spiros, and Gautam Mitra. 2003. *Decision Modelling and Information Systems: The Information Value Chain*. Dordrecht, Netherlands: Kluwer Academic.

Kraay, Aart, Daniel Kaufmann, and Massimo Mastruzzi. 2010. "The Worldwide Governance Indicators: Methodology and Analytical Issues." Policy Research Working Paper, No. 5430, World Bank, Washington, DC.

Kraay, Aart, Pablo Zoido-Lobaton, and Daniel Kaufmann. 1999. "Governance Matters." Policy Research Working Paper, No. 2196, World Bank, Washington, DC.

Kraay, Aart, Pablo Zoido-Lobaton, and Daniel Kaufmann. 2002. "Governance Matters II: Updated Indicators for 2000–01." Policy Research Working Paper, No. 2772, World Bank, Washington, DC.

Kramer, Franklin D., Stuart H. Starr, and Larry K. Wentz, eds. 2009. *Cyberpower and National Security*. Dulles, VA: Potomac Books.

Kratochwil, Friedrich, and John G. Ruggie. 1986. "International Organization: A State of the Art on an Art of the State." *International Organization* 40 (4): 753–775.

Kruzel, Joseph, and James N. Rosenau, eds. 1989. *Journeys Through World Politics: Autobiographical Reflections of Thirty-Four Academic Travelers*. Lexington, MA: Lexington Books.

Kuehls, Thom. 1998. "Between Sovereignty and Environment: An Exploration of the Discourse of Government." In *The Greening of Sovereignty in World Politics*, edited by Karen T. Litfin, 31–54. Cambridge, MA: MIT Press.

Kuhn, Thomas S. 1962. *The Structure of Scientific Revolutions*. Chicago: University of Chicago Press.

LACNIC. 2017. "Delegated-Lacnic-Extended-Latest." Accessed November 24, 2017. ftp://ftp.lacnic.net/pub/stats/lacnic/delegated-lacnic-extended-latest.

Lagazio, Monica, Nazneen Sherif, and Mike Cushman. 2014. "A Multi-Level Approach to Understanding the Impact of Cyber Crime on the Financial Sector." *Computers & Security* 45: 58–74.

Lang, Winfried, ed. 1995. *Sustainable Development and International Law*. London: Graham & Trotman.

Lasswell, Harold D. 1936. *Politics: Who Gets What, When, How*. London: McGraw-Hill.

Lasswell, Harold D. 1941. "The Garrison State." *American Journal of Sociology* 46 (4): 455–468.

Latham, Robert, ed. 2003. *Bombs and Bandwidth: The Emerging Relationship Between Information Technology and Security*. New York: New Press.

Lawrence, Steve, and C. Lee Giles. 1999. "Accessibility of Information on the Web." *Nature* 400 (6740): 107.

Lawson, Chappell. 2007. "New Media Undermining Elite Control of Public Diplomacy." Internal memorandum, Department of Political Science. Massachusetts Institute of Technology, Cambridge, MA.

Lazer, David, Alex Pentland, Lada Adamic, Sinan Aral, Albert-László Barabási, Devon Brewer, Nicholas Christakis, et al. 2009. "Computational Social Science." *Science* 323 (5915): 721 LP–723.

Lessig, Lawrence. 1997. "The Constitution of Code: Limitations on Choice-Based Critiques of Cyberspace Regulation." *CommLaw Conspectus* 5 (2): 181–191.

Lessig, Lawrence. 1999. *Code: And Other Laws of Cyberspace*. New York: Basic Books.

Lessig, Lawrence. 2001a. *The Future of Ideas: The Fate of the Commons in a Connected World*. New York: Random House.

Lessig, Lawrence. 2001b. "The Internet Under Siege." *Foreign Policy* 127: 56–65.

Levy, David L., and Peter Newell, eds. 2005. *The Business of Global Environmental Governance*. Cambridge, MA: MIT Press.

Levy, Jack S. 1989. "The Causes of War: A Review of Theories and Evidence." In *Behavior, Society, and Nuclear War*, edited by Philip E. Tetlock, Jo L. Husbands, Robert Jervis, Paul C. Stern, and Charles Tilly, 209–333. New York: Oxford University Press.

Lewin, Roger. 1992. *Complexity: Life at the Edge of Chaos*. New York: Macmillan.

Lewontin, Richard. 1968. "The Concept of Evolution." In *International Encyclopedia of the Social Sciences*. Vol. 5, edited by David L. Sills, 202–210. New York: Macmillan.

Libicki, Martin C. 2007. *Conquest in Cyberspace: National Security and Information Warfare*. Cambridge: Cambridge University Press.

Livnat, Adi, and Marcus W. Feldman. 2001. "The Evolution of Cooperation on the Internet." *Complexity* 6 (6): 19–23.

Lofdahl, Corey L. 2002. *Environmental Impacts of Globalization and Trade: A Systems Study*. Cambridge, MA: MIT Press.

Lucas, George R. 2016. *Ethics and Cyber Warfare: The Quest for Responsible Security in the Age of Digital Warfare*. New York: Oxford University Press.

Lynn, William J. III. 2010. "Defending a New Domain." *Foreign Affairs* 89 (5): 97–108.

Mahan, Alfred T. 1894. *The Influence of Sea Power upon History, 1660–1783*. New York: Dover.

Mahoney, James, and Kathleen A. Thelen. 2010. *Explaining Institutional Change: Ambiguity, Agency, and Power*. Cambridge: Cambridge University Press.

"Malware on the Move." 2014. *MIT Technology Review* 117 (4): 16.

Mance, Henry. 2013. "Huawei Defends UK Internet Filtering Role." *FT.com*, July 26.

Mandiant. 2014. "APT1: Exposing One of China's Cyber Espionage Units." https://www.fireeye.com/content/dam/fireeye-www/services/pdfs/mandiant-apt1-report.pdf.

Mann, Catherine L., Sue E. Eckert, and Sarah C. Knight. 2000. *Global Electronic Commerce: A Policy Primer*. Washington, DC: Institute for International Economics.

Mann, Charles C. 2001. "Taming the Web." *MIT Technology Review* 104 (7): 44–51.

Mann, Charles C. 2014. "The Myth of a Free Internet." *MIT Technology Review* 117 (3): 92.

March, James G., and Johan P. Olsen. 1984. "The New Institutionalism: Organizational Factors in Political Life." *The American Political Science Review* 78 (3): 734–749.

March, James G., and Johan P. Olsen. 1989. *Rediscovering Institutions: The Organizational Basis of Politics*. New York: Free Press.

March, James G., and Johan P. Olsen. 1999. "The Institutional Dynamics of International Political Orders." In *Exploration and Contestation in the Study of World Politics*, edited by Stephen D. Krasner, Robert O. Keohane, and Peter J. Katzenstein, 303–329. Cambridge, MA: MIT Press.

March, Salvatore, Alan Hevner, and Sudha Ram. 2000. "Research Commentary: An Agenda for Information Technology Research in Heterogeneous and Distributed Environments." *Information Systems Research* 11 (4): 327–341.

Matis, Michael S. 2012. *The Protection of Undersea Cables: A Global Security Threat*. Carlisle, PA: United States Army War College.

Maugis, Vincent, Nazli Choucri, Stuart E. Madnick, Michael D. Siegel, Sharon E. Gillett, Farnaz Haghseta, Hongwei Zhu, et al. 2005. "Global E-Readiness—for What? Readiness for E-Banking." *Information Technology for Development* 11 (4): 313–342.

Mayer-Schönberger, Viktor. 2009. *Delete: The Virtue of Forgetting in the Digital Age*. Princeton, NJ: Princeton University Press.

Mayer-Schönberger, Viktor, and Deborah Hurley. 2000. "Information Policy and Governance." In *Governance in a Globalizing World*, edited by Joseph S. Nye, Jr. and John D. Donahue, 330–346. Washington, DC: Brookings Institution Press.

Mayer-Schönberger, Viktor, and David Lazer, eds. 2007. *Governance and Information Technology: From Electronic Government to Information Government*. Cambridge, MA: MIT Press.

Mayer, Franz C. 2001. "Review Essay: The Internet and Public International Law—Worlds Apart?" *European Journal of International Law* 12 (3): 617–622.

Mazarr, Michael J., ed. 2002. *Information Technology and World Politics*. New York: Palgrave Macmillan.

McCoy, Damon, Hitesh Dharmdasani, Christian Kreibich, Geoffrey M. Voelker, and Stefan Savage. 2012. "Priceless: The Role of Payments in Abuse-Advertised Goods."

In *Proceedings of the 2012 ACM Conference on Computer and Communications Security*, 845–856. New York: ACM.

McGee, John. 2003. "Strategy as Orchestrating Knowledge." In *Images of Strategy*, edited by Stephen Cummings, and David Wilson, 136–163. Malden, MA: Blackwell.

McNeal, Ramona, Kathleen Hale, and Lisa Dotterweich. 2008. "Citizen–Government Interaction and the Internet: Expectations and Accomplishments in Contact, Quality, and Trust." *Journal of Information Technology & Politics* 5 (2): 213–229.

Merali, Yasmin. 2016. "Complexity and Information Systems: The Emergent Domain." In *Enacting Research Methods in Information Systems*. Vol. 3, edited by Leslie P. Willcocks, Chris Sauer, and Mary C. Lacity, 251–281. New York: Palgrave Macmillan.

Michael, David C., and Greg Sutherland. 2002. *Asia's Digital Dividends: How Asia-Pacific's Corporations Can Create Value from E-Business*. Singapore: Wiley.

Midlarsky, Manus I., ed. 1989. *Handbook of War Studies*. Ann Arbor: University of Michigan Press.

Midlarsky, Manus I., ed. 2000. *Handbook of War Studies II*. Ann Arbor: University of Michigan Press.

Miller, David, and Sohail H. Hashmi, eds. 2002. *Boundaries and Justice: Diverse Ethical Perspectives*. Princeton, NJ: Princeton University Press.

Miller, John H., and Scott E. Page. 2007. *Complex Adaptive Systems: An Introduction to Computational Models of Social Life*. Princeton, NJ: Princeton University Press.

Modelski, George, and Kazimierz Poznanski. 1996. "Evolutionary Paradigms in the Social Sciences." *International Studies Quarterly* 40 (3): 315–319.

Moore, Gordon E. 1965. "Cramming More Components onto Integrated Circuits." *Electronics* 38 (8): 114–117.

Morowitz, Harold J. 2002. *The Emergence of Everything: How the World Became Complex*. New York: Oxford University Press.

Mueller, Milton. 2004. *Ruling the Root: Internet Governance and the Taming of Cyberspace*. Cambridge, MA: MIT Press.

Mueller, Milton, and Mawaki Chango. 2008. "Disrupting Global Governance: The Internet Whois Service, ICANN, and Privacy." *Journal of Information Technology & Politics* 5 (3): 303–325.

Murdoch, Steven J., and Ross Anderson. 2008. "Tools and Technology of Internet Filtering." In *The Access Denied: Practice and Policy of Global Internet Filtering*, edited by Ronald J. Deibert, John G. Palfrey, Rafal Rohozinski, and Jonathan Zittrain, 57–72. Cambridge, MA: MIT Press.

Nakamoto, Satoshi. n.d. "Bitcoin: A Peer-to-Peer Electronic Cash System." http://bitcoin.org/bitcoin.pdf.

Natural Earth. 2018. "1:10m Cultural Vectors (Admin 0—Countries)." http://www.naturalearthdata.com/downloads/10m-cultural-vectors/.

Neef, Dale. 1998. *The Knowledge Economy.* Boston: Butterworth-Heinemann.

Negroponte, Nicholas. 1994. *Being Digital.* New York: Knopf.

NETmundial. 2014. "Contributions." http://content.netmundial.br/docs/contribs/.

"Net Support." 2008. *OECD Observer*, 268 (July): 8–9.

Network Resource Organization. 2017a. "About the NRO." https://www.nro.net/about-the-nro/.

Network Resource Organization. 2017b. "RIR Governance Matrix." https://www.nro.net/about-the-nro/rir-governance-matrix/.

Newman, Abraham L. 2015. "What the 'Right to Be Forgotten' Means for Privacy in a Digital Age." *Science* 347 (6221): 507 LP–508.

Newman, M. 2003. "The Structure and Function of Complex Networks." *SIAM Review* 45 (2): 167–256.

Nordstrom, Timothy, Jon Pevehouse, and Megan Shannon. 2010. "Intergovernmental Organizations (v2.3)." In *The Correlates of War Project.* June 30. http://www.correlatesofwar.org/data-sets/IGOs.

Norris, Pippa. 2001. *Digital Divide? Civic Engagement, Information Poverty, and the Internet Worldwide.* Cambridge: Cambridge University Press.

North, Robert C. 1990. *War, Peace, Survival: Global Politics and Conceptual Synthesis.* Boulder, CO: Westview Press.

Nye, Joseph S., Jr. 2004. *Soft Power: The Means to Success in World Politics.* New York: PublicAffairs.

Nye, Joseph S., Jr. 2011. "Nuclear Lessons for Cyber Security?" *Strategic Studies Quarterly* 5 (4): 18–38.

Nye, Joseph S., Jr. 2012. *The Future of Power.* New York: PublicAffairs.

Nye, Joseph S., Jr. 2014. "The Regime Complex for Managing Global Cyber Activities." Global Commission on Internet Governance Paper Series No. 1, Centre for International Governance Innovation and the Royal Institute for International Affairs, London.

OECD, and European Commission. 2008. *Handbook on Constructing Composite Indicators: Methodology and User Guide.* Paris: OECD.

Ohmae, Kenichi. 1990. *The Borderless World: Power and Strategy in the Global Marketplace*. London: HarperCollins.

OpenSeaMap. 2018. "OpenSeaMap—The Free Nautical Chart: Full Screen Chart." May 9. http://map.openseamap.org.

Ostrom, Elinor. 1990. *Governing the Commons: The Evolution of Institutions for Collective Action*. Cambridge: Cambridge University Press.

Ostrom, Elinor. 2005. *Understanding Institutional Diversity*. Princeton, NJ: Princeton University Press.

Ostrom, Elinor, Joanna Burger, Christopher B. Field, Richard B. Norgaard, and David Policansky. 1999. "Revisiting the Commons: Local Lessons, Global Challenges." *Science* 284 (5412): 278 LP–282.

Ostrom, Elinor, and Charlotte Hess, eds. 2007. *Understanding Knowledge as a Commons: From Theory to Practice*. Cambridge, MA: MIT Press.

Packet Clearing House. 2018. "Internet Exchange Directory." May 4. https://www.pch.net/ixp/dir.

PeeringDB. 2018. "PeeringDB facilitates the exchange of information related to Peering." May 6. https://www.peeringdb.com.

Pevehouse, Jon C., Timothy Nordstrom, and Kevin Warnke. 2004. "The COW-2 International Organizations Dataset Version 2.0." *Conflict Management and Peace Science* 21: 101–119.

Pimm, Stuart L., Márcio Ayres, Andrew Balmford, George Branch, Katrina Brandon, Thomas Brooks, Rodrigo Bustamante, et al. 2001. "Can We Defy Nature's End?" *Science* 293 (5538): 2207 LP–2208.

Pollins, Brian M., and Randall L. Schweller. 1999. "Linking the Levels: The Long Wave and Shifts in U.S. Foreign Policy, 1790–1993." *American Journal of Political Science* 43 (2): 431–464.

Pouzin, Louis. 1976. "Virtual Circuits vs. Datagrams: Technical and Political Problems." In *AFIPS '76; Proceedings of the June 7–10, 1976, National Computer Conference and Exposition*, 483–494. New York: ACM.

Press, William H. 2013. "What's So Special About Science (And How Much Should We Spend on It?)." *Science* 342 (6160): 817 LP–822.

Rady, Mina. 2013. "Anonymity Networks: New Platforms for Conflict and Contention." Department of Political Science Research Paper 2013–5, Massachusetts Institute of Technology, Cambridge, MA.

Raiu, Costin, David Emm, and Sergey Lozhkin. 2014. "IT Security Threats and Data Breaches Perception versus Reality: Time to Recalibrate." Global IT Risks Report 2014, Kaspersky Labs, Woburn, MA.

Rattray, Gregory J. 2001. *Strategic Warfare in Cyberspace*. Cambridge, MA: MIT Press.

Rayman, Noah. 2014. "The World's Top 5 Cybercrime Hotspots." *Time*, August 7, 2014.

Reardon, Robert, and Nazli Choucri. 2012. "The Role of Cyberspace in International Relations: A View of the Literature." Paper presented at ISA Annual Convention 2012: Power, Principles and Participation in the Global Information Age, San Diego, CA, April 1–4.

Reddy, Raj. 1996. "The Challenge of Artificial Intelligence." *Computer* 29 (10): 86–98.

Redner, Sidney. 2002. "Networking Comes of Age." *Nature* 418 (6894): 127–128.

Regalado, Antonio. 2014a. "Spying Is Bad for Business." *MIT Technology Review* 117 (3): 67–69.

Regalado, Antonio. 2014b. "Before Snowden, There Was Huawei." *MIT Technology Review* 117 (3): 70–71.

Reidenberg, Joel R. 1997. "Governing Networks and Rule-Making in Cyberspace." In *Borders in Cyberspace: Information Policy and the Global Information Infrastructure*, edited by Brian Kahin and Charles R. Nesson, 85–105. Cambridge, MA: MIT Press.

Réseaux IP Européens (RIPE). 2017a. "Delegated-Ripencc-Extended-Latest." Accessed November 24, 2017. ftp://ftp.ripe.net/pub/stats/ripencc/delegated-ripencc-extended-latest.

Réseaux IP Européens (RIPE). 2017b. "The History of RIPE." https://www.ripe.net/participate/ripe/history/the-history-of-ripe.

Rodrigue, Jean-Paul, Theo Notteboom, and Brian Slack. 2017. *The Geography of Transport Systems*, 4th edition. New York: Routledge.

Rogers, Richard. 2004. *Information Politics on the Web*. Cambridge, MA: MIT Press.

Rosecrance, Richard N. 1999. *The Rise of the Virtual State: Wealth and Power in the Coming Century*. New York: Basic Books.

Roser, Max. 2016. "War and Peace." https://ourworldindata.org.

Rucker, Rudy. 1987. *Mind Tools: The Five Levels of Mathematical Reality*. Boston: Houghton Mifflin.

Sawyer, Steve, Rolf T. Wigand, and Kevin Crowston. 2005. "Redefining Access: Uses and Roles of Information and Communication Technologies in the US Residential

Real Estate Industry from 1995 to 2005." *Journal of Information Technology* 20 (4): 213–223.

Schmidt, Eric, and Jared Cohen. 2010. "The Digital Disruption." *Foreign Affairs* 89 (6): 75–85.

Schmitt, Michael N. 2007. "Grey Zones in the International Law of Cyberspace." *Yale Journal of International Law* 42 (2): 1–21.

Schmitt, Michael N., ed. 2013. *Tallinn Manual on the International Law Applicable to Cyber Warfare: Prepared by the International Group of Experts at the Invitation of the NATO Cooperative Cyber Defence Centre of Excellence.* Cambridge: Cambridge University Press.

Schmitt, Michael N., ed. 2017. *Tallinn Manual 2.0 on the International Law Applicable to Cyber Operations.* Cambridge: Cambridge University Press.

"Security and the Internet." 2008. *OECD Observer*, 268 (July): 10–11.

Shane, Peter M., and Jeffrey A. Hunker, eds. 2013. *Cybersecurity: Shared Risks, Shared Responsibilities.* Durham, NC: Carolina Academic Press.

Sheffi, Yossi. 2005. *The Resilient Enterprise: Overcoming Vulnerability for Competitive Advantage.* Cambridge, MA: MIT Press.

Shepsle, Kenneth A. 1989. "Studying Institutions: Some Lessons from the Rational Choice Approach." *Journal of Theoretical Politics* 1 (2): 131–147.

Shi, Xiaoqing, and Hai Zhuge. 2011. "Cyber Physical Socio Ecology." *Concurrency and Computation: Practice and Experience* 23 (9): 972–984.

Simon, Herbert A. 1968. *The Sciences of the Artificial.* Cambridge, MA: MIT Press.

Simon, Herbert A. 1983. *Reason in Human Affairs.* Stanford, CA: Stanford University Press.

Simonite, Tom. 2014. "Silicon Valley to Get a Cellular Network, Just for Things." *MIT Technology Review* 117 (4): 79.

Singer, Peter W., and Allan Friedman. 2014. *Cybersecurity and Cyberwar What Everyone Needs to Know.* New York: Oxford University Press.

Smith, M., J. Bailey, and Erik Brynjolfsson. 2000. "Understanding Digital Markets: Review and Assessment." In *Understanding the Digital Economy: Data, Tools, and Research,* edited by Erik Brynjolfsson and Brian Kahin, 99–136. Cambridge, MA: MIT Press.

Software Engineering Institute (SEI). 2017. "About Us." Pittsburgh, PA: Carnegie Mellon University. http://www.cert.org/about/.

Sola Pool, Ithiel de, and Manfred Kochen. 1978. "Contacts and Influence." *Social Networks* 1 (1): 5–51.

Solla Price, Derek J. de. 1965. "Networks of Scientific Papers." *Science* 149 (3683): 510 LP–515.

Solum, Lawrence, and Minn Chung. 2003. "The Layers Principle: Internet Architecture and the Law." *Notre Dame Law Review* 79 (3): 815–948.

Souter, David. 2008. "Louder Voices and the International Debate on Developing Country Participation in ICT Decision Making." In *Governing Global Electronic Networks: International Perspectives on Policy and Power*, edited by William J. Drake and Ernest J. Wilson III, 429–462. Cambridge, MA: MIT Press.

Spinello, Richard A. 2002. *Regulating Cyberspace: The Policies and Technologies of Control*. Westport, CT: Quorum Books.

Standage, Tom. 1998. *The Victorian Internet: The Remarkable Story of the Telegraph and the Nineteenth Century's On-Line Pioneers*. New York: Walker.

Star, Susan L., and Karen Ruhleder. 1996. "Steps Toward an Ecology of Infrastructure: Design and Access for Large Information Spaces." *Information Systems Research* 7 (1): 111–134.

Starosielski, Nicole. 2015. *The Undersea Network*. Durham: Duke University Press.

Starr, Chauncey, and Chris Whipple. 1980. "Risks of Risk Decisions." *Science* 208 (4448): 1114 LP–1119.

Stefik, Mark J. 1999. *The Internet Edge: Social, Technical and Legal Challenges for a Networked World*. Cambridge, MA: MIT Press.

Stokes, Bruce, and Shane Harris. 2008. "China's Cyber-Militia." *National Journal* 40 (21): 32.

Talbot, David. 2010. "Moore's Outlaws." *MIT Technology Review* 113 (4): 36–43.

Talbot, John, and Dominic Welsh. 2006. *Complexity and Cryptography: An Introduction*. Cambridge: Cambridge University Press.

TeleGeography. 2018. "Submarine Cable Map: How Can I Download the KML or a CSV of the Dataset?" October 23, 2018. https://github.com/telegeography/www.submarinecablemap.com.

Testart, Cecilia. 2014. "Understanding ICANN's Complexity in a Growing and Changing Internet." Paper presented at NETMundial: Global Multistakeholder Meeting on the Future of Internet Governance, Sao Paulo, Brazil, April 23–24.

Tor Metrics. 2018a. "Estimated Number of Clients in the Tor Network." In *Pre-Aggregated Statistics Files Used on This Website*. Accessed May 20, 2018. https://metrics.torproject.org/stats.html#clients.

Tor Metrics. 2018b. "Top-10 Countries by Bridge Users." Accessed May 20, 2018. https://metrics.torproject.org/userstats-bridge-table.html?start=2016-01-01&end=2016-12-31.

Tor Metrics. 2018c. "Top-10 Countries by Relay Users." Accessed May 20, 2018. https://metrics.torproject.org/userstats-relay-table.html?start=2016-01-01&end =2016-12-31.

Trossen, Dirk, and George Parisis. 2012. "Designing and Realizing an Information-Centric Internet." *IEEE Communications Magazine* 50 (7): 60–67.

Tu, Yuhai. 2000. "How Robust Is the Internet?" *Nature* 406 (6794): 353–354.

Tyugu, Enn. 2011. "Artificial Intelligence in Cyber Defense." In *2011 3rd International Conference on Cyber Conflict*, edited by Christian Czosseck, Enn Tyugu, and Thomas Wingfield, 1–11. Tallinn, Estonia: NATO CCD COE.

Underwood, Todd. 2008. "Wrestling With the Zombie: Sprint Depeers Cogent, Internet Partitioned." *Dyn Guest Blogs*, October 31. https://dyn.com/blog/wrestling -with-the-zombie-spri/.

United Nations. 1945a. "1. Charter of the United Nations." In *Chapter I Charter of the United Nations and Statute of the International Court of Justice*. San Francisco: Secretary-General of the United Nations. https://treaties.un.org/doc/Publication/UNTS/No Volume/Part/un_charter.pdf.

United Nations. 1945b. "2. Declarations of Acceptance of the Obligations Contained in the Charter of the United Nations—Admission of States to Membership in the United Nations in Accordance with Article 4 of the Charter." In *Chapter I Charter of the United Nations and Statute of the International Court of Justice*. San Francisco: Secretary-General of the United Nations. https://treaties.un.org/doc/Publication /MTDSG/Volume I/Chapter I/I-2.en.pdf.

United Nations. 1992. "Rio Declaration of Environment and Development." In *Agenda 21: Earth Summit. The United Nations Programme of Action from Rio*, 7–11. New York: United Nations Division for Sustainable Development.

United Nations. 1993. *The Global Partnership for Environment and Development: A Guide to Agenda 21 Post Rio Edition*. New York: United Nations.

United Nations. 2009. "UN-Backed Anti-Cyber-Threat Coalition Launches Head-quarters in Malaysia." *UN News Center*, March 20.

United Nations. 2017a. "UNdata: A World of Information." http://data.un.org.

United Nations. 2017b. "We Can End Poverty: Millennium Development Goals and Beyond 2015." http://www.un.org/millenniumgoals/.

United Nations: Department of Economic and Social Affairs. 2002. *World Population Prospects: The 2000 Revision*. Vol. 3, *Analytical Report*. New York: United Nations.

United Nations: Department of Economic and Social Affairs. 2004. *World Population Prospects: The 2002 Revision*. Vol. 3, *Analytical Report*. New York: United Nations.

United Nations: Department of Economic and Social Affairs. 2005. "Table 1. E-Government Readiness Index 2005." In *UN Global E-Government Readiness Report 2005: From E-Government to E-Inclusion*, 196–199. New York: United Nations.

United Nations: Department of Economic and Social Affairs. 2006. *World Population Prospects: The 2004 Revision*. Vol. 3, *Analytical Report*. New York: United Nations.

United Nations: Department of Economic and Social Affairs. 2015a. "Table 1: International Migrant Stock at Mid-Year by Sex and by Major Area, Region, Country or Area, 1990–2015." In *Trends in International Migrant Stock: The 2015 Revision (United Nations Database, POP/DB/MIG/Stock/Rev.2015)*. New York: United Nations.

United Nations: Department of Economic and Social Affairs. 2015b. "Table 3: International Migrant Stock as a Percentage of the Total Population, 1990–2015." In *Trends in International Migrant Stock: The 2015 Revision (United Nations Database, POP/DB/MIG/Stock/Rev.2015)*. New York: United Nations.

United Nations: Department of Economic and Social Affairs. 2016. "Table 2. E-Government Development Index (EGDI)." In *United Nations E-Government Surveys: 2016 E-Government for Sustainable Development*, 154–158. New York: United Nations.

Van Valen, Leigh. 1973. "A New Evolutionary Law." *Evolutionary Theory* 1 (January): 1–30.

Valeriano, Brandon, and Ryan C. Maness. 2014. "The Dynamics of Cyber Conflict Between Rival Antagonists, 2001–11." *Journal of Peace Research* 51 (3): 347–360.

Waltz, Kenneth N. 1959. *Man, the State, and War: A Theoretical Analysis*. New York: Columbia University Press.

Watts, Duncan J. 2003. *Six Degrees: The Science of a Connected Age*. New York: Norton.

Weiner, Myron. 1995. *The Global Migration Crisis: Challenge to States and to Human Rights*. New York: HarperCollins.

Wellenius, Björn, Carlos A. P. Braga, and Christine Z. Qiang. 2000. "Investment and Growth of the Information Infrastructure: Summary Results of a Global Survey." *Telecommunications Policy* 24 (8): 639–643.

Werbach, Kevin. 2002. "A Layered Model for Internet Policy Symposium—The Regulation of Information Platforms: Telecommunications Regulation." *Journal on Telecommunications & High Technology Law* 1: 37–68.

Westland, Christopher J., and Theodore H. K. Clark. 2001. *Global Electronic Commerce: Theory and Case Studies*. Cambridge, MA: MIT Press.

Wheeler, Quentin D., Peter H. Raven, and Edward O. Wilson. 2004. "Taxonomy: Impediment or Expedient?" *Science* 303 (5656): 285 LP–285.

Whitt, Richard S. 2004. "A Horizontal Leap Forward: Formulating a New Communications Public Policy Framework Based on the Network Layers Model." *Federal Communications Law Journal* 56 (3): 587–672.

Wickboldt, Anne-Katrin, and Nazli Choucri. 2006. "Profiles of States as Fuzzy Sets: Methodological Refinement of Lateral Pressure Theory." *International Interactions* 32 (2): 153–181.

"Widening Broadband's Reach." 2008. *OECD Observer*, 268 (July): 14–15.

Wiener, Norbert. 1961. *Cybernetics or Control and Communication in the Animal and the Machine.* 2nd ed. Cambridge, MA: MIT Press.

Wilson, Ernest J., III. 2006. *The Information Revolution and Developing Countries.* Cambridge, MA: MIT Press.

Wilson, Ernest J., III, and Kelvin R. Wong, eds. 2006. *Negotiating the Net in Africa: The Politics of Internet Diffusion.* Boulder, CO: Lynne Rienner.

World Bank. 2003. *World Development Report 2003: Sustainable Development in a Dynamic World—Transforming Institutions, Growth, and Quality of Life.* Washington, DC: World Bank.

World Bank. 2016a. "Government Effectiveness: Estimate (GE.EST)." *Worldwide Governance Indicators.* October 19, 2016. Washington, DC: World Bank. http://databank .worldbank.org/data/home.aspx.

World Bank. 2016b. "The Global Knowledge Partnership on Migration and Development (KNOMAD): Bilateral Migration Matrix" 2013. Accessed November 13, 2017. Washington, DC: World Bank. https://www.knomad.org/data/migration/emigration.

World Bank. 2016c. "Voice and Accountability: Estimate (VA.EST)." *Worldwide Governance Indicators.* October 19, 2016. Washington, DC: World Bank. http://databank .worldbank.org/data/home.aspx.

World Bank. 2017a. "CO_2 Emissions (Kt) (EN.ATM.CO2E.KT); CO_2 Emissions (Metric Tons per Capita) (EN.ATM.CO2E.PC)." *World Development Indicators.* November 21, 2017. Washington, DC: World Bank. http://databank.worldbank.org/data/home.aspx.

World Bank. 2017b. "Exports of Goods and Services (Constant 2010 US$) (NE. EXP.GNFS.KD); Exports of Goods and Services (Annual % Growth) (NE.EXP.GNFS. KD.ZG)." *World Development Indicators.* November 21, 2017. Washington, DC: World Bank. http://databank.worldbank.org/data/home.aspx.

World Bank. 2017c. "GDP Deflator (Base Year Varies by Country) (NY.GDP.DEFL. ZS); DEC Alternative Conversion Factor (LCU per US$) (PA.NUS.ATLS); ICT Service Exports (% of Service Exports, BoP) (BX.GSR.CCIS.ZS); Service Exports (BoP, Current US$) (BX.GSR.NFSV.CD); ICT Goods Exports (% of Total Goods Exports) (TX. VAL.ICTG.ZS.UN); Goods Exports (BoP, Current US$) (BX.GSR.MRCH.CD)." *World*

Development Indicators. November 21, 2017. Washington, DC: World Bank. http://databank.worldbank.org/data/home.aspx.

World Bank. 2017d. "GDP per Capita (Constant 2010 US$) (NY.GDP.PCAP.KD); GDP per Capita Growth (Annual %) (NY.GDP.PCAP.KD.ZG)." *World Development Indicators.* November 21, 2017. Washington, DC: World Bank. http://databank.worldbank.org/data/home.aspx.

World Bank. 2017e. "MEC Dataset: Sumwi (Weight of the Country in Terms of Values)." 2015Q2. January 2017. Washington, DC: World Bank. https://mec.worldbank.org/downloads_data_availability_and_metadata.

World Bank. 2017f. "Personal Remittances, Received (Current US$) (BX.TRF.PWKR.CD.DT)." *World Development Indicators.* November 21, 2017. Washington, DC: World Bank. http://databank.worldbank.org/data/home.aspx.

World Bank. 2017g. "Population, Total (SP.POP.TOTL); Individuals Using the Internet (% of Population) (IT.NET.USER.ZS)." *World Development Indicators.* November 21, 2017. Washington, DC: World Bank. http://databank.worldbank.org/data/home.aspx.

World Bank. 2017h. "Population, Total (SP.POP.TOTL); Population Growth (Annual %) (SP.POP.GROW); Population Density (People per Sq. Km of Land Area) (EN.POP.DNST)." *World Development Indicators.* November 21, 2017. Washington, DC: World Bank. http://databank.worldbank.org/data/home.aspx.

World Bank. 2017i. "Population, Total (SP.POP.TOTL); Surface Area (Sq. Km) (AG.SRF.TOTL.K2); GDP (Constant 2010 US$) (NY.GDP.MKTP.KD)." *World Development Indicators.* November 21, 2017. Washington, DC: World Bank. http://databank.worldbank.org/data/home.aspx.

World Bank. 2017j. "What Is The Difference Between Current And Constant Data?" https://datahelpdesk.worldbank.org/knowledgebase/articles/114942-what-is-the-difference-between-current-and-constan.

World Bank. 2017k. "What Is Your Constant U.S. Dollar Methodology?" https://datahelpdesk.worldbank.org/knowledgebase/articles/114943-what-is-your-constant-u-s-dollar-methodology.

WSIS. 2006. "Basic Information: About WSIS." http://www.itu.int/wsis/index.html.

Yangyue, Liu. 2015. "China's Perspective on Cyber Security." In *Perspectives on Cybersecurity,* edited by Nazli Choucri and Chrisma Jackson. Cambridge, MA: Massachusetts Institute of Technology.

Yannakogeorgos, Panayotis A., and Adam Lowther, eds. 2014. *Conflict and Cooperation in Cyberspace the Challenge to National Security.* Boca Raton, FL: Taylor & Francis.

Zacher, Mark W. 2001. "International Organizations." In *The Oxford Companion to Politics of the World,* edited by Joel Krieger, 418–20. New York: Oxford University Press.

Zhang, Lixia, Alexander Afanasyev, Jeffrey Burke, Van Jacobson, Kimberly C. Claffy, Patrick Crowley, Christos Papadopoulos, et al. 2014. "Named Data Networking." *ACM SIGCOMM Computer Communication Review* 44 (3): 66–73.

Zhao, HongXin. 2002. "Rapid Internet Development in China: A Discussion of Opportunities and Constraints on Future Growth." *Thunderbird International Business Review* 44 (1): 119–138.

Zittrain, Jonathan L. 2005. "Technological Complements to Copyright." New York: Foundation Press.

Zittrain, Jonathan L. 2008. *The Future of the Internet and How to Stop It*. New Haven, CT: Yale University Press.

Zittrain, Jonathan L. 2009. "Law and Technology: The End of the Generative Internet." *Commun. ACM* 52 (1): 18–20.

Zook, Matthew. 2000. "Internet Metrics: Using Host and Domain Counts to Map the Internet." *Telecommunications Policy* 24 (6): 613–620.

Index